DISABILITY ALLIANCES AND ALLIES

RESEARCH IN SOCIAL SCIENCE AND DISABILITY

Series Editors: Sharon N. Barnartt and Barbara M. Altman

Recent Volumes:

Volume 1:	Expanding the Scope of Social Science Research on Disability – Edited by Sharon N. Barnartt and Barbara M. Altman
Volume 2:	Exploring Theories and Expanding Methodologies: Where We Are and Where We Need to Go – Edited by Sharon N. Barnartt and Barbara M. Altman
Volume 3:	Using Survey Data to Study Disability: Results from the National Health Interview Survey on Disability – Edited by Barbara M. Altman, Sharon N. Barnartt, Gerry E. Hendershot and Sheryl A. Larson
Volume 4:	International Views on Disability Measures: Moving Toward Comparative Measurement – Edited by Barbara M. Altman, Sharon N. Barnartt, Gerry E. Hendershot and Sheryl Larson
Volume 5:	Disability as a Fluid State – Edited by Sharon N. Barnartt
Volume 6:	Disability and Community – Edited by Allison C. Carey and Richard K. Scotch
Volume 7:	Disability and Intersecting Statuses – Edited by Sharon N. Barnartt and Barbara M. Altman
Volume 8:	Environmental Contexts and Disability – Edited by Sharon N. Barnartt and Barbara M. Altman
Volume 9:	What Did We Know and When Did We Know It – Edited by Sara Green and Sharon N. Barnartt
Volume 10:	Factors in Studying Employment for Persons with Disability: How the Picture Can Change – Edited by Barbara M. Altman and Sharon N. Barnartt
Volume 11:	New Narratives of Disability: Constructions, Clashes, and Controversies – Edited by Sara E. Green and Donileen R. Loseke

RESEARCH IN SOCIAL SCIENCE AND DISABILITY (RSSD)
VOLUME 12

DISABILITY ALLIANCES AND ALLIES: OPPORTUNITIES AND CHALLENGES

EDITED BY

ALLISON C. CAREY
Shippensburg University, Shippensburg, PA, USA

JOAN M. OSTROVE
Macalester College, St. Paul, MN, USA

TARA FANNON
New York City Department of Education, New York, NY, USA

emerald
PUBLISHING

United Kingdom – North America – Japan
India – Malaysia – China

Emerald Publishing Limited
Howard House, Wagon Lane, Bingley BD16 1WA, UK

First edition 2021

British Library Cataloguing in Publication Data
A catalogue record for this book is available from the British Library

ISBN: 978-1-83909-322-7 (Print)
ISBN: 978-1-83909-321-0 (Online)
ISBN: 978-1-83909-323-4 (Epub)

ISSN: 1479-3547 (Series)

Printed and bound by CPI Group (UK) Ltd, Croydon, CR0 4YY

ISOQAR certified Management System, awarded to Emerald for adherence to Environmental standard ISO 14001:2004.

ISOQAR REGISTERED
Certificate Number 1985
ISO 14001

INVESTOR IN PEOPLE

CONTENTS

PART II
RELATIONAL DYNAMICS OF ALLIANCE BUILDING

LIST OF TABLES

ABOUT THE CONTRIBUTORS

Sharon Barnartt is Professor Emeritus of Sociology at Gallaudet University. She coauthored *Deaf President Now: The 1988 Revolution at Gallaudet University* (with John Christiansen) and *Disability Protests: Contentious Politics 1970- 1999* (with Richard Scotch). She has served as president of the Society for Disability Studies, Chair of the Disability and Society Section of the American Sociological Association, and Chair of the American Sociological Association Status Committee on Persons with Disabilities in Sociology. She is currently a coeditor of *Research in Social Science and Disability*.

Allison C. Carey is a professor of Sociology at Shippensburg University. She is a coauthor of *Allies and Obstacles: Disability Activism and Parents of Children with Disabilities* (Temple University Press, 2020, with Pamela Block and Richard Scotch) and the author of *On the Margins of Citizenship: Intellectual Disability and Civil Rights in Twentieth Century America* (Temple University Press, 2009). She has coedited two volumes, including RSSD's volume 6 *Disability and Community* (Emerald, 2011, with Richard Scotch).

Christopher Constantino lives in Tallahassee with his wife Megan and son Augustine. He is a person who stutters. He works as a speech-language pathologist and assistant professor at Florida State University. He teaches classes on counseling and stuttering and studies how the subjective experience of stuttering interacts with culture and society.

Danielle DeNigris, PhD, is an Assistant Professor of Psychology at Fairleigh Dickinson University. Earlier, she served as Coordinator for Project REACH at the College of Staten Island, CUNY. Her research is two-pronged: (1) the experiences of autistic undergraduates and (2) the development of temporal cognition in children.

Ina Dimitrova received her PhD in social and political philosophy from Bulgarian Academy of Sciences, Institute for the Study of Knowledge and Societies, and currently is an associate professor at Plovdiv University "Paisii Hilendarski" in social philosophy and bioethics.

Patrick Dwyer is a psychology graduate student at UC Davis. His research is primarily focused on understanding the sensory experiences of autistic people, both at the group level and the individual level, and he uses electrophysiology and questionnaires to explore auditory processing, cross-modal integration, and attention in autism.

Eric Endlich, PhD, is a clinical psychologist, educational consultant, and autistic self-advocate who coauthored an international study of 150 older autistic adults. He helps autistic students transition to higher education, provides training on managing a neurodiverse workforce, and writes and presents regularly on related topics.

Tara Fannon is a gender and disability sociologist and interdisciplinary scholar working in disability advocacy. Her research bridges sociology, disability studies, and narrative studies and examines the relationship between self, identities, and social-structural access. She has been an editor of *Endangered Bodies NYC* and *Masculinities 101* blogs and a contributor to others such as *Gender & Society* and *The Good Men Project*. Her academic work has been published in *Research in Social Science and Disability, Symbolic Interaction, Disability Studies Quarterly,* and the *Norton Reader*. Her current work focuses on using story-telling in the public sphere as an alliance building tool and medium for advocacy and policy development.

Morton Ann Gernsbacher is a Vilas Research Professor and the Sir Frederic Bartlett Professor of Psychology at the University of Wisconsin-Madison. Her research examines human communication, including typical, atypical, and virtual.

Mark Halley, PhD, NIC is an Assistant Professor of American Sign Language/English Interpreting at the University of North Florida. He conducted his doctoral research in the Department of Interpretation and Translation at Gallaudet University in Washington, DC. He has also been an interpreter in private practice since 2011.

Emily Hotez, PhD, is a research scientist at the UCLA Center for Healthier Children, Families and Communities. Her research interests include utilizing participatory and mixed-methods approaches to designing, implementing, and evaluating interventions that reflect the needs, experiences, and priorities of the populations they seek to serve.

Shixin Huang is a PhD candidate in the Henry M. Jackson School of International Studies, University of Washington. Her research focuses on the disability rights movement in China, especially how local disability organizations and activists deploy the international discourses and approach of disability rights to claim their identity and citizenship on the ground.

Steven K. Kapp is a developmental psychologist. He is a Lecturer in Psychology at the University of Portsmouth with expertise in autism and neurodiversity. His academic background includes psychology, education, public policy, and disability studies, with additional publications in anthropology, medicine, and neuroscience reaching diverse audiences and readerships.

Erika Katzman, PhD, is a registered Occupational Therapist and Assistant Professor in Disability Studies at King's University College (Western University) in

London, Ontario, Canada. Her research is informed by critical feminist and disability studies. Areas of focus include invisible work, care work, caregiving relationships, occupational justice, and disability representation in health professional education.

Bella Kofner is a senior at the College of Staten Island who is majoring in mathematics education with a minor in disability studies. She is an autistic self-advocate who coleads Project REACH structured group meetings, does participatory research and does presentations about autism (gender inequality in autism and neurodiversity to name one of the many).

Kristen Gillespie-Lynch is an Associate Professor of Psychology at the College of Staten Island & The Graduate Center (CUNY). In collaboration with autistic people, she coconstructs supports to empower autistic people and reduce stigma. She developed a participatory mentorship program for autistic college students and evaluates autism trainings internationally.

Melinda Leigh Maconi is a doctoral candidate in the Sociology Department at the University of South Florida, United States. Her areas of research include disability, health and illness, education, the arts, and identity. Her current projects examine the ways in which these artists with disabilities incorporate art into their identity.

Stephen Meyers is an Assistant Professor of Law, Societies & Justice; International Studies; and Disability Studies at the University of Washington, Seattle. His research explores the interaction between grassroots disabled persons organizations and older persons associations with local and international laws and policies in the Global South.

Joan M. Ostrove is a Professor of Psychology and the Director of the Jan Serie Center for Scholarship and Teaching at Macalester College in Saint Paul, Minnesota. Her current research examines the qualities that members of marginalized groups look for in dominant-group allies, specifically in the domains of disability and race. Ostrove has coedited special issues of the *Journal of Social Issues* and *Disability Studies Quarterly*, and her work has been published in the *Journal of Applied Social Psychology, Feminism & Psychology, Review of Higher Education*, and *Journal of Higher Education*, among others.

Nicki Pombier is an oral historian, writer, and educator. She is a part-time faculty member at the College of Performing Arts at The New School University and on faculty in the Oral History Master of Arts program at Columbia University. She lives in Brooklyn, New York.

Helen Rottier is a graduate student in disability studies at the University of Illinois at Chicago. Her research focuses on academic ableism, empowering autistic scholars, and radically reimagining autistic knowledge production in and out of the academy.

Ariana Riccio is a doctoral candidate at the Graduate Center of the City University of New York. Her research interests include design and evaluation of employment and educational transition services for autistic adolescents and young adults, expressions of disability and autistic identity, and engaging in participatory research design.

LIST OF CONTRIBUTORS

Sharon Barnartt	Department of Sociology, Gallaudet University, Washington, DC, USA
Allison C. Carey	Department of Sociology and Anthropoplogy, Shippensburg University, Shippensburg, PA, USA
Christopher Constantino	College of Communications and Information, Florida State University, Tallahassee, FL, USA
Danielle DeNigris	Department of Psychology and Counseling, Fairleigh Dickinson University, Madison, NJ, USA
Ina Dimitrova	Departments of Philosophy and History, Plovdiv University – Paisii Hilendarski, Plovdiv, Bulgaria
Patrick Dwyer	Department of Psychology, University of California, Davis, Davis, CA, USA
Eric Endlich	Independent Scholar and Educational Consultant, Top College Consultant, Needham, MA, USA
Tara Fannon	New York City Department of Education, New York City, USA
Morton Ann Gernsbacher	Department of Psychology, University of Wisconsin–Madison, Madison, WI, USA
Mark Halley	Department of Exceptional, Deaf, and Interpreter Education, College of Education and Human Services, University of North Florida, Jacksonville, FL, USA
Emily Hotez	Center for Healthier Children, Families and Communities, University of California, Los Angeles, Los Angeles, CA, USA
Shixin Huang	Henry M. Jackson School of International Studies, University of Washington, Seattle, WA, USA
Steven K. Kapp	Department of Psychology, University of Portsmouth, Portsmouth, Hampshire, UK
Erika Katzman	Department of Interdisciplinary and Disability Studies, King's University College, Western University, London Ontario, Canada

Bella Kofner	School of Education, College of Staten Island – City University of New York, New York, NY, USA
Kristen Gillespie-Lynch	Department of Psychology, College of Staten Island & CUNY Graduate Center – City University New York, NY, USA
Melinda Leigh Maconi	Department of Sociology, University of South Florida, Tampa, FL, USA
Stephen Meyers	Department Law, Societies and Justice, University of Washington, Seattle, WA, USA
Joan M. Ostrove	Department of Psychology and Jan Serie Center for Scholarship and Teaching, Macalester College, Saint Paul, MN, USA
Nicki Pombier	Oral History Master of Arts Program at Columbia University and College of Performing Arts at The New School University, New York, NY, USA
Helen Rottier	Department of Disability and Human Development, University of Illinois at Chicago, Chicago, IL, USA
Ariana Riccio	Department of Psychology, CUNY Graduate Center – City University of New York, New York, NY, USA

INTRODUCTION: EXPLORING THE OPPORTUNITIES AND CHALLENGES OF ALLIANCES AND ALLYSHIP IN THE LIVES OF PEOPLE WITH DISABILITIES

Allison C. Carey, Tara Fannon and Joan M. Ostrove

INTRODUCTION

In 2019, when we (Allison, Joan, and Tara) issued the call for papers for this volume, we aimed to draw attention to the opportunities and challenges of alliances within, among, and beyond disability communities. We set out to encourage challenging conversations, focusing on issues such as power, shared and conflicting interests, and voice. As we moved toward finalizing the volume, the political landscape changed dramatically. The spread of the novel coronavirus and the protests following the killing of George Floyd by a police officer shone a spotlight on the devastating consequences of social oppression and thrust the meaning and practice of allyship into the foreground of national dialogue.

As the contributing authors revised their accepted chapters in March of 2020, the novel coronavirus was rapidly spreading across the United States, and stay-at-home orders were put in place to slow transmission and try to prevent the health care system from being overwhelmed. Most people experienced social upheaval, but precarity and social marginalization heightened the threats faced by people with disabilities. Social distancing upended established relationships of support upon which people with disabilities relied, and disruptions to supply chains and economic hardship undercut access to vital resources. Disability communities drew on their vast repertoire of strategies and marshaled mutual aid efforts – grounded in the principles of disability justice and modeled on the long-standing alliance-building strategies – to provide one another with needed support to live full lives (Bak, 2020; Sins invalid, 2020). In the absence of adequate

Disability Alliances and Allies
Research in Social Science and Disability, Volume 12, 1–16

ISSN: 1479-3547/doi:10.1108/S1479-354720200000012002

support from the state and local communities, though, too many were left without the care and resources they needed. Disabled people, especially Black, Indigenous, and people of color (BIPOC) and people in poor communities, as so often happens disproportionately bore the brunt of devastation (Lederer, 2020; Prior, 2020) and double-downed on efforts to provide support and resource to one another. As the United States learned the value of the social model of disability, it simultaneously Exceptionalized and disregarded the needs of disabled people in increasingly blatant economic calculations designed to reignite capitalist engines (Kukla, 2020; Ladau, 2020; Ne'eman, 2020).

Final submissions for the volume came due at the end of May 2020, just days after the horrifying murder of George Floyd at the hands (or more precisely the knee) of the Minneapolis Police Department. The massive uprisings that ensued, led by community members and activists demanding #justiceforGeorgeFloyd and reminding the world – once again – that #BlackLivesMatter, forced another important reckoning about what it means to be an ally in the fight for racial justice, the dismantling of white supremacy, and the end of anti-Blackness (Stewart, 2020). Coalitions emerged among many different groups to organize mutual aid, to promote efforts to defund the police, invest in public services, and demand a broad array of changes. Recognizing the intersection of race, disability, gender, and class provided new opportunities for collective mobilization and "radical inclusivity," while others used Floyd's health and disability status to skirt responsibility for police brutality (see #DisabilitySolidarity, #DisabilityJustice, #BlackBrilliance; Ankel & Mahbubani, 2020).

Through the tumultuous spring, the meaning of and practical strategies for alliance became a key part of national and international dialogues. Activists instructed allies to check their privilege, build their knowledge, teach anti-oppression strategies to their children, create change in their local communities, and support (not usurp) BIPOC and disabled leaders. Highlighting power imbalances, activists called for "accomplices" who would use and sacrifice their privilege – such as risking police violence and the loss of employment – in the fight for social justice. Silence and complicity were identified as acts of violence themselves (Wyatt, 2020).

National and international conversations have certainly changed in the past year. The chapters in this volume unfortunately do not attend to the novel coronavirus or the Black Lives Matter movement. Fortunately, they do provide an academic foundation for our work in understanding and forging alliances to create change. They present varied conceptualizations of alliance, explore the factors that encourage and discourage alliance building, demonstrate both the consequences of alliance and the absence of alliance, and consider the processes and characteristics of effective alliances often across significant differences and inequalities. It is clearer than ever that we must work together toward social transformation, but the road to alliance is not smooth; it is forged through hard work, sacrifice, humility, and acts of connection and reconnection. We hope this volume offers a substantive contribution toward imagining and achieving new paths to collective activism and resisting acts in the name of alliance that actually serve to maintain inequality.

To frame the contributions of this collection, below we offer a discussion of several key issues related to alliance and disability. We then briefly introduce the chapters and their contributions to the field.

KEY ISSUES IN THE SOCIAL SCIENCES OF ALLIANCES, ALLIES, AND DISABILITY

Alliance at its simplest is a strategy by which individual or organizational entities join in partnership with others to achieve mutual benefit or common purpose. Our world is relational – identities are enacted through interaction; resources flow unequally and inequitably across groups; rights represent claims by which we demand others respect our freedoms and needs; and social change occurs as we influence the beliefs and social structures that shape behavior. Despite the American emphasis on individualism, our lives intertwine with and depend on a vast array of other people. As such, alliance is one of the central strategies by which we navigate social life, forming partnerships as we seek to meet our needs, achieve our interests, and shape our world.

Within social sciences, the concept of alliance has received scant attention. When it is studied, it tends to be addressed in two particular ways. At the macro level, alliances are seen as one of the variables affecting social movements and change. As such, scholars examine the factors that shape political alliances and the consequences of these alliances or lack thereof (e.g., Barnartt & Scotch, 2001; Carey, Block, & Scotch, 2019, 2020; Schweik, 2011; Taylor, 2009; Van Dyke & McCammon, 2010). On a more micro level, the concept of allyship evokes the often explicit act of relationship building, at times among people of similar social status and at times across majority–minority or superordinate–subordinate lines. In the psychological research literature, allies are typically described as members of dominant groups who are committed to and work on behalf of the liberation of a nondominant group (e.g., Brown, 2015; Case, 2012; Droogendyk, Wright, Lubensky, & Louis, 2016; Fingerhut, 2011; Selvanathan, Techakesari, Tropp, & Barlow, 2017). In both circumstances, alliances are political; they involve the conferring, sharing, or mutual challenging of power. Other types of relationships, such as friendships, family, or "helping" relationships, likely involve power and shared interests, but in alliances issues of power, process, and the pursuit of shared interests come to the fore.

Alliance Building among the Powerful

Alliance building is a key strategy of the powerful in the pursuit of power, and this often is experienced as a coercive external constraint by people with disabilities. This can be seen in several arenas in society. In the classic sociological work *The Power Elite,* C. Wright Mills (1956) demonstrated that politicians, military leaders, and capitalists do not act as independent actors or even within independent sectors; instead, they coordinate their actions, share resources, and consolidate power within the "military industrial complex." Alliances across sectors benefit actors in these sectors and reinforce the power of elites, and thus they enable widespread economic exploitation, oppression, and even warfare to benefit themselves. Everyday citizens can hardly prevail over this political goliath, and instead experience disablement, poverty, exploitation, and alienation as the rich get richer (Charlton, 2000).

Another structural alliance that reinforces power for elites while devastating poor, marginalized communities, including people with disabilities, is the prison industrial complex. This represents "a complex web interweaving private business and government interests in the growing industry of incarceration and prison development" (Chapman, Carey, & Ben-Moshe, 2014, p. 13); economic and political elites ally with agents of incarceration to warehouse and disempower segments of the population deemed dangerous or unproductive, particularly men of color, while profiting directly and indirectly from their incarceration (Ware, Ruzsa, & Dias, 2014). The prison industrial complex infiltrates the school systems that label children as disabled and delinquent and channel them into the "prison pipeline," while it also produces disability through the abusive conditions of prison life (Erevelles, 2014; Ware et al., 2014).

Via the "criminal justice–social service alliance," marginalized communities are surveilled and policed under the guise of benevolent assistance (Dewey & St Germain, 2016; Hewlett & West, 1998; Ladd-Taylor, 2017). Social services coerce people with disabilities into institutional settings, encourage sterilization and birth control, and impose social control mechanisms in exchange for providing the resources needed for survival. While portraying themselves as allies of the poor, social workers may instead serve the interests of elites who seek to discourage deviance and dependence (Chapman & Withers, 2019; Ladd-Taylor, 2017).

In each of these structural alliances, we see cooperation across macro social systems and the official actors within them that facilitates a political agenda, threatens the well-being of the most vulnerable, and leaves little opportunity for resistance. Disability is central to this system of stratification. Economic exploitation and war produce disability; medical systems and social services individualize and pathologize the experience of disability while overlooking oppression; and incarceral settings (including medical institutions) disempower people with disabilities (Charlton, 2000; Erevelles, 2014). People with disabilities as a group rarely exercise significant control over these structures and therefore experience them primarily as coercive external forces rather than as effective avenues to attain their own interests.

Alliance Building as an Act of Social Resistance

Alliance, however, is not solely a tool of the elite; it is an essential component of social resistance. As such, alliance building – both internal and external – has been a valuable strategy within disability activism. According to the theory of resource mobilization (McCarthy & Zald, 1977; Morris, 1984; Zald & McCarthy, 1997), social movements are likely to be successful to the extent that they can mobilize people and their resources (e.g., money, political influence, symbolic authority, physical presence at protests, knowledge). Therefore, alliance building is critical to success.

While there are many dimensions by which to consider alliances, here we will distinguish between internal and external alliances (Barnartt, this volume). Internal alliance building involves the work of uniting those most directly affected to engage in activism. Social networks – radically reconfigured and expanded in an era of social media – often provide the pathways by which individuals gain exposure to and encouragement to participate in activism. Participation fosters an "oppositional consciousness" (Groch, 1994), the framing of an individuals' experiences as a collective phenomenon rooted in shared oppression and best addressed through social change. Barnartt and Scotch (2001. p. 17) wrote, "One of the most important tasks that social movements actively engage in is the production of meaning for participants, antagonists, and observers." For people with disabilities, the consciousness achieved via engaging with social movements likely upends prior views of disability and self-identity (Darling, 2013). The 504 sit-ins, for example, cultivated a collective identity rooted in the shared experience of ableism and a sense of political efficacy among participants, many of whom had only experienced social isolation and dependency (Fleischer & Zames, 2011; Pelka, 2012).

Through alliances, people with disabilities sought to remake the political landscape. In the early and mid-twentieth century, distinct disability communities formed organizations, such as the League of the Physically Handicapped and the National Association of the Deaf (Fleischer & Zames, 2011; Nielsen, 2012). Over time, cross-disability organizations and alliances grew more widespread. Often, activists worked with distinct populations on distinct issues, creating in effect multiple disability movements; yet, they also allied when mutually agreeable, creating the potential for mass collaborative action (Barnartt & Scotch, 2001; Charlton, 2000; Pelka, 2012). Through this decentralized structure, disability activists forged a major civil rights movement, nurtured politicized identities, and fostered disability pride.

External alliances also play a crucial role in social movements. External alliances broaden the reach of a movement's message, tap into key roles and institutions necessary to enact social change, and expand the pool of resources (Van Dyke & McCammon, 2010). Since broad social change must be institutionalized and enacted across diverse settings and groups, alliance building across groups is essential. To address employment discrimination, for example, disability activists must work with politicians, employers, social security experts, social service officials, other civil rights groups, and others.

Among external allies, some are more closely aligned with the interests of disability activists than others. Parents, for example, are often keenly aware of the disadvantages experienced by their disabled children, experience secondary discrimination themselves, and may participate in the front lines of disability activism (e.g., Blum, 2015; Carey, Block, & Scotch, 2020; Charmak, 2008; Panitch, 2008; Rosqvist, Brownlow & O'Dell, 2015). Civil rights organizations at times offer support to affirm the value of civil rights, resist oppression, and build connections across marginalized populations such as between BIPOC and the disability community (Frederick & Shifrer, 2018; OToole, 2015; Schweik, 2011), although at other times they disregard the centrality of disability to their work. Some organizations led primarily by nondisabled people explicitly ally with the disability community, although their commitment to widespread, systemic changes varies widely (Maconi, this volume).

Disability politics may also inspire "strange bedfellows" – alliance between unexpected groups who share a specific interest but otherwise embrace divergent or even contrary goals. Giric (2016) offers the example of the alliance between the Christian Right and disability activists. The values of the Christian Right, such as limited social spending and freedom from government intervention and mandates regarding civil rights, clash with the goals of many disability activists. The Christian Right and disability activists, though, have allied to ensure protections to newborns with disabilities (Giric, 2016; Staggenborg, 2010).

The Social Factors that Encourage or Hinder Alliances

Various factors hinder or encourage alliances, and people with disabilities experience particular challenges to alliance building. Macro systems such as government and economy shape the feasibility of activism and alliance building. Activism and alliances tend to thrive in democratic systems with vibrant civil societies and where people's basic needs are met, whereas state repression, civil unrest, and poverty undermine such activities. Even in democratic societies, though, barriers to disability activism abound (Scotch, 1988). Most people become engaged in activism via their social networks, but poverty, limited education, and social isolation mean that people with disabilities enjoy less access to and control over valuable social institutions like government and policy-making, research institutes, and media outlets. People with disabilities may rely on family members and/or paid staff for transportation and support, but this assistance may be more or less available; family and staff may even see activism as a threat and actively discourage it (Friedman & Beckwith, 2014). Inaccessibility in transportation, communication, information, and physical structures hinders participation in activism. Furthermore, the disproportionate poverty of people with disabilities limits their ability to engage in particular strategies of activism, impeding access to dues-based organizations, protests that require travel, and activities that require time, resources, and childcare.

In addition to logistical issues, identification and framing shape decisions of how and with whom to ally. Many people with physical and mental limitations do not identify as "disabled." Their disinclination to identify might be relatively unconscious or might involve an explicit "dis-identification" – a rejection of the label of "disabled" (Darling, 2013; Egner, 2018; Nario-Redmond, 2020). They may focus instead on their abilities, assign spiritual or other explanations for their experiences, or prioritize other identity affiliations. People who become disabled later in life, for example, are less likely to identify as "disabled" or to engage in activism as disabled people, thwarting alliance despite shared concerns (Darling, 2013; Kahana & Kahana, 2017; Meyers, this volume). For African-Americans, the long history of medical discrimination and the use of psychiatric diagnosis as a means of pathologizing resistance to oppression fostered community suspicion of stigmatizing diagnoses and focused energies on race-based inequities (Metzl, 2010).

Activists with similar needs may disagree on the framing of the problem, policies, and solutions. For example, neoliberalism fractures potential partners as they fight over scarce resources. In this competitive environment, some activists fight for resources by playing into neoliberal demands for productivity, while others resist the commodification of human worth (Fritsch, 2013; Russell, 1998; Dimitrova, this volume).

When we consider the factors that make organizational alliance more likely, several factors stand out. Shared interests and framing, known as ideological alignment, encourages agreement regarding the perceived problems and solutions and thereby facilitates cooperation (Carey et al., 2019; Gerhards & Rucht, 1992; McCammon & Van Dyke, 2010; Snow & Benford, 1992; Snow, Rochford, Worden, & Benford, 1986; Staggenborg, 2010). Shared interests and framing may not be sufficient, however; a sense of shared threats and/or perceived political opportunities may be necessary to motivate groups to work together (McAdam, 1996; Van Dyke & McCammon, 2010). For example, threats in 2017 to the Affordable Care Act brought many formerly disparate groups to Washington DC to protest together, while bipartisan support among politicians for the ABLE Act encouraged various organizations to work together. Shared membership may also serve to bridge organizational divides, such as people who belong to both disability and LGBT + groups who act as "bridge-builders," helping each group understand their shared interests and concerns (Fernández, Bosch, & Samarach, 2017). New technologies have upended traditional movement strategies; now a tweet or online call to action can "go viral" and influence people far outside traditional organizational bounds.

Power Imbalances within and across Alliances

Within alliances, tensions are common as disparate parties negotiate interests, tactics, and power. People and groups bring different levels of power and privilege into activism, and inequality among partners threaten a sense of solidarity. Racial privilege is one such type of inequality. Among activists with disabilities, white, educated, physically disabled people have often positioned themselves in the forefront of the movement, failed to encourage leadership by BIPOC, and disregarded the intersectional nature of oppression (Berne, 2015; Erkulwater, 2018; Moore, Lewis, & Brown, 2016). American disability organizations dominated by white activists, for instance, thereby discouraging cross-race alliance. Describing the Center for Independent Living at Berkeley in the 1970s, Corbett OToole (2015) explains that white activists focused on achieving rights and accessibility, which they thought helped everyone, but they ignored the range of access needs across diverse populations. She writes,

> While the local independent living center fought hard for access to the library, they rarely fought for access to a battered women's shelter or for interpreters for the Gay Pride Parade and English-as-a-second-language classes. Many disabled people of color and disabled queers were left on their own to fight for their access rights (2015, p. 101).

People with other types of disabilities, including intellectual and mental disabilities, also felt excluded by the power of activists with physical disabilities and their focus on physical access (Pelka, 2012).

Others criticized disabled leaders for buying into a neoliberal agenda to secure rights and employment for those most easily integratable while minimizing, or even ignoring, the pressing needs of people who could not work, have complex medical needs, need extensive supports, and/or belong to communities impacted by multiple vectors of oppression (Berne, 2015; Fritsch, 2013; Mingus, 2014). By supporting the idea that disability rights would minimize dependency, activists secured rights legislation but subverted claims to a widespread redistribution of resources and ignored the intersecting factors hindering basic survival (Huang, this volume; Russell, 1998).

Alliances with external parties are similarly fraught with competing interests and complex power dynamics. For example, people with disabilities and care providers share many interests related to the provision of high quality care, yet their alliance falters at times when the goal of higher wages or better working conditions for care providers jeopardizes the hours of care for people with disabilities (Chang, 2017; Katz, this volume). Civil rights organizations at times express concern that the expansion of civil rights laws undercuts their own hard-won victories (Scotch, 1984).

When interests compete, issues of power come to the fore. External allies who enter the relationship with greater power may have greater power to shape the goals, message, and tactics of the movement, in effect undercutting the goal of self-determination (Russell & Bohan, 2016). The role of parents as allies highlights the advantages and disadvantages of external allies. Parents often see themselves as not only allies but as leaders in disability activism (Jones, 2010). They bring considerable resources and symbolic authority to the fight, but they also may subvert self-determination and empowerment of people with disabilities (Carey et al., 2019, 2020; Landsman, 2009; McGuire, 2016; Rottier & Gernsbacher, this volume). Academics and researchers also frequently seek to ally with marginalized communities, yet the power and interests of academics threaten to overwhelm these partnerships (see Pombier, this volume).

Because allies may hold privilege and act in deeply ableist ways, disability organizations struggle to balance the needs of their disabled members with the desire to welcome potential allies (Gillespie-Lynch et al., this volume). Allyship simultaneously may confer resources but also threaten the goals of the movement and even the well-being of disabled activists (Piepzna-Samarashinha, 2018; Moore et al., 2016).

The Work of Allyship

While alliances may be formed around any issue and are used for a variety of purposes, activists often desire allies who are trustworthy and act as "co-conspirators" or "accomplices" in the fight for social change. Acting in ways that are both interpersonally affirming and politically and socially informed (Brown & Ostrove, 2013), allies from dominant groups should be willing not only to critically examine their own privileged identity/identities but also to act as "ally activists" (Curtin, Kende, & Kende, 2016), to affiliate with and take action on behalf of the liberation of nondominant groups. This may include recognizing the oppression faced by groups with whom they are in alliance; understanding and opposing their own group's role in creating and sustaining that oppression; and working toward dismantling the systems that support and maintain hierarchy, power imbalances, and unequal distribution of resources (Rottier & Gernsbacher, this volume; Pombier, this volume).

Gill (2001) emphasizes both the structural/political and interpersonal dimensions of being a nondisabled ally to disabled people. Being an ally requires one to recognize ableism ("knowing and despising it when you see it"), make an effort to "learn who their disabled associates are in their full glory and full ordinariness," and, in short, "get it" (Gill, 2001, p. 368). More recently, Forber-Pratt, Mueller, and Andrews (2019) proposed that nondisabled individuals could demonstrate allyship by "showing up" in a number of specific ways, including by understanding intersectionality; asking and respecting language and terminology choices; embracing principles of universal design; acting as an ally (for example, by making accessibility-related changes related to accessibility, or interrogating organizational policy); recognizing problematic representations of disability in the media that reinforce pity, objectification, and an emphasis on "overcoming" disability; being aware of current disability rights issues facing the community; checking internal ableist biases; and honoring the experiences and perspectives of *all* disabled people (across, and regardless of, the type of disability/impairment).

Qualitative studies of the characteristics that disabled or deaf people encourage, value, and look for in nondisabled or hearing allies reveal a number of common themes. Disabled and deaf people want their nondisabled/hearing allies to be respectful, encouraging, accommodating, and appropriately helpful, while simultaneously recognizing and supporting their autonomy and multiple identities. They appreciate nondisabled people who can be trustworthy in their understanding of identity, make personal connections, advocate and act against ableism, be willing to learn, and communicate effectively (e.g., Evans, Assadi, & Herriott, 2005; Halley, this volume; Ostrove & Crawford, 2006; Ostrove, Cole, & Oliva, 2009; Ostrove, Kornfeld, & Ibrahim, 2019).

While alliances always involve some negotiation of power, these negotiations are particularly complex and fraught within "new social movements," which focus on creating social change in identity, lifestyle, and culture, rather than striving to address material inequality alone. In new social movements, issues of control and voice are significant because they are goals in and of themselves (Pichardo, 1997). One cannot achieve respect and equality broadly in society if one cannot achieve these goals within one's own movement among one's allies. Carey et al. (2020, p. 181) write,

> ...new social movements seek allies who not only share a specific goal or a broader frame around that goal but also display a commitment to the identity politics of the movement. This commitment entails respecting who 'owns' the issue, placing the value of collaboration at times above one's own specific interests, and sharing a sense of grievance when an ally is wronged, even if it doesn't immediately affect you.

Through "bridging work" (Beamish & Luebbers, 2009) activists look to move "from alliance to trust," building the structure and tactics needed to foster the mutual recognition of needs, sense of belonging, and affirmation of respect and dignity (Fernández, Bosch, & Samaranch, 2017).

Alliance and Allyship as Contested Concepts

Not only are the desired actions of allies negotiated, but the concept of allyship itself is contested among social justice organizers as well as within the academy. Some cast a wide net, viewing any person who provides resources, support, or even shares a particular belief as an "ally." Some emphasize that "ally" must be understood as a verb, rather than a noun, to emphasize that being an ally is an ongoing process grounded in critical self-reflection and engaged action, not a label or an identity, especially not one that one can confer on oneself (peernetbc.com, n.d.). Others see allies as those who are guided by the leadership of the most vulnerable and who collaboratively engage in building communities of care and support that center mutual aid, dignity of all, and respect (Piepzna-Samarasinha, 2018). Still others offer cogent critiques of the term itself, arguing that true liberation will only come when dominant group members are willing to "weaponize their privilege" as accomplices in the struggle, not as "allies" (Indigenous Action, 2014, p. 6).

Despite these differences, disabled activists seek to envision possible futures which embrace and value people in all their diversity, futures only possible through massive social change. Alison Kafer (2013, p. 28) writes:

> To put it bluntly, I, *we*, need to imagine crip futures because disabled people are continually being written out of the future, rendered as a sign of the future no one wants. This erasure is not mere metaphor. Disabled people—particularly those with developmental and psychiatric impairments, those who are poor, gender-deviant, and/or people of color, those who need atypical forms of assistance to survive—have faced sterilization, segregation, and institutionalization; denial of equitable education, health care and social services; violence and abuse; and the withholding of the rights of citizenship. . . . It is my loss, our loss, not to take care of, embrace, and desire all of us. We must begin to anticipate presents and to imagine futures that include all of us.

THIS VOLUME

The chapters in this volume are split into two parts. Part I focuses on the structures and systems that shape alliances, and explores instances of cooperation and conflict in advocacy and activism across social movements, organizations, and institutions. Part II engages the relational dynamics of everyday life interactions and intersections.

In Part I, topics include the factors influencing the formation of new alliances, what happens when interests collide, how institutional power is leveraged to meet political ends, and the social and economic challenges of forming coherent unions between groups with distinct priorities. It opens with studies of alliance building and fragmentation in three nations: China, Jamaica, and Bulgaria. In Chapter 1, Shixin Huang examines the discrepancies between the Western-centered international disability rights model and disability activism in China. Although the dissemination of the disability rights model has "opened spaces of resistance," Huang argues that it remains divorced from the everyday struggles of people struggling with poverty under an authoritarian government. He proposes transnational alliances that rely on grass roots knowledge to address how globalization processes uniquely affect socioeconomic life in disability communities.

Chapters 2 and 3 examine political conflict between social movements whose intersecting interests could instead encourage alliance. Stephen Meyers writes about specific social and political factors driving deep disconnects between the disability and older persons' movements in Jamaica. In their pursuit of separate rights campaigns, each often relies on ageism and ableism to advance their interests – disability activists emphasizing its young and productive members and older activists focusing on its healthy and vibrant members. Thus, despite the similar goals and needs of the two movements, they have not embraced alliance. Next, Ina Dimitrova develops a "productivist" analysis of the discord between parents of disabled children engaged in grass roots activism and national disability rights organizations embedded in the state infrastructure in Bulgaria. Her analysis reveals how neoliberalism and the national commitment to productivity divided disability activists, pitting those who wanted employment opportunities against those who wanted to retain a government safety net for people with disabilities. While very distinct in their foci and analysis, each of the first three chapters engage with the themes of neoliberalism and the impact of Western disability politics in nations with very different sociopolitical realities.

Chapters 4 and 5 examine alliances within the United States, one on an organizational level and the other on a national level. Melinda Leigh Maconi examines an arts-based nonprofit organization and reveals its use of competing organizational narratives. One narrative centers the empowerment of disabled artists and resists disability stereotypes, while another, aimed at potential donors, draws on stereotypes of the art as therapeutic and "helpful" to people with disabilities. Thus, their alliance with disabled artists is tempered by its reliance on traditional models of fundraising. Concluding Part I, Sharon Barnartt explores what constitutes an ally in disability social movements and offers a robust, multilayered historical analysis of the forms and functions of *internal*, *external*, and *individual* protest allies. She documents shifts in participation over five decades of work on disability activism and across a range of potential allies. Barnartt finds multiple impairment single issue organizations to be the most likely internal ally, veterans groups the most common external organizational ally, and parents the most common individual ally.

Part II of this volume takes on agency and autonomy in interpersonal relationships and brings attention to the role of power and status between individuals, with a particular focus on alliance dynamics between disabled and nondisabled people. The chapters explore identity, self-advocacy, and representation in everyday life in relation to practices of help, parenting, care, and independent living. It opens with Erika Katzman's ethnography of a direct-funded support services organization in Ontario, Canada. She reveals how insufficient funding and the direct funding model of service leads disabled self-managers to use a variety of strategies to maximize their hours of care, bringing into clear relief the social stratification of interests and related tensions between care workers and disabled service users. The interrelated coinciding of social and economic needs of disabled self-managers and care workers offer a coalition-building opportunity, undermined by the meager social service infrastructure and scarce resources.

In Chapter 7, Helen Rottier and Morton Ann Gernsbacher bring attention to the discordant history of autism advocacy in the United States by examining key debates between autistic adults, who fight for visibility, and nonautistic parents, who often seek cure, research, and interventions. They identify common ground to form a united front based on the actionable principles of resource allocation, recognition, and autonomy. Following this, in Chapter 8 Mark Halley studies the events of 1988 *Deaf President Now* protest and traces the political alliances formed between the Deaf community and American Sign Language interpreters. Halley examines various possible roles of interpreters and what it means for interpreters to act within the "ally model."

Chapter 9 offers a reflexive piece in which Kristen Gillespie-Lynch, Steven K Kapp, Ariana Riccio, Danielle DeNigris, Jin Delos Santos, Eric Endlich, Jessye Herrell, Emily Hotez, Bella Kofner, and Naveen Hadi examine the origins and application of the concept of neurodiversity in diverse communities and organizations, with particular attention to the benefits and challenges of alliance building. The authors identify core aspects of the neurodiversity paradigm and argue that through a commitment to these core aspects we can foster alliances across diverse perspectives. Oral historian Nicki Pombier authors the final chapter. In conversation with a self-advocate, Pombier explores how academics can serve as allies, and in particular, how self-advocacy narratives can be used to re-tell [and re-construct] cultural representations of Down syndrome. Together they reflect on the methodological value [and implications] of "narrative allyship," using story-telling methods to cultivate relationships that validate disability identity and lived experience. This reflection, along with analysis of previous efforts at narrative allyship, yields a framework for the practice of narrative allyship, prioritizing that the narratives produced further the interests of narrators as the narrators define them, optimize the autonomy of narrators, and tell stories with, instead of about, narrators.

Overall, the chapters in this volume broaden and diversify the existing alliances literature. They offer new and nuanced interpretations of the meaning and practice of being an ally and ways of building thoughtful, effective alliances that reflexively account for the structural, individual, and interpersonal challenges of doing this work and, importantly, seek to amplify disabled voices and center disability lived experience.

ACKNOWLEDGMENTS

We wish to thank all of the authors in this volume for their hard work and insightful scholarship. We also thank the reviewers who provided thoughtful feedback. As coeditor of the series, *Research in Social Science and Disability,* Sharon Barnartt provided invaluable guidance. And, of course, we thank the team at Emerald Press for supporting this series and for their work on this particular volume.

REFERENCES

Ankel, S., & Mahbubani, R. (2020, May 30). George Floyd autopsy shows no sign of traumatic asphysia or strangulation. *Insider*. Retrieved from https://www.insider.com/george-floyd-non-responsive-before-officer-took-knee-off-neck-2020-5

Bak, J. (2020, March 26). Coronavirus shows care work isn't just for disabled communities any more. *BitchMedia*. Retrieved at https://www.bitchmedia.org/article/care-work-disability-framework-becomes-coronavirus-response

Barnartt, S., & Scotch, R. (2001). *Disability protests: Contentious politics: 1970-1999*. Washington, DC: Gallaudet University Press.

Beamish, T. D. & Luebbers, A. J. (2009). Alliance building across social movements. *Social Problems, 56*(4), 647–676.

Berne, P. (2015). Disability justice – A working draft. *Sins Invalid*. Retrieved from sinsinvalid.org/blog/disability-justice-a-working-draft-by-patty-berne

Blum, L. (2015). *Raising generation Rx: Mothering kids with invisible disabilities in an age of inequality*. New York, NY: New York University Press.

Brown, K. T. (2015). Perceiving allies from the perspective of non-dominant group members: Comparisons to friends and activists. *Current Psychology: A Journal for Diverse Perspectives on Diverse Psychological Issues, 34*, 713–722. doi:10.1007/s12144-014-9284-8

Brown, K. T., & Ostrove, J. M. (2013). What does it mean to be an ally?: The perception of allies from the perspective of people of color. *Journal of Applied Social Psychology, 43*, 2211–2222. doi: 10.1111/jasp.12172

Carey, A. C., Block, P., & Scotch, R. K. (2019). Sometimes allies: Parent-led disability organizations and social movements. *Disability Studies Quarterly, 39*(1). Retrieved from https://dsq-sds.org/article/view/6281

Carey, A. C., Block, P., & Scotch, R. K. (2020). *Allies and obstacles: Disability activism and parents of children with disabilities*. Philadelphia, PA: Temple University Press.

Case, K. A. (2012). Discovering the privilege of whiteness: White women's reflections on anti-racist identity and ally behavior. *Journal of Social Issues, 68*, 78–96. doi:10.1111/j.1540-4560.2011.01737

Chang, G. (2017). Inevitable intersections: Care, work, and citizenship. In M. Rembis (Ed.), *Disabling domesticity* (pp. 163–194). New York, NY: Palgrave Macmillan.

Chapman, C., Carey, A. C., & Ben-Moshe, L. (2014). Reconsidering confinement: Interlocking locations and logics of incarceration. In L. Ben-Moshe, C. Chapman, & A. C. Carey (Eds.), *Disability incarcerated: Imprisonment and disability in the United States and Canada*. (pp. 3–24). New York, NY: Palgrave Macmillan.

Chapman, C., & Withers, A. J. (2019). *A violent history of benevolence: Interlocking oppression in the moral economies of social working*. Toronto, ON: University of Toronto Press.

Charlton, J. I. (2000). *Nothing about us without us: Disability oppression and empowerment*. Berkeley, CA: University of California Press.

Charmak, B. (2008). Autism and social movements: French parents' associations and international autistic individuals' organizations. *Sociology of Health & Illness, 30*(1), 76–96.

Curtin, N., Kende, A., & Kende, J. (2016). Navigating multiple identities: The simultaneous influence of advantaged and disadvantaged identities on politicization and activism. *Journal of Social Issues, 72*, 264–285, doi:10.1111/josi.12166

Darling, R. B. (2013). *Disability and identity: Negotiating self in a changing society*. Boulder, CO: Lynne Rienner Press.

Dewey, S., & St Germain, T. (2016). *Women of the street: How the criminal justice - social service alliance falis women in prostitution*. New York, NY: New York University Press.

Droogendyk, L., Wright, S. C., Lebensky, M., & Louis, W. R. (2016). Acting in solidarity: Cross-group contact between disadvantaged group members and advantaged group allies. *Journal of Social Issues*, *72*, 315–334. doi:10.1111/josi.12168

Egner, J. E. (2018). "The disability rights community was never mine": Neuroqueer disidentification. *Gender & Society*, *33*(1), 123–147.

Erkulwater, J. L. (2018). How the nation's largest minority became white: Race politics and the disability rights movement, 1970-1980. *Journal of Policy History*, *30*(3), 367–399.

Evans, N. J., Assadi, J. L., & Herriott, T. K. (2005). Encouraging the development of disability allies. In R. D. Reason, E. M. Broido, T. Davis, & N. J. Evans (Eds). *Developing social justice allies: New directions for student services* (pp. 67–79). San Francisco, CA: Jossey-Bass.

Erevelles, N. (2014). Crippin' Jim Crow: Disability, dis-location, and the school-to-prison pipeline. In L. Ben-Moshe, C. Chapman, & A. C. Carey (Eds.), *Disability incarcerated: Imprisonment and disability in the United States and Canada* (pp. 81–100). New York, NY: Palgrave Macmillan.

Fernández, A. G., Bosch, N. V., & Samaranch, E. A. (2017). "From alliance to trust": Constructing crip-queer intimacies. *Journal of Gender Studies*, *26*(3), 269–281.

Fingerhut, A. W. (2011). Straight allies: What predicts heterosexuals' alliance with the LGBT community? *Journal of Applied Social Psychology*, *41*(9), 2230–2248. doi:10.1111/j.1559-1816.2011.00807.x

Fleischer, D. Z., & Zames, F. (2011). *The disability rights movement: From charity to confrontation*. Philadelphia, PA: Temple University Press.

Forber-Pratt, A. J., Mueller, C. O., Andrews, E. E. (2019). Disability identity and allyship in rehabilitation psychology: Sit, stand, sign, and show up. *Rehabilitation Psychology*, *64*(2), 119–129. doi:10.1037/rep0000256

Frederick, A., & Shifrer, D. (2018). Race and disability: From analogy to intersectionality. *Sociology of Race and Ethnicity*, *5*(2), 200–214.

Friedman, M., & Beckwith, R. (2014). Self-advocacy: The emancipation movement led by people with intellectual and developmental disabilities. In L. Ben-Moshe, C. Chapman, & A. C. Carey (Eds.), *Disability incarcerated: Imprisonment and disability in the United States and Canada*. (pp. 237–254). New York, NY: Palgrave Macmillan.

Fritsch, K. (2013). The neoliberal circulation of affects: Happiness, accessibility and the capacitation of disability as wheelchair. *Health, Culture and Society*, *5*(1), 135–149.

Gerhards, J., & Rucht, D. (1992). Mesomobilization: Organizing and framing in two protest campaigns in West Germany. *American Journal of Sociology*, *98*, 555–595.

Gill, C. J. (2001). Divided understandings: The social experience of disability. In G. L. Albrecht, K. D. Seelman, & M. Bury (Eds.), *Handbook of disability studies* (pp. 351–372). Thousand Oaks, CA: SAGE Publications.

Giric, S. (2016). Strange bedfellows: Antiabortion and disability rights advocacy. *Journal of Law and the Biosciences*, *3*(3), 736–742.

Groch, S. (1994). Oppositional consciousness: Its manifestations and development. The case of people with disabilities. *Sociological Inquiry*, *64*(4), 369–395.

Hewlett, S. A., & West, C. (1998). *The war against parents: What we can do for America's beleaguered moms and dads*. Boston, MA: Houghton Mifflin Company.

Indigenous Action (2014, May 4). Accomplices not allies: Abolishing the ally industrial complex. Retrieved from http://www.indigenousaction.org/accomplices-not-allies-abolishing-the-ally-industrial-complex

Jones, L. A. (2010). Doing disability justice. Lulu.com.

Kafer, A. (2013). *Feminist queer crip*. Bloomington, IN: Indiana University Press.

Kahana, J. S., & Kahana, E. (2017). *Disability and aging: Learning from both to empower the lives of older adults*. Boulder, CO: Lynne Rienner Press.

Kukla, E. (2020, March 19). My life is more 'disposable' during this pandemic. *New York Times*. Retrieved at https://www.nytimes.com/2020/03/19/opinion/coronavirus-disabled-health-care.html

Ladau, E. (2020, March 25). As a disabled person, I'm afraid I may not be deemed worth saving from the coronavirus. *HuffPost*. Retrieved from https://www.huffpost.com/entry/coronavirus-healthcare-rationing-medical-ethics-disability_n_5e7a2b0dc5b6f5b7c54bb117

Ladd-Taylor, M. (2017). *Fixing the poor: Eugenic sterilization and child welfare in the twentieth century*. Baltimore, MD: Johns Hopkins University Press.

Landsman, G. (2009). *Reconstructing motherhood and disability in an age of "perfect" babies*. New York, NY: Routledge.

Lederer, E. (2020, May 6). UN leader says 1B people with disabilities hard hit by virus. *Associated News*. Retrieved from https://apnews.com/c753de7283390477e007b0aeb4d09e3c

McAdam, D. (1996). Political opportunities: Conceptual origins, current problems, future directions. In D. McAdam, J. D. McCarthy, & M. N. Zald (Eds.), *Comparative perspectives on social movements* (pp. 20–40). Cambridge: Cambridge University Press.

McCammon, H. J., & Van Dyke, N. (2010). Applying qualitative comparative analysis to empirical studies of social movement coalition formation. In N. Van Dyke & H. J. McCammon (Eds.), *Strategic alliances: Coalition building and social movements* (pp. 292–325). Minneapolis, MN: University of Minnesota Press.

McCarthy, J. D., & Zald, M. N. (1977). Resource mobilization and social movements: A partial theory. *American Journal of Sociology*, *82*(6), 1212–1241.

McGuire, A. (2016). *War on autism: On the cultural logic of normative violence*. Ann Arbor, MI: University of Michigan Press.

Metzl, J. (2010). *The protest psychosis: How schizophrenia became a black disease*. Boston, MA: Beacon Press.

Mills, C. W. (1956). *The power elite*. Oxford: Oxford University Press.

Mingus, M. (2014). Reflection toward practice: Some questions on disability justice. In C. Wood (Ed.), *Criptiques* (pp. 107–114). San Bernardinao, CA: May Day Publishers. Retrieved from criptiques.files.wordpress.com/2014/05/crip-final-2.pdf

Moore, L. F. Jr, Lewis, T. A., & Brown, L. X. Z. (2016). Accountable reporting on disability, race, & police violence: A community response to the "Ruderman white paper on the media coverage of use of force and disability". Retrieved from https://harriettubmancollective.tumblr.com/post/174479075753/accountable-reporting-on-disability-race-and

Morris, A. D. (1984). *The origins of the civil rights movement: Black communities organizing for change*. New York, NY: Free Press.

Nario-Redmond, M. R. (2020). *Ableism: The causes and consequences of disability prejudice*. Hoboken, NJ: Wiley Blackwell.

Ne'eman, A. (2020, March 23). I will not apologize for my needs. *New York Times*. Retrieved from https://www.nytimes.com/2020/03/23/opinion/coronavirus-ventilators-triage-disability.html

Nielsen, K. (2012). *A disability history of the United States*. Boston, MA: Beacon Press.

Ostrove, J. M., Cole, E. R., & Oliva, G. A. (2009). Toward a feminist liberation psychology of alliances. *Feminism & Psychology*, *19*, 381–386. doi:10.1177/0959353509105629

Ostrove, J. M., & Crawford, D. (2006). "One lady was so busy staring at me she walked into a wall": Interability relations from the perspective of women with disabilities. *Disability Studies Quarterly*, *26*(3).

Ostrove, J. M., Kornfeld, M., & Ibrahim, M. (2019). Actors against ableism?: Qualities of non-disabled allies from the perspective of people with physical disabilities. *Journal of Social Issues*, *75*, 924–942.

OToole, C. (2015). *My fading scars: My queer disability history*. Fort Worth, TX: Autonomous Press.

Panitch, M. (2008). *Disability, mothers, and organization: Accidental activists*. New York, NY: Routledge.

Pelka, F. (2012). *What we have done: An oral history of the disability rights movement*. Amherst, MA: University of Massachusetts Press.

Pichardo, N. A. (1997). New social movements: A critical review. *Annual Review of Sociology*, *23*, 411–430.

Piepzna-Samarashinha, L. L. (2018). *Care work: Dreaming disability justice*. Vancouver, BC: Arsenal Pulp Press.

Prior, R. (2020, April 8). Coping with disease and disability in the time of coronavirus. *CNN*. Retrieved from https://www.cnn.com/2020/04/08/health/coronavirus-disability-and-chronic-illness-wellness/index.html

Rosqvist, H. B., Brownlow, C., & O'Dell, L. (2015). An association for all': Notions of the meaning of autistic self-advocacy politics within a parent-dominated movement. *Journal of Community and Applied Psychology*, *25*(3), 219–231.

Russell, M. (1998). *Beyond ramps: Disability at the end of the social contract*. Monroe, ME: Common Courage Press.

Russell, G. M., & Bohan, J. S. (2016). Institutional allyship for LGBT equality: Underlying processes and potentials for change. *Journal of Social Issues*, *72*(2), 335–354.

Schweik, S. (2011). Lomax's matrix: Disability, solidarity, and the black power of 504. *Disability Studies Quarterly*, *31*(1). Retrieved from https://dsq-sds.org/article/view/1371/1539

Scotch, R. K. (1984). *From good will to civil rights: Transforming federal disability policy*. Philadelphia, PA: Temple University Press

Scotch, R. K. (1988). Disability as the basis for a social movement. *Journal of Social Issues*, *44*(1), 159–172.

Selvanathan, H. P., Techakesari, P., Tropp, L. R., & Barlow, F. K. (2017). Whites for racial justice: How contact with Black Americans predicts support for collective action among White Americans. *Group Processes & Intergroup Relations*, *21*, 893–912, doi:10.1177/1368430217690908

Sins Invalid. (2020, March 19). Social distancing and crip survival: A disability centered response to COVID-19. *Sins Invalid*. Retrieved from https://www.sinsinvalid.org/news-1/2020/3/19/social-distancing-and-crip-survival-a-disability-centered-response-to-covid-19

Snow, D. A., & Benford, R. D. (1992). Master frames and cycles of protest. In A. D. Morris & C. M. Mueller (Eds.), *Frontiers in social movement theory* (pp. 133–155). New Haven, CT: Yale University Press.

Snow, D. A., Rochford, B. E. Jr, Worden, S. K., & Benford, R. D. (1986). Frame alignment processes, micromobilization, and movement participation. *American Sociological Review*, *51*(4), 464–481.

Staggenborg, S. (2010). Conclusion: Research on social movement coalitions. In N. Van Dyke & H. J. McCammon (Eds.), *Strategic alliances: Coalition building and social movements* (pp. 316–330). Minneapolis, MN: University of Minnesota Press.

Stewart, E. (2020, June 2). How to be a good white ally, according to activists. Vox.com. Retrieved from https://www.vox.com/2020/6/2/21278123/being-an-ally-racism-george-floyd-protests-white-people

Taylor, S. J. (2009). *Acts of conscience: World War II, mental institutions, and religious objectors*. Syracuse, NY: Syracuse University Press.

Van Dyke, N., & McCammon, H. J. (2010). *Strategic alliances: Coalition building and social movements*. Minneapolis, MN: University of Minnesota Press.

Ware, S., Ruzsa, J., & Dias, G. (2014). It can't be fixed because it's not broken: Racism and disability in the prison industrial complex. In L. Ben-Moshe, C. Chapman, & A. C. Carey (Eds.), *Disability incarcerated: Imprisonment and disability in the United States and Canada*. (pp. 163–184). New York, NY: Palgrave Macmillan.

Wyatt, M. (2020). Myne Wyatt's monologue on racism. *Guardian Australia*. Retrieved from https://www.youtube.com/results?search_query=meyne+wyatt+silence+is+violence

Zald, M. N. & McCarthy, J. D. (1997). *Social movements in an organizational society: Collected essays*. New York, NY: Routledge.

PART I

STRUCTURES AND SYSTEMS THAT SHAPE ALLIANCES

Chapter 1

INTERNATIONAL RIGHTS AND LOCAL REALITIES: TRANSNATIONAL ALLIES OF THE DISABILITY RIGHTS MOVEMENT IN CHINA

Shixin Huang

ABSTRACT

Purpose: *The purpose of this chapter is to scrutinize the apparent alliance between international and local disability rights movements by contextualizing the process in which the disability rights model is being diffused globally. It seeks to critically examine the transplantation and promotion of the international disability rights movement's rights-based model in China.*

Approach: *This chapter draws from 18 in-depth interviews with local and international disability rights activists through multisite ethnographic fieldwork in China in 2019.*

Findings: *This chapter finds that despite opening up spaces for resistance and emancipation locally, the international disability rights movement nevertheless constitutes what I call an* enclave of rights *that insulates the international rights model from the political, social, and economic realities on the ground. In the case of China, the authoritarian politics that define the relationship between the state and civil society, as well as the economic vulnerability of people with disabilities in the post-socialist market economy, limit, if not invalidate, the rights model espoused by the international disability rights movement.*

Disability Alliances and Allies
Research in Social Science and Disability, Volume 12, 19–39

ISSN: 1479-3547/doi:10.1108/S1479-354720200000012004

Implications: *The findings of this chapter challenge and complicate the current scholarship of the transnational disability rights movement beyond its normative claims of emancipation. They also explore potential spaces and direction for building a new transnational alliance that takes into account the local experience of disability in a rapidly globalized world.*

Keywords: Disability rights movement; the rights model of disability; China; transnational alliance; conventions on the rights of persons with disabilities; transnational disability studies

INTRODUCTION

On June 7th, 2014, Li Jinsheng, a 46-year-old blind man from Zhumadian, a village in central China, walked proudly on his way to take the *Gaokao,* or College Entrance Exam, after graduating from high school 26 years before (Di, 2014; Tatlow, 2013). He was the first blind student in China to take the exam in Braille, after a years-long advocacy campaign of disability rights activists. Before that, most people with disabilities in China studied in special schools, with rarely any reasonable accommodation provided for the college entrance exam. Li challenged this discrimination by signing up for the exam and applying for reasonable accommodations to the local educational authority. When speaking to national media outlets, Li framed access to higher education as a "basic legal right of people with disabilities" because "the Conventions on the Rights of People with Disabilities (CRPD) took effect in China in 2008, which prohibits all discrimination on the basis of disability, including refusal to provide reasonable accommodation" (Liu & Guo, 2014). Regardless of the initial refusal of the local educational authority, Li's application was accepted and finally led to a national policy from the Ministry of Education mandating the provision of reasonable accommodations in the exam for students with visual, hearing, and physical impairments (Huang, 2019).

Why did a disabled man such as Li who is from a remote village in Central China engage and maneuver the transnational rights discourse of reasonable accommodation and nondiscrimination that is remote from his everyday life? In other words, why and how do disability rights discourses diffuse globally? And, finally, what is the role of international disability rights movement allies in the diffusion process?

Heyer (2015) identifies the making of the disability rights model and its globalization as "the disability revolution." Since the 1960s, a disability rights movement launched by people with disabilities in the United States and United Kingdom has striven for the equal rights of the disability community. According to Heyer, a major output of the movement was a revolutionary rights model of disability that sees disability as a human rights issue rather than an object of charity issue. Even though the disability rights movement and its rights-based model were primarily developed in the Western democracies, this rights agenda diffuses globally through transnational institutions and becomes the agenda of disability rights development of these societies in the age of globalization, not only in developed countries such as Germany, Japan (Heyer, 2015), Taiwan

(Chang, 2007), and Denmark (Vanhala, 2015) but also in developing states such as Ukraine (Phillips, 2010), Nicaragua (Meyers, 2014), India (Kalyanpur, 2015), and China (Zhang, 2017).

The CRPD has triggered a new wave of global disability rights movements that are funded and promoted by international civil society and governmental organizations. The CRPD institutionalized the rights model of disability that emerged from the Western disability rights movement and provides both the goals and tools of disability rights mobilizations globally, especially in developing countries. According to a report that traces human rights grants globally, a lump sum of $246.8 million dollars and a total number of 3,312 grants on disability rights were endowed from 2011 to 2015 (Foundation Center and Human Rights Funders Network, 2019). Both disability-specific organizations such as Disability Rights Fund and Humanity and Inclusion (former Handicap International) and mainstream organizations such as European Union and the Ford Foundation adopt this new human rights framework to fund projects on disability rights locally.

At first glance, the international disability rights movement, comprised of international organizations, funders, and networks that are predominantly based in the global North, can be contended as a desirable and beneficial ally to local disability activists beyond the global North. Mobilized around the rights model as "means and tools of communication" (Heyer, 2015, p. 203), the alliance of international and local disability activism constitutes what scholars of international human rights movements define as transnational advocacy networks. On the one hand, as informed by resource mobilization theorists of social movements (McAdam, McCarthy, Zald, & Meyer, 1996; McCarthy & Zald, 1977; Tarrow, 2011), international disability rights actors serve as powerful allies of local social movements by providing resources for effective mobilization, including the formation of professional organizations, financial support, information, institutional access of international advocacy, etc. On the other hand, this global–local alliance in turn transforms domestic norms and on the ground practices regarding human rights. For example, Risse, Ropp, and Sikkink (1999) propose a "spiral model" that captures the socialization process by which international human rights norms are incorporated into the domestic practices of states. In this socialization process, a vibrant transnational advocacy network and a corresponding domestic civil society are seen as vital. Keck and Sikkink (2014) suggest a "boomerang pattern" in which domestic civil society actors can direct information and appeals to the transnational advocacy networks including foreign states, regional and international organizations, which respond by mobilizing external pressure against the norms-violating state. As proposed by this strand of research, the alliance of international and local disability rights movements can potentially lead to the diffusion and domestication of disability rights transnationally.

On the surface, the story of Li Jinsheng, presented at the beginning of this chapter, represents a successful story of alliance between international and local disability rights movements, signaled by the transplantation of the rights model into a domestic political process. Upon closer examination, however, there are gaps to be filled in understanding this linear, and in a certain extent, positivist process of alliance building and rights model proliferation. Does Li Jinsheng, a man with visual disabilities who runs a small blind massage shop in a village of central China, perceive rights in the same way as a disabled activist in North America does? In other words, do rights connote different meanings across culture and space? More importantly, how do political, economic, social, and cultural processes on the ground mediate and shape the localization of the global discourses of rights?

In my efforts to study the global–local interface of disability rights movements, I am following Ingstad and Whyte's (1995, 2007) attempts to problematize the "universal" definition of disability through cross-cultural, comparative perspectives. Their earlier work insightfully argued that the universal standards and rights model of disability was predicated on European and North American assumptions of disability, emerging out of "a framework of state, legal, economic, and biomedical institutions" (Ingstad & Whyte, 1995, p. 10). Therefore, they posit:

> ...the energizing potential of human-rights declarations, progressive policies, and international statements of intent toward disabled citizens has to be measured in the context of local worlds (1995, p. 10).

This chapter scrutinizes the apparent alliance between international and local disability rights movements by contextualizing the process in which the disability rights model is being diffused globally. I argue that in the context of China, although the international disability rights movement has opened up spaces for resistance and emancipation locally, it nevertheless constitutes what I call an *enclave of rights* that insulates the international rights model from the political, social, and economic realities on the ground. The implementation of the international rights model is complicated by both the authoritarian politics that confine the relationship between state and civil society, as well as the economic vulnerability of people with disabilities in the post-socialist market economy. By identifying the gaps between international and local disability rights movements, I seek not to renounce the alliance between the two, nor to reject the emancipation potential of the rights model; instead, I intend to explore potential spaces and directions for building a new transnational alliance that takes into account the local experience of disability in a rapidly globalizing world.

INTERNATIONAL RIGHTS, LOCAL REALITIES

The disability right movement is also known as the "last civil rights movement." People with disabilities in the United Kingdom have mobilized around the issues of segregated residential care, domination of medical professionals, and economic exclusion since the late 1960s (Barnes & Mercer, 2010). In 1976, the Union of the Physically Impaired Against Segregation published the Fundamental Principles of Disability, which proposed the idea of the social model of disability that sees social barriers, instead of individual impairments, as the source of disability. The social model of disability, born in the British disability rights movement, soon became the central concept around which disabled people began to interpret their own experiences and organize their own political movement (Oliver, 1996). While the British movement created significant ideological discourses of political mobilization, disability activists in the United States made legal mobilization discourse a dominant repertoire of strategy. Learning from the success of the civil rights movement in the 1960s, the US disability rights movement also mobilized around the principles of nondiscrimination and equal treatment through legal mobilization (Heyer, 2015). This repertoire of strategies is based on the notion that people with disabilities are equal citizens and a political minority, subject to civil rights protection. As a result, people with disabilities in the United States mobilized around antidiscrimination legislation to claim equal citizenship, which led to the passage of Section 504 of the Rehabilitation Act and the Americans with Disabilities Act. These Anglo-American political discourses have traveled and diffused globally, leading to disability antidiscrimination legislation in more than 40 countries during the 1990s (Kanter, 2014). In 2006, the CRPD was adopted by the UN General Assembly. The CRPD adopts the rights model of disability comprehensively and marks the institutionalization of the normative claims coming out of the international disability rights movement.

Emerging from the international disability rights movements of the United States and the United Kingdom, the rights model of disability inevitably reflects the agenda, repertoires of strategies, assumptions, as well as the economic, social, political, and political processes that shaped disability rights in Western societies. The rights model of disability entails four fundamental and interrelated perspectives about emancipating people with disabilities. First and foremost, it puts great emphasis on the struggle for citizenship to affirm choice, independence, and control of people with disabilities (Barton, 1993). Closely related to this assumption of equal citizenship is the model's focus on the state both as duty bearers and rights violators. The international disability rights movement targets the state to undertake responsibility in eliminating attitudinal, institutional, and environmental barriers that prohibit equal participation of people with disabilities. Furthermore, the movement views legal mobilization that aims at new legislation and institutional transformation as the most effective way of realizing rights and equal citizenship (Vanhala, 2010). Nondiscrimination legislation and policy-making in the realms of education, employment, and accessibility more broadly are promoted as essential components of protecting the rights of people with disabilities. Last but not least, the rights model believes in the importance of civil society empowerment, usually in the form of facilitating the development of Disabled Persons' Organizations (DPOs) (Meyers, 2014; Meyers & Lockwood, 2014).

In recent years, a growing body of work has emerged as comparative and international disability studies, which seeks to understand the manifestation of disability in different social, political, and economic contexts beyond North America and Western Europe (Cobley, 2018; Grech, 2014; Kiuppis & Soorenian, 2017). These scholars challenge the assumptions that the experiences of people with disabilities, and the relevance of the rights model of disability, are universal and that the experience of the international disability rights movement can be applied throughout the world. For example, Ingstad's (1995) early ethnographic fieldwork in Botswana provides a re-examination of the Anglo-American rights model of disability. She found that in Botswana Society, disability can be seen as a positive identity because it is *mpho ya modimo*, or a gift from God. Berghs (2017) proposes a relational approach to disability which differs from the rights model's emphasis on independence and autonomy. He argues that the conceptualization of disability in Africa is centered around the idea of *Ubuntu*, which refers to a local philosophy of shared collective humanness and responsibility.

Recognizing that the experience of disability is contingent on local cultural, social, economic, and political processes, other scholars also examine the global diffusion of the rights model of disability in the context of the global South. Chataika, Berghs, Mateta, and Shava (2015) argue that the disability rights approach in international development is rooted in the neocolonialism and charity model, as well as embedded in the neoliberal hegemony of the West. They propose a more nuanced examination of disability activism in Africa under the influence of the international disability rights movement. The authors highlight the undemocratic imposition of the rights paradigm, the neoliberal development discourse that promotes disability as a "big business," the superficial participation of DPO in the development process, and the inability of the international rights discourse to address local reality. Similarly, Grech (2014) adopts a critical stance and argues that the rights-based model of development entails an epistemological hegemony of neocolonialism, imposed on the global South by the Western disability studies paradigm. He further proposes that a re-examination of the Southern "space of poverty" would potentially challenge and even reconstruct the Eurocentric knowledge of disability.

These previous works insightfully identify the political economy of colonialism in shaping the international organizations' imposition of the rights model of disability in the context of underdeveloped countries in South America and Africa. In this chapter, I follow the inquiry of this body of work in comparative and international disability studies to examine the dynamics of a transnational alliance of disability rights movements in the context of a post-socialist, authoritarian regime. In an upper-middle income country that has undergone radical socioeconomic transformation from a collective to market economy, as well as an authoritarian regime that demonstrates strong state capacity to exercise repression against rights-oriented civil society activism, how does this transnational movement coalition manifest?

CONTEXTUALIZING DISABILITY RIGHTS IN CHINA

In order to explore the coalition between the international and local disability rights movements, it is necessary to explore the context in which a disability rights movement has developed in China. I discuss the socioeconomic factors that conditioned the diffusion of disability rights as an international agenda in the context of post-socialist China, as well as the authoritarian politics that defined state and civil society relations underlying local disability activism.

People with disabilities are arguably one of the most stigmatized and marginalized social groups in China. As the world's most populous country, China has the largest number of people with disabilities in the world. According to the most recent official disabled population census, there are more than 83 million people with disabilities in China, although the actual number is significantly higher according to World Health Organization (WHO)'s estimation[1]. Even though China is now an upper-middle–income country, people with disabilities substantially lag behind in the economic development process. Approximately 75% of people with disabilities live in the countryside, 21% of them live under the poverty line, and almost a half of people with disabilities over the age of 15 are illiterate. Yeo and Moore (2003) argue that people with disabilities in China are trapped in a "vicious circle" of poverty because of exclusion from social, economic, and political opportunities, as well as limited access to public services.

This socioeconomic vulnerability of people with disabilities should be understood in relation to the post-socialist state's reform toward a market economy and a retrenchment in welfare provision. Since 1978, the Chinese Communist Party has launched the "open door reform" that shifted away from its collectivist, planned economy toward a market economy. This radical socioeconomic reorganization also fundamentally transformed the everyday life of people with disabilities. The most significant influence originated from the privatization of the collective and state-owned enterprises, as well as the reduction of "welfare enterprises (福利企业)." During the socialist period, the state had an all-encompassing influence on individual lives, from work arrangements to social welfare provision through these collectivist organizations. Even though disability was not a policy priority at the time, people with disabilities were seen as members of the masses and were entitled to the "iron rice bowl (铁饭碗)" placements in the collective economy that guaranteed them access to employment and social welfare (Fjeld & Sagli, 2011). In the wave of privatization, these collectivist organizations have been dismantled, leading to a massive wave of lay-offs among both people with disabilities and workers in general. Coupled with this trend was the state's retrenchment of social welfare services such as health care and housing. Moreover, market reform opened up spaces for the proliferation of neoliberal values that emphasize productivity and entrepreneurship (Zhang & Ong, 2008), which further stigmatizes people with disabilities by generating discourses of welfare dependency and disability as an individual responsibility. These socioeconomic transformations in the post-socialist society exacerbated the economic vulnerability of people with disabilities and marginalized them as one of the "losers" of the reform.

Along with China's integration in global capitalism, Western notions of biomedicine and public health have also been infused in the post-socialist state, shaping the ways in which disability is perceived and responded to in a local context. The international notion of medicalization plays out by defining what constitutes a healthy, functional, "normal," and desirable body in China. This transformation is best shown in the first national census on people with disabilities in the 1990s. According to Kohrman (2005), international influence was prominent in generating China's first statistical survey on people with disabilities. He traces the census back to the early 1980s when the United Nations and international organizations such as Rehabilitation International first came to

China. These international organizations increasingly brought the global agenda of "data collection" and managing disability as an epidemiological issue into China, a country in which disability was never an object of national survey nor were "people with disabilities" a homogenous group. These international pressures converged with the post-socialist state's nationalist projects of achieving modernization and gaining positive foreign assessment. The result was a new national classification of disability into five separate categories: hearing and speech disability, intellectual disability, visual disability, physical disability, and psychiatric disability, in accordance with international benchmarks.

Even though international conceptions of biomedicine and rehabilitation diffused and influenced disability politics on the ground, the authoritarian state still plays a significant role in defining and channeling the ways in which disability rights are protected and claimed. Rather than taking the form of bottom-up grassroots mobilization, disability rights advocacy is institutional advocacy that is incorporated closely within the ideology and bureaucracy of the post-socialist state. China Disabled People's Federation (CDPF) was founded in 1988 by Deng Pufang, the son of Deng Xiaoping, the paramount leader of China who initiated market reform. CDPF is defined as a "mass organization" that people with disabilities join voluntarily. It is also known as a government-owned nongovernmental organization (NGO) in China. Kohrman (2005) argues that the CDPF is, in essence, a state apparatus that redistributes public resources and monopolizes welfare provision. CDPF takes the administrative power as commissioned by the party-state to develop, implement, and supervise disability-related legislation, policies, and affairs. While coordinating disability policy horizontally across different administrative bodies, the CDPF also establishes networks in different administrative levels vertically, from national, provincial, and municipal to township levels (CDPF, 2018).

As an authoritarian regime, the party-state also executes strict social control over civil society activism. After the pro-democracy movement in 1989, scholars argue that the state adopted a corporatist approach to organizing civil society, such as enforcing registration of and sponsoring social organizations (White, Howell, & Shang, 1996). Other studies show that civil society in China is subjected to the regulation and guidance of the state, rather than acting autonomously (Ma, 2005; Teets, 2015). Recent scholars identify a differentiated approach adopted by the state, repressing the rights-based advocacy of NGO that are not in line with the state's goals on the one hand, while tolerating, incorporating, and promoting service-delivery NGOs that provide public goods for the state on the other hand (Dickson, 2016; Howell & Pringle, 2019). The state is particularly hostile toward civil society organizations such as foreign NGOs and local NGOs with foreign connections. The Law on the Management of Overseas Non-Governmental Organisations' Activities within Mainland China, which is also widely known as the Foreign NGO Law, was enacted on January 1st, 2017. The Foreign NGO Law has been seen as a new initiative of the party-state to tighten control over activities of foreign NGOs and their domestic grantees in China, especially those with an orientation toward civil and political rights (Feng, 2017; Sidel, 2019). Under this law, all foreign NGOs in China are required to register formally under the Ministry of Public Security and report their activities regularly. This new wave of legislation and political tightening poses a threat to the development of a disability rights movement, hindering the extent to which the international agenda of rights advocacy can be adopted and appropriated by local disability activists.

In sum, the international disability rights movement's global diffusion did not occur in a vacuum. In the context of China, the market economy transition and the retrenchment of welfare services in the post-socialist era shaped the socio-economic vulnerability of people with disabilities. However, the authoritarian state regulates disability rights, both through its administrative apparatus of CDPF and the political control over civil society groups, especially those with foreign backgrounds. These economic, social, and political dynamics on the ground condition the coalition between international and local disability rights movements, a theme that I will explore in the following parts of this chapter.

METHOD

This chapter is part of a broader research project of understanding the disability rights movement in China that originated from my embodied experience as a person with hearing disability and as a disability rights activist. Between 2013 and 2016, I worked in the field of disability rights advocacy in China and was deeply inspired by the rights discourse mandated by the CRPD. At the time, China's ratification of CRPD triggered a considerable wave of international funding to support projects on disability rights. I had been involved in this process by working in a foreign-funded NGO that promoted disability rights locally during a period in which the transnational alliance of disability rights was at its peak in the country. As time passed, however, my colleagues and I began reflecting on the applicability of the rights model in the local context, as well as the personal and social consequences the international model brought with it.

In the summer of 2019, I conducted three months of ethnographic fieldwork in China. This chapter draws from 18 in-depth interviews I conducted over this period. The interviews were conducted in multiple field sites, including Hong Kong, Guangzhou, Yantai, and Seattle, Washington. I interviewed founders and staff members of local NGOs and DPOs working on disability rights, directors and staff of international organizations that fund and collaborate with local partners, as well as people with disabilities who were engaged in disability rights advocacy. Many of these interviewees no longer work in the same organizations, as political repression against civil society organizations with foreign connections has steadily escalated since 2015. I conducted the interviews in Mandarin, Cantonese, and English according to the language spoken by the interviewee, and then translated the Mandarin and Cantonese interviews into English. I conducted semistructured interviews that lasted for about two to three hours. The information provided by interviewees was triangulated both with other informants and with other data sources such as news reports and official websites of organizations.

Receiving foreign funding and engaging in rights advocacy can be politically sensitive in China, shaping how I collected data. Most of the interviews were recorded and transcribed in the language that the interviews were conducted in. One interviewee refused to be recorded, but allowed me to take notes during the interview. Another interviewee requested that I delete the recording after transcribing, due to safety considerations. During my fieldwork, a director and two staff members of an NGO in southern China that advocates for the rights of "vulnerable groups" including people with disabilities were arrested on suspicion of state subversion, partly due to their international connections (Feng, 2019; Kuo, 2019). This event escalated concern among some of my informants about the shrinking spaces for rights advocacy and international funding. In order to protect their safety, all the interviewees and their organizations are anonymized and their identifiable information is removed.

RESULTS

The Diffusion of the Rights Agenda through Transnational Coalition

Under the rights model of disability, international organizations have shifted their local funding agenda from medical rehabilitation to promoting human rights of people with disabilities. This new funding agenda also applied to the case of China. China's ratification of the CRPD in 2008 opened up space for the introduction of the rights model as an international norm. A founder of a renowned national disability organization contended that funding from the international disability rights movement was precious to local organizations, saying,

> At the beginning, the state provided no service nor resource to people with disabilities. People with intellectual disabilities were not taken good care of. We can only rely on foreign funding.

Another experienced disability rights activist reflected on how they started to work in the field of disability rights:

> ...our organizations had no experience working on disability rights. However, we had accumulated effective policy advocacy experiences in the realms of public health. Probably because of the influence of China's ratification of CRPD, our donors at the time started to purposely ask us if we wanted to pay attention to other realms such as disability rights.

Since 2008, international funders and organizations have supported disability-related projects and activities among local NGOs and DPOs in China within the framework of human rights. These dynamics significantly transformed the landscape of disability politics in China.

The introduction of the rights discourses such as equality, nondiscrimination, and the social model from the international disability rights movement cultivated a new generation of activists with rights consciousness. Local disability activists believe that the rights model fundamentally transformed their way of understanding a person with a disability from an object of charity to an equal citizen.

An NGO staff member recalled her first time learning the rights model from a training about mental disability in 2010:

> The teacher was a founder of a mental disability NGO in Europe and he gave us a training about legal capacity. It was really progressive at the time! He introduced the definition of disability and CRPD to us. No one had heard of them before. It was so eye-opening! I had never thought that one can think about disability like that. Because when you talked about disability in the past, you might just think about it as an individual problem. But the training about CRPD made you believe that disability is not about individual, but about the structure. I was really amazed at the time.

An activist with a visual disability also found the rights discourse fundamentally transformed his perception of his own and his community's situation:

> It was so natural that I connected my situation with the vision of the CRPD. In the past, I always had a strong sense of unfairness. Why do I have to work as a blind massager and cannot get rid of it? Why do I have to work like cattle every day? Why can't I have my own space of living?[2] The social model and CRPD gave me answers to all those questions.

As a result of this new funding agenda, the rights language has become the legitimated and widely used language to frame and approach disability issues. An NGO staff member made a joke that the rights language is the slang of those worked with disability issues.

> It is like, people think that if you work on disability issue without talking about CRPD or the social model, then you are an outsider of the field and you know nothing... If you talk about rights, then you belong to the community of disability rights. So it became a common language, jargon, or slang that everyone who works in the field of disability rights share.

It is also through this process that disability activists in China started to implement the rights model into their everyday work of service provision and policy advocacy. The founder of the national organization mentioned above said that they purposively transplanted the international tools including "ICF (International Classification of Functioning, Disability and Health), CBR (Community-based Rehabilitation Guidelines), and CRPD" to their regional partners.

> No matter what program you are designing, the first thing you should do is to check the CBR from WHO (World Health Organization). Then you should check which CRPD articles that CBR program refers to. There are a lot of programs in CBR and what you simply need to do is just to pick one from it, localize the program, and make a budget of the program.

Disability rights activists in China have adopted the rights model and launched campaigns focused on nondiscrimination legislation, rights to employment, inclusive education, gender equality, legal capacity, physical and informational accessibility, and so forth. These local activists have led the CRPD's right-based language and mechanisms to be adopted by the state in disability rights policies and legislation. Since 2008, the rights model's core concept of discrimination and reasonable accommodations has been included in revisions to the Mental Health Law (2012), Disability Regulations for Education (2017), Regulations for Disability Prevention and Rehabilitation (2017), and

Measures for the Administration of Air Transport for the Disabled (2015), and other areas of law and policy. The feminist disability perspective was also introduced into China's 2015 domestic violence legislation through articles emphasizing the needs and mechanisms of "special protection" for domestic violence victims with disabilities as a result of civil society action.

The transnational coalition of disability rights movements, in the narratives of local disability activists, was formed during this period of rapid expansion of international funding for rights-based programs and projects. What came after this funding is the transplantation of the rights discourses and rights-based programs that originated from the international disability rights movement into China. The question then becomes, to what extent has the transplantation of the rights model transformed everyday lives of people with disabilities on the ground?

Can Rights Buy Me Rice and Oil?

While the rights model is deeply rooted in persons with disabilities' experience in the disability rights movement in the West, this model came into China as a set of rights discourses on paper as promoted by transnational institutions. Local practitioners, many of them keen believers in the model, worked to find a way to translate the model into their own context. However, they soon found that this approach was not viable because these abstract "rights" were too far away from the everyday struggles of people with disabilities.

The majority of disability rights programs in China focused on capacity building and policy or legislation advocacy, echoing the international disability rights movement's agenda. A former NGO staff illustrated the way he delivered capacity training:

> We mainly conducted rights education. We taught people what rights are and what rights they ought to have. The trainings and workshops we delivered all had a similar structure. In the first day, we conducted DET (Disability Equality Training)[3], in which we taught the three models of disability and principles of the CRPD. In the second day, we taught the slogan of "nothing about us without us" and the idea of self-advocacy. In the last day, we formed people into small group to form action plans and hoped that activists could be cultivated out of such an assembly line-like training.

Through introducing the concepts of the social model, equality, nondiscrimination, advocacy, and participation during capacity training, local practitioners aimed at transforming people with disabilities' understanding of disability, which would in turn cultivate them into activists who advocate for disability rights.

However, the agenda of the rights model supported by local rights advocates, often illustrated by a set of legal rights on paper, departed from the local realities experienced by people with disabilities on the ground. A disability activist told me:

> In 2012, I went to a remote village in the countryside to deliver a disability awareness training. In the training, I was challenged by a disabled famer in that village. He said, "Do not talk about rights and awareness to me! Can rights buy me rice and oil?" From then on, I started to realize that the rights that I was talking about everyday cannot solve people's everyday life challenges. I even asked myself, "Why am I doing this job?"

A legal specialist who worked for a disability rights organization also explained this gap vividly:

> There was a time we conducted a disability rights training for the Deaf. We were talking about concepts of disability, how should we understand disability, what kinds of legal rights we should enjoy, and so forth. The Deaf participants were signing all the time down there and I asked the interpreter what they were talking about. It turned out that they were talking about whose money was defrauded, why the Deaf cannot enjoy free public transportation as other people with disabilities and so on. Our agenda was that disability should be deemed as normal and people with disabilities should enjoy equal rights to be civil servants. But the Deaf have no access to education at all, it is so far away to talk about being a civil servant to them.

Increasing this gap is the international partners' preferences toward advocacy-oriented programs instead of services provision, even though the latter is important to realize rights of people with disabilities. Scholars who study local disability rights movements observe the same dynamics of the international organizations' overemphasis on political empowerment over material needs (Meyers, 2019). A former staff member of an international organization bluntly said that most foreign funding only supports advocacy-oriented projects:

> If you want to apply for a project that provides counseling service to people with disabilities, then you can get nothing. But if you are applying for a legal aid or policy advocacy project, then you can get the money. It is understandable because if you work with individuals, there are a massive number of individuals. But if you work with institutions, then you can change individuals through institutional transformation.

Even local activists who conduct rights advocacy have to follow the "hierarchy of rights" that prioritizes political and civil rights over social, economic, and cultural rights. A founder of an advocacy-oriented NGO explained the topics they worked on over the past few years:

> At the beginning, we still hadn't got foreign funding regarding disability rights and we started to work on the issue in a small scale. We started by getting in touch with people with disabilities to know what kind of topics they deemed as important. Because people with disabilities are generally living in poor condition, they want economic assistance or allowance from the society, or from the government. So, at the beginning, we worked a lot on legal cases of free public transportation.

Later on, however, the organization shifted from "needs-based" to "rights-based" because of criticisms from other disability organizations:

> For them, it (welfare) should not be…a priority. It would conversely strengthen the stereotypes of people with disabilities as a disadvantaged group that need to be rescued, and as object of charity…It is just strengthening stereotypes. Therefore, there were very few people who pay attention to these concrete needs of people with disabilities. But for the community, it is what they really care about and it is needs-based. Later on, we learned about CRPD and used the social model of CRPD as the blueprint of our work. These concepts guided us to promote disability rights and the social model in order to promote the implementation of CRPD in China. We would think about our work from this direction. It is not about needs-based and about doing whatever *canyou* (friends with disabilities) think we should do anymore… Instead, we turned to work in the field of employment discrimination and seek to promote non-discrimination legislation in China.

It is striking that the local disability activists distinguish rights from the needs of the community, illustrating the international rights agenda's fissure from local realities. A by-product of this gap is the underrepresentation of people with disabilities in the local disability rights movement. In other words, the local disability rights movement that adopted their international allies' agenda, ironically, marginalized participation by people with disabilities. The use of legal mobilization as a main repertoire of strategy means that disability activists have to be acquainted with domestic laws and policies, as well as international human rights mechanisms. Working with international partners also requires a solid command of English. Actually, several staff members and founders I interviewed have overseas educational backgrounds and went to graduate school in law. Others have university degrees from domestic colleges. A person with disability who only graduated from primary school once got an opportunity to work as an intern with a professional rights advocacy NGO as part of a community empowerment program. He described his experience in this way,

> I felt myself not competent with this job at all. There were all kinds of project documents to process and all kinds of advocacy campaigns to design. And then I have to follow their financial procedures of reimbursement. How could I do it?

With more than 40% of people with disabilities over 15 years old are illiterate in China (National Bureau of Statistics, 2007), only a small number of people with disabilities who possessed a university degree can be lucky enough to work in these disability rights NGOs as staff members. A nondisabled activist reflected:

> There is an apparent phenomenon in our field. That is, within the disability community, there is a huge gap between the so-called elites and the so-called grassroots. The elites are using the language of CRPD to promote rights, and do rights advocacy; on the other hand, the grassroots are using another set of language. There is a huge gap between them... The distribution of people with disabilities in different social classes is not even. We can see that people [with disabilities] around us have always been the same group of people. Imagine there are 86 million people with disabilities in the country and there have always been the same small group of people [with disabilities] and people without disabilities like us in the field! Oh my god!

The rights model of disability as actively promoted by the international disability rights movement departs from the local reality on the ground, where the lives of people with disabilities are characterized by economic insecurity and educational deprivation. While the local community's immediate needs are livelihood and social welfare, the international agenda predominantly focuses on legal mobilization to enforce the civil and political rights of people with disabilities. This gap constituted the first dimension of what I call the *enclave of rights*, which asserts that the international disability rights movement generated a symbolic and materialist terrain mirroring the international agenda of rights. This terrain, however, insulates itself from lived experiences of disabled people characterized by socioeconomic vulnerability on the ground.

Advocating Against the State

In this section, I propose the second dimension of the *enclave of rights*: that the international disability rights movement failed to generate a meaningful local movement in the context of an authoritarian party-state. That is, the state–society relationship in an authoritarian regime is fundamentally different from that in the liberal democratic states, which hindered the potentials of the movement to permeate throughout China and take effect.

Adopting the rights mandate from their international counterparts required that local actors hold the state responsible for protecting the equal citizenship of people with disabilities through policy and legislative change. An example of this approach is the local NGOs and DPOs' engagement with the CRPD's reporting mechanism in 2011–2012. The CRPD mandated that domestic NGOs and DPOs can submit a civil society shadow report in addition to the State Party Report to the Committee on the Rights of People with Disabilities. This mechanism is said to be an effective way of monitoring a states' obligation to protect the rights of people with disabilities (Stein & Lord, 2010). The international partners introduced this international disability rights mechanism to local NGOs and DPOs mainly through trainings, visiting trips to foreign countries, etc. In 2011, when it came to the fourth year of China's ratification of CRPD, the Chinese government initiated the procedure of submitting the State Party Report[4]. Local DPOs and NGOs also felt motivated to engage in the process. A founder of an NGO that submitted a shadow report explained that they wrote the report because

> I had to take the responsibility as a legal practitioner. This was the first time I had the opportunity (to participate in the monitoring mechanism)... Moreover, we have followed up the whole process of CRPD's introduction into China, we couldn't lag behind in this important part of the mechanism. I think I did it out of a sense of mission.

More activists, however, expressed concerns about the safety for themselves and their organizations because of the political risks associated with participating in the international human rights mechanism. Even an international partner who was engaged in promoting this monitoring mechanism hesitated. She said:

> In our rights education training, one of my main purposes was to encourage participants to write the shadow report. But later I found it was kind of wrong to do so. On the one hand, it is unrelated to the local needs; on the other hand, it is really risky when it comes to practice. So, we stopped promoting this agenda in the end.

This concern proved to be valid. The NGO that submitted the shadow report to the Committee through the official mechanism was later shut down by the state. Other NGOs and DPOs who tried to participate in the mechanism had to do so strategically. One interviewee, for example, explained that they did not submit the report in the name of the organization; instead, their international partner submitted the report in another name. After the wave of shadow report submissions, domestic NGOs and DPOs involved in the process experienced differing levels of state repressions, from organization shut down to police interrogations of staff members. By far, no local NGO or DPO has submitted a shadow report since the Chinese government submitted its second State Party Report in 2018.

The international disability rights movement's emphasis on state obligation and civil society participation manifested differently in China, as the authoritarian state plays a more significant role in shaping social movements than the democratic states (Zhao, 2010). State–civil society relations in China are characterized by state control over civil society activities that threat state authority, although a certain degree of consultation and symbiosis coexist between the state and NGOs (Spires, 2011; Teets, 2014). While the rights model was developed and gained its success in the Anglo-American contexts, its direct transplantation in an authoritarian state unintentionally exposed disability rights activists on the ground to risks of state repression.

As a result of constant political repression, the NGOs and DPOs that adopt a repertoire of rights advocacy against the state turn out to be precarious and marginalized, especially during the cycle of tightening political control. In the face of constant harassment and even imprisonment, not only were NGOs and DPOs unable to maintain organizational survival and development in the short term but they were also unable to launch consistent campaigns for policy and legislative change that require continuous efforts over time. An NGO founder recalled that a few years ago a peer NGO decided to make a strategic adjustment to the organization and emphasize community empowerment. As a result, one of the founders of the organization was arrested and the organization was then dismantled. An interviewee also reported the police's constant intervention in their work that provided legal aid to people with disabilities. This interference has increased since the Foreign NGO Law enacted in 2017, which illegalized all unregistered activities funded by their international partners and therefore posed heightened risks to local activists. The local and international disability rights activists I interviewed all sought some form of transformation after the Foreign NGO Law. While some left their previous organizations by going to graduate schools abroad or changing their jobs, others who continue to work on disability rights had to adopt a different approach to seek domestic legitimacy. Amid the uncertainty they are facing, a local disability rights activist maintains his optimism, saying:

> Throughout this process, I feel that the adaptability of disability organizations is getting stronger and stronger. No matter what approaches we are taking, as long as we are not dead, we can continue our work; and as long as we continue our work, people with disabilities are taken care of. Then it is still better than doing nothing.

In sum, the boundary of the disability rights movement in the context of an authoritarian regime is confined by the state. The tendency of the international disability rights movement toward targeting the state as a rights violator and duty bearer has been introduced into China by the international allies. This transplantation, however, does not come without consequences. Local activists have been exposed to risks of political repression because of the state's hostility toward rights advocacy and international connections, which in turn destabilizes and marginalizes the movement and reinforce the *enclave of rights* that international allies have created.

CONCLUSION AND DISCUSSION

An activist who had worked in disability rights for 6 years left the field in 2017. She concluded her reflection on conducting rights advocacy in the following way:

> Advocacy sometimes pays no attention to people. I used to say that the focus of human rights lies only on *rights* and ignores the *human* component. It became 'rights human' and put rights ahead of human. We used to adopt the rights-first approach and just want to change policy and laws; then we think about what we should do from this starting point. We rarely paid attention to the person herself. What is the person's internal motivation? What is her biggest concern? Maybe her biggest concern is that she cannot survive by her disability allowance. The process of rights advocacy muted so many life experiences that are real and important.

While the international disability rights movement opens up new spaces for resistance and renegotiation of disability rights, in the local context of China, this transnational alliance also creates a fissure in relation to local realities and generates what I term the *enclave of rights*. On the one hand, the international movement's rights model fails to respond to the socioeconomic vulnerability of people with disabilities in the post-socialist market economy. On the other hand, the authoritarian regime with a strong state capacity to enforce political repression confines the boundary of local disability rights movements, limiting the extent to which the rights mandate can be fulfilled while posing the risk of repression for local activists. These findings encourage us to reexamine the conventional wisdom about the apparent alliance between international and local disability rights movements and the triumph of the disability revolution globally.

The case of China provides an invaluable opportunity to rethink what constitutes effective alliances in disability rights movements transnationally. First and foremost, local activists' embodied experiences in disability activism reinforced previous findings of comparative and international disability studies that socioeconomic vulnerability constitutes the major barrier faced by people with disabilities in the global South. Relying on its rights model that predominantly emphasizes promoting civil and political rights through legal and policy advocacy, international partners fail to address the immediate concerns faced by the local community. A robust and genuine alliance should therefore expand the universal visions of what constitute rights from civil and political rights to include socioeconomic rights and address the issues of poverty and livelihood in developing countries.

Moreover, the international disability rights movement should shift away from its narrow repertoire of rights to include culture-relevant and context-sensitive approaches to advancing the rights of people with disabilities on the ground. Previous scholars of disability rights movements rarely pay attention to disability activism in authoritarian regimes. As the case of China illustrates, political repression compromises the effectiveness of the Anglo-American strategy of targeting the state. Instead, this strategy endangers local activists and marginalizes the movement, hindering the extent to which the rights of people with disabilities can be realized.

Perhaps the most important insight gained is to adopt a human-centered rather than rights-centered approach, similar to an approach called for by the local activist at the beginning of this section. While advancing the mission of promoting disability rights globally, the international disability rights movement has unexpectedly silenced the voices and concerns of both people with disabilities and disability rights activists in local contexts. In the process of alliance building and movement formation, the local disability community found their immediate socioeconomic needs being left-out in the international agenda of rights. Moreover, people with disabilities are, ironically, woefully underrepresented in this movement that claims to advance their rights. Local disability rights activists are also disproportionately endangered by state repression for their rights advocacy campaigns. All of these problems illustrate that the transnational alliance of disability rights movements should move away from its emphasis on rights toward a human-centered approach that recognizes and includes the life experiences of people with disabilities on the ground.

ACKNOWLEDGMENTS

The fieldtrip for this research was not possible without the support of the Harlan Hahn Award from the Disability Studies Program, University of Washington. In addition, I am grateful to my advisor Stephen Meyers who has always been supportive of my work and with whom I developed the ideas for this chapter. I thank Heather D. Evans for being my best reader and offering very constructive comments about my arguments and writing with tremendous patience. I also thank the editors and reviewers for their feedbacks and comments. The last remark is to my interviewees and those who are still on the frontlines and working to advance disability rights in China: Thank you for sharing your gripping stories with me.

NOTES

1. According to The World Report on Disability (WHO, 2011), about 15% of the world's population live with some form of disability. The prevalence is even higher in low- and middle-income countries compared to higher-income countries.

2. In China, more than 90% of people with visual disabilities in job market work as masseurs (Chu & Xu, 2012). The CDPF that is responsible of enforcing disability-related policy has been actively promoted massage as the "most suitable job for the blind because their special advantage of tactile sensation and concentrated mind" (GOSC, 1999). Disability rights activists, however, have been criticizing this policy reinforcing stereotype against people with visual disabilities and resulting in employment segregation. The poor working environments and long working hours also led to health issues among those working in the industry.

3. DET is "a participatory process where people are introduced to the real issues and discrimination facing all disabled people with a view to them changing their behavior, policies, and practices" (Carr, Darke, & Kuno, 2012). This method of training was developed by people with disabilities in the United Kingdom originally in the 1970s (Kuno, 2009). Now, DET becomes a training program that is actively promoted by international

organizations promoting disability rights, especially the UN agencies. The DET facilitator training in China, for example, was introduced by the UN agencies in 2014 (China Development Brief, 2018).

4. The Chinese government submitted its first State Party Report in 2011 and did not submit the second report until 2018.

REFERENCES

Barnes, C., & Mercer, G. (2010). *Exploring disability: A sociological introduction.* (2nd ed.). Cambridge; Malden, MA: Polity Press.

Barton, L. (1993). The struggle for citizenship: The case of disabled people. *Disability, Handicap & Society*, *8*(3), 235–248.

Berghs, M. (2017). Practices and discourses of ubuntu: Implications for an African model of disability? *African Journal of Disability (Online)*, *6*, 1–8.

Carr, L., Darke, D., & Kuno, K. (2012). *Disability equality training: Action for change.* Kuala Lumpur: MPH Publishing.

Chang, H. H. (2007). Social change and the disability rights movement in Taiwan 1981–2002. *Review of Disability Studies: An International Journal*, *3*(1&2).

Chataika, T., Berghs, M., Mateta, A., & Shava, K. (2015). From whose perspective anyway? The quest for African disability rights activism. In A. de Waal (Ed.), *Advocacy in conflict: Critical perspectives on transnational activism* (pp. 187–211). London: Zed Books.

China Development Brief. (2018). *Call for application – disability equality training of facilitators in Beijing (DET-TOF)*. Retrieved from http://www.chinadevelopmentbrief.cn/events/call-for-application-disability-equality-training-of-facilitators-in-beijing-det-tof/?fbclid5IwAR1pJZDibFp5ri4TM4VB7HhydX7_llcNa_0EBw2dYUZ4j0oZa5DaiTyLIyo

China Disabled Persons' Federation (CDPF). (2018). *Constitution of the China disabled persons' federation.* Retrieved from http://www.cdpf.org.cn/83/201810/t20181023_639741.shtml

Chu, H., & Xu, M.(2012). Current situations and policy research of the health of blind masseurs. *Journal of Changchun University*, *10*, 1236–1238.

Cobley, D. (2018). *Disability and international development: A guide for students and practitioners (rethinking development)*. London; New York, NY: Routledge.

Di, Y. (2014, April 23). China to allow the blind to take college entrance exams. *cn.NYTimes.com.* Retrieved from https://cn.nytimes.com/china/20140423/c23blind/zh-hant/dual/

Dickson, B. (2016). *The dictator's dilemma: The Chinese communist party's strategy for survival.* Oxford: Oxford University Press.

Feng, C. (2017). The NGO law in China and its impact on overseas funded NGOs. *Cosmopolitan Civil Societies: An Interdisciplinary Journal*, *9*(3), 95–105.

Feng, E. (2019, September 6). Inside China's crackdown on human rights advocates. *National Public Radio.* Retrieved from https://www.npr.org/2019/09/06/753478775/inside-chinas-crackdown-on-human-rights-advocates?fbclid=IwAR3Pp1XaRoZj8cUqsYCkdqNdMNURUDTOiJ4fLiwSHfPkfpMK7decioEwGQ8.

Fjeld, H., & Sagli, G. (2011). Disability, poverty and healthcare: Changes in the canji ('disability') policies in the history of the people's Republic of China. In A. H. Eide & B. Ingstad (Eds.), *Poverty and disability: A global challenge* (pp. 31–53). Bristol; Portland, OR: Policy Press.

Foundation Center & Human Rights Funders Network. (2019). Advancing human rights: Trends in global foundation grantmaking. Retrieved from https://humanrightsfunding.org/wp-content/themes/advancing-human-rights/images/Infographic_FINAL_web.pdf.

General Office of the State Council of the People's Republic of China (GOSC). (1999). *Notice of promoting employment and work of disabled people.* Retrieved from http://www.gd.gov.cn/gkmlpt/content/0/136/post_136964.html#7

Grech, S. (2014). The spaces of poverty: Renegotiating place and disability in the global South. In K. Soldatic, H. Morgan, & A. Roulstone (Eds.), *Disability, spaces and places of policy exclusion* (pp. 48–63). Abingdon, Oxfordshire; New York, NY: Routledge.

Heyer, K. (2015). *Rights enabled: The disability revolution, from the US, to Germany and Japan, to the United Nations.* Ann Arbor, MI: University of Michigan Press.

Howell, J., & Pringle, T. (2019). Shades of authoritarianism and state–labour relations in China. *British Journal of Industrial Relations*, *57*(2), 223–246.

Huang, S. (2019). Ten years of the CRPD's adoption in China: Challenges and opportunities. *Disability & Society*, *34*(6), 1004–1009.

Ingstad, B. (1995). *Mpho ya modimo* – a gift from god: Perspectives on 'attitudes' toward disabled persons. In B. Ingstad & S. R. Whyte (Eds.), *Disability and culture* (pp. 246–263). Berkeley, CA: University of California Press.

Ingstad, B., & Whyte, S. R. (Eds.). (1995). *Disability and culture*. Berkeley, CA: University of California Press.

Ingstad, B., & Whyte, S. R. (Eds.). (2007). *Disability in local and global worlds*. Berkeley, CA: University of California Press.

Kalyanpur, M. (2015). Mind the gap: Special education policy and practice in India in the context of globalization. In S. Rao & M. Kalyanpur (Eds.), *South Asia and disability studies: Redefining boundaries and extending horizons* (pp. 49–72). New York, NY: Peter Lang.

Kanter, A. S. (2014). *The development of disability rights under international law: From charity to human rights*. Abingdon, OX: Routledge.

Keck, M. E., & Sikkink, K. (2014). *Activists beyond borders: Advocacy networks in international politics*. Ithaca, NY: Cornell University Press.

Kiuppis, F., & Soorenian, A. (2017). Bridging continents, cultures, and crip theories; teaching comparative and international disability studies in education and sociology. *Scandinavian Journal of Disability Research*, *19*, 118–128.

Kohrman, M. (2005). *Bodies of difference: Experiences of disability and institutional advocacy in the making of modern China*. Berkeley, CA: University of California Press.

Kuno, K. (2009). Disability equality training (DET): Potentials and challenges in practice in developing countries. *Asia Pacific Disability Rehabilitation Journal*, *20*(1), 4–51.

Kuo, L. (2019, August 29). Staff of NGO linked to Hong Kong arrested in southern China. *The Guardian*. Retrieved from https://www.theguardian.com/world/2019/aug/29/staff-of-changsha-funeng-ngo-hong-kong-arrested-in-southern-china?fbclid=IwAR0aNEfJQo0UaNnvoEfD04I1Y1nT_siH4XzU_kKeGh0I6akFjaYGe8cjLC8

Liu, T., & Guo, B. (2014, June 26). Mangren Li Jinsheng "pobing" putong gaokao [Li Jinsheng, a blind person, took part in general college entrance exams]. *Zhongguo jiaoyu xinwen wang*. Retrieved from http://www.jyb.cn/gk/ksjy/201406/t20140626_587739.html?fbclid=IwAR0M25JdBlGRv7H-Vl7xz-se3zTBt-tTik4JNnDcn0wwWxic896DDoVWR1E

Ma, Q. (2005). *Non-governmental organizations in contemporary China: Paving the way to civil society?*. London; New York, NY: Routledge.

McCarthy, J. D., & Zald, M. N. (1977). *The trend of social movements in America: Professionalization and resource mobilization*. Morriston, NJ: General Learning Press.

Meyers, S. (2014). Global civil society as megaphone or echo chamber?: Voice in the international disability rights movement. *International Journal of Politics, Culture, and Society*, *27*(4), 459–476.

Meyers, S. (2019). *Civilizing disability society: The convention on the rights of persons with disabilities socializing grassroots disabled persons' organizations in Nicaragua*. Cambridge: Cambridge University Press.

Meyers, S., & Lockwood, E. (2014). The tale of two civil societies: Comparing disability rights movements in Nicaragua and Uruguay. *Disability Studies Quarterly*, *34*(4).

National Bureau of Statistics. (2007, May 28). *Data report of the second national census of disabled people*. Retrieved from http://www.stats.gov.cn/tjsj/ndsj/shehui/2006/html/fu3.htm

Oliver, M. (1996). *Understanding disability: From theory to practice*. New York, NY: St. Martin's Press.

Phillips, S. D. (2010). *Disability and mobile citizenship in postsocialist Ukraine*. Bloomington, IN: Indiana University Press.

Risse, T., Ropp, S. C., & Sikkink, K. (Eds.). (1999). *The power of human rights: International norms and domestic change* (*Vol. 66*). Cambridge: Cambridge University Press.

Sidel, M. (2019). Managing the foreign: The drive to securitize foreign nonprofit and foundation management in China. *Voluntas: International Journal of Voluntary and Nonprofit Organizations*, *30*(4), 664–677.

Spires, A. (2011). Contingent symbiosis and civil society in an authoritarian state: Understanding the survival of China's grassroots NGOs. *American Journal of Sociology*, *117*(1), 1–45.

Stein, M., & Lord, J. E. (2010). Monitoring the convention on the rights of persons with disabilities: Innovations, lost opportunities, and future potential. *Human Rights Quarterly*, *32*(3), 689–728.

Tarrow, S. G. (2011). *Power in movement: Social movements and contentious politics*. Cambridge: Cambridge University Press.

Tatlow, D. K. (2013, December 18). Barred from college entrance exams, in a blow for China's blind. *The New York Times*. Retrieved from https://sinosphere.blogs.nytimes.com/2013/12/18/blind-man-barred-from-college-entrance-exams/?_ga=2.16344758.1661769846.1569286502-245885540.1565075571

Teets, J. C. (2014). *Civil society under authoritarianism: The China model*. Cambridge: Cambridge University Press.

Teets, J. C. (2015). The evolution of civil society in Yunnan province: Contending models of civil society management in China. *Journal of Contemporary China*, *24*(91), 158–175.

Vanhala, L. (2010). *Making rights a reality?: Disability rights activists and legal mobilization*. Cambridge: Cambridge University Press.

Vanhala, L. (2015). The diffusion of disability rights in Europe. *Human Rights Quarterly*, *37*(4), 831–853.

White, G., Howell, J. A., & Shang, X. (1996). *In search of civil society: Market reform and social change in contemporary China*. Oxford; Hong Kong: Clarendon Press.

World Health Organization. (2011). *World report on disability 2011*. Geneva: World Health Organization.

Yeo, R., & Moore, K. (2003). Including disabled people in poverty reduction work: "Nothing about us, without us". *World Development*, *31*(3), 571–590 doi:10.1016/S0305-750X(02)00218-8

Zhang, C. (2017). 'Nothing about us without us': The emerging disability movement and advocacy in China. *Disability & Society*, *32*(7), 1096–1101.

Zhang, L., & Ong, A. (Eds.). (2008). *Privatizing China: Socialism from afar*. Ithaca, NY: Cornell University Press.

Zhao, D. (2010). Authoritarian state and contentious politics. In K. T. Leicht & J. C. Jenkins (Eds.), *Handbook of politics: State and society in global perspective*. New York, NY: Springer.

Chapter 2

ALLIES, ENEMIES, OR INDIFFERENT? THE DISABILITY AND OLDER PERSONS' MOVEMENTS UNDER NEOLIBERALISM IN JAMAICA

Stephen Meyers

ABSTRACT

Purpose: *Researchers and advocates alike have noted that persons with disabilities and older persons are the two groups most marginalized by neoliberal economic policies and therefore could come together as a broad-based movement against the roll back of their rights. Yet, these two groups fail to collaborate, and instead compete against one another for an ever-shrinking pool of benefits. This chapter explores the barriers to their collaboration within the context of structural adjustment in Jamaica.*

Methods/Approach: *The author engages in a critical analysis of neoliberalism's effect on the advocacy strategies of the disability and older persons' movements in Jamaica based on 32 semi-directed depth interviews, participant observation of numerous events, and a survey of media written by local advocates.*

Findings: *The disability movement makes claims on behalf of their members by focusing on the potential returns that society will gain by providing the opportunities that will make young persons with disabilities productive employees over their lifetime. The older persons' movement advocates by portraying themselves as "vibrant" and worthy of social investment because of the contributions they*

Disability Alliances and Allies
Research in Social Science and Disability, Volume 12, 41–65

ISSN: 1479-3547/doi:10.1108/S1479-354720200000012006

make. Both of these arguments for inclusion are also exclusionary. The disability movement excludes older persons as potential contributors and the older persons' movement similarly excludes persons with disabilities.

Implications: *The only way neoliberalism will successfully be rolled back and universal rights returned is if the disability movement and older persons' movements build an alliance that is more inclusive, including of one another, by rejecting the language of investment and productivity, and instead focus on rights and inherent dignity.*

Keywords: Jamaica; social movements; aging; disability; neoliberalism; ableism; ageism

INTRODUCTION

For several decades now, Jamaica has been a crucible for the development of new rights and services for both persons with disabilities and older persons in the Global South. Demographic change, local leadership, and outreach from international NGOs have pushed Jamaica to become the first country in its region to enact a national policy for senior citizens, a move that garnered widespread international attention in 1997 (Ministry of Labor & Social Security [MLSS] of Jamaica, 1997, p. 1), and to be the first country to become States Party to the United Nations Convention on the Rights of Persons with Disabilities in 2007 (White-Jennings, 2019).

During that same time period, Jamaica has also been the site of the implementation of neoliberal Structural Adjustment Policies (SAP), which were introduced in 1983 (Robinson, 1994). Economic policies introduced under structural adjustment have been catastrophic for Jamaica's citizenry. Economic liberalization policies not only severely damaged Jamaica's agricultural sector, but currency devaluations reduced purchasing power so much that the average weight of Jamaica's children dropped precipitously because low-income families could no longer afford basic food (Handa & King, 2003). Two of the constituencies most affected by structural adjustment have been persons with disabilities and older persons. Neoliberal International Monetary Fund and World Bank policies forced Jamaica's Ministry of Labour and Social Security (MLSS) to make deep cuts. MLSS agencies, including the Jamaica Council for Persons with Disability and the National Council for Senior Citizens, have had to cut disability and elder benefits and services despite already low levels of coverage (Lavigne & Vargas, 2013). Many of the funds left are now distributed in limited quantities to individuals who must apply and qualify for basic subsistence grants, financial support to start small businesses, mobility aids, and so forth. Many of these benefits come from HEART (Human Employment and Resource Training) Trust, which was established at the beginning of Jamaica's structural adjustment program to "create a vibrant, dynamic, inspired, highly competent workforce" and thereby make Jamaica more productive and competitive while also reducing the roles of persons receiving public assistance (HEART, 2020).

During that same period of structural adjustment, Jamaica's grassroots disabled persons' organizations (DPOs) and older peoples' associations (OPAs) played an instrumental role in pushing Jamaica to recognize the rights of these two important populations. A shared strategy that both movements have used is to incorporate the neoliberal language of structural adjustment by promoting a new identity for their group as potential contributors to society. The Combined Disability Association (CDA), for example, lists "To create public awareness of the capabilities of persons with disabilities in the Jamaican society" as first among its aims and objectives (CDA, 2019), and the Caribbean Community of Retired Persons (CCRP) claims "to ensure that retired persons are allowed to contribute to national and regional development as we acknowledge their vast resource of expertise, and experience" as one of their main goals (CCRP, 2019).

This identity specifically uses the neoliberal framework by portraying their members as "good investments" that will garner society major returns if barriers to their participation are removed and new opportunities are provided so that they too can be a part of a "highly competent workforce." It specifically appeals to public agencies, such as the HEART Trust, to set aside additional monies for disabled persons and older persons. As such, both movements support their cause using an economic logic of productivity, rather than civil rights or social justice logic based on equality and human dignity.

While the strategy of both the disability movement and older persons' movement directly responds to neoliberalism, it also perpetuates both ableism and ageism by buying into what Kelly Fritsch calls "a happy affective economy" (2013; 2015; 2017) that ultimately limits inclusion by marginalizing disabled and older persons who are not deemed as having productive potential. The disability movement's specific argument, for example, focuses on educational investments in *youth* with disabilities and argues that those investments will result in decades of gainful employment and taxable earnings. As a result, older persons with disabilities are excluded from advocacy, including those that did not receive education when they were young. The older persons' movement similarly excludes large swathes of their members by promoting the image of themselves as healthy and "*vibrant*" older people. This image excludes the majority of senior citizens with chronic conditions and/or impairments. These strategies result in DPOs steering resources away from their older members by prioritizing the young and OPAs excluding older persons with disabilities from membership, including by holding meetings in inaccessible locations and organizing events, such as dances, where access is limited and accommodations are unavailable. At a national level, the separate advocacy campaigns also drive a wedge between the disability and older persons' movements in Jamaica by pitting them against each other as they compete for ever scarcer resources within a political culture where governments dole out benefits to distinct constituencies for their loyalty rather than promote and protect universal rights and benefits (Weis, 2005).

As a case study, Jamaica lends considerable insight into the way in which neoliberalism co-opts movements by creating a paradoxical logic whereby the argument for inclusion is, in fact, exclusionary. It also explains why activists and policymakers that have pinned their hope in bridging disability and age, and thereby mobilizing the sort of mass, multiclass movement necessary to fight neoliberalism, have had little success on the ground.

Bridge-building between the Disability Rights and Aging Movements

For decades, disability rights advocates have sought to broaden their allies by arguing that everyone benefits from disability rights, especially as they age. In an op-ed in *Forbes* on traveling with a disability, for example, the author argues that the Americans with Disabilities Act needs to be applied to airlines (currently they are only required to follow the lenient Air Carrier Access Act) by not only explaining his difficulties of traveling with a disability as a relatively young man, but by arguing that "Aging makes disability concerns almost universal" after pointing to US Census data that shows nearly 40% of people above 60 years and 50% of those above 70 years have some form of disability (Pfeffer, 2015). The intent is clear; the author is attempting to mobilize senior citizens as allies in his advocacy to extend the coverage of the ADA. In other cases, allyship is based on both groups being discriminated against, whether they share disability or not. At the global level, for example, major organizations such as Humanity & Inclusion (formerly Handicap International) and HelpAge International have joined forces in research to show that persons with disabilities and older persons are systematically excluded from foreign development aid and humanitarian assistance (Handicap International & HelpAge International, 2012). Research such as this supported their advocacy, which led to the United Nations adopting the specific language barring discrimination on the basis of "*age*, gender, *disability*, and other characteristics" in the Sustainable Development Goals (my emphasis, UNPD, 2019). This international advocacy, however, has not led to similar collaboration between grassroots DPOs and OPAs at the community level, despite many being funded by international NGOs such as Humanity & Inclusion or HelpAge International.

Perhaps the most significant attempt to bring persons with disabilities and older persons together for advocacy is the Toronto Declaration on Bridging Knowledge, Policy and Practice in Aging and Disability, which was adopted at the 2011 Growing Older with a Disability Conference (Bickenbach et al., 2012). This declaration notes that persons with disabilities and older persons constitute two of the largest minority groups in the world today, yet receive far less international attention than others. It calls for all stakeholders to collaborate and find common ground, in order to defeat the twin barriers of ableism and ageism, that prevent persons with disabilities and older persons from participating as full citizens in society (Naidoo, Putnam, & Spindel, 2012). While bridging initiatives between disability and aging policy advocacy have been adopted by important circles of researchers and policymakers (see Leonardi, Bickenback, & Leroy, 2012; Salvador-Carulla, Putnam, Bigby, & Heller, 2012), there is little evidence of bridging initiatives on the grassroots level.

In this chapter, I use Jamaica as a case study for understanding why, despite both facing discrimination, cuts in public services, and other barriers to participation, organizations representing persons with disabilities and older persons fail to collaborate in advocacy, even when they apparently have an interest in doing so. Instead, in Jamaica I find that rather than create a united front to fight neoliberal policies that have rolled back shared benefits, such as pensions and health benefits, the disability and older persons' movements put forth identities representing themselves as potentially productive citizens worthy of investment that are not only exclusionary of one another, but exclude vast numbers of their own members.

Neoliberalism, Identity Politics, and the Happy Effects of Capacitation in Jamaica

Neoliberalism, dubbed by *The Guardian* newspaper as "the idea that swallowed the world" (Metcalf, 2017), is an economic philosophy that dates back to the 1930s. It rose to the top of the global economic policy agenda in the 1980s with Reaganomics and Thatcherism in the United States and United Kingdom, respectively, and with the so-called "Washington consensus" Structural Adjustment Programs of the International Monetary Fund and the World Bank for much of the rest of the world. At its core, neoliberalism seeks to institutionalize free markets through deregulation, privatization, and austerity policies that shrink governments and put their citizens at the whims of global capitalism. The putative outcome is growth, although in many societies it has resulted in booms and busts, increased inequality, and stagnation. Structural Adjustment Programs (SAPs) are policy sets that countries must agree to in order to restructure existing debt or qualify for new loans from the World Bank and IMF. Standard SAPs include the devaluation of currencies, liberalization of trade policies, privatization of publicly owned businesses and services, and reductions in government spending. These policies are meant to lead to export-led growth and quicker debt repayment (Easterly, 2003). The human effect, however, is a reduction of people's purchasing power; the elimination of whole swathes of industries as the local market is flooded by cheaper imports; the elimination of publicly backed jobs; severe reductions in public health care, education, and benefits; and the mass violation of basic human rights (Abouharb & Cingranelli, 2007; Peabody, 1996).

Persons with disabilities and older persons are perhaps the two groups that face the greatest violation of rights under neoliberal policies in the Global North and SAPs in the Global South. Social security and public pension benefits for both persons with disabilities and older persons are inevitably targeted for cuts despite the existence of hard won laws on the books that protect these benefits (see George & George, 2013; Grover & Soldatic, 2013; Polivka, 2012). Health care, especially benefits for rehabilitation, geriatric medicine, and even mobility aids and personal care assistance, are also reduced or eliminated, thereby robbing persons with disabilities and older persons of not only their access to specialized care, but also the means for independent living (e.g., McGregor, 2001; Sakellariou & Rotarou, 2017).

Neoliberalism's singular focus on increasing economic productivity leads to an evaluation of citizens on the basis of their potential contribution to the economy, rather than their inherent value and right to have rights. The only justification left within neoliberal citizenship for public services is if they are used as social investments as a means for increasing the productive capacity of citizens (Jenson, 2012). Persons with disabilities and older persons, therefore, are put in a position where they must prove themselves to be good investments.

Kelly Fritsch's work on neoliberalism points to the ways in which the disability movement has succumbed to the neoliberal logic by portraying disabled people as active citizens who make a contribution to society. As such, she argues that "Disability can be capacitated by neoliberal practices of inclusion: that is if one can be captured by market rationality, or market values" such as being incorporated into the labor force or as consumers (2013, p. 142). In short, "bodies are included because they can be predictably productive under neoliberalism and as such are rewarded and trumpeted as evidence of an inclusive society" (p. 142). That inclusion, however, comes at the cost of every government "investment" in education, health, and other public programs being evaluated according to the returns gained from increased health, wealth, and productivity (Puar, 2012, p. 155) of persons with disabilities and older persons. Those that fail to become upwardly mobile – the oldest and "most disabled" – then, are sacrificed for more productive others. This means that the argument for inclusion is paradoxically exclusionary, as both the disability and older persons' movements justify cutting benefits to some of their members (those deemed unproductive) in order to gain benefits for the rest.

Fritsch (2013) portrays this neoliberal politics of inclusion/exclusion as a "happy affective economy" centered on compulsory able-bodiedness where persons with disabilities, and as I argue, older persons, must prove themselves to be healthy, productive, and, basically not *too disabled* or *too old* in order to be deemed worthy of inclusion as citizens.

The use of identity as an organizing principle in political movements (or "identity politics"), in contrast to broad-based party politics that bring diverse groups together into one coalition, has a similar effect of mobilizing while also marginalizing. Of particular importance is the fact that while movements organized around identity can promote the equality of specific groups, the movements as such can also be exclusionary of other identities (Neofotistos, 2013), including identities ostensibly within their own group (e.g., feminist movements that exclude working class or queer women). Social movements that use identity politics often draw stark lines regarding who is in and who is out. Whereas many identity movements may self-proclaim their motivations in terms of "social justice," the specific rights and recognition they press for are often narrow and circumscribed to those matters that directly affect their group. Cohen (2000), for example, emphasizes the way in which identity movements draw strict "boundaries" regarding who they include and exclude, and thus what they lobby for and do not lobby for. This "boundedness" of identity-based movements can present a significant obstacle to coalition building.

Identity politics can exacerbate inequalities between groups because it "hardens rather than redefines differences in status identities that are the basis for inequality" (Cohen, 2000, p. 56). In this vein, Meekosha and Pettman (1991) argue that "category politics" (i.e., identity politics) can be exclusionary despite emancipatory intentions, because the use of a single identity as an organizing principle means that "some members outside the category may be silenced by those inside the category, intimidated by being denied the right to speak" despite experiencing similar forms of denial and discrimination within society (p. 75). Such critiques are often met with calls for identity politics' replacement with more pluralist forms of organizing (see, for example, Dalmia, 2019) that include everyone or, at the very least, recognize a broad set of intersecting identities or larger, society-wide systems of exploitation or oppression.

The disability and older persons' movement both utilize identity politics that are, in Fritsch's framework, simultaneously inclusionary and exclusionary. In her seminal work, Renee Anspach (1979) argued that the disability movement was as much about altering the self-concept of its members as it was about creating social change. In the contemporary era of global aging, this may prove to be true for older persons as well. Fundamental to disability rights advocacy has been replacing the "sick" or "dependent" identity of persons with disabilities with new identities that center on the contributions persons with disabilities make to society. This new identity, however, excludes persons with disabilities, especially older persons with disabilities, who are seen as too sick to be potentially productive citizens. Thus, while the disability movement focuses on issues, such as education and the transition into the labor market, it also prioritizes young persons with disabilities by arguing that their inclusion will result in socioeconomic benefits for the whole society (see Priestley, 2003, pp. 88–115). Older persons with disabilities are marginalized as "disability activism has tended to focus on issues affecting those of working age or below" (Priestley, 2003, p. 143). Disability activism's *ageism* results in older persons with disabilities being excluded. Similarly, as older persons seek their own international human rights convention (see HelpAge International, 2019), older persons' organizations around the world are similarly doing significant work to disrupt stereotypes regarding older persons as dependent, instead presenting them as active contributors to society. The new, age-positive identity that they seek to promote is one of health, vitality, and, importantly, *nondisabled* (See Gibbons, 2016), thus excluded disabled older persons.

"Successful aging" campaigns are inherently ableist (Gibbons, 2016). Successful aging is defined as maintaining a "low risk of disease and disease-related disability," a "high mental and physical function," and an "active engagement in life" (Rowe & Kahn, 1997). This goal has made its way into international policy, evidenced by the World Health Organization's promotion of 2020–2030 as the *Decade of Healthy Ageing* (WHO, 2019). That goal of healthy aging has filtered its way down into grassroots Older People's Associations that engage in group exercise and health-maintenance activities (see HelpAge International, 2016). These initiatives are expressly for disability prevention. At the grassroots level, many senior organizations and OPA networks exclude older persons with disabilities because they are viewed as antithetical to the organizations' efforts to promote an "active lifestyle" (Raymond & Lacroix, 2016).

Given the shared marginalization of both persons with disabilities and older persons under neoliberalism, the exclusionary consequences of both movements' advocacy helps explain why broad-based mobilization has failed, and why the elimination of universal social rights is accepted through a strategic retreat that focuses on gaining individual social investments for the few at the exclusion of others.

The Importance and Relevance of Jamaica

Jamaica, the second poorest country in the Caribbean, is an important site for comparing persons with disabilities and older persons' mobilization for four reasons: population, politics, law, and neoliberal structural adjustment policies. First, Jamaica has a very significant and growing population of both persons with disabilities and older persons. Currently, 15% of the population is persons with disabilities and over 12% is older persons, a percentage set to double to 25% by 2050 (where Japan is currently). There is a significant intersection between these two populations, as disabled people are living longer (in the past, many persons with disabilities from birth or childhood lived significantly shorter lives than the general population), and older persons are more likely to develop disabilities in comparison to other age cohorts.

The demographic shift in Jamaica that is increasing the number of both older persons and persons with disabilities is based on a fertility rate that has plummeted from 5.4 children in the 1960s to just 2.0 today, and a life expectancy that has increased from 64 to 76 years in the same period (World Bank, 2016). Similar "development success" has also moved Jamaica from an agricultural economy to an urban, industrial/services economy, which has introduced new, disabling chronic diseases, such as untreated diabetes within the population, while past causes of impairment persist. This new economy also marginalizes disabled and older persons from the labor force in ways that were not an issue under a subsistence farming economy. A 2016 World Bank study found that only 1% of Jamaicans with severe disabilities were formally employed and older persons in Jamaica are often barred from formal employment due to mandatory retirement policies that force women to leave work at 60 and men at 65, often with no pension or savings (Luton, 2015). The National Insurance Scheme currently pays the small number of eligible disabled persons, which is a mere fraction of the total population of persons with disabilities, pensions ranging from USD 2.50–25.00 per week (5%–50% of the national minimum wage) based on "degree of disability" and pays the 10% of senior citizens who qualify for a pension on average just 11% of the national wage, meaning that "benefits under the Scheme are not adequate – at any income level" (Ministry of Labor and Social Security, Jamaica, 2014, p. 4). Both groups are also less educated than the general Jamaican population. Special schools for persons with disabilities often do not teach basic literacy; older persons, who grew up prior to major investments in public education, have a literacy rate of only 68% overall and just 43% for women above 60 years, whereas literacy for youth is now over 90% (KNOEMA, 2015). Finally, disabled persons and older persons face barriers to political participation. A Human Rights Watch report on the 2011 Jamaican National Election recorded the majority of polling stations as inaccessible for persons with disabilities, and local newspapers reported older persons being denied the vote, especially in rural areas (Gleaner, 2016).

Secondly, the number of grassroots disabled persons and older persons' advocacy groups in Jamaica is rapidly growing. In 2017, for example, alone, two new older persons groups – Intergenerational Caribbean and the St Elizabeth Intergenerational Foundation – were formed, joining the already existing Alliance for Ageing, Association of Returning Residents, Caribbean Community of Retired Persons, HelpAge-Jamaica, and dozens of local National Council for Senior Citizens' Senior Citizens Clubs. The older persons' population has also received new dynamism as returning residents from the Windrush generation (Jamaicans who immigrated to the UK as laborers between 1948 and 1971 as part of a post-World War II program) are voluntarily returning or being forcibly sent back to Jamaica for retirement; subsequently many join older persons' advocacy organizations. The disability field is similarly growing. In 2016 and 2017, the Kingston-based Combined Disability Association created three new regional affiliates (St Ann Disabilities Association, Cornwall Combined Disabilities Association, Eastern Disability Association), and a new national advocacy network, Jamaica Empowerment Partnership for Persons with Disability, was established.

Next, government disability and older persons' law and policy is up for debate. Jamaica's Vision 2030 National Development Plan's Vision Statement specifically states that "our elderly and persons with disabilities [will be] fully integrated within society, have access to appropriate care and support services and are treated as valuable human resources." That vision, however, has not been turned into a specific policy or implementation plan. In 2018, the Parliament announced that the 20-year-old National Policy for Senior Citizens would be reviewed and revised during 2019, which has served as a clarion call for older persons' organizations to mobilize. The disability community is equally mobilized because the Disabilities Act was already reviewed and revised in 2014, but has since then languished; it has not been defined in statute (entered into the Gazette) and has remained unimplemented with no end in sight. Both groups are also focused on a current review of the National Insurance Scheme, which has been identified for reform by the InterAmerican Development Bank. Reforms may result in an increase (or more likely decrease) in disability and old age pensions. In these ways, Jamaica offers an especially fertile ground for comparative study of the disability and older persons' movements in a specific context.

Finally, disability and older persons' rights mobilization occurs in the context of neoliberal structural adjustment in Jamaica, which has divided Jamaica in multiple ways. Jamaica, which began as a colony first of Spain, and then of the UK, did not become independent until 1962. When the UK pulled out, it left behind a society where the local citizens had originally been slaves, and following emancipation been transformed into day labor on British-owned sugar plantations. Virtually no investments were made in health, education, or economic diversification. With Jamaica's independence came social reforms focused on equality. Just as these programs began to take hold, the oil crisis hit the Caribbean, which forced Jamaica to take on enormous levels of public debt. Beginning in the early 1980s, Jamaica was forced to accept a Structural Adjustment Program from the IMF and World Bank to begin paying down that debt. In fact, Jamaica became one of the first countries to "accept" structural adjustment, and "became almost a byword for 'structural adjustment'" (Dearden, 2013). The neoliberal policies accepted, however, did not result in a strengthened economy, but instead decimated Jamaica's agricultural sector as cheap imports of rice and other food stuffs put local farmers out of business and mass layoffs across the civil service sector occurred, as public employees were fired or their jobs were privatized.

As old loans did not generate the economic growth needed to pay them off, Jamaica was forced to accept new loans with ever stricter conditions, including further cuts in public services in order to make payments to the IMF and World Bank. Today, Jamaica spends twice as much on debt repayments than public education and health combined (Dearden, 2013). Within a decade, inequality, already high, skyrocketed; as the lucky few involved directly in trade (i.e., export–import businesses) benefited, the vast majority of Jamaicans were pushed further into poverty. The only positive growth has been through remittances sent back by Jamaica's growing diaspora as Jamaicans seek work in North America and Europe (Handa & King, 1997). As Jamaica's economy continues to stagnate under structural adjustment and debt payments increase, leading to ever increasing struggle for survival (Harrison, 2014), the population's health, income, and general well-being have continued to decline.

In addition to the human costs of neoliberal structural adjustment in Jamaica, there has also been a breakdown in civil society. As benefits and services are rolled back, various groups have had to fight ever harder to maintain or gain access to a decreasing supply. Politicians have used this to their advantage by establishing a patronage politics that rewards some and punished others, thereby pitting groups and individuals in society against one another (Auyero, Lapegna, & Poma, 2009; Weis, 2005). This has led to incivility across social movements, where once broad-based coalitions have broken down. Jamaica, which was once capable of unifying broad swathes of the public through the labor movement that fought for independence, is now balkanized into tiny movements defined by incivility and infighting, which has become the defining politics of the "people on the margins" (Johnson, 2005). As people are increasingly pit against each other through government roll backs and patronage politics, universal rights have continued to decrease as they are converted into programs that individuals must qualify for (Weis, 2005). Increasingly, the public programs left, such as the HEART Trust (Human Employment and Resource Training), are based on criteria that disqualifies the oldest and most disabled as "bad investments," and only rewards those who can prove their potential to earn income and be gainfully employed.

METHOD

In the summers of 2017, 2018, and 2019, I collected 32 semi-directed depth interviews, participated in numerous events and activities, and conducted over 30 site visits to government agencies, academic research institutions, DPOs, OPAs, and disability and ageing-focused NGOs in Jamaica. I also collected articles published online from Jamaica's two national newspapers – *The Jamaica Observer* and *The Gleaner* – using the "disability," "disabled" "special needs," "older persons," "elderly," "aging," and "senior citizen" as search terms, and followed DPOs and OPAs on Facebook. Relevant articles, social media postings, transcribed interviews, and field notes were subsequently coded according to an interpretative analysis (Ruiz, 2009) that focused on the ways in which persons with disabilities and older persons are presented in discourse. Coding was done through a grounded process that involved two steps. The first step identified key, overarching themes, which were subsequently recoded to identify more specific trends and patterns.

RESULTS AND DISCUSSION

Today, DPOs and OPAs in Jamaica are mobilized in a fight for access to a meager array of services and benefits for their members, each by alternatively portraying disabled persons or older persons as active contributors to the community. These arguments for inclusiveness are also the basis of each movement's exclusion of others. New organizations that represent persons with disabilities and older persons also continue to be established throughout the island nation, including relatively remote areas. For example, in 2018 seniors came together in St Elizabeth, a parish (i.e., province) in central Jamaica, to create Intergenerational St Elizabeth for the purpose of advancing "the economic, social, and cultural rights" of older people and multigenerational households in the local community and to "promote the role of older persons as active participants and contributors to their families, communities, and society" (Intergenerational St Elizabeth, 2017). Likewise, persons with disabilities in the northern parish of St Ann came together and organized the St Ann Disability Association to bring persons with disabilities together to demand for more opportunities for disabled persons in their area by arguing, in the words of their president, that persons with disabilities "are people with real abilities" and therefore have a right to "participate in the social, economic, and political life of the community" (Combined Disabilities Association, 2019).

The new identities that each movement deploys are expressly designed to subvert negative beliefs about the abilities of disabled persons and older persons. These beliefs, however, share the same *ableist* root by alternatively depicting disabled persons as incapable of contributing to society, and portraying older persons as disabled. These ableist beliefs are precisely what each movement seeks to address, although in very different ways. The disability movement tackles *ableism* by celebrating youth with disabilities as potential contributors to society when they are properly invested in. The older persons' movement combats *ableism* by arguing that it is false to equate age with disability as because many older persons remain active in old age.

Both movements – membership organizations, disability or older persons–focused organizations, and other allies and advocates – use these new identities as a strategy for combating stigma, as well as advocating for rights and services that directly contribute toward the ability of their groups to be active participants in society. To this end, DPO and OPA representatives and other advocates share press releases, submit editorials, and organize advocacy campaigns that call upon the government to remove barriers and provide opportunities that will ensure their constituency's participation. Both groups primarily focus on issues of employment, education, accessibility, health care, pensions, and social stigma. For example, in a 2018 letter to the editor published in *The* Gleaner, one of Jamaica's largest newspapers, a disability advocate argued that persons with disabilities are "dehumanized" and denied their basic rights in Jamaica because they "have limited or virtually no access to basic amenities and social services," in part due to inaccessible "public sidewalks, crosswalks, roadways, and other infrastructural developments" (Quest, 2018, September 22). The letter goes on to explain that the lack of accessible public spaces prevented persons with disabilities from being employed, gaining educations, and contributing to the community. Similarly, a senior citizens' advocate profiled by *The Gleaner* demanded that seniors' "right to access public services" be recognized by the government, and sited an incident where an elderly woman "had to be assisted up three flights of stairs to attend court because of nonfunctioning elevators at the Supreme Court building" (2015). Her inability to participate in court meant that she could not represent herself in legal disputes that directly determined her ability to remain independent. The similarity in these public statements provides evidence of shared strategies across DPOs and OPAs, yet the movements have never made such statements together. In a similar vein, leaders of both movements quite literally pass one another in the halls as they lobby Members of Parliament or meet with the Ministry of Labour and Social Security to push for reforms, particularly regarding pension reforms, which have been under discussion in recent years, of which changes would have a disproportionate impact on both older persons and persons with disabilities.

The intersection in strategy and tactics of the disability movement and older persons' movement in Jamaica is profound. Indeed, the intersection between these two groups goes beyond mere similarities in advocacy. In theory, they represent overlapping populations as those most hurt by structural adjustment policies. They also overlap in other ways. The largest age cohorts of persons with disabilities are people over the age of 60, and a large number of senior citizens in Jamaica – an estimated 40% – have one or more disabilities. Yet, despite the intersection and overlap between each movement, when leaders of DPOs are asked about older persons or leaders of OPAs are asked about persons with disabilities, they often treat the question as an opportunity to distance themselves from that group and deny and form of commonality.

During the summer of 2017, I asked the president of one of Jamaica's largest disability advocacy associations about whether or not they reached out to senior citizens as potential members. She responded "You mean the elderly? Well, no – I mean, they are for the Council for Senior Citizens" (this DPO's main governmental partner was the Jamaican Council for Persons with Disabilities). After I explained that many older persons had disabilities, she finally responded

> Oh yes, of course, we include some elderly. You know, there are lots of our original members who joined in the 1980s – many then were affected by the polio as children, and they are now getting to be in their sixties. We represent them.

Her answer indicated that senior citizens experiencing new disabilities were not considered part of the organization's constituency, but only long-time members with disabilities who had joined when young and then subsequently aged. The organization's programmatic activities further demonstrated that recruitment was overwhelmingly focused on youth, despite their mission to reach out and represent all persons with disabilities in Jamaica.

Similarly, in the summer, 2019, while attending a senior citizens' club meeting, one of my students, whom I was leading on a study abroad program on disability and aging in Jamaica, asked the senior citizens' club director if their club included persons with disabilities. The club president immediately answered "Oh no! None of our members have disabilities, we've never had one – It has never been an issue for us. No, this club – this club is for *vibrant seniors!*" She went on in a loud and energetic voice to emphasize the "vibrancy" and "health" of their members. When pressed on the fact that many older people have disabilities, the club president continued to insist that the club was for vibrant seniors. This insistence seemed to demonstrate that the identity of "senior citizen" that the club promoted was constructed in contrast to persons with disabilities. Later, during the meeting, we learned that as a club, they did outreach to "shut-ins," who were older people whom they described as "bedridden" (i.e., disabled), but these individuals were not members of the club, but objects of their volunteerism and charity.

My objective in comparing and contrasting the disability and older persons' movement in Jamaica is driven by a desire to understand why these two movements, which ostensibly share so much in common, remain so distant and divided from one another. As this chapter unfolds, I explain this puzzle in regards to the ways in which both groups seek to change the negative societal belief that they are inevitably dependents by promoting a new identity. This identity work, however, diverges in both means and ends. The disability movement's new identity is specifically focused on the potential productivity of persons with disabilities if investments are made and barriers removed in early life. As such, it focuses on youth with disabilities, and celebrates narratives of young persons with disabilities overcoming barriers in their youth, and becoming productive adults. This narrative has little room for older persons, and is, in fact *ageist.* In contrast, the older persons' movement constructs the identity of senior citizens in a very different way. Instead, their identity centers on "vibrancy" and "healthy" to argue that just because someone is 60 or 70 (or, indeed 80 or 90), they can still remain active and independent contributors and, in effect, not be disabled dependents. This argument is, obviously, *ableist.* The divergent identities mobilized by DPOs and OPAs, thus, work against any possibility that the two movements will come together in a coalition to ultimately push back the neoliberal structural adjustment policies that are at the root of their marginalization.

Youth Focus in Disability

Of the more than 20 disability organizations or programs visited, all but one focused on young persons with disabilities or persons with disabilities in general. The majority of the programs were focused on early diagnosis, education, rehabilitation, and employment of children and youth with disabilities. This was true of both public and private services *for* persons with disabilities and DPO-run programs *by* persons with disabilities. Successful transition to adulthood was a central focus and the potential for lifelong contributions to society were the primary justification.

The emphasis on youth is a critical part of the stories that many of Jamaica's most important disability advocates use to make their case that persons with disabilities can be productive members of society when barriers are removed, services provided, and opportunities created at an early age.

The most important personal narrative circulated in Jamaica regarding what is possible for persons with disabilities is that of Senator Floyd Morris, who recently published *By Faith, Not by Sight: The Autobiography of Jamaica's First Blind Senator* (2017). Now 50 years old, Morris traces his success to a mix of his own gumption as a youth and the services he accessed as a young man that ensured his disability would not stop him from achieving great things.

Morris, who lost his sight as a teenager, summarizes his situation before he accessed services as:

> At 17 years old… I knew enough to realise that if I stayed at home, a severely visually impaired, uneducated boy without a skill, my life would be a tragic tale of abject poverty, sickness and uselessness… (Morris, 2017, p. vii)

Indeed, he had failed out of high school because they did not provide him any accommodations, which meant he could not take his graduation exams. The story, however, changes when he learns about the Jamaican Society for the Blind.

Once Morris learns about the JSB, which was located in Kingston, he packed his bags and immediately moved to the capital, where he began a rehabilitation program with JSB to learn how to walk with a white cane, use public transportation, read Braille, and other skills. Morris summarizes his experiences there as: "Upon completing the rehabilitation training, I was a new man. I was so excited by my new skills. I could operate and function more independently as a blind person" (Morris, 2017, p. 29). From that point further, Morris commences a speedy climb through high school completion, university and graduate school, political success, business-ownership, appointment as a government minister, hiring as a university lecturer, and eventually becoming the president of Jamaica's upper chamber of Parliament.

It is no surprise, then, that Morris, who shepherded through the 2014 Disability Act, emphasizes access to education and rehabilitation for children and young persons with disabilities. In an interview, he proudly proclaimed that Jamaica was a shining example in the Caribbean for its advances in accessible and inclusive education opportunities. But, he also emphasized his own role in inspiring others, especially young persons with disabilities, explaining "Much is owed by one to whom much has been given." As such, Morris takes a special interest in addressing the barriers that he faced himself, such as access to accommodations in education. To that end, he founded the Centre for Disability Studies at the University of West Indies, which houses the university's Office of Special Student Services. Special Student Services does the work that Morris wishes had been done for him as a young man, such as providing Braille or audio versions of texts for students with visual impairments, and basic accommodations for Deaf students, students with physical disabilities, and others.

Similarly, when I met with a leader of the Combined Disability Association, Jamaica's most prominent DPO at the national level, she recounted the ways in which, as a youth with visual impairments, she fought hard against a system that lacked access, but also benefited from disability services being provided by disability organizations in Jamaica.

The director of CDA also explained that she and other prominent members of the disability movement, such as Morris, "came up together," and have known each other since their youth. They now saw it as their responsibility to remove the barriers that they had encountered so that the next generation of persons with disabilities would have more opportunities than they did. As a result, even though CDA represented all persons with disabilities, it was CDA's leader who responded to my inquiry regarding older persons with disabilities

> Oh yes, of course, we include some elderly. You know, there are lots of our original members who joined in the 1980s – many then were affected by the polio as children, and they are now getting to be in their sixties. I'm getting on up there too [laughter]. We represent them.

But, when I asked about outreach to "new" older persons with disabilities, making it clear that I was not referring to people who have been part of CDA previously as a youth, but had gained their disability as an older adult, she answered "Well no, we don't do anything with them. I think maybe they might be for the senior citizens [organizations.]" This demonstrates how there is little interest in including older persons with disabilities in the movement who do not share the disability experience as a youth.

Morris' and CDA's youth-focused narrative and programmatic focus is reflected across disability organizations and DPOs in Jamaica. For example, the Abilities Foundation in Kingston focuses on vocational training and job placement. The front page of its website highlights a 22-year-old graduate from one of their programs, a place-and-train employment service:

> Through initiatives such as the Social and Economic Inclusion Grant for Persons with Disabilities, Richard Spragg was placed on the paid 6-week work Apprenticeship Program at Sweetie Confectionery Company Limited, Kingston. The company has since offered Richard full-time employment. This opportunity has positioned Richard to gain experience, improve his

> skill level, contribute to his family and the productivity of the country. (Abilities Foundation, 2019, p. 1)

The description of the program and Richard's experience is followed by a testimonial made by Richard himself, which reflects the youth narrative of the disability movement by acknowledging the blend of personal attributes plus opportunities leading to a life as a productive citizen:

> At Abilities Foundation, I worked very hard to pass my exams and I liked learning about information technology. I am a pleasant and confident person and having the right attitude helped me to obtain a job at the Sweetie Confectionery Company as a production assistant. At work, I am helpful and I support my coworkers. My goal is to continue learning and improving my manufacturing skills so that I may become more successful in the field. (Abilities Foundation, 2019, p. 1)

One of the most prominent DPOs in Jamaica, which has garnered widespread media attention and public support, is Deaf Can Coffee, a young Deaf persons-operated coffee roasting and barista business. Deaf Can sells hundreds of pounds of coffee throughout the world and operates coffee kiosks across the island, including one in the US Embassy, and a coffee trailer that is in constant demand for music festivals and other events. Their narrative again affirms the idea of young persons overcoming barriers through belief in self and opportunities. Their "Story" states:

> At the root of Deaf Can! Coffee is the belief that Deaf people can do anything and lack nothing, even though we don't hear with our ears. Society however doesn't always agree and Deaf youth often face a negative stigma in their environment that creates a L-A-C-K in their life by excluding them and preventing access to Language, Affirmation, Community and Knowledge…

The narrative goes on to recount a group of young Deaf persons from a Deaf school visiting a Deaf man who had his own coffee farm in Jamaica.

> With his inspiration and challenge, the teen students began roasting, packaging and selling coffee. Then they began brewing the coffee and a few months later opened up a small coffee shop at their school. Out of this was born the social enterprise Deaf Can! Coffee. (Deaf Can! 2018, p. 1)

During a panel Q & A with Deaf Can, I pointed out that they only included *young* Deaf persons (the oldest was 25), but there were obviously many Deaf older persons who lacked employment and could certainly benefit from Deaf Can. I asked if they would ever consider including older persons in their training and employment opportunities. The young man, however, appeared flummoxed by the question. He then signed that "I have never thought about that before. I do not know."

Deaf Can's answer reflects a much larger phenomenon in Jamaica's disability movement: Older persons with disabilities are simply "not thought of." In fact, the only disability-focused organization out of dozens to actively develop a program that intentionally worked with older persons with disabilities was Mustard Seed Communities, a Catholic service-provision organization that runs eight residences for persons with disabilities in Jamaica. Seven are homes that work with children and young adults. Their most recent residence, however, is Jacob's Ladder, a community and farm built explicitly for adults with disabilities, including older persons with disabilities. The director of Jacob's Ladder explained that for decades they had nothing, but realized that many graduates of their homes and programs had nowhere to go or anyone to support them, and were thus being made homeless when they aged out of their services. Thus, they built Jacob's Ladder a few years ago, and it included some persons with disabilities in their sixties. Yet, two items remain significant. The first is the service was almost exclusively for persons with disabilities who had entered the Mustard Seed programming as younger persons and, second, their work with the older persons was not acknowledged on their public materials. Instead, they explained Mustard Seed as serving "over 400 children, young adults, and families" (Mustard Seed, 2019).

In all of the interviews and site visits, only one other program was proactively thinking about the inclusion of older persons with disabilities, although they had not yet developed or piloted any programs. It was, like Mustard Seed, not a DPO, but a disability services organization.

In response to learning that of their eight service areas, which ranged from early intervention and special education to partnerships with parents, none included older persons with disabilities, I asked the new director of the Jamaica Association for Intellectual Disabilities regarding services for older persons with disabilities. The director responded:

> Yes! Let me tell you what has concerned me over the years, and now that I sit in this chair [i.e., leadership position], I am equally concerned, because we have not been reaching out in any significant and targeted way to the persons with ID who are ageing. And, if they lack the support when they are younger, how much more are they needing when they are ageing.

I asked what she had done regarding her concern, which revealed what little interest older persons' organizations have in persons with disabilities.

> My first step was I reached out to the council for the aged…senior citizens [National Council for Senior Citizens]. I called and asked for a meeting, but I haven't gone [haven't had] that meeting yet. I wanted to look at partnerships between the senior citizens and the persons with disabilities who are also senior citizens. 'Cause what is happening is that in all the mainstream programs, the focus is on mainstream people. So usually they don't think about the ones with disabilities who are also ageing – who are also senior citizens.

Despite the call having been made many months earlier, the director of JAID had not received any response from the council, nor had the director found any other willing partners with older persons' organizations.

Healthy Aging Focus in Aging

Whereas the disability movement in Jamaica is organized around a focus on youth, the older persons' movement in Jamaica is organized around health and nondisability. The goal of "healthy aging" is ubiquitous across OPAs and older persons–focused organizations. As the prevention of chronic disease or disability is the primary measure of healthy aging, older persons *with* disabilities are not the focus. Instead, older persons who do not have a disability are. This means that while older persons with disabilities are not explicitly excluded – and, in fact, receive important benefits and services – they are marginalized within the movement, as they are not seen as fitting within the narrative that older persons are and can continue to be active contributors to the community.

Hailee Gibbons (2016) discusses the discourse of "successful aging" extensively in her work regarding the intersection of ableism and ageism. Whereas Jamaica does not use the specific term "successful" aging, the import of healthy aging is the same: Older persons with disabilities are a failure – and, in terms of counteracting the societal narrative of older persons being dependent, they have no place. Thus, their presence within older persons' organizations is not encouraged, although some do include them, but portray them as active *despite* their disability.

The most prominent organization focused on older persons' rights in Jamaica is the Mona Ageing and Wellness Centre (MAWC). It was established in 2005 at the University of West Indies to address rapid aging in Jamaica, as the older persons' population in Jamaica was and still is growing exponentially in comparison to many other countries. The MAWC's mission statement includes three areas for policy development: teaching, research, and outreach. It goes on to state that its primary outreach effort is to "Promote healthy aging throughout the life course" (MAWC, 2019a).

In a recent press release promoting "Age Equality" for the 2019 International Day for Aging, MAWC does clearly state that

> We recognize as a result of the increase in Chronic Non Communicable Diseases (CNDCs), some older adults may become dependent on others for caregiving support and assistance with activities of daily living,

but then rather than explicitly recognize their equal rights, continues on to state

> We salute the persons who are involved in both the formal and informal care sector and acknowledge this as a valuable contributor of decent work and the well-being of older adults. (MAWC, 2019b, p. 1)

The focus is, therefore, on those who have stepped up to care for dependents, rather than the dependents themselves. In fact, during an interview in 2017, the director of MAWC explained to me that her priorities had shifted. The mission continued to be on promoting healthy aging, but she felt their biggest impact could be made in the prevention of chronic disease, many of which were considered disabling, by focusing on reaching children, youth, and adults up through their 40s. As such, the goal was explicitly on healthy aging rather than those who had aged and acquired disabilities during their transition to becoming an older person.

MAWC's mission of healthy aging is reflected in the newly proposed Senior Citizens Policy. It states that the first pillar of the policy is to promote "Active and productive aging for national development," which is done, in part, by promoting "a culture of wellness through healthy lifestyle choices and practices." Whereas persons with disabilities are not mentioned in the draft policy *per se*, they are alluded to as the unhealthy and unwell. The rationale for the policy is borne out in a number of statistics regarding older persons, including a prominently displayed health status and disability occurrence table, which highlights chronic illness, physical disability, sight only disabilities, and mental retardation, and is included in the Green Paper for the policy as its justification for increased government investment in healthy aging (Ministry of Labor and Social Security, 2018, pp. 16–17). Leaders of OPAs at the local level also emphasize addressing stigma and promoting healthy aging. The emphasis on "vibrancy," however, as evidenced in the senior citizens club mentioned earlier, suggests a level of ableism in their practices, which can mean the exclusion of some older persons with disabilities.

The importance of counteracting stigma, including the stigma associated with the assumption that all older persons are disabled, is a strong concern among local advocates, including OPA leaders. During a panel discussion with Julian Davis, a researcher associated with MAWC, Davis explained that when she asks her university students to tell her the first word they think of when they think of an older person, they say "miserable." She went on to explain that many young people see older people as "useless." Davis was followed by a board member of the Caribbean Community of Retired Persons, an older woman, who picked up on that theme to talk about how CCRP specifically plans activities that counter those beliefs. She detailed a night out they organized at a dance club. She asked my students "Can you imagine what people must of thought, seeing a group of us seniors dancing to the music at Waterfalls [a prominent nightclub in Kingston]?" as she moved her shoulders to an imagined beat. She went on to recount how her granddaughter, now a university student, and she communicate by WhatsApp, a popular smartphone app, to the surprise of her granddaughter's roommate. She continued with anecdotes meant to surprise my students in the audience, emphasizing how active and involved older persons were.

In a separate interview with two of CCRP's board members, I also learned that, like the disability rights movement, they recognized accessibility as a key issue in their advocacy. Both explained that waiting hours in line at either the bank or hospital were difficult because many older persons had issues with their knees and hips. The result of the bank advocacy was a policy of banks designating a special line for senior citizens that provided chairs they could sit in.

One CCRP board member went on to recount her own advocacy to have railings installed for the outside steps of a post office, which older persons struggled to mount. When I mentioned that her actions complemented many DPO's advocacy to create greater accessibility, she dismissed my point by saying "Oh no, this is different – They [disabled persons] are asking for ramps and all of that. We [seniors] are still active, we just have some difficulties now and then." Her response is indicative of how older persons view persons with disabilities as a separate category of people with whom they have nothing in common, even if they both struggle with stigma that sees them as unable, and want accommodations to ensure that they can, in fact, participate in society.

The categorical separation between older persons and persons with disabilities was affirmed during a discussion that included the local parish-level organizer in Manchester Parish for the National Council for Senior Citizens, who had primary responsibility for supporting senior citizens' clubs in the area. One of my students asked if her work included persons with disabilities. The organizer answered "Persons with disabilities? No, we have another entity for them. Just like we have a council for senior citizens, we also have a council for the disabled." While the questioner intended the question to be about *senior citizens* with disabilities, the organizer's ready assumption that any person with a disability was not under her purview demonstrates how disability is the primary identity given by others, even if the disability identity easily intersects with another aspect of identity, such as age.

As such, our site visits revealed that while many OPAs met in locations that were easy to walk to (i.e., few stairs), none were wheelchair accessible. Similarly, there were few accommodations offered, and none of the organizations we visited included persons who were blind, Deaf, or persons with obvious mobility disabilities (i.e., using a wheelchair or crutches). The stated intent of all was continued activity into old age. For example, one seniors' group on the north coast organized a weekly water exercise class on the beach. Many of the participants explained their commitment to it as "keeping us young," and stressed the way in which working out in the warm waters kept them active. But, they also stressed the importance of access. When they first formed as a group, several years earlier, they had used an adjacent beach that had been public, but then was sold to a resort group that closed it down from public access. The members had organized a protest, where they went to government meetings, wrote letters, and undertook other activities with the intention of reversing the decision. They even supported a court case, which was now sitting before the Privy Council (the Commonwealth's highest court), regarding the legality of the sale. One member explained that the government wants them (older persons) to stay active, but, with the loss of the beach, was not providing them the means (accessible space) to do it. To her, it meant a violation of rights.

A final example is the Recycled Teenagers, which is perhaps the most well-known grassroots OPA. Whereas Deaf Can! Coffee is pointed to constantly as a demonstration of what the disability rights movement in Jamaica is trying to accomplish – show that young persons with disabilities can become productive, contributing members of the community – the Recycled Teenagers are the most pointed to group among older persons. The Recycled Teenagers is a senior citizens' dance group that is featured frequently in the press and came up in virtually every discussion regarding OPAs. My students and I met with them and, in fact, received an unexpected dance lesson to a disco beat that surprised us, which is precisely what the group intended to do. While the founder of the group justified it on health grounds by telling a local newspaper that dancing stimulates their memory and enhances "active ageing ... [and] really provides an outlet for seniors who would otherwise be bored and inactive" (Williams, 2015).

Its true purpose, in addition to the enjoyment participants gain, seems to be to change attitudes regarding older persons. The National Council for Senior

Citizens ensures that they perform at major public events and, to many of the older persons we spoke to, they pointed to it as an exemplar of active older persons.

CONCLUSION

Throughout 2019, both the disability movement and the older persons' movement in Jamaica focused on pointing out the ways in which Jamaican society excludes them, and advocating that the government does more to be inclusive. A disability advocate wrote the following to the *Jamaica Observer* an op-ed titled "Disabled and Disrespected":

> There remains a need for further strengthening of these efforts [government initiatives promoting disability rights], especially as some social and cultural practices continue to impede the progress made in promoting the rights of all *children* in Jamaica... Overall, it was perceived that all ministries need to engage in greater public awareness of the existing programmes or services from which PWDs could benefit; expand the services and programmes offered to ensure that all PWDs have equal and fair access; and engage in continuous sensitisation sessions with staff. (emphasis added; Hall, 2019, p. 1)

In this op-ed, the advocate makes an explicit connection between a discriminatory culture and the need for government to get involved in tackling stigma, including sensitization of their own staff. It also, importantly, frames the argument in the "rights of all *children* in Jamaica," even though the article's title and other sections refer to the "Disabled" and persons with disabilities. Disability advocacy, in this way, continues to use references to youth a key part of their argument and as a justification for more state services that may generate a return over the lifetime of a productive disabled person.

In a similar work of advocacy, again published in the *Jamaica Observer,* an older persons advocate makes the case that stigma is the main problem, and connects age-based discrimination to the lack of "protection or safety net for the aged." The advocate also argues that the state's main responsibility is to "empower older people in all dimensions of development, including promoting their active participation" by going on to argue the following is essential for *active* participation:

> Jamaica has a long way to go to effectively tackle ageism... Our policymakers need to redouble their efforts in ensuring that there is neither inequity nor discrimination against older Jamaicans. There is an urgent need to engage the society with the aim of returning to the time in our culture when respect for the aged was evident and promoted through all aspects of our culture. (Campbell, 2019, p. 1)

Again, tackling stigma is seen as the solution, although in this case the advocate alludes to a time when stigma was not an issue.

The disability movement and the older persons' movement in Jamaica represent two of the most important groups in the population. Both face stigma that views them as unproductive dependents on society, both face barriers in everyday life, and both argue that the government needs to do more to ensure their rights and address their needs. Perhaps the most important commonality, however, is that they are two groups that have experienced the greatest cuts due to neoliberal structural adjustment as Jamaica reduces public services in order to repay its debt.

Despite these obvious areas where the disability movement and the older persons' movement have commonalities in their objectives, they not only do not work together, but ignore, if not actively distance themselves from one another. Because of a breakdown in civil society in Jamaica, different groups engage in a zero sum game in which they exclude others in order to see themselves included. The disability movement's prioritization of youth by emphasizing the potential of persons with disabilities to be productive over their lifetimes excludes older persons. The older persons' movement similarly leaves out persons with disabilities in their attempt to make the case that older persons are important contributors to society. They do so by only focusing on "vibrant" older people, who are by definition (in their minds) nondisabled. In short, the identity-based politics of the disability movement is ageist and the identity-based politics of older persons' movement is ableist. Thus, mutual cooperation between the movements is unlikely, if not impossible, and thus structural adjusment's logic again divides and conquers.

Researchers of structural adjustment's effects on civil society in Jamaica have recorded the ways in which social movements themselves have paved the way for the roll back of universal rights by fighting against one another rather than joining forces to form a common front against the government and the neoliberal financial institutions (i.e., IMF and World Bank) behind them. International policymakers and researchers interested in reversing the effects of neoliberalism have both noted that there is a significant intersection across persons with disabilities and older persons, and surmised that in an era of government cut backs, there is an opportunity for both groups to come together as allies, and push with a single voice (see, for example, AGE Platform Europe, 2019). In regards to Jamaica, if not elsewhere, that hope in a larger coalition seems ill founded. Whereas the needs may be the same, such as pensions, access, nondiscrimination protections, and simple respect, the identities of each movement are not only different, but opposed. At this moment, there seems to be little room for their coming together if they must keep their new identities intact. Thus, the "happy affective economy" (Fritsch, 2013) of neoliberalism appears to be here to stay, as disabled persons and older persons argue for their inclusion at the expense of one another and their most marginalized members.

REFERENCES

Abilities Foundation. (2019). Home. Retrieved from https://www.abilitiesfoundationja.com/

Abouharb, M. R., & Cingranelli, D. (2007). *Human rights and structural adjustment*. Cambridge: Cambridge University Press.

AGE Platform Europe. (2019, May 06). Ageing and disability: The intersection needs urgent exploring, conference finds. *European Commission* Retrieved from https://www.age-platform.eu/policy-work/news/ageing-disability-intersection-needs-urgent-exploring-conference-finds

Anspach, R. R. (1979). From stigma to identity politics: Political activism among the physically disabled and former mental patients. *Social Science & Medicine, 13*, 765–773.

Auyero, J., Lapegna, P., & Poma, F. P. (2009). Patronage politics and contentious collective action: A recursive relationship. *Latin American Politics and Society, 51*(3), 1–31.

Bickenbach, J., Bigby, C., Salvador-Carulla, L., Heller, T., Leonardi, M., LeRoy, B., & Spindel, A. (2012). The Toronto declaration on bridging knowledge, policy and practice in agingand disability: Toronto, Canada, March 30, 2012. *International Journal of Integrated Care, 12*, 4.

Campbell, W. (2019, October 21). Jamaica must prepare for its ageing population. *Jamaica Observer*. Retrieved from http://www.jamaicaobserver.com/opinion/jamaica-must-prepare-for-its-ageing-population_177601?profile=1096

CCRP. (2019). About us. Retrieved from https://www.ccrponline.org/about

Cohen, A. (Ed.). (2000). *Signifying identities: Anthropological perspectives on boundaries and contested values*. New York: Routledge.

Combined Disability Association. (2019). Mission & vision. Retrieved from https://www.combined-disabilities-association.org/mission-vision/

Combined Disability Association. (2019, July 11). *Posts*. Retrieved from https://www.facebook.com/pg/CombinedDisabilitiesAssociation/posts/

Dalmia, S. (2019, March 17). The rights' identity politics is more dangerous than the left's. *Reason*. Retrieved from https://reason.com/2019/03/17/why-the-rights-identity-politics-is-more/

Deaf Can Coffee. (2018). It's a long story. https://www.deafcancoffee.com/

Dearden, N. (2013, April 16). Jamaica's decades of debt are damaging its future. *The Guardian*, April 16. Retrieved from https://www.theguardian.com/global-development/poverty-matters/2013/apr/16/jamaica-decades-debt-damaging-future

Easterly, W. (2003). IMF and World Bank structural adjustment programs and poverty. In M. P. Dooley, & J. A. Frankel (Eds.), *Managing currency crises in emerging markets* (pp. 361–392). Chicago, IL: University of Chicago Press.

Fritsch, K. (2013). The neoliberal circulation of affects: Happiness, accessibility and the capacitation of disability as wheelchair. *Health, Culture and Society, 5*(1), 135–149.

Fritsch, K. (2015). Gradations of debility and capacity: Biocapitalism and the neoliberalization of disability relations. *Canadian Journal of Disability Studies, 4*(2), 12–48.

Fritsch, K. (2017). Contesting the neoliberal affects of disabled parenting: Toward a relational emergence of disability. In M. Rembid (Ed.), *Disabling domesticity* (pp. 243–267). New York, NY: Palgrave Macmillan.

George, P., & George, J. (2013). Interrogating the neoliberal governmentality of the Old Age Security Act: The case of sponsored immigrant seniors. *Canadian Social Work Review/Revue canadienne de service social, 30*, 65–81.

Gibbons, H. M. (2016). Compulsory youthfulness: Intersections of ableism and ageism in "successful ageing" discourses. *Review of Disability Studies: International Journal, 12*(2&3), 13.

The Gleaner. (2015, January 21). Seniors rights advocate chides Gov't. *Jamaica Gleaner*. Retrieved from http://jamaica-gleaner.com/power/57862

The Gleaner. (2016, February 25). Disabled at risk of being disenfranchised. *Jamaica Gleaner*. Retrieved from http://jamaica-elections.com/general/2016/news/article-1098.html

Grover, C., & Soldatic, K. (2013). Neoliberal restructuring, disabled people and social (in) security in Australia and Britain. *Scandinavian Journal of Disability Research, 15*(3), 216–232.

Hall, A. (2019, May 5). Disabled and disrespected. *Jamaica Observer*. Retrieved from http://www.jamaicaobserver.com/news/disabled-and-disrespected-new-study-underscores-that-life-remains-brutish-for-most-jamaican-children-with-disabilities_163848?profile=1373. Accessed on June 10, 2019.

Handa, S., & King, D. (1997). Structural adjustment policies, income distribution and poverty: A review of the Jamaican experience. *World Development, 25*(6), 915–930.

Handa, S., & King, D. (2003). Adjustment with a human face? Evidence from Jamaica. *World Development, 31*(7), 1125–1145.

Handicap International/HelpAge International. (2012). A study of humanitarian financing for older people and people with disabilities, 2010-2011. Retrieved from https://www.helpage.org/

newsroom/press-room/press-releases/helpage-and-handicap-international-study-shows-less-than-1-of-humanitarian-aid-targets-older-people-or-people-with-disabilities/

Harrison, F. V. (2014). The gendered politics and violence of structural adjustment: A view from Jamaica. In L. Lamphere, H. Ragoné, & P. Zavella (Eds.), *Situated lives: Gender and culture in everyday life* (pp. 451–468). Hoboken, NJ: Taylor & Francis.

HEART Trust. (2020). About. Retrieved from https://www.heart-nta.org/about/

HelpAge International. (2016). Older people's associations: A briefing on their impact, sustainability and replicability. Retrieved from https://www.ageing.ox.ac.uk/download/199

HelpAge International. (2019). Towards a UN convention on the rights of older people. Retrieved from https://www.helpage.org/what-we-do/rights/towards-a-convention-on-the-rights-of-older-people/

Intergenerational St. Elizabeth. (2017). *Articles of incorporation.*

Jenson, J. (2012). Redesigning citizenship regimes after neoliberalism: Moving towards social investment. *Towards a Social Investment Welfare State? Ideas, Policies and Challenges, 1*, 61–87.

Johnson, H. N. (2005). Incivility: The politics of 'people on the margins' in Jamaica. *Political Studies, 53*(3), 579–597.

KNOEMA. (2015). *Jamaica – Youth illiterate population.* Retrieved from https://knoema.com/atlas/Jamaica/topics/Education/Literacy/Youth-illiteracy

Lavigne, M., & Vargas, L. H. (2013). Social protection systems in Latin America and the Caribbean: Jamaica. Retrieved from https://repositorio.cepal.org/handle/11362/4068\

Leonardi, M., Bickenbach, J., & Leroy, B. (2012). International initiatives on bridging knowledge, policy and practice. *International Journal of Integrated Care, 12*, e203 doi:10.5334/ijic.1084

Luton, D. (2015, August 28). Mandatory retirement for teachers too rigid. *The Gleaner.* Retrieved from http://jamaica-gleaner.com/article/lead-stories/20150828/mandatory-retirement-teachers-too-rigid-says-thwaites

McGregor, S. (2001). Neoliberalism and health care. *International Journal of Consumer Studies, 25*(2), 82–89.

Meekosha, H., & Pettman, J. (1991). Beyond category politics. *Hecate, 17*(2), 75.

Metcalf, S. (2017, August 18). Neoliberalism: The idea that swallowed the world. *The Guardian.* Retrieved from https://www.theguardian.com/news/2017/aug/18/neoliberalism-the-idea-that-changed-the-world

Ministry of Labour and Social Security. (2014, February 7). Actuarial analysis roadmap and reform agenda for strengthening the role of the national insurance scheme in Jamaica. Retrieved from https://jis.gov.jm/?sfid=192533&_sf_s=audit

Ministry of Labour & Social Security. (2018). Green paper: National policy for senior citizens, 2018. Government of Jamaica. Retrieved from https://jis.gov.jm/?sfid=192533&_sf_s=audit

Ministry of Labour & Social Security of Jamaica. (1997). National policy for senior citizens. National Council for Senior Citizens. Retrieved from https://www.ifa-fiv.org/wp-content/uploads/2012/11/061_Jamaica-National-Policy-for-Senior-Citizens.pdf

Mona Ageing and Wellness Centre (MAWC). (2019a). Ageing and wellness Centre. Retrieved from https://www.pressreader.com/jamaica/jamaica-gleaner/20190529/282071983382275

Mona Ageing and Wellness Centre (MAWC). (2019b, September 30). The journey to age equality. Press Release. Retrieved from https://www.facebook.com/uwimawc/photos/a.882987475102036/2466968196703948/?type=3&theater

Morris, F. (2017). *By faith, not by sight: The autobiography of Jamaica's first blind senator.* Kingston: Imagination Books.

Mustard Seed. (2019). Our work. Retrieved from https://www.mustardseed.com/our-work/where-we-serve/jamaica

Naidoo, V., Putnam, M., & Spindel, A. (2012). Key focal areas for bridging the fields of aging and disability: Findings from the growing older with a disability conference. *International Journal of Integrated Care, 12.*

Neofotistos, V. (2013). *"Identity politics." Oxford Bibliographies.* Oxford: Oxford University Press. Retrieved from https://www.oxfordbibliographies.com/view/document/obo-9780199766567/obo-9780199766567-0106.xml

Peabody, J. W. (1996). Economic reform and health sector policy: Lessons from structural adjustment programs. *Social Science & Medicine*, *43*(5), 823–835.

Pfeffer, K. (2015, July 14). Why disability rights is everyone's business. *Forbes*. Retrieved from https://fortune.com/2015/07/14/disability-rights/

Polivka, L. (2012). The growing neoliberal threat to the economic security of workers and retirees. *The Gerontologist*, *52*(1), 133–144.

Priestley, M. (2003). *Disability: A life course approach*. Cambridge, MA: Polity.

Puar, J. K. (2012). Coda: The cost of getting better: Suicide, sensation, switchpoints. *GLQ: A Journal of Lesbian and Gay Studies*, *18*(1), 149–158.

Quest, A. (2018, September 22). Stop dehumanizing the disabled. *Jamaica Gleaner*. Retrieved from http://jamaica-gleaner.com/article/letters/20180922/stop-dehumanising-disabled

Raymond, E., & Lacroix, N. (2016). To include or not to include them? Realities, challenges and resistance to the participation of people with disabilities in seniors' organizations. *Review of Disability Studies: International Journal*, *12*(2&3), 17–18.

Robinson, J. W. (1994). Lessons from the structural adjustment process in Jamaica. *Social & Economic Studies*, *43*(4), 87–113.

Rowe, J. W., & Kahn, R. L. (1997). Successful ageing. *The Gerontologist*, *37*(4), 433–440.

Ruiz, J. R. (2009, May). Sociological discourse analysis: Methods and logic. *In Forum qualitative sozialforschung/Forum: Qualitative social research*, *10*(2), 32.

Sakellariou, D., & Rotarou, E. S. (2017). The effects of neoliberal policies on access to healthcare for people with disabilities. *International Journal for Equity in Health*, *16*(1), 199.

Salvador-Carulla, L., Putnam, M., Bigby, C., & Heller, T. (2012). Advancing a research agenda for bridging ageing and disability. *International Journal of Integrated Care*, *12*, 22.

UNDP. (2019). The 2030 agenda for sustainable development. Retrieved from https://sustainabledevelopment.un.org/post2015/transformingourworld

Weis, T. (2005). A precarious balance: Neoliberalism, crisis management, and the social implosion in Jamaica. *Capital & Class*, *29*(1), 115–147.

White-Jennings, D. (2019). Statement by Mrs Dione White-Jennings, Chief Technical Director of the Ministry of Labour & Social Security to the 12th Session of the Conference of States Parties to the Convention on the Rights of Persons with Disabilities. June 11–13, 2019. Permanent Mission of Jamaica to the United Nationshttps.Retrieved from //www.un.int/jamaica/sites/www.un.int/files/Jamaica/national_statement_-_12th_cop-crpd_june_2019.pdf

World Bank. (2016). Jamaica: Country profile. Retrieved from https://www.worldbank.org/en/news/feature/2016/04/18/acting-on-disability-discrimination-jamaica

World Health Organizations. (2019). Decade of Healthy Ageing. Retrieved from https://www.who.int/ageing/decade-of-healthy-ageing

Chapter 3

IMPASSES OF DISABILITY ALLIANCE BUILDING IN BULGARIA: SUCCESSFUL PHANTOM ACTIVISM AND TOXIC GRASSROOTS MOBILIZATION

Ina Dimitrova

ABSTRACT

Purpose: *In this chapter, I explore the current activist disability landscape in Bulgaria, focusing on its apparent insusceptibility to change. My objective is to examine the interplay between the conflicting parties, focusing on the factors that conditioned their successes and failures.*
Methods/Approach: *Relying mainly on directed content analysis, I analyzed website publications, online discussions, official statements released during the protests, as well as 18 interviews of mothers of children of disabilities and the data from five focus groups.*
Findings: *On the local disability scene, we discern two types of collective action – phantom disability activism and toxic grassroots mobilization. The first one held strongly to the traditionally construed notion of disability as confined in the need-based system and defined solely as medical condition. The second one – although very important for putting on the agenda issues as personal assistance and demedicalization – embraced deeply disturbing and toxic activist rhetoric, giving rise of an "abled-disabled" citizen thus reinforcing neoliberal images of human worth and failure.*
Implication/Value: *This chapter offers a closer look at the different meanings and implications of success, failure, and enabling or halting political renewal*

Disability Alliances and Allies
Research in Social Science and Disability, Volume 12, 67–85

ISSN: 1479-3547/doi:10.1108/S1479-354720200000012005

with regard to disability. On an empirical level, it adds more to the existing knowledge about the opportunities for, the role, the outcomes, and the specific features of alliance building in a context as Bulgaria, which presents us with specific combination of socialist legacies, post-socialist ways of abandoning disabled people, and, at best, short-term and transient embodiments of the "Nothing about us without us" tenet.

Keywords: Disability activism; parental mobilizations; post-socialism; alliance building; Bulgaria; "abled-disabled" citizen

INTRODUCTION

The social activism in the post-socialist countries has been sustainably in the focus of social scientists' interest as a "complex nexus of state–society–market relations" (Jacobsson, 2015, p. 3), operating in a specific context of diverse socialist legacies, interacting with the current neoliberal policies and imperatives. This chapter adds to this field of research by exploring the current activist disability landscape in Bulgaria, addressing the broad issue of how individuals and groups are effectively recruited to participate in collective action.

The local post-socialist disability politics has been marked by a controversy between two visions about disability. The first is embodied by the nationally representative organizations of and for people with disabilities which are institutionally closely connected with the state and receive public funding. The second is embraced by some grassroots mobilizations which preserve their independence from the state, contest the status quo, and struggle for political renewal and transformation of disability policies, identities, and public attitudes. Since 2012, some parental organizations have tried to effectively confront and transform the way disability is governed and to realize the tenets of United Nations Convention on the Rights of Persons with Disabilities (CRPD). In 2018, this tension gave rise to a clash, which brought disability issues to the fore of public attention for more than one year – an unprecedented event in the local disability history. The clash commenced with two marches. The first was organized by parents (predominantly mothers) of children with disabilities, which embraced the slogan of independent living, followed by a four-month-long sit-in protest in front of the Bulgarian National Assembly building. In almost all big cities across the country, tent protests arose in solidarity with the mothers at the capital. The second march was assembled by the nationally representative organizations, which defended the status quo.

The march by mothers raised high hopes that it could turn into a "window of opportunity" (Kingdon, 1984) and instigate radical social change in the way disability is governed and lived. Unfortunately this window soon was closed and the local disability landscape imploded, returning to its usual condition.

Thus, my main interest in this chapter is exploring and discussing this apparent insusceptibility to change. More concretely, my objective is to try to examine the interplay between the conflicting parties, focusing on what factors conditioned their successes and failures. I argue that this issue could be fruitfully analyzed if we pay attention to the different strategies they mobilized in order to recruit allies and build coalitions. Drawing on the rich research on social movements and grassroots activism, I offer one possible explanation as to why the grassroots mobilization of the mothers largely failed to make a considerable difference, while the adversarial party that formed around the nationally representative organizations could be assessed as a successful alliance that reached its reactive objectives.

I hope to demonstrate that with regard to the local disability activism it would be beneficial to differentiate between notions of success and of making real political difference. During the protests and the public confrontation that followed, it became relatively easy to discern, on the one hand, the existence of a *phantom disability activism,*[1] which *nonetheless* achieved successful alliance woven around the nationally representative organizations, and, on the other hand, an authentic but toxic grassroots mobilization by mothers which mostly failed due to its unfortunate choice of narrating and representing disability. The framing adopted by the mothers blocked their alliance-building opportunities, mainly because it drew a fundamental divide between "worthy" and "unworthy" disabled. This key moral-epistemic grid rested on an imperative to participate in the work-based system (Stone, 1984) and elevated it to the rank of a measure of human worth and deservingness of respect and support. The counter-framing, embraced by the national organizations, relied, respectively, on the alleged values of the need-based system (Stone, 1984) and allowed for the maintenance of effective structural alliances.

This chapter is structured as follows. The first section briefly sketches the local disability landscape. The second introduces the theoretical background of the analysis. Then I describe the data and method used. The third and the fourth sections present and discuss the specific features of the conflicting parties. Finally, a conclusion follows, offering some reflections on the future of solidarity and disability activism locally.

The contribution of this chapter is the closer look it offers at the different meanings and implications of success, failure, and enabling or halting political renewal in terms of disability empowerment. On an empirical level, it adds to the existing knowledge about the opportunities for, and the role, the outcomes, and the specific features of alliance building. It specifically discusses the Bulgarian context, which presents us with a specific combination of socialist legacies in governing disability, post-socialist ways of abandoning disabled people, and, at best, short-term and transient embodiments of the "Nothing about us without us" tenet.

SETTING THE STAGE

Before proceeding further, it is important to clarify the local status quo with regard to disability politics against the normative horizon of the present study. The normative horizon is crucial for understanding what is assumed here to mean *a movement to make difference* in the context of disability in Bulgaria. I construe this in terms of getting closer to, enacting and affirming key tenets of the social model of disability and independent living philosophy. Notwithstanding the diverse conceptual and practical issues haunting these perspectives (e.g., Hughes & Paterson, 1997; Kittay, 2011; Mladenov, 2015; Shakespeare, 2006; Shakespeare & Watson, 2001), what they achieve is beyond all doubt a certain level of empowerment of the disabled. It has been extensively argued "that [the social model] is a powerful tool for producing social and political change, for discussing the socio-historic oppression of disabled people and for driving emancipatory research" (Owens, 2015, p. 385). But the slogan "Nothing about us without us," which in the Global North serves as a shorthand for this transformative political project, aiming at rights, independence, self-determination, and self-sufficiency and entails radical resistance to paternalistic and medicalized approaches to disability, has never been broadly embraced on the Bulgarian disability scene. Using as a grid the distinction between the social and the medical model, I will briefly sketch how it is structured and how the existing organizations position themselves.

The social model has been advocated and promoted by the Center for independent living – Sofia (CIL) since 1995. The Center has been and continues to be a stronghold of the independent living philosophy and is quite significant event on the local disability scene, but its impact on the identity construction unfortunately has not been strong enough to inspire broader disability rights movement. Among its other initiatives, the Center struggled for the adoption of a Law on Personal Assistance with the intention to make this mechanism of support nationally available (Mladenov, 2017, p. 93)[2]. Later on, the adoption of such a law and its implementation as a crucial aspect of the realization of the United Nations CRPD became one of the main demands of the mothers' grassroots mobilization. It gained visibility in 2012, when the mothers took to the streets for the first time. The ideals they promoted were strongly focused on the integration, empowerment, and independence of the disabled. This may seem ironic, since often in the history of the disability struggles in the West, parental organizations have been seen as an obstacle for the genuine liberation of the disabled, subverting their authentic self-determination (Carey, Block, & Scotch, 2019). But locally this is not exactly the case, and the reason should be sought in the specific context of the quite unfavorable legacy with regard to disability activism in which the mothers had to struggle for the rights of their disabled children.

A key factor in this legacy undoubtedly is the historical absence of disability rights activism. The socialist way of governing disability was largely characterized by multifaceted paternalism, expressed in medicalization and segregation in residential institutions and in sheltered workshops. This kind of treatment as well as the political and cultural isolation from the West and the general lack of information about activist struggles abroad stifled any grassroots initiatives in this period. A closely related aspect playing a decisive role for the specific profile of the local activist scene is the general absence of strong voices of disabled self-advocates. In the context of the disability rights movement in the West, such figures and mobilizations have a crucial impact. One straightforward reason for their absence locally is that there are not many adults with certain types of disabilities – those on the autism spectrum or Down syndrome, for example – who have received proper education and treatment, permitting them to develop their full potential and become self-advocates or important figures in activist struggles. This is another unfortunate consequence of the socialist treatment of disabilities, which limited professional educational opportunities to the field of defectology, a pedagogical approach focused on keeping the children who needed special education segregated rather than integrating them with the help of extra support (Kalinnikova & Trygged, 2014, p. 243).

Crucial for the specific structuring of the disability scene are the nationally representative organizations of and for people with disabilities, which are closely connected to the state. These may sound as an equivalent to the Western organizations which are controlled and run by the disabled themselves – a key feature of the social model inspired disability activism – but in fact they "display some or all of the characteristics, attributed by British [social model] analysts and activists exclusively to 'organizations *for*' [people with disabilities]," rather than organizations *by* people with disabilities (Mladenov, 2009, p. 40; emphasis added). They are supported financially by the government, which makes them indispensable part of the state structures in the sphere of disability politics. This not only gives them an opportunity to exert pressure and to influence some policies from within the system but also makes them totally inept at advocating for radical transformation. Consequently, they largely remain in the medicalized needs-based perspective, which traditionally is the dominant policy approach adopted by the Bulgarian state.

These organizations are legally defined as such on the basis of territorial coverage and membership:

> ...the territorial structures of the organizations should "cover more than 30 percent of the municipalities in the country" [and] should "have no less than 1,600 members, no less than 50 percent of whom should be people with permanent disabilities.[3] (Mladenov, 2009, p. 42)

It is obvious that these purely quantitative criteria for representation are fundamentally flawed. One consequence is that numerous organizations of people with certain disabilities simply cannot attain such status. Besides that limitation, the actual social and activist involvedness of the organizations is not relevant as a condition for receiving their annual subsidies. Thus, totally passive and even "fake" organizations have the opportunity to receive public funding. The subsidy is not the single preference which these organizations are given. For example, only they can apply for funding under the European Union Operational Programs and receive a number of advantages when participating in public procurement (Runevski, 2014). Another factor, determining their general position as an arm of the state in disability politics, is their participation in the National Council for Integration of People with Disabilities (NCIPD), which will be discussed in more detail in the section on the preexisting ties.

That said, it must be noted that some of these organizations really offer support in the everyday lives of their constituency, including the provision of free medical treatment for their members, organizing celebrations, excursions, sightseeing tours, and museum visits, and arranging talks with doctors, nurses, and social services employees (Mladenov, 2017, p. 42). There are also exceptions as, for example, the Bulgarian Association of Persons with Intellectual Disabilities, which advocates tenets generally in line with the CRPD. But this is of little comfort given the quite unfavorable general context, which largely stalls radical transformation of the local disability scene.

ALLIANCE BUILDING, NOTIONS OF SUCCESS, AND MEANING-MAKING WORK OF MOVEMENTS

Previous research on social movements' capacity to provoke social change usually links their success with building extensive and viable alliances and assembling collaborating social actors (Beamish & Luebbers, 2009; Carey et al., 2019; Gamson, 1990; Polanska, 2015; Van Dyke, 2003; Van Dyke & McCammon, 2010). Thus, the scholarly attention has been focused on the factors facilitating and promoting ally recruitment. Diverse factors have been studied in this respect, including specific features of political and cultural opportunity structures, cultural resonance of the symbolic work done, identity alignment, shared framing of values, goals, and interests, preexisting social ties, etc. In this chapter, I focus mainly on two of these factors, which I consider of key importance for the dynamics and the specific profile of Bulgarian disability activism during the clash of grievances and the subsequent gradual fragmentation of the mothers' camp. These two factors are the meaning-making efforts of the activists on the one hand, and the preexisting ties on the other.

Meaning-making work is explored from the perspective of culturalist approaches within social movement theory. In these approaches, the main interest is how culture is used in order to pursue one's activist aspirations (Williams, 2004, p. 93). In other words, the focus is on the construction, mobilization, and alignment of symbols, frames, and cultural repertoires, which shape the conceptual space of a movement, as well as its effective interplay with the cultural environment and possible allies (Benford & Snow, 2000; Jasper, 1997; Snow & Benford, 1992; Williams, 2004; Williams & Benford, 2000). Analysis of such signifying, meaning-producing work, which makes certain nodes of meaning salient and others invisible, is usually referred to as frame analysis. This concept has gained prominence across varied strands of social sciences and is often employed in research on social movements and different types of collective mobilizations (Benford & Snow, 2000; Goffman, 1974; Snow & Benford, 1992).

The mothers' mobilization deployed mainly on the level of such symbolic work. The other party, which was formed around the nationally representative organizations, constructed a counternarrative only due to necessity to offer an adversarial ideology and disability identity; in other words, its symbolic work was simply a countermeasure. The real strength of the alliance work by the nationally representative organizations lay in its strong embeddedness in preexisting social ties, including links with the state. Thus, in order to understand its successful alliance building, I rely on the existing conceptualizations of social ties as key factor for alliance building (McAdam & Paulsen, 1993; Polanska, 2015; Van Dyke & McCammon, 2010). As Polanska and Piotrowski (2015, p. 280) note

> … the formation of alliances and cooperation is not always grounded on rational decisions. Instead, in many cases already existent social relations play a decisive role in individuals and organizations' choices of partners to cooperate or build alliances with. This could be explained by the (inter-personal and inter-organizational) trust built in already existing relations and the formation of strong social ties.

I would like to add here some comments on the difficult and contentious conceptual issue of how to define "success" of social movements. According to Steven Epstein, for example, who considers it with regard to patient movements (Epstein, 2011), we should diversify our assessment criteria, which would allow us to trace the intended as well as the unintended outcomes of actors' activities, framing choices, and so on. Thus, success could be understood as "achieving the movement's stated objectives, but also the capacity of an alliance to persist and thus continue to be a viable vehicle for social change" (Beamish & Luebbers, 2009, p. 648). The phantom activism of the nationally representative organizations demonstrates the need to divorce the notion of *success* of an alliance and provoking *social change* or *making real difference*. Relying on its social ties this coalition was really successful, but this is mostly an unfortunate fact, since it more or less cemented the status quo.

DATA AND METHOD

This chapter is based on qualitative data from a variety of sources. Since a substantial part of the popularization and the heated discussions between the conflicting parties took place on the Internet, I have followed the relevant websites and online discussions since the beginning of the controversy in April 2018 until January 2019. Most data come from the largest Facebook groups ("The system kills us/you" and "Our system kills – national protests for disability reform") that were promoting the mothers' protests and their proposals for legislative changes as well as from the public profiles of the key public figures representing the demands of the parties. Additional textual resources include official statements released by the activist groups, publications in newspapers, and social media, assembled also during the period indicated above.

An important source of additional information are 18 semistructured interviews with mothers of children with disabilities and five focus groups (between five and eight participants each), conducted in Sofia, Varna, and Plovdiv in 2018. The interviews and the focus groups are part of the fieldwork conducted in the period 2017–2018 as part of the project "*Generational Patterns of Coping with Life Crisis: Biographical, Social and Institutional Discourses,*" financially supported by the Bulgarian scientific fund and carried out by researchers from five academic institutions (Sofia University, Bulgarian Academy of sciences, New Bulgarian University, and Plovdiv University[4]). It is important source of information, since the respondents were supporters of the protest "The system kills us" in the respective cities in the country. All respondents' names are anonymized and pseudonyms are used in the quotations. Their age and their child's condition are identified since the general objective of the project was to gain a grasp on the generational patterns of living with disability in Bulgaria and on the care contexts of the diverse conditions. All respondents have signed informed consent forms to participate in the study.

Data are obtained also from the websites of several nationally representative organizations; among them are the Union of the Deaf in Bulgaria, The Union of the Blind in Bulgaria, and the Union of the Invalids in Bulgaria, Bulgarian Association of Persons with Intellectual Disabilities, Bulgarian Association for Recreation and Tourism, Bulgarian Association for Recreation, Integration, and Sport.

I relied mainly on directed content analysis, which uses "existing theory or prior research [in order to identify] key concepts or variables as initial coding categories" (Hsieh & Shannon, 2005, p. 1281). As described by Hsieh and Shannon (2005, p. 1282), it involves developing operational definitions of these predetermined categories, followed by careful review of data, highlighting all that appears to pertain to each of them. After coding for each category, the data are examined to determine whether subcategories are needed. Thus, I used three broad categories and searched for statements which fall into each of them. The categories were largely derived from two normative clusters of meaning, namely the already mentioned above work- and need-based systems (Stone, 1984). Each category was further broken up into three elements, in order to be able to identify if there are combinations of them across the initial categories. These elements could be differentiated into a core tenet (work vs need), and their respective moralized and practical consequences.

The first category – the value of work – was characterized by a vocal appeal to inclusion in the paid employment. It is traditionally construed as the most effective tool for integration in society (UPIAS/Disability Alliance, 1976). Its moralized retinue of images encompasses being worthwhile, having social value, being a deserving citizen, being independent and productive, and as the interviews showed "being a taxpayer." Its corresponding policy manifestation is the personal assistance model since this is the tool which can "[help the disabled] to make whatever contribution they can in ordinary work situations" (UPIAS/Disability Alliance, 1976, p. 17), which was the ultimate goal of the mothers' protest.

The second cluster is centered around the assumption that the disabled belong exceptionally to the need-based system. This is accompanied by the moralized images of burdensomeness, undeservingness, dependency, lack of self-sufficiency, etc. Its policy manifestation stays close to the medical model and in the local context relies on a purely medical disability assessment mechanism. I assumed that a third cluster could transpire during the content analysis, a cluster I dubbed "nonculpable vulnerability." Its core tenet was expected to be, briefly stated, a caring variety of accepting the universal human weakness, provoking feelings of solidarity. Its practical consequences are promoting and defending both generous public assistance without stigmatizing it, stable network of social services, as well as effective mechanisms of supporting employment and independent living of the disabled. As I will note and briefly discuss mainly in the conclusion, this category was largely absent from the local disability activism landscape.

CREATING A TOXIC DIVIDE: MOTHERS' MOBILIZATION AND LABOR-CENTERED FRAMES

In order to better understand the rise and fall of the mothers' mobilization, some context is needed. The April march of the mothers of children with disabilities has been the sixth annual protests, taking place since 2012. This time the slogan was "The system kills us," referring to the radical ineptness and ineffectiveness of the existing disability policy. The protesters were really adamant. They demanded radical reform of the disability policy in tune with the general tenets, adopted by the United Nations Convention for the Rights of People with Disabilities, which has been ratified by Bulgaria since 2012, but not followed by any decisive steps for its implementation. The protesters called for change in the disability assessment mechanism, which is entirely medicalized, and for the introduction of effective personal assistance legislation. As already mentioned the provision of personal assistance was conceived as the key tool, which could integrate the disabled in the world of work (as well as the mothers themselves), and empower them to live independently as the social model advocates. The medicalized logic of the disability assessment was seen as a key obstacle since it does not provide an assessment of the individual need of support, which could more effectively help the person with disability to be independent, integrated in society, and, possibly, also work.

The demand in general and especially the bill provoked vocal contestation of the large coalition which formed around the nationally representative organizations of and for people with disabilities. They claimed that such legislative reforms are not just, since not all disabled people would benefit from them, and also because changes in the assessment mechanism would be misused in order to deprive many of their disability pensions and allowances. Here, I will not discuss the actual effects of the concrete legislative changes which were demanded and some of them implemented, since this goes beyond the focus of this chapter.

As mentioned above, the Bulgarian parents of children with disabilities find themselves in a complex and ambivalent situation, trying to fight the consequences of the socialist institutional, cultural, and political "erasure" of the people with disabilities, to ensure decent living, education, training, etc., of their children largely without the support from the state, and at the same time to respond to the neoliberal ideology requiring one to be able to demonstrate that one is a deserving, efficient, productive, self-reliant citizen, passionately rejecting social assistance, and desiring economization.

The need to make the framing, mobilized by the mothers, culturally resonant (Williams & Kubal, 1999) with this broadly embraced neoliberal ideology, determined its sheer labor-centeredness. From here ensued the effort to narrate the relation between disabled people and society as a relation of investment and payback, in which any good and wise investment pays back. A good example is the following statement from an interview of a mother who was among the main activists during the early stages of the protest:

> The individual assessment [of the needs of the disabled person] will provide everyone with access to education and work – even if work means only to press a button [...] on the production-line for plastic bags [...]. Then significant number of people with disabilities who receive support will be able to work and contribute with their labor and productivity to society. I can assure you that no one wants to live like a parasite and depend on social assistance [...]. A lot of useful potential is lost.

This was, in fact, the backbone of the narrative that these activists mobilized not only in 2018 but also in the previous protests. In 2017, the key message was similar: "the integration of children with disabilities will make them more useful to the state. Leaving them neglected will in no way be cheaper for the public funds" (New protest of mothers of children with disabilities, n.d.).

In the semistructured interviews and in the focus groups with mothers of children with disabilities, the same basic node emerged. Here is how a mother from Varna comments on her child's ability to work, emphasizing that "employment" is very important, and so whenever she has the opportunity, she wants the issue to be discussed among the local parenting community: "[The disabled child] will be aware that she does something and most importantly – that she will contribute to society" (respondent 3, focus group 2, Varna).

In the semistructured interviews, the notions of "investment" and "exchange" appear quite often. Indicative is the following statement:

> ...all expenses that are made for people with disabilities, and for children with disabilities, and for their parents are a kind of investment. It pays back but you need to know where to invest, what activities to support in order to make them useful for the others. People with disabilities are not dependent, needy, they can be useful to society... (Stanimira, 34, caring for daughter with spina bifida)

Here, in a completely unambiguous and spontaneous way, we see what is conceived as the real threat and as the most radical negation of being useful and deserving citizen: it is the dependency on social assistance or being "needy." The contempt in these words could hardly be concealed. In such a way, the need-based system was radically stigmatized and demonized by the mothers' protest. I will return to this point in more detail below.

Another mother shares her concern about the future of her daughter, who has "a preserved intellect to some extent" but nonetheless she will never be able to find a place in the world or work, even in supported employment. Therefore, the mother strives to launch some kind of social enterprise, in order to provide her daughter with a "place under the sun," even if that means "that she will only press the button of a dough mixer." To the interviewer's comment that the girl could also read and write, the mother replies: "Yes, she can write, but it is necessary that she produces some output" (Nesrin, caring for daughter with cerebral palsy). In a similar manner a mother of a son with Asperger's syndrome says that

> ...he has to work [in order] to feel that he is useful. Now we are trying to organize social enterprises so that these young people can work... Otherwise [...] what is the point of all our efforts, which we have invested in these kids? (Catherina, 51)

The work-and-productivity–centered logic is particularly obvious in one very common rhetorical node that mobilizes the image of "paying taxes" as a proxy for individual utility and productivity. This "contribution" to society and the ubiquitous image of the "worthy taxpayer" is repeatedly mobilized by the activists. Similar statements were often made during the protests and in the interviews. Here is what one of the mothers, who was among the most active at the start of the April 2018 protests, said:

> I have good education, which could provide me good job and good income, which can respectively be taxed by the state – in such a sense I could contribute seriously to the budget revenues as all normal people (key protest activist).

Impressive here is the obviously deeply ingrained assumption that "normality" can be attained through paying taxes. Another mother, also among the most prominent activists in the early stages, used the same argument:

> Suppose I have motor impairment but also the cognitive capacity of Bill Gates… and can make a lot of money and respectively, the state could take a lot as taxes. In this way I could support the state budget… (key protest activist).

The statements cited so far demonstrate the activists' belief that economic "utility" and the logic of exchange are basic legitimating conditions, which allow making demands on society. The following statement shows that this is not merely a strategic decision, but a deeply ingrained conviction:

> We have a useful move […] and this useful move is to continue with protests but not because we suffer, but because there is an unfair distribution and harmful and incompetent spending of money… With this logic we can ask for the support of the society, and not because we suffer (key protest activist).

This implies that suffering is always a personal, individual tragedy that does not permit seeking collective and structural support or change. This was a key feature of the protests: although some of the demands were rhetorically similar to the tenets of the social model – namely rights, independence, dignity – in their essence they were fundamentally distinct since they framed disability as individual problem and conveyed the message that the broader public could be recruited among the allies if and only if a payback could be guaranteed. That is why these activists mobilized rhetoric based mainly on the idea that society rests on relationships of exchange, resembling the economic ones, and not on commonality of precariousness and interdependence, for example.

The other affective node that stood out, both in the personal narratives and in the frames mobilized by the activists, was the loathing of "parasitism," i.e., of life within the need-based system. It was construed as the utmost human failure and the most undesirable kind of subjectivity. Here are some of the activist voices: "I love my child, but I want to work, in order not to turn into a parasite for the state" (key activist, mother of daughter with severe multiple disabilities). The same mother also says:

> For years we have been pleading not to be treated as burden of society – we do not want social assistance, we want rights. But [our government] obviously thinks that our children do not have rights and will continue to be nothing more than benefit dependents.

Indicative is also the emotional exclamation in a Facebook post of another key activist, with which she refers to the members of the nationally representative organizations in the following way: "Their protest affirms INVALIDITY! They want their pensions, they want to be pitied. That's what they want!"

In the interviews, this sentiment was clearly present and usually was shared by the respondents in an unsolicited and spontaneous manner. The mothers say, for example: "do you know how humiliating is the dependence on these meager allowances" (Kalina, 40, caring for son with cerebral palsy); or

> ...we are seen by the rest as people who do not contribute in any way ... I know that the workforce has shrunk and many like us hinge on it and suck up its blood as ticks (Tsvetana, 55, caring for daughter with intellectual disability)

or "we do not want to be seen as beggars" (respondent 1, focus group 1, Varna) and as people, who "merely ask and wait for charity" (respondent 2, focus group 1, Varna). Frequently the respondents characterize themselves and their children as "burden on the state" (respondent 4, focus group 1, Varna).

This way of selecting words and images for self-description confronts us, I believe, with an instance of a grassroots appropriation of a normative regime of valuation of life – with but also without disability – through gradation of capacity and debility (Puar, 2017). It produces the mentioned above crucial divide between the "abled-disabled" (Titchkosky, 2003) and the "invalids," who are unable and unwilling to be productive and responsible. This kind of framing, constructed and affirmed by the mothers' coalition, gave rise to a "disability spectrum," ranging from the "abled-disabled" to the undeserving "welfare scroungers." The latter were framed as being content with living as "parasites," letting themselves to be manipulated and duped by the existing system and as consciously rejecting the "abled-disabled" lifestyle of self-sufficiency, responsibility, economized existence, and active seeking of independence. This division can be especially cruel and harmful when it ranks the suffering experienced in the context of different disabilities, as in the following example from an online discussion:

> I am fed up with people saying that I am a loafer, parasite and fake disabled... The fact that people with paresis can move, although with great difficulty, and that (some of them) can find a job, doesn't mean that there aren't others – with paraplegia or other impairments, who cannot even get up from the bed... So, those like me – the paraplegics – are loafers and fake disabled in comparison to you, the "active" disabled?"

Deeply disturbing are the words of one supporter of the mothers' protest, directed to a blind woman:

> Nothing is wrong with you! If you were like our children, you would have known what real suffering is. In your condition you cannot feel pain... You just sit and receive money from the state without working (online discussion)

It should be recognized that the mothers' protest was perhaps the most vocal instance of demands, appealing to radical redefinition of disability and distancing it from the need-based approach. They empathically and consciously embraced the neoliberal narrative of work, productivity, and deservingness in order to justify their demands and to recruit supporters from the broader nondisabled public. As Michel Callon convincingly argues, the efficiency of any activist performance depends on the ability of the concerned groups to make themselves recognized by future allies, who are not standing in their shoes (Callon, 1999, pp. 92, 93). The mothers tried to achieve exactly this, but along the path they left behind the disabled themselves. The framing, stressing the desirability and even the moral indispensability of attaining an "abled-disabled" subjectivity by all disabled, appeared to be deeply problematic. It individualized disability, stigmatized and further marginalized those who simply cannot fulfill such requirements and need assistance for various reasons, thus further entrenching the neoliberal mode of construing citizenship and human worth, which is palpably present in the post-socialist context (Phillips, 2010).

The mothers obviously believed that the best strategy to make themselves heard was to employ a work-and-productivity logic, which could be boiled down to the following: "disabled people could be useful and productive members of society and *that is why* they deserve support." The mothers' rhetoric, suffused with this ethos, undermined the possibilities for solidarity among the disabled people themselves as well as with other vulnerable groups. Moreover, this framing obscured the broader implications of the notion and practice of personal assistance, whose aim is not only access to the world of work but also to fight the diverse societal mechanisms, which oppress people with disability.

NATIONALLY REPRESENTATIVE ORGANIZATIONS AND THEIR ALLIES: PHANTOM DISABILITY ACTIVISM IN A NETWORK OF PREEXISTING TIES

This section traces the network-building work of the coalition which grew around the nationally representative organizations. I rely on a notion of alliances, which identifies their existence through the "ability to engage in joint action despite differences in claims and strategies" that connects two or more social sites and in this way contributes to reaching "greater level of achievement in social movements" (Polanska, 2015, p. 197). Achievement or success in its turn, although a complex conceptual issue as already stressed above, would be understood here as accomplishing "the movement's stated objectives, but also [as] the capacity of an alliance to persist" (Beamish & Luebbers, 2009, p. 648). Thus, it could be argued that the nationally representative organizations succeeded in building a stable and enduring alliance, which accomplished its objectives, namely to act as an adversarial force with regard to the mothers and to subvert their framing on an ideological level. However, the real strength of this coalition is rooted in the social ties, including its close connections to the state.

These connections are multifaceted but of key importance is the financial dependence. These organizations can be defined as government-operated nongovernmental organizations, which turns them into an extension of the state apparatus (Mamonova & Visser, 2014, p. 501). They receive annual public subsidies and are "representative" in terms of territorial coverage and number of members and not in terms of giving voice to and defending the rights of disabled people. This significantly contributes to the current state of depoliticization of these largest organizational bodies (Mladenov, 2009, p. 42). As I already mentioned, their efforts are focused on providing free medical treatment for their members, organizing excursions and social activities, and arranging talks with doctors, nurses, and social services employees, which only perpetuates their state of learned helplessness (Mladenov, 2009, p. 42).

This could be clearly seen also throughout the pages of the newspaper *Courage*, the official periodical of the Union of the Invalids, which is published online on the Internet site of the organization. The reader encounters predominantly depictions and photographs of diverse social events as celebrations of official and religious holidays, anniversaries, contests, excursions, museum, and exhibition visits, organized for the disabled and their families in different regions of the country. Certainly, this is valuable experience for them, since otherwise they would be almost totally isolated, but still it cannot contribute to recasting disability identities and bringing them closer to the empowering ideas of the social model and the independent living philosophy.

Besides the financial connection with the state, most of these organizations have representatives in the NCIPD. There are independent sociological analyses that have demonstrated the fundamental flaws in the functioning of this body:

> National Council for Integration of People with Disabilities (NCIPD) has redefined its role from an arena for deliberation between equal partners to a "marriage of convenience", in which the state simply purchases the legitimacy of its decisions and the silence of the "beneficiaries" with an annual subsidy. These beneficiaries – almost always – do not justify properly the expenses made (Center for Independent Living-Sofia & Trust for Civil Society in Central and Eastern Europe, 2011, p. 2).

Another important feature of these organizations and of the alliance that grew around them is the firm embeddedness in the medical model. In a historical perspective, this is due to the socialist legacy with regard to the totally medicalized disability assessment mechanism. But if we look closely, we see the importance of the close personal ties between the leaders and representatives of these organizations and the main figures in the medical establishment and in the structure, known as the national and territorial expert medical commission (NEMC, TEMC). The most prominent figure during the mothers' protests, who contested the mothers' demands, was the chairwoman of the Association of the Medical Specialists from TEMC, Boryana Holevich. She was one of the most vocal opponents of the proposed reforms, whose aim was to distance disability assessment from its purely medical character. Holevich (Holevich, 2019) repeatedly stated that:

> The proposed model for individual assessment envisions serious interference in the most intimate spheres of the lives of the disabled by staff with no medical education. The social worker has no medical education. My personal opinion is that the task of social workers is to comply with the opinion and the prescriptions of doctors and not to assess impairments.

It is important to note here that since the expert certificate received from these medical commissions is the "standard basis for getting access to all disability-related welfare structures and processes in the country" (Mladenov, 2016, p. 6), protecting and justifying it amounts to perpetuating the traditional confinement of disabled people entirely in the need-based system.

Another vehement opponent of the reforms and of the mothers' demands for introducing personal assistance was the labor union "Confederation of Labor *Podkrepa*" (meaning "support" in Bulgarian), which is also represented in the NCIPD. The organization strongly opposed the passing of a law of personal assistance in its official statement (Confederation of Labor *Podkrepa,* 2018). Its representative in the National Council and economic adviser, Vanya Grigorova, strongly criticized the participation of social workers in the process of assessment, claiming that they do not have the necessary medical education and training in order to objectively assess the functional deficits of the disabled person, thus echoing the mentioned above opinion of Holevich and backing the heavily medicalized profile of the assessment. The importance of the personal ties can be very clearly seen in the fact that Holevich was the chairwoman of the committee, which supported Grigorova to run as an independent candidate in the European Parliamentary elections in May 2019.

Among the arguments of the labor union against the user-led personal assistance was that it practically amounts to exploitation of personal assistants by the mothers of disabled children or by the disabled themselves, since the latter hire them, fire them, and determine the timing of the performed activities. Concerns about the working conditions and protection of personal assistants have been raised (Watson, McKie, Hughes & Gregory, 2004).[5] Also battles between disability movements and organized labor are not something novel and sometimes have been really acute (Bagenstos, 2017). What is worrisome in the local context is the fact that this concern was couched as an unequivocal repudiation of the very idea of personal assistance. To declare officially that personal assistance amounts to exploitation could be deeply harmful in a context such as Bulgaria, in which the service awaits its effective implementation. Not less problematic is the unconditional support for a totally medicalized disability assessment.

The other allies from this coalition were some leftist NGOs which, despite some differences, support each other and share some common objectives (as, for example, supporting Vanya Grigorova during the mentioned above elections). They fiercely attacked the mothers' proposals for legislative changes and defended TEMC as a bastion of just and fair support for the disabled (Parvanov, 2018). This comes as no surprise, since here again the social ties are obvious. Besides being a consensual figure among the members and supporters of these NGOs, seen as an embodiment of their key political leftist goals, Vanya Grigorova is the president of one of these NGOs, Association "Solidary Bulgaria." Thus, her close connections with a significant number of the allies in this coalition make her perhaps the main actor in this alliance, who could be identified as broker or bridge builder (Bandy & Smith, 2005; Obach, 2004).

It could be summarized that the nationally representative organizations succeeded in weaving around themselves quite a stable network, which mobilized a counter-framing strategy in order to more effectively resist the mothers' attempts to recruit supporters. Accordingly, the script, which they devised, pertained to the cluster of meanings typical for the need-based system. The main contention was that satisfying mothers' demands would lead to deprivation for many disabled people of their benefits, since they would be declared able to work but in the same time would be unable to find a job. In this way, the most vulnerable would be completely deprived of support. The disabled were framed as dependent, incapacitated, in constant need of care, and the mothers as a conduit of neoliberal influence that comes to shatter the last remains of the welfare state. This repertoire succeeded in discrediting the grievances of the mothers' mobilization by pointing exactly the toxicity of the divide which they drew across the disability communities. In the public consciousness mothers' demands were stigmatized as another attempt to "drain the budget." This trapped disability activism in an insidious situation, in which it could not appeal neither to demands for more generous state assistance nor to values as independence, self-sufficiency, and productivity.

CONCLUSION

My aim in this chapter was to discuss the recent divides, which cut across the local disability landscape, and gave rise to two specific strains of collective action, which I dubbed phantom disability activism and toxic grassroots mobilization. The first one held strongly to the traditionally construed notion of disability as confined in the need-based system and defined solely as medical condition. The second one – although very important for putting on the agenda issues as personal assistance and demedicalization – embraced deeply disturbing activist rhetoric, giving rise to an "abled-disabled" citizen thus reinforcing neoliberal images of human worth and failure.

Both parties however could not succeed in inventing and in practicing novel ways of framing, rooted in modes of togetherness and solidarity. This was evidenced by the total absence of the mentioned above category of "nonculpable vulnerability." Premising social belonging either on usefulness and payback as the mothers did or on a perpetual confinement in the need-based system as the nationally representative organizations insisted led to the closure of the window of opportunity and stalled radical policy changes. This activist impasse perhaps signals that the local grassroots disability organizations and disability academics should search for alternative frameworks for thinking about definitions of disability and about recruiting allies. As Quirici (2019, p. 2) states, the challenges facing activists and scholars today are connected primarily to "questions of coalition and inclusion: [w]ho should be part of the movement?" The disability justice movement [...] attempts to propose a viable option and to imagine "new ways of countering oppression and generat[ing] new forms of being-in-common" (McRuer, 2018, p. 24) rooted in the commonality of vulnerability, interdependency, and failure to live up to the neoliberal requirements. Locally, this looks to be an inspiring perspective, since the economic hardships and poverty, the corrupted health care system and the social and political precarity literally pour out debility (Puar, 2017). This could make one think that there are many potential allies, which could easily be recruited in a large coalition, glued together by human weakness and state of social abandonment. But the local disability activism has not yet recognized and recasted vulnerability as a hopeful horizon for solidarity.

ACKNOWLEDGMENTS

I would like to thank the two anonymous reviewers and Allison Carey whose comments and suggestions greatly helped to improve this chapter.

NOTES

1. Mamonova and Visser (2014) discuss a phenomenon, which they call phantom movement organizations and define them as "nontransparent, occasionally (at most) active social organizations that pursue goals often different from the ones officially declared – in particular, pursuing the aims of umbrella organizations and/or the leaders' personal aims instead of defending the interests of their declared constituencies" (p. 508). I use the phrase "phantom activism" in a different way, stressing simply the fact of its superficial role with regard to real political transformation.
2. The Center never succeeded in this respect, but was the main factor for the successful implementation of a scheme for the provision of personal assistance by Sofia Municipality in 2007. For more details see Mladenov (2017).
3. There is additional reduction of this number for the blind and deaf (no less than 400 members) and for the little people (no less than 150).
4. The author of this chapter is member of the project team and has participated in the interviewing process.
5. For discussion of this issue, based on the results of recently conducted study on personal assistance, conducted among users and members of the independent living movement in Europe, see Mladenov (2019).

REFERENCES

Bagenstos, S. (2017). Disability rights and labor: Is this conflict really necessary? *Indiana Law Journal*, *92*(1), 277–298.

Bandy, J., & Smith, J. (2005). *Coalitions across borders: Transnational protest and the neoliberal order*. Lanham, MD: Rowman and Littlefield.

Beamish, T. D., & Luebbers, A. J. (2009). Alliance building across social movements. *Social Problems*, *56*(4), 647–676.

Benford, R., & Snow, D. A. (2000). Framing processes and social movements: An overview and assessment. *Annual Review of Sociology*, *26*, 611–639.

Callon, M. (1999). The role of lay people in the production and dissemination of scientific knowledge. *Science Technology & Society*, *4*(1), 81–94.

Carey, A., Block, P., & Scotch, R. K. (2019). Sometimes allies: Parent-led disability organizations and social movements. *Disability Studies Quarterly*, *39*(1). doi:10.18061/dsq.v39i1.6281

Centre for Independent Living-Sofia & Trust for Civil Society in Central and Eastern Europe. (2011). Analysis of the activities of the national council for integration of people with disabilities. Retrieved from https://cil.bg/wp-content/uploads/2020/03/Report-NSIHU-2011_final.pdf

Confederation of Labor Podkrepa. (2018). Official statement, regarding the personal assistance bill. Retrieved from http://podkrepa.org/

Epstein, S. (2011). Measuring success: Scientific, institutional, and cultural effects of patient advocacy. In B. Hoffman, N. Tomes, R. Grob, & M. Schlesinger (Eds.), *Patients as policy actors* (pp. 257–277). London: Rutgers University Press.

Gamson, W. A. (1990). *The strategy of social protest*. Belmont: Wordsworth.

Goffman, E. (1974). *Frame analysis: An essay on the organization of experience*. Boston, MA: Northeastern University Press.

Hsieh, H.-F., & Shannon, S. E. (2005). Three approaches to qualitative content analysis. *Qualitative Health Research*, *15*(9), 1277–1288.

Hughes, B., & Paterson, K. (1997). The social model of disability and the disappearing body: Towards a sociology of impairment. *Disability & Society*, *12*(3), 325–340.

Holevich, B. (2019). People with disabilities suffer folly after folly. Retrieved from https://frognews.bg/inteviu/holevich-horata-uvrejdaniia-tarpiat-bezumie-sled-bezumie.html

Jacobsson, K. (Ed.). (2015).*Urban grassroots movements in Central and Eastern Europe*. Farnham: Ashgate.

Jasper, J. M. (1997). *The art of moral protest: Culture, biography, and creativity in social movements*. Chicago, IL: University of Chicago Press.

Kalinnikova, L., & Trygged, S. (2014). A retrospective on care and denial of children with disabilities in Russia. *Scandinavian Journal of Disability Research*, *16*(3), 229–248.

Kingdon, J. W. (1984). *Agendas, alternatives, and public policies*. Boston, MA: Little Brown & Co.

Kittay, F. E. (2011). The ethics of care, dependence, and disability. *Ratio Juris*, *24*(1), 49–58.

Mamonova, N., & Visser, O. (2014). State marionettes, phantom organizations or genuine movements? The paradoxical emergence of rural social movements in post-socialist Russia. *Journal of Peasant Studies*, *41*(4).

McAdam, D., & Paulsen, R. (1993). Specifying the relationship between social ties and activism. *American Journal of Sociology*, *3*, 640–667.

McRuer, R. (2018). *Crip times: Disability, globalization, and resistance*. New York, NY: New York University Press.

Mladenov, T. (2009). Institutional woes of participation: Bulgarian disabled people's organizations and policy-making. *Disability & Society*, *24*(1), 33–45.

Mladenov, T. (2015). Neoliberalism, postsocialism, disability. *Disability & Society*, *30*(3), 445–459.

Mladenov, T. (2016). Postsocialist disability matrix. *Scandinavian Journal of Disability Research*. doi: 10.1080/15017419.2016.1202860.

Mladenov, T. (2017). Governing through personal assistance: A Bulgarian case. *Scandinavian Journal of Disability Research*, *19*(2), 91–103.

Mladenov, T. (2019). What is good personal assistance made of? Results of a European survey. *Disability & Society*. doi:10.1080/09687599.2019.1621740.

New protest of mothers of children with disabilities. (n.d). Retrieved from https://maikomila.bg

Obach, B. K. (2004). *Labour and the environmental movement: A quest for common good*. Cambridge, MA: MIT Press.

Owens, J. (2015). Exploring the critiques of the social model of disability: The transformative possibility of Arendt's notion of power. *Sociology of Health & Illness*, *37*(3), 385–403.

Parvanov, K. (2018). These are the "fake" invalids. Retrieved from https://baricada.org/2018/12/28/eto-gi-falshivite-invalidi-video-i-snimki/

Phillips, S. (2010). *Disability and mobile citizenship in postsocialist Ukraine*. Bloomington and Indiana: Indiana University Press.

Polanska, D. V. (2015). Alliance-building and brokerage in contentious politics: A case–study of the polish tenants' movement. In K. Jacobsson (Ed.), *Urban movements in Central and Eastern Europe* (pp. 195–218). Farnham: Ashgate.

Polanska, V. D., & Piotrowski, G. (2015). The transformative power of cooperation between social movements: Squatting and tenants' movements in Poland. *City*, *19*(2–3), 274–296.

Puar, J. (2017). *The right to maim: Debility, capacity, disability*. Durham, NC: Duke University Press.

Quirici, M. (2019). *Disability studies. The year's work in critical and cultural theory*. Oxford: Oxford University Press. doi:10.1093/ywcct/mbz015

Runevski, N. (2014). On the business with disabilities. *Legal World*. Retrieved from http://legal-world.bg/37025.za-biznesa-s-uvrejdaniia.html. Accessed on April 9, 2020.

Shakespeare, T. (2006). *Disability rights and wrongs.* Oxford and New York, NY: Routledge.

Shakespeare, T., & Watson, N. (2001). The social model of disability: An outdated ideology? *Research in Social Science and Disability, 2*, 9–28.

Snow, D. A., & Benford, R. (1992). Master frames and cycles of protest. In A. D. Morris, & C. M. Mueller (Eds.), *Frontiers in social movement theory* (pp. 133–155). New Haven, CT: Yale University Press.

Stone, D. (1984). *The disabled state.* Philadelphia, PA: Temple University Press.

Titchkosky, T. (2003). Governing embodiment: Technologies of constituting citizens with disabilities. *Canadian Journal of Sociology, 28*(4), 517–542.

UPIAS/Disability Alliance. (1976). *Fundamental Principles of Disability: Being a summary of the discussion held on 22nd November, 1975 and containing commentaries from each organization.* London: The Union of the Physically Impaired Against Segregation and the Disability Alliance.

Van Dyke, N. (2003). Crossing movement boundaries: Factors that facilitate coalition protest by American college students, 1930–1990. *Social Problems, 50*, 226–250.

Van Dyke, N., & McCammon, H. (2010). *Strategic alliances: Coalition building and social movements.* Minneapolis, MN: University of Minnesota Press.

Watson, N., McKie, L., Hughes, B., Hopkins, B., & Gregory, S. (2004). (Inter)dependence, needs and care: The potential for disability and feminist theorists to develop an emancipatory model. *Sociology, 38*(2), 331–350.

Williams, R. H. (2004). The cultural contexts of collective action: Constraints, opportunities, and the symbolic life of social movements. In D. Snow, S. Soule, & H. Kriesi (Eds.), *The Blackwell companion to social movements* (pp. 91–115). Malden, MA: Blackwell Publishing.

Williams, R. H., & Benford, R. D. (2000). Two faces of collective action frames: A theoretical consideration. *Research in Social Movements, Conflicts and Change, 20*, 127–151.

Williams, R. H., & Kubal, T. (1999). Movement frames and the cultural environment: Resonance, failure, and the boundaries of the legitimate. *Research in Social Movements, Conflicts and Change, 21*, 225–248.

Chapter 4

"I'VE USED MY WIDE ARRAY OF SKILLS TO CREATE A LIFE FOR MYSELF": MANAGING NARRATIVES WITH COMPETING GOALS IN AN ARTS-BASED DISABILITY ALLY ORGANIZATION

Melinda Leigh Maconi

ABSTRACT

Purpose: *Artists with disabilities use their bodies and minds to create art. Yet, the prevailing cultural narrative that art is "therapeutic" for people with disabilities shifts attention from their creative accomplishments to their disabilities. Some ally organizations attempt to challenge the narrative that art is merely therapy for people with disabilities. However, drawing on narratives of "helping" people with disabilities attracts funding. This chapter examines how organizations navigate empowering allies while still maintaining funding.*

Methods/Approach: *This chapter uses narrative analysis of material accessed through a nonprofit arts-based disability ally organization's website to address two research questions: 1. How do ally organizations both draw on and resist cultural narratives of disability in order to garner public support?; and 2. How do personal narratives of disabled artists associated with ally organizations support and/or resist organizational and cultural narratives about the connection between disability and art?*

Disability Alliances and Allies
Research in Social Science and Disability, Volume 12, 87–109

ISSN: 1479-3547/doi:10.1108/S1479-354720200000012007

Findings: *The organization uses narratives to address important and sometimes conflicting goals. Personal narratives from artists with disabilities that are available through the website tell a range of stories about art and disability. The organization draws on these heterogeneous stories to position itself as an ally. By including such personal narratives on its website, the organization challenges the cultural narrative that the art produced by disabled artists is merely therapeutic.*

Implication/Value: *Much of the work on allyship focuses on how individuals can be allies. Examining ways in which organizations frame themselves as allies can help us to more fully understand allyship on multiple levels of social life.*

Keywords: Disability; narratives; allyship; ally organizations; art; disabled artists

INTRODUCTION

Disability scholarship has long documented the ways in which people with disabilities are excluded, devalued, and stigmatized in both institutional settings and everyday life (Allen, 2010, 2014; Calderón-Almendros & Calderón-Almendros, 2016; Coriale, Grant, & Robertson, 2012; Egilson & Traustadottir, 2009; Goffman, 1963; Lenakakis & Koltsida, 2017; Manago, Davis, & Goar, 2017; Oliver & Barnes, 2012; Shakespeare, 2014; Zederayko & Ward, 1999). Through social movements and academic research, organizations and policy-makers have made some efforts to make spaces more accessible and inclusive (Patterson, 2012; Shah & Priestley, 2010; Shaw, 2015). In order to reach these goals of accessibility and inclusiveness, many individuals and organizations have sought to become allies to people with disabilities and disability rights–based social movements (Carey, Block, & Scotch, 2019; Evans, Assadi, & Harriott, 2005; Ostrove, Kornfeld, & Ibrahim, 2019; Patterson, 2012; Van der Klift & Kunc, 2019).

However, in many cases, "accessibility" and "inclusion" have become poorly defined, catchall terms that are used with little discussion on what specifically is meant and how this concept will be practically implemented. This is further complicated in that many organizations seeking to be allies by "helping" people with disabilities do so without necessarily consulting people with disabilities on what they find "helpful" (Cahill & Eggleston, 1994; Carey et al., 2019; Evans et al., 2005; Gill, 2001; Ostrove et al., 2019). As Carey et al. (2019) demonstrate well-meaning organizations led by parents and/or professionals may push agendas that may not align with, or may even conflict with, the goals and needs of people with disabilities. Some allies, both individuals and organizations, may fail to recognize their privilege and cling to condescending narratives of helping people with disabilities, with the underlying assumption that people with disabilities cannot help themselves. Ostrove et al. (2019) assert that

> Disabled people have experienced a long history of exploitation as research participants, and knowledge about people with disabilities has often been used for 'management and control' rather than to achieve social justice (p. 928).

Thus, in studying organizations that frame themselves as allies, we must look at how people with disabilities perceive the role of allies and the impact, positive or negative, that this alliance has on people with disabilities.

This chapter will focus on an organization, *Arts4All Florida*, which seeks to be an ally by training teachers to make art classrooms more accessible to students with disabilities. They are unusual in not conceptualizing themselves as providing art therapy. Rather, they promote inclusion and active participation in the arts as a human right. In rejecting the art therapy label, they also challenge existing culture narratives and understandings of disability as a personal tragedy and instead draw from aspects of the social model of disability (Oliver & Barnes, 2012) and Goffman's (1963) concept of stigma to illuminate barriers to participation, to challenge negative assumptions about people with disabilities. In this chapter, I use narrative analysis of material accessed through the *Arts4All Florida* website to address two interrelated research questions: 1. How do ally organizations both draw on and resist cultural narratives of disability in order to garner public support?; and 2. How do personal narratives of disabled artists associated with ally organizations support and/or resist organizational and cultural narratives about the connection between disability and art?

Why Study Ally Organizations?

Good intentions are not enough for a person or organization to be an ally. Positive action for meaningful change is needed (Brown & Ostrove, 2013; Carey et al., 2019; Evans et al., 2005; Forber-Pratt, Mueller, & Andrews, 2019; Russell, 2011; Russell & Bohan, 2016). Russell and Bohan (2016) make a distinction between "first-order" and "second-order" changes as a result of allyship. First-order changes are defined as "superficial changes that were compatible with existing power dynamics, with no substantive challenge to institutional structures," while second-order changes work to "alter structures and challenge hierarchies of power" (Russell & Bohan, 2016, p. 342). In their study on LGBTQ+ "allyship" within a church, Russell and Bohan (2016) found that much of the alliance focused on token ideas of "acceptance" without ever challenging heteronormativity, thus allowing "allies" to feel that they were being helpful, good people without challenging any power structures or making changes in their own lives.

Forber-Pratt et al. (2019) outline ways in which medical/rehabilitative professionals can be allies to patients with disabilities. Traditionally, rehabilitative practitioners interact with and think about their patients using a medical model lens. They are also often working with people with acquired disabilities who also have a tendency to use a medical model lens. Forber-Pratt et al. (2019) propose that rather than adhering to medical savior narratives of the relationship between medical professionals and people with disabilities, medical professionals should work to help clients develop a disability identity. "Psychologists, along with other rehabilitation practitioners, have an inherent ethical obligation to function as allies, activists, and advocates as part of professional responsibility and identity" (Forber-Pratt et al., 2019, p. 123).

However, Carey et al. (2019) argue that not all of those attempting to be allies are truly helpful to people with disabilities. Organizations led by stakeholders who do not have disabilities themselves are sometimes at odds with, and even in opposition to, the goals of organizations led by people with disabilities. Those with more power and cultural capital may have lower expectations about the quality of life for people with disabilities and can exert their own interests more easily. Furthermore, in focusing solely on the intentions of allies, the perspective of the privileged is prefaced with little to no focus on what this allyship means for marginalized groups, or if marginalized groups even view the privileged group as allies at all (Carey et al., 2019; Russell & Bohan, 2016). Russell and Bohan (2016) assert that

> ...nontarget allies retain the power to define the problem and provide solutions that sustain their own position as knowledgeable and powerful agents of social change, even as members of the target group tend to be portrayed as victims lacking in personal agency and unable to define for themselves the direction that change should take (p. 346).

In their study on organizations led by parents of children with disabilities and organizations led by people with disabilities, Carey et al. (2019) found that some organizations led by parents proposed goals of "cure," which are at odds with more social model–oriented organizations led by people with disabilities. Perhaps most insidious, some organizations even sought to give parents more rights to usurp the rights of their children in adulthood, even to the point of institutionalization without their child's consent if it's what the parents thought was best (Carey et al., 2019). Thus, while claiming to be an ally to people with disabilities, some of these organizations pushed for measures that would further oppress people with disabilities. In not including people with disabilities in the leadership process, well-intentioned "allies" are able to push their own agenda at the expense of those with whom they claim to be allies. Still, some organizations and activists have taken up the cause of facilitating the active participation of people with disabilities in previously exclusive spaces. The purpose of this chapter is to examine how one such organization constructs narratives in the context of the competing goals of disability empowerment and fundraising.

Why Study Organizational Narratives?

Donileen Loseke (2007) describes the ways in which the world is made up of stories. There are many different levels of narratives, each of which are "created for different purposes, do different types of work, and are evaluated by different criteria." Narratives of disability have traditionally been ones of personal tragedy (Coriale et al., 2012; Jung, 2003; Oliver & Barnes, 2012; Shah & Priestley, 2010; Shakespeare, 2014). Yet, as this chapter will explore, there are multiple types of competing narratives told throughout all levels of social life (Loseke, 2007). These narratives are not fixed, but instead are fluid and ever-changing. Moreover, different narratives will be deployed at different times for different purposes. Loseke (2007) identifies different levels of narratives, such as cultural narratives, institutional narratives, organizational narratives, and personal narratives. These narratives may overlap, contradict each other, or sometimes do both.

Cultural narratives refer to the collective representation or categories of people depicted through widely told cultural stories. Typically, there are characters, often heroes, victims, and villains who follow a familiar plot. Within the context of western capitalism, the predominant cultural narrative frames disability as a personal, tragic, biomedical problem. This understanding focuses exclusively on what tasks a person cannot do, which in turn defines what counts as disability (Coriale et al., 2012; Jung, 2003; Oliver & Barnes, 2012; Shah & Priestley, 2010; Shakespeare, 2014). Pity and tragedy arising from this narrative give people that status of "victims" of the feared villain, disability. These devalued identities allow people with disabilities to obtain services. Often, these services, and their providers, are the "heroes" of this story. However, victimhood and passivity are not seen as desirable in a culture that values independence and agency (Best, 1997; Dunn, 2004; Kimball, Moore, Vaccaro, Troiano, & Newman, 2016; Loseke, 2007).

Competing narratives of disability such as the Social Model (Oliver & Barnes, 2012) and Crip Theories (Kafer, 2013) have offered more empowering ideas about disability as well as offering a collective disability identity. The Social Model narrative has informed the organizational narratives of some disability-centered nonprofit organizations that demand that people, particularly policy-makers, examine the negative consequences of social and physical environments that restrict the ability of people with impairments to participate in their communities (Oliver & Barnes, 2012). This paradigm has influenced public policy and practices by focusing attention on accessibility of public spaces, education, employment, housing, and all areas of social life, including art programs. This disability rights narrative has begun to compete with the narrative of personal tragedy in widely circulating understandings of disability in the United Kingdom, United States, and Europe. Social Model (Oliver & Barnes, 2012) and Crip Theories (Kafer, 2013) understandings of disability offer a newer, more nuanced narrative for people with disabilities and ally organizations alike, mainly in that these narratives may offer paths for people with disabilities and their allies to fill the "heroic" role without objectifying people with disabilities for the horror or inspiration of able-body/minded people.

Social Model and Crip understandings of disabilities challenge the traditional narrative where external forces in society "rescue" people with disabilities. People with disabilities are recognized as being capable of making high quality art. However, art created by people with disabilities is not often depicted in mainstream venues, either because art classes are not disability accessible and lack the adaptive tools for people with disabilities to learn and practice their craft (Taylor, 2005; Young, 2008; Zederayko & Ward, 1999) or when people with disabilities do create art, it is presented as a niche category separate from "real art" (Cooley & Fox, 2014:; Fox, 2015; Solvang, 2012; Wexler & Derby, 2015). This is present in ally-art programs for people with disabilities, in that by not making art accessible for would-be artists with disabilities, society misses out on the visual and performance art that people with disabilities could offer the art world.

Organizations that view themselves as disability allies may choose to adopt or challenge cultural narratives of disability, depending on the goals of the organization and what it is trying to achieve at a particular point in time. Stories told for one purpose may inadvertently negate other organizational goals. For example, the narrative of a "heroic" organization, helping those in need by providing a path to change and/or betterment, makes the organization look good, which can result in more funding and support. However, such stories may be off-putting to potential clients who resist the narrative of disability as an inferior way of being. To ensure that their message is not at odds with the people they serve, organizations may use personal narratives to emphasize their allyship and the congruence between the organization's goals and the goals of their clients. As we will see in this chapter, organizations also make use of personal narratives to advance organizational goals.

Thus, organizations must construct and circulate narratives that depict themselves as heroes without completely stripping its clients of agency or hope. This may involve borrowing from both the tragic and the inspirational narratives of disability, in which the organization provides a pathway for their client to become "inspirational." Still, other organizations may reject both cultural narratives outright, instead, offering a counternarrative for those who are dissatisfied with the cultural narratives to rally behind, as seen in many nongovernmental social movement organizations (Fox, 2015; Oliver & Barnes, 2012; Patterson, 2012; Solvang, 2012). Ally organizations serving marginalized groups may achieve this through stressing similarities their clients have to hegemonic groups, rejecting definitions of the dominant group, or sometimes a combination of the two. Egner (2019b)

> explores the degree to which these organizations stress sameness and/or difference in relation to the dominant group in establishing collective identity and collective consequences, and how this emphasis informs their position in relation to and the use of queer/crip or hegemonic discourses (p. 141).

Some organizations that view themselves as allies encourage "normality" and assimilation tactics to gain more "political room." However, these tactics may contradict the goals and outcomes that clients are seeking (Egner, 2019b). Yet, when stressing sameness, some people with multiple marginalized identities may find their needs ignored or even rejected by organizations that claim to help them, leading them to disidentify with the organization or the identity as a whole (Egner, 2019a). Organizations that strive to be allies must recognize the heterogeneousness of their target group, or risk failing the segments of the population the organization claims to serve. Thus, some ally organizations seek to "Crip" the boundaries of their organization, by challenging existing concepts of "normal" and the binary logic of "disabled/not disabled" (Egner, 2019b; Kafer, 2013). While this may complicate the process of "boundary work," a process by which organizations articulate who they serve and implicitly, who they do not, such ally organizations may be more aware of the heterogeneous needs of their clients (Egner, 2019a, 2019b).

Ally organizations must also be explicit about who they are serving to avoid co-optation. Carey et al. (2019) examined the ways in which supposed ally organization run by parents of people with disabilities sometimes had goals diametrically opposed to the goals of people with disabilities. This is further complicated in that some of these parents are well-intentioned in their goals. Thus, the voices of people with disabilities must be the center of ally organizations' decisions and goals. This can be achieved by including people with disabilities in leadership positions within the organization. However, since that information was not available for this project, this chapter will instead focus on the ways that organizational narratives align with or contradict the narratives actually told by people with disabilities.

Organizations, like culture and individuals, are not static, unchanging entities. The narratives they tell may shift and evolve over time, in concert with or resistance to changing cultural narratives. The subject of this case study, *Arts4All Florida*, the organization is currently in the process of rebranding itself, including changing its name, after some changes in funding and affiliations. Organizations are responsive to both their clients and funding sources. Furthermore, organizations may deploy different narratives in different circumstances for different purposes. Sometimes, organizations may use testimonials and personal narratives to build the narrative they use for themselves.

This last point highlights the importance of personal narratives. Personal narratives can be a form of agency for individuals telling their own stories. People tell stories to make sense of the world and these stories can reify or subvert cultural narratives. Adopting and creating personal narratives can be a means of advocacy in and of itself. Kimball et al. (2016) discussed the ways in which university students with disabilities viewed self-advocacy and storytelling as a form of collective action. Many students saw educating others about their experience to raise awareness about what people with disabilities need. This form of storytelling as a type of advocacy was empowering to students in a way that allowed them to control the narrative, avoid victimhood, avoid objectification, and still claim need for services (Kimball et al., 2016).

Personal narratives told by people with disabilities and their families often draw from multiple understandings of disability (Darling, 2013; Green, Darling, & Wilbers, 2017). While people with disabilities experience fulfilling lives, they do not live in a cultural vacuum. People with disabilities, particularly those who develop disability later in life, may subscribe to some aspects of the cultural narrative of biomedical tragedy (Darling, 2013). Furthermore, people with disabilities are also interacting with people who believe this cultural narrative. Thus, relying on biomedical understandings of disability may be used to communicate more efficiently with others. For example, Manago et al. (2017) found in their interviews with parents of children with disabilities that parents used both the Social Model *and* the Biomedical models in order to advocate for their children.

People with disabilities must also make sense of their lives and identities within institutional and organizational narrative identities. Organizational narratives are created to evaluate who they help and how they help them. While people can create personal narratives that are subversive to the cultural and organizational narratives, going against these narratives can lead people to be cut off or to lose services (Dunn, 2004; Loseke, 2007).

Why Study Art Programs?

Like other artists, artists with disabilities want to be recognized for their artistic talents (Cooley & Fox, 2014; Fox, 2015; Lenakakis & Koltsida, 2017). However, when people with disabilities who engage in the arts do get recognition, they are often praised for having disabilities, rather than for the art they produce (Rousso, 2013). In this paradigm, art is assumed to be "therapeutic" for people with disabilities rather than as a craft requiring skill and dedication (Kafer, 2013; Lenakakis & Koltsida, 2017; Rousso, 2013; Solvang, 2012). Even people with disabilities who are actively pursuing the arts receive subtle messages that their bodies do not belong. Disabled bodies are not the subject of portraits and are rarely seen in the performing arts. In her interview with students pursuing college-level art degrees, Taylor (2005) found that her participants "rarely encounter a disabled artist as a role model and none of the students I interviewed had been taught by a disabled teacher before they came to college" (p. 766).

Art can be a powerful way to resist dominant narratives about disability and to draw attention to inequalities. Allen (2014) asserts that

> ...the arts have emerged as an important site of activism for inclusion, as a 'force that draws people into participation,' and a political vehicle for centering 'normally silenced or disenfranchised voices (p. 518).

For many participants, art may be a desired path toward income and possibly independence.

This brings up another seemingly contradictory issue. Since organizations experience courtesy stigma (Goffman, 1963), mainstream customers may refuse to even consider resulting products and performances as true art.[1] However, such organizations sometimes work together to sell and showcase art and/or performances created by people with disabilities, opening up a market for alternative sources of art and a specific place to buy and sell such pieces. Therefore, such organizations have practical implications for artists with disabilities in addition to social ones. In opening up these possibilities, organizations also offer up new avenues for creating more empowered personal and organizational narratives.

Art also falls into an interesting category when it comes to tracking and disability access in the educational system. Wexler and Derby (2015) point out that "the art room has often been the first regular classroom where disabled learners are placed; yet, the needs of disabled learners have often gone unmet" (p. 129). Zederayko and Ward (1999) outline inclusion is not the mere presence of people with disabilities in a room. Unless active participation is possible, the space is still exclusionary. This is particularly salient in art classrooms. While this appears to be one of the more inclusive spaces in schools, in terms of who is invited to be in the classroom, some art classrooms lack the assistive technology needed to facilitate participation for students with disabilities. Furthermore, multiple studies show that while art teachers are interested in making their lessons accessible to students with disabilities, they lack knowledge on how to bring this goal to fruition. Zederayko and Ward (1999) detail this process in describing a general art classroom with two students with disabilities. Since each of the students shared an aide, at least one of the students had to observe and not participate at any given time. Furthermore, well-meaning aides sometimes overaccommodate and do too much of the artwork for the student, meaning that neither student was truly engaged in the artistic process (Coleman & Cramer, 2015; Coleman, Cramer, Park, & Bell, 2015; Young, 2008; Zederayko & Ward, 1999). Thus, while the art classroom, on the surface, appeared to be the most accessible classroom space, the presence of a person with disabilities in the classroom does not necessarily indicate that the classroom or the content are accessible. Taylor (2005) describes the ways in which assistive technology can become an extension of oneself in the creation of art. She attributes the under-representation of artists with disabilities to both negative attitudes about disability, and the lack of equipment provided in many classrooms to account for students' impairments. Taylor (2005) asserts that "enabling support/classroom assistance is critical in the potential that it has to create access to the arts for all students, regardless of their support requirements" (p. 766).

Multiple studies, both in the United States and abroad, have documented a gap between the knowledge held by art educators and the knowledge held by Special Education educators. Art educators overwhelmingly agree with the statement that students with disabilities should be included in art classrooms but lack confidence or knowledge on how to implement inclusion, via assistive technologies or otherwise. Similarly, Special Education instructors agree that art is beneficial for students with disabilities but lack confidence or knowledge about how to teach arts to their students (Coleman et al., 2015:; Coleman & Cramer, 2015; Cramer, Coleman, Park, Bell, & Cole, 2015; Lenakakis & Koltsida, 2017; Loesl, 2012; Penketh, 2014; Taylor, 2005; Zederayko & Ward, 1999). Bridging this knowledge gap could increase inclusiveness in art classrooms and programs, which is beneficial for students, regardless of their artistic aspirations (Coleman et al., 2015; Coleman & Cramer, 2015; Lenakakis & Koltsida, 2017; Loesl, 2012; Penketh, 2014; Taylor, 2005; Wexler & Derby, 2015; Young, 2008; Zederayko & Ward, 1999). For this reason, bridging this gap is one of the stated goals of the organization that is the focus of this chapter.

RESEARCH METHODS

Site Selection – Why Arts4All Florida*?*

Arts4All Florida, originally called Florida Arts for the Handicapped Program and formerly part of the Very Special Arts (VSA) program, was founded in 1981 by the Florida Department of Education and Floridan Department of State, Division of Cultural Affairs. Since then, the organization has undergone multiple name and policy changes, most recently changing its name to *Arts4All Florida* and undergoing major changes as far as affiliations and funding are concerned. One of the main services provided by *Arts4All Florida* is assigning trained "teaching artists," into K-12 schools and to juvenile correctional facilities, in order to create accessible art spaces. The *Arts4All Florida* website defines a teaching artist as

> ...a professional who has the experience and knowledge to teach their craft to students and adults with various disabilities in a school setting, Department of Juvenile Justice facility, or adult program (http://arts4allflorida.org/).

This includes, but is not limited to, having a working knowledge of assistive technologies, and teaching other art teachers and/or Special Education teachers to implement these technologies to make the arts more accessible for people with disabilities. Assistive technology is a key to increasing accessibility in art programs (Coleman et al., 2015; Coleman & Cramer, 2015; Loesl, 2012; Penketh, 2014; Zederayko & Ward, 1999). However, more than half of the instructors in Coleman et al.'s (2015) study had rarely to never used assistive technologies, as many did not have training on what was available or how to use such technologies.

According to the Mission Statement on the homepage of their website, *Arts4All Florida* aims to "provide, support, and champion arts education and cultural experiences for, and by people with disabilities" (www.arts4allflorida.org/). Much of this is done through providing disability-accessible art programs in schools, community centers, and juvenile correctional facilities throughout the state of Florida. The organization also works to promote artists with disabilities and provide training to art educators on disability accessibility. This statewide organization must manage multiple, sometimes competing, narratives to appeal to participants and their families, the educational facilities they wish to maintain ties with, along with donors, and funding sources. This makes it an ideal site for addressing my research questions.

Why Websites?

Since the advent of the Internet, online spaces have increasingly become spaces for organizations to promote themselves *and* places for people of marginalized groups to converge and tell stories that had previously been silenced (Egner, 2019a, 2019b; Hine, 2000; Maloney, 2013). Hine (2000) coined the term "virtual ethnography" to describe the process of recognizing that online forums can create cultural meanings in the same ways that physical spaces can. "Virtual ethnography is useful in exploring the ways in which the Internet is and becomes socially meaningful, allowing researchers to examine the Internet as both culture and artifact" (Egner, 2019a, p. 131).

Websites can be updated and changed in real time as the organizations or groups update or change their position on an issue or as more information is added. This will be particularly of interest as the *Arts4All Florida* website includes name changes and changes in affiliations over the years. In her work on Social Movement Organizations, Egner (2019b) illustrates how organizations' websites can communicate vast amounts of information that may not be easily available through traditional qualitative methods including how pictures and narratives are a type of boundary work, designating an in-group and, therefore, an out-group, even among organizations that state that their goal is to be inclusive.

Another important feature that online spaces provide is the ability to connect people who are geographically far apart yet share understandings and lived experiences. This is particularly useful for people with disabilities who may be prevented from interacting with other people with similar shared experiences due to inaccessible environments (Egner, 2019a). This may be the case for artists with disabilities who tell their stories in the registry, as some artists indicate that they engage in art and sell art online as an adaptation to not being able to fit in to a rigid time schedule or inaccessible physical spaces.

In the following sections, I will explore in more detail what narratives are communicated through the organization's website, the purposes these narratives serve, and the ways in which they resist or reify cultural understandings of people with disabilities. I will do this by examining the history of the organization, as described on the website, and testimonials from teachers, parents, and artists with disabilities.

Data Collection and Analysis

Upon going to the *Arts4All Florida* website, I immediately began searching for stories.[2] I found most of these in the Annual Reports and in the Artist Registry to identify organizational narratives and personal narratives, respectively. These different levels of narratives accomplish different things for both the organizations and the people within them (Loseke, 2007, 2012). Organizational narratives are unique in that if the narrative is not told in a way that appeals to both clients and donors, the organization may cease to exist (Loseke, 2007). Thus, *Arts4All Florida* must offer up a narrative that resonates with various audiences to serve the purposes for the organization.

Organizational narratives create easily recognizable stories in which the organization itself is one of many characters. These stories must identify who the organization helps and how it helps them in an easy to understand way. For this type of narrative, the organization must be a major "character" who plays a role that is both necessary and evaluated as morally good. Without these components, potential donors may question the need for the organization to exist. The most obvious and easily recognizable role for organizations in their narratives is for the organization to fill a hero role, in which they save their clients from a perceived barrier or villain. However, such stories may be off-putting to potential clients who resist the cultural narrative that imagines their selves as deficient, their lives as inferior (Loseke, 2012). Thus, organizations like *Arts4All Florida* must construct a narrative that depicts the organization as heroic without sacrificing the dignity of their clients.

Personal narratives are stories that individual people tell about themselves. On the surface, it may be easy to assume that these narratives are pure, without an agenda, or free of outside influence. Yet, it's still important to remember that neither individual people nor their personal narratives exist in a vacuum (Loseke, 2007). Individual people draw on cultural narratives, organizational narratives, and even other people's individual narratives when making sense of their lives. In the Artist Registry, artists are free to offer up their own narrative with little to no censoring from *Arts4All Florida*. In that sense, the artists are offering up their own personal narratives. However, like organizational narratives, these stories still have a goal – to sell art – and include familiar characters such as themselves,

Arts4All Florida, and even more abstract characters, such as art itself. Personal narratives help individual people present themselves in a way that makes sense to them, and often with the hope that the narrative will appeal to others. Individuals will often, though not always, portray themselves as being morally "good." Yet, often, in the act of storying themselves, people highlight things they *do*, showing agency and intent. This is where the personal narratives of clients may clash with the organizational narratives of nonprofits and governmental organizations. Individual people may not want to be pitied; they may want to be their own hero. Yet, in being their own hero, there may not be an obvious need for an organization to exist (Loseke, 2007, 2012).

The annual reports provide an important part of the organizational narrative as this is the document sent out to sponsors and potential clients. These stories are crafted for the particular purpose of attracting donors and clients. Even stories that appear to be personal narratives, such as those from employees about what they do for the organization, were picked based on the degree to which they support the organization's goals.

I also explored the personal narratives told in the Artist Registry, where artists with disabilities shared their stories and showcased artwork to sell. Additionally, I watched any promotional videos provided on the website to analyze the stories told via video. I specifically selected stories where artists talked about how their disability is related to their art.[3] Unlike the stories told in the annual reports, stories told in the artist registry are from the artist themselves. Some artists told stories that aligned with those told in the annual reports, but others did not. Stories in the Artist Registry are organized by alphabetical order of the artists' name. They are not selected or organized by *Arts4All Florida* to highlight stories that make the organization look good.

I conducted a narrative analysis to look at how the organization and artists with disabilities constructed their stories. To use narrative analysis, as outlined by Loseke (2007), one must first determine the context of the narrative, including who wrote the narrative, for whom it was written, and for what purpose it was constructed. In the case of *Arts4All Florida*, spokespeople of the organization write narratives for a variety of reasons that center around attracting clients and funding, as is the case of many nonprofits. Artists may have similar goals, as many sell their work on the website through the Artist Registry. However, the degree to which artists include stories of their disability, if at all, may vary.

Following this, I did a close reading of the narratives to fully ascertain the plot and the content of each narrative. This separates narrative analysis from thematic analysis in that narratives must, to some extent, have a beginning, middle, and end with some degree of conflict, whether explicitly or implicitly included. From there, I determined who the characters in this story were. In each story, I sought to identify the villain, the hero, and the role that art played in the story. These characters do not always have to be human but can instead be ideas, such as disability or art itself.

To fully analyze the narrative, one must also unpack symbolic codes embedded in the narratives. This includes, but is not limited to, ideas about what is moral/immoral, what is considered normal/abnormal, and what is considered desirable or bad. To do so, I considered the following questions posed by Loseke (2012):

> What knowledge about the world does this statement assume? What would I need to believe about the world for this statement to be believable and important? What specific values are being reflected/transmitted? (p. 262).

FINDINGS

To provide context for the discussion of the three themes that emerged in the narrative analysis, I first outline the mission and history of this ally organization. Following this, I use personal narratives from artists with disabilities on the artist registry and compare and contrast these stories with stories that make up the organizational narrative. For the purposes of this chapter, I include stories from staff members as part of the organizational narrative as they are speaking as representatives of the organization. All the names of artists, clients, and staff members are pseudonyms.

Arts4All Florida*: Mission, Vision, and Guiding Principles*

An essential part of any organizational narrative is the official mission statement. The inviting and uncluttered *Arts4All Florida* homepage (http://arts4allflorida.org/) displays its mission, along with a concise plan as to how it will carry out this mission. The statement includes the following:

> The mission of Arts4All Florida is to provide, support, and champion arts education and cultural experiences for and by people with disabilities. Our vision is to create a world in which the arts are universally accessible. We do this by:

- Conducting art education programs in schools, Department of Juvenile Justice facilities, and community centers
- Promoting the accomplishments of artists with disabilities through our artist registry, exhibitions, and performances
- Increasing access to the arts through professional development workshops

By including a clear and concise description of its goals, the organization can then provide evidence of its effectiveness in carrying out these goals The website offers several kinds of proof that it has taken the actions outlined in the bullet points above: (1) pictures and testimonials from programs in schools (located in the Annual Reports under http://arts4allflorida.org/content/our-impact); (2) an artist registry where artists with disabilities can showcase their work and link to personal pages where they sell their art (http://arts4allflorida.org/artist-registry); and (3) a schedule of upcoming webinars about setting up accessible art classes (http://arts4allflorida.org/content/webinars). Through its mission statement, goals, and these three types of evidence, the organization begins to tell a story in which it serves as a morally worthy ally to disabled artists by countering forces of exclusion and promoting the talent and value of the creative endeavors of artists.

As we will see in the following sections, however, the story is more complex than the mission statement might at first suggest. My narrative analysis of personal and staff stories that are featured on, or can be accessed through, the website identified three types of stories with three different types of villains: (1) Stories in which disability is not a villain, but a source of artistic creativity; (2) Stories of overcoming disability, in which a biomedical notion of disability is the villain; and (3) Stories of adapting to disability, in which the villain is a more nuanced, social model understanding of disability as barriers and negative attitudes. Taken together, these stories reveal tensions between cultural, organizational, and personal ideas about the relationship between art and disability.

Personal Narratives: Disability as a Source of Creativity

A few artists featured on the website rejected the cultural code of disability as a villain entirely, instead, crediting some of their creativity and personal identity to their disability. This sentiment was not echoed in most of the promotional material put forward by the organization, perhaps because this narrative theme does not as clearly establish a need for the programs offered through *Arts4All Florida*. Still, such stories were found among the descriptions and stories told by artists with disabilities. Trey Littles, for example, credits his synesthesia for his unique use of color.

> As a child, my autism prevented me from communicating through traditional means until my mother used her experience in art therapy to open my eyes to all the world has to offer. Today I'm confident in my artistic abilities and have grown into an adult who uses his synesthesia, autism, and emotions to create unique and expressive pieces...I communicate my feelings through my color choices utilizing my synesthesia which involves a link between my emotions and colors[...] I intend to make a difference in the world by being an artist.-Trey Littles (http://arts4allflorida.org/artist-registry)

In this narrative, Littles acknowledges both positive and negative aspects of his experience with a disability. His disabilities are not treated as unequivocal "heroes" in his narrative. He did talk about difficulties he experienced due to autism. However, his story highlights ways in which disability also helps him express himself though art.

Other artists cited their disability as a call to use art to connect to others with similar disabilities. While the story above discusses how visual and sensory perceptions influence visual arts, Sydney Glenn, who uses multiple mediums including "painting, sculpture, video, installation, performance and storytelling," uses disability as a theme across her artistic mediums – a theme she came to through her own personal experience.

> Deformity, adversity, and empowerment- these are the themes of my work. Having been born with seven fingers total, (five fingers on my left-hand and two fingers on my right-hand) as an artist, I have chosen to take this unique personal experience and transform it into a shared experience with my audiences. I have created four distinct characters that represent different developmental stages a person born with a physical defect goes through [...] Birth defects occur in all groups of people and the adversity of the disabled can truly touch us all, especially when the adversity is overcome and the deformed then become the empowered.- Sydney Glenn (http://arts4allflorida.org/artist-registry)

I would like to stress that I am by no means suggesting that these artists do not experience any difficulties or barriers related to their disabilities. Rather, I am saying that life with a disability, as an artist, or anyone for that matter, is not an inferior, negative way of being. These narratives stick out because they counter the narrative that disability can only cause negative experiences.

In having an identity that is culturally devalued, it is assumed that people with certain disabilities are not able to produce high quality art. People with disabilities are often assumed to be less capable than people without disabilities in all activities (Cahill & Eggleston, 1994; Calderón-Almendros & Calderón-Almendros, 2016; Goffman, 1963; Lenakakis & Koltsida, 2017; Solvang, 2012; Zederayko & Ward, 1999). When it comes to art, there are some exceptions, where people with disabilities are considered to be more artistic or creative (Chan & Sireling, 2010; Foucault, 1965/1988). However, this is for the most part associated with mental illness. While this may appear positive and empowering, even "positive" stereotypes can be harmful. It takes away from the process of identity-making in that it is cultural stories, rather than the person themselves, deciding *which* talents, crafts, or skills artists with disabilities should excel.

Arts4All Florida offers the space and resources for such empowered artists to create and sell their art. However, these narratives are not highlighted in the same ways as other, more traditional, narratives about disability. On one hand, these stories can only be told by the artists with disabilities themselves. Supportive others, such as family members or art educators, cannot say where an individual artist's inspiration and creativity come from, as this assessment belongs to the artist alone. However, there is also a practical purpose to not highlighting these narratives front and center, mainly in that it does not focus on any need for the organization.

Personal Narratives: Overcoming Disability

In contrast to narratives that highlight disability as being a source of creativity, some artists portrayed disability as a barrier to be overcome. This is not surprising since disability is often culturally coded as a tragedy (Jung, 2003; Loseke, 2007; Oliver & Barnes, 2012; Shah & Priestley, 2010), making this narrative readily available and easy to use. It also easily suits the needs of the organization and the teachers in the organization, as well as some of the artists with disabilities. Disability itself is the villain of this story. It is portrayed as a barrier that prevents the person with a disability from communicating with others, experiencing the world, or participating in the arts. Despite the drawbacks of this narrative, some people with disabilities may view themselves as the heroes who overcome their circumstances. Some stories told by the artists themselves also echoed similar narratives.

> As an individual with Epilepsy and Asperger's syndrome - a form of autism, I often felt like I could not do anything, but because of my life and social experience, I have overcome many challenges. Today I am the International spokesperson for the Center for Autism and Related Disabilities at [a large public university in the Southeastern United States] and was just elected to the constituency board… I also was with several organizations that provide services to

> individuals with disabilities including therapy such as occupational and physical along with music and art therapy. My plan for the future is to graduate from [my university] with a PHD in education, open my own school and work with children with disabilities. Monica Bakerson (http://arts4allflorida.org/artist-registry)

Monica has a story of overcoming her disabilities and moving from the initial conflict (difficulty with social experiences and confidence) to becoming a spokesperson for CARD and other organizations as well as working on a postgraduate degree. Yet, while it vilifies her disability, Monica's agency is not entirely stripped away. Monica maintains her agency by making a separation between herself and her disability. Unsurprisingly, organizational narratives echo this sentiment, in that this type of narrative provides the most direct link between the organization and a necessary hero role. Such narratives do serve a purpose for helping organizations, illustrating both the need for such programs and the positive results creates.

Personal Narratives: Adapting to Disability

In stories of adaptation, the person with a disability has more agency in their interactions with their surroundings. While disability is often still cast as the implicit villain, it also addresses other aspects of the inaccessible policies or environment as villains. In many of these stories, artists address the inflexible work hours and schedules as a barrier to full employment for people with disabilities, congruent with those described by Social Models of disability (Oliver & Barnes, 2012). For many artists, art offered not only a source of fulfillment but also a career path for people whose disabilities require a more flexible schedule.

> I'm a certified professional photographer, visual artist and licensed clinical social worker living in Florida. I live with several chronic illnesses that prevent me from working your typical 9-5, so I've used my wide array of skills to create a life for myself that prioritizes self-care and allows me to be self-employed -Ashely Peters (http://arts4allflorida.org/artist-registry)

While Ashley still attributes some difficulties to her chronic illnesses, she changes her career options, rather than "overcoming" aspects of the disability itself. In addition to adapting to new work schedules and careers, some artists also discussed the available mediums for creating art. Technology has offered many opportunities to make both art spaces and art skills more accessible. Anthony Blake, an artist with limited mobility and use of his hands, discusses in his video, "Painting with One Finger," the use of technology to create art, which he displays and sells professionally.

> I started in art because I love it! I have a passion for it. When I was younger, I would paint traditionally. I used the paintbrush and acrylics just like any other artist would and as my disease progressed, I began to lose the use of my hands and was forced to transfer into more of a digital medium. I was fortunate enough to develop and understand how to use the computer and the computer software to my advantages early on and that's kind of how it started....I paint with my left hand but more specifically, I only paint with one finger on my left hand. I really only have, you know, two or three inches range of motion, left to right, and up and down, and that's it, right there. And I'm able to use the mousepad to do the brush strokes ... I always say, if J. Lo. is gonna

> insure her butt for a million dollars, I should insure my hand for a million dollars, because it's definitely my million dollar finger.-Anthony Blake (http://arts4allflorida.org/artist-registry; https://www.youtube.com/watch?time_continue=140&v=IbRwnnnlogc)

While this seems like the stories about overcoming disability, Blake's story focuses on the use and availability of adaptive technology, with somewhat minimal focus on the impairment aspect of his disability. The two narratives are very similar and have overlapping, though not identical, implications and uses for *Arts4All Florida*. Adaptation stories place more onus on policies, tools, and the environment in terms of accessibility/inaccessibility. *Arts4All Florida* is an organization that can offer such tools, teach artists how to use adaptive technologies, and advocate for art spaces to be accessible.

Organizational Narratives: Overcoming Disability

Organizational Narratives and Personal Narratives meet at an interesting intersection via the testimonials from staff members of the organization that are chosen to be included in the annual reports. While these are narratives from people, they can overlap into the world of organizational narratives in that staff members are often speaking on behalf of the organization. In their stories as representatives of the organization, it is unsurprising that they highlight the ways that the organization helps its clients, often resulting in narratives of people overcoming their disability with the help of the organization. Either explicitly or implicitly, *Arts4All Florida* is framed as the hero.

In the 2017–2018 Annual Report, a document that is linked to under the "Impact Tab" (http://arts4allflorida.org/content/our-impact), the following story is told by an educator employed by the organization:

> Lisa is a non-verbal student and usually communicates through a Promethean board. Ever since she started the dance residency two semesters ago, Lisa now uses non-verbal language to communicate with classmates and teachers. Lisa has also increased the use of sounds and is able to follow directions without re-direction…Lisa had trouble sitting down on the floor and getting back up, but ever since we began our dance creative process, Lisa sits and gets back up without any assistance and quicker than when we started. Lisa is a pure example of how the arts creates transformations and assists in growth and increase of skills. (2017–2018 Annual Report)

This short story has a clear beginning, conflict, resolution, and happy ending. In the beginning, Lisa has a problem, and the conflict is that she is unable to communicate with others, due to her disability, the barrier/villain. In this story, *Arts4All Florida* offers a dance program and through this dance program, the conflict is resolved as her behavior and communication have improved – *Arts4All Florida* has saved the day. It's a familiar and easy story to understand.

The story of Lisa, an image of an organization that is a worthy investment for grants and funding. Still, these narratives are not entirely money driven. I firmly believe that educators and participants do indeed find the programs to be beneficial to people with disabilities and derive joy from seeing students improve and gain new skills.

> I discovered one girl IS AN AMAZING talented, natural artist. She has had difficulty with verbal & written comprehension & expression. HER JOY of drawing, painting, creating, and sharing-further developed her individuality & processing skills in my class. STEP BY STEP directions help her significantly. She smiles in the world of color!! Learning in a multi-sensory environment is essential. (Site Evaluation Annual Report 2016–2017)

These narratives still have elements of *Arts4All Florida* as a hero that helps students to "overcome" their disabilities. Still, showing progress in students does offer an avenue for people with similar disabilities to identify programs that could, in fact, benefit themselves in some way.

Organizational Narratives: Adapting to Disability

Given the potential usefulness of the narrative that disability is a barrier to be overcome, it would not be surprising if this was the organizational narrative *Arts4All Florida* chose to center. However, many of the organization's narratives highlighted the ways that *Arts4All Florida* teaches people to adapt to sociocultural and economic expectations of society as opposed to teaching clients to adapt to their disabilities per se. While the narratives as told by spokespeople were highlighted in the annual reports, the website's impact tab is prefaced with the following narrative:

> For 38 years, Arts4Fall Florida has provided programs that make it possible for people with disabilities to contribute to the social, cultural, and economic life of Florida. Our programs have demonstrated success in increasing *artistic skills*, fostering creativity, promoting social skills, *creating self-confidence*, *teaching marketable skills* and providing *new ways of communication* for people with disabilities. (emphasis added) (https://arts4allflorida.org/about-and-impact.html)

The successes touted by the organization revolve around teaching artistic skills as a craft, and marketable skills to help promote oneself economically. Neither of these are inherent to disability and, thus, it is not necessarily disability that is being overcome. Instead, artists are taught how to handle socially imposed barriers, such as lack of art training due to inaccessible art classes, and low confidence stemming from low expectations surrounding disability. *Arts4All Florida* trains artists, which can help them to find niches outside of a typical 8-hour a day, 40-hour workweek which may be inaccessible for some of these artists with disabilities. Additionally, annual reports, particularly more recent ones, also shifted the focus from overcoming disabilities to narratives more focused on access.

> In an effort to help schools and other organizations provide accessible art instruction, Arts4All Florida coordinated an adapted art tool and material fund for classroom teachers, teaching artists, and cultural organizations. (https://arts4allflorida.org/assets/docs/2018-2019%20Annual%20Report%20Arts4All%20FLORIDA-r.pdf)

By drawing on social model understandings of disability, *Arts4All Florida* can be an ally to people with disabilities by helping them overcome inaccessible environments without objectifying people with disabilities as victims of their body/minds. It is also worth noting that more recent annual reports draw on stories of adaptation and social model understandings of disability more clearly than older reports, showing that the organization itself also adapts to be a better ally to its clients as more empowering narratives become available. This ability to shift from traditional narratives of overcoming disability, in which the organization is the clearly identified hero, to one in which the organization is more of a side kick or helper shows a commitment to empowering clients, shows a commitment to allyship and support for the flourishing narratives of adapting to disabling situations becomes a more positive narrative for artists with disabilities.

DISCUSSION

This chapter explores the plurality of narratives about and within an ally organization that supports arts education for people with disabilities. Narratives can be used to support or subvert understandings of disability. While much of the promotional materials subscribed to more traditional understandings of disability, in which the organization, to an extent, "saves" students with disabilities, *Arts4All Florida* has increasingly begun to put narratives of adaption to inaccessible societies front and center as their organizational narrative, which better empowers artists with disabilities. While this chapter is somewhat critical toward the cultural narratives of disability, the stories told support the claim that many students who have taken programs though *Arts4All Florida* did experience benefits, whether artistically or otherwise. Telling such stories could reach families that may also benefit from such programs.

I was particularly interested in the variability among the stories of artists with disabilities. Some artists did not tell stories at all, instead, preferring to give a brief description of the type of art they do with a link to their website where they sell their art. This, to some extent, echoes Gill's (2001) findings that people with disabilities do not necessarily want to be praised for routine things they do in their lives simply because they have a disability. For some of these artists, their disability may be irrelevant to their art and the organization is an ally only insofar as it provides another forum for them to sell their artwork. Other artists told long stories about their experience with disability, how they initially got involved in creating art, and their hopes about creating art or pursuing other goals in the future. I focused on the latter, as this gave me more of a snapshot into the artist's identity and their understanding of their disability.

As discussed earlier, it is important to be wary of organizations that are led primarily by those who adopt an identity as ally, as opposed to people with disabilities themselves. *Arts4All Florida* had its beginnings being funded primarily be the government and run by people who may not have had disabilities themselves. However, *Arts4All Florida* has since undergone extensive changes. By providing spaces for people with disabilities to tell their own stories and sell their own work, the organization is attempting to shift toward an organization that highlights the voices of people with disabilities. It is important to note that there is no attempt to silence or hide voices whose narrative seems to contradict the larger overarching narrative of the organization.

Additionally, *Arts4All Florida* does take actions, rather than simply preaching mere acceptance. It actively devotes resources to making art classrooms more accessible and promoting artists with disabilities. *Arts4All Florida* also confronts token-style inclusion that only considers whether persons with disabilities are in the classroom, without assessing the degree to which they have the resources to actively participate and express themselves with art. This action component of *Arts4All Florida's* mission is perhaps the most important component of the organization's allyship.

Artists who told stories about overcoming disability are not wrong to conceptualize their experience in this way. Sharing such stories can be powerful and for some people overcoming difficulties stemming from their disability still allows them to be the hero of their own story. My goal is not to critique those who experience disability through this lens. Instead, I seek to answer questions of "what?" and "how?" narratives make up our world to such an extent that we do not think about how we narrate ourselves or how our narratives changes from context to context. Identifying different types of narratives, even when the differences are subtle, as is the case for overcoming versus adaptation narratives, can open different understandings of what disability is and how it is experienced.

Discussions of finding funding and sponsors may appear cold and rational on the surface. However, many of the programs offered through *Arts4All Florida,* seeking to make art classrooms more accessible for students with disabilities, could not exist without money. Thus, attracting donors is not only practical but arguably moral, in making is possible for organizers to fulfill a calling.

Additionally, understanding the different purposes that narratives serve gives us a better understanding of the complexity of social reality and bridges gaps in our understanding. A purpose can be as simple as trying to bridge a gap in understanding. The organizers who chose which stories to highlight in their promotional material are no more calculating than I am in choosing narratives to serve the interest of writing this chapter. In short, the goal of this chapter is to better understand conceptions of disability and how organizations that wish to be allies draw on these conceptions of disability in ways that promote or contradict the narratives of their clients.

CONCLUSION

As with all research, there are limitations. Perhaps most noticeably, this is a case study of only one organization that offers art programs to people with disabilities. This was done to explore the full depth that this organization's website had to offer. With this information, future research may explore other websites to see if these themes reach across organizations. Additionally, in future research with artists with disabilities, it may be informative to also reach out to artists who did *not* include information about their disability in their artist registry. Artist who do not discuss their disability on the Artist Registry may have their own reasons for doing so and may have a different perspective as to the role of art or *Arts4All Florida* in their lives. As stated multiple times, the narratives on this website are very short snapshots, some being only a few sentences long. In-depth interviews with artists, employees, or board members of *Arts4All Florida* may offer a better, more wholistic understanding into the organization and/or the lives and identities of artists with disabilities. Each of these pieces will offer a deeper understanding of the role narratives play in shaping organizations and what it means for organizations to consider themselves as allies.

ACKNOWLEDGMENTS

I would like to thank my wonderful mentor, Sara E. Green, and my colleague, Richard Chapman, for supporting and encouraging me through the writing and editing process.

NOTES

1. Courtesy stigma refers to stigma experienced by a person or organization due to its association with someone who has a stigmatized identity. People working with this organization would be what Goffman (1963) refers to as "the wise" meaning "persons who are normal but whose special situation has made them intimately privy to the secret life of the stigmatized individual" (p. 28).
2. This study using personal stories posted online to the *Arts4All Florida* website was deemed exempt for research with human subjects by the International Review Board at the University of South Florida.
3. There were many narratives on the Artist Registry that did not mention disability at all. Some artist simply wanted to talk about the art that they sold and this was just one of many platforms where they advertised their art. This, in itself, is an interesting finding. However, since this chapter is about narratives of disability and allyship, narratives that did not mention disability were a bit beyond the scope of this chapter.

REFERENCES

Allen, J. (2010). The sociology of disability and the struggle for inclusive education. *British Journal of Sociology of Education*, *31*(5), 603–619.

Allen, J. (2014). Inclusive education and the arts. *Cambridge Journal of Education*, *44*(4), 511–523.

Best, J. (1997). Victimization and the victim industry. *Society*, *34*, 9–17.

Brown, K. T., & Ostrove, J. M. (2013). What does it mean to be an ally? The perception of allies from the perspective of people of color. *Journal of Applied Social Psychology*, *43*, 2211–2222.

Cahill, S. E., & Eggleston, R. (1994). Managing Emotions in Public: The case of wheelchair users. *Social Psychology Quarterly*, *57*(4), 300–312.

Calderón-Almendros, I., & Calderón-Almendros, R. (2016). 'I open the coffin and here I am': Disability as oppression and education as liberation in the construction of personal identity. *Disability & Society*, *31*(1), 100–115.

Carey, A. C., Block, P., & Scotch, R. K. (2019). Sometimes allies: Parent-led disability organizations and social movements. *Disability Studies Quarterly*, *39*(1).

Chan, D., & Sireling, L. (2010). I want to be bipolar...A new phenomenon. *The Psychiatrist*, *34*, 103–105.

Coleman, M. B., & Cramer, E. S. (2015). Creating meaningful art experiences with assistive technology for students with physical, visual, severe, and multiple disabilities. *Art Education*, *68*(2), 6–13.

Coleman, M. B., Cramer, E. S., Park, Y., & Bell, S. M. (2015). Art educators' use of adaptations, assistive technology, and special education supports for students with physical, visual, severe, and multiple disabilities. *Journal of Developmental and Physical Disabilities*, *27*(5), 637–660.

Cooley, J., & Fox, A. M. (2014). Disability art, aesthetics, and access: Creating exhibitions in a liberal arts setting. *Disability Studies Quarterly*, *34*(1).

Coriale, L., Grant, L., & Robertson, J. (2012). Exploring the educational experience of a social work student with a disability: A narrative. *Social Work Education*, *31*(4), 422–434.

Cramer, E. S., Coleman, M. B., Park, Y., Bell, S. M., & Cole, J. (2015). Art Educators' knowledge, attitudes, and experiences working with students who have physical, sensory, severe, or multiple disabilities. *Studies in Art Education*, *57*(1), 6–20.

Darling, R. B. (2013). *Disability and identity: Negotiating self in a changing society*. Boulder, CO; London: Lynne Rienner Publishers.

Dunn, J. (2004). The politics of empathy: Social movements and victim repertoires. *Sociological Focus*, *37*(3), 235–250.

Egilson, S. T., & Traustadottir, R. (2009). Assistance to pupils with physical disabilities in regular schools: Promoting inclusion or creating dependency? *European Journal of Special Needs Education*, *24*(1), 21–36.

Egner, J. E. (2019a). The disability rights community was never mine: Neuroqueer disidentification? *Gender & Society*, *33*(1), 123–147.

Egner, J. E. (2019b). Hegemonic or queer?: A comparative analysis of five LGBTQIA/disability intersectional social movement organizations. *Humanity and Society*, *43*(2), 140–178.

Evans, N. J., Assadi, J. L., & Harriott, T. K. (2005). Encouraging the development of disability allies. In R. D. Reason, E. M. Broido, T. Davis, & N. J. Evans (Eds.), *Developing social justice allies: New directions for student services* (pp. 67–79). San Francisco, CA: Jossey-Bass.

Forber-Pratt, A. J., Mueller, C. O., & Andrews, E. E. (2019). Disability identity and allyship in rehabilitation psychology: Sit, stand, sign and show up. *Rehabilitation Psychology*, *64*(2), 119–129.

Foucault, M. (1988). Vintage Books. *Madness and civilization: A history of insanity in the age of reason*. New York, NY: Random House. Original Work Published 1965.

Fox, A. (2015). Invigorating disability aesthetics through art and performance: A report from the bodies of work festival of disability arts and culture 2013. *Journal of Literary & Cultural Disability Studies*, *9*(3), 349–355.

Gill, C. J. (2001). Divided understandings: The social experience of disability. In G. L. Albrecht, K. D. Seelman, & M. Bury (Eds.), *Handbook of disability studies* (pp. 351–372). Thousand Oaks, CA: SAGE Publications.

Goffman, E. (1963). *Stigma: Notes on management of spoiled identity*. New York, NY: Simon & Schuster.

Green, S. E., Darling, R. B., & Wilbers, L. (2017). Struggles and joys: A review of research on the social experience of parenting disabled children. In S. E. Green & S. N. Barnartt (Eds.), *Sociology looking at disability: What did we know and when did we know it?* (pp. 39–56). Bingley: Emerald Publishing Limited.

Hine, C. (2000). *Virtual ethnography*. London: SAGE Publications.

Jung, K. E. (2003). Chronic illness and academic accommodation: Meeting disabled students' "unique needs" and preserving the institutional order of the university. *Journal of Sociology & Social Welfare*, *30*(1), 91–112.

Kafer, A. (2013). *Feminist queer crip*. Bloomington, IN: Indiana University Press.

Kimball, E. W., Moore, A., Vaccaro, A., Troiano, P. F., & Newman, B. M. (2016). College students with disabilities redefine activism: Self-advocacy, storytelling, and collective action. *Journal of Diversity in Higher Education*, *9*(3), 245–260.

Lenakakis, A., & Koltsida, M. (2017). Disabled and non-disabled actors working in partnership for a theatrical performance: A research on theatrical partnerships as enablers of social and behavioral skills for persons with disabilities. *Research in Drama Education: The Journal of Applied Theatre and Performance*, *22*(2), 251–269.

Loesl, S. (2012). The adaptive art specialist: An integral part of a student's access to art. *The intersection of arts education and Special Education: Exemplary programs and approaches* (pp. 47–68). Washington, DC: International Organization on Arts and Disability.

Loseke, D. R. (2007). The study of identity as cultural institutional, organizational, and personal narratives: Theoretical and empirical integrations. *The Sociological Quarterly*, *48*, 661–688.

Loseke, D. (2012). The empirical analysis of formula stories. In J. Holstein & J. Gubrium (Eds.), *Varieties of narrative analysis* (pp. 251–271). Los Angeles, CA: SAGE Publications.

Maloney, P. (2013). Online networks and emotional energy. *Information, Communication & Society*, *16*(1), 105–124.

Manago, B., Davis, J. L., & Goar, C. (2017). Discourse in action: Parents' use of medical and social models to resist disability stigma. *Social Sciences & Medicine*, *184*, 169–177.

Oliver, M., & Barnes, C. (2012). *The new politics of disablement*. New York, NY: Palgrave Macmillian.

Ostrove, J. M., Kornfeld, M., & Ibrahim, M. (2019). Actors against ableism? Qualities of nondisabled allies from the perspective of people with physical disabilities. *Journal of Social Issues*, *75*(3), 924–942.

Patterson, L. (2012). Points of access: Rehabilitation centers, summer camps, and student life in the making of disability activism, 1960-1973. *Journal of Social History*, *46*(2), 473–499.

Penketh, C. (2014). Putting disability studies to work in art education. *International Journal of Art and Design Education*, *33*, 291–300.

Rousso, H. (2013). *Don't call me inspirational: A disabled feminist talk back*. Philadelphia, PA: Temple University Press.

Russell, G. M. (2011). Motives of heterosexual allies in collective action for equality. *Journal of Social Issues*, *67*, 358–375.

Russell, G. M., & Bohan, J. S. (2016). Institutional allyship for LGBT equality: Underlying processes and potentials for change. *Journal of Social Issues*, *72*(2), 335–354.

Shah, S., & Priestley, M. (2010). Home and away: The changing impact of educational policies on disabled children's experiences of family and friendship. *Research Papers in Education*, *25*(2), 155–175.

Shakespeare, T. (2014). *Disability rights and wrongs revisited*. (2nd ed.). Cornwall, ON: Routeledge.

Shaw, C. (2015). We have no need to lock ourselves away: Space, marginality, and negotiations of Deaf identity in Late Soviet Moscow. *Slavic Review*, *74*(1), 57–78.

Solvang, P. K. (2012). Research paper: From identity politics to dismodernism? Changes in the social meaning of disability art. *European Journal of Disability Research*, *6*(3), 178–187.

Taylor, M. (2005). Self-identity and the arts education of disabled young people. *Disability & Society*, *20*, 763–778.

Van der Klift, E., & Kunc, N. (2019). Segregation versus solidarity: Rethinking the uncritical commitment to inclusion. In K. Scorgie, & C. Forlin (Eds.), *Promoting social inclusion: Co-creating environments that foster equity and belonging* (pp. 17–24). Bingley: Emerald Publishing Limited.

Wexler, A. J., & Derby, J. (2015). Arts in institutions: The emergence of (disabled) outsiders. *Studies in Art Education*, *56*, 127–141.

Young, G. C. (2008). Autonomy of artistic expression for adult learners with disabilities. *International Journal of Art and Design Education*, *27*, 116–123.

Zederayko, M. W., & Ward, K. (1999). What to do when students can't hold a pencil. *Art Education*, *52*(4), 18–22.

Chapter 5

ALLYSHIP CHANGES IN AMERICAN DISABILITY PROTESTS OVER FIVE DECADES: AN EMPIRICAL ANALYSIS

Sharon Barnartt

ABSTRACT

Purpose: *To examine empirical patterns of participation of allied groups in disability protests from 1970 to 2016 in the United States.*

Methods/approach: *Uses event history to analyze 1,268 cases of disability protests quantitatively. Internal and external allied groups and types of individual protestors are analyzed over the entire period and by decade.*

Findings: *Multiple impairment, single issue organizations were a more common type of "internal" ally than were either single impairment, multiple issue organizations or multiple impairment, multiple issue (truly cross-disability) organizations. External ally groups with a wide range of concerns were less common than internal ally groups but were most represented during the 1990s. Veterans groups were the most common type of external ally, while parents were the most common type of individual allies.*

Implications/values: *Two topics need more attention: How ally participation in disability protests compares to that in protests in other social movements, and what types of changes over time emerge. Explanations relating to movement trajectories and other social movement characteristics are presented, and the need for a more nuanced conceptualization of protest allies is discussed.*

Disability Alliances and Allies
Research in Social Science and Disability, Volume 12, 111–129

ISSN: 1479-3547/doi:10.1108/S1479-354720200000012008

Keywords: Protest; disability movement; protest allies; ally types; social movement trajectories; social movement organizations; cross disability organizations

INTRODUCTION

Sun Tzu, Chinese philosopher of war strategy, wrote that "If you do not seek out allies and helpers, then you will be isolated and weak." While this chapter is discussing social movements, not wars, the principle is not so different. Social movements are comprised of groups whose needs or demands have not been successfully satisfied by conventional political processes. They lack power to affect political decision-making; if they had power within the traditional political processes, they would already have used it to attain their demands (Piven & Cloward, 1979). They often succeed either by disruption, which poses a threat, or by persuasion, which provokes sympathy (Andrews, 2002, p. 109). Social movements conduct many types of actions, some of which are normatively acceptable within the cultural context of a particular society but most of which are not.[1] They may conduct many separate incidents and types of collective action over extended periods of time, on many fronts at the same or different times, using many different tactics and conducted by many different groups.

Members of a social movement form an amorphous social entity. Movements are comprised of groups who may share one belief or many, who work together always or sometimes, and who may or may not have overlapping members. Although there may be offices, organizations, and membership lists, these do not form the whole of the movement – and some movements do not have them anyway. Social movements are "clusters of . . . overlapping networks and individuals" who share goals and collective identities (Whittier, 1997, p. 761) – although we would note that some supporting individuals may not be on any membership list and the networks may be extremely fluid. Despite the centrality of this notion of overlapping networks to discussions of social movements, there has not been much attention paid to the role of allies as part of those networks.

One type of action which occurs in most social movements is protests. Protest actions are collective, contentious (Tarrow, 1996), angry, demanding, and ideologically based, challenging the power structure, and seeking social, as opposed to individual, change. Protests are often, although not always, shorter than other types of actions. Because they are usually both finite and obvious, identifying allies in protests is easier than it might be for other types of social movement actions.

Allies in protests may be somewhat different than other types of the (presumably longer term) allies identified in the literature on social movements. Ferree and Hess (1994) discuss allies as being part of coalitions, whereas Finnegan (2003) sees allies as coprotesters who might not agree on much of anything other than the need for that specific protest. In fact, Finnegan uses the word "affinity groups" to describe the allies in one protest they studied, who varied from ... "Teamsters on the right ... to, on the left, a dozen or so anarchist factions" (p. 215). Goffman identifies one category of allies whom he calls "'the wise' as being persons who are normal (*sic*) but whose special situation has made them intimately privy to the secret life of the stigmatized individual and sympathetic with it, and who find themselves accorded a measure of acceptance, a measure of courtesy membership in the clan" (1963, p. 28). The "wise" may be mobilized to become protest allies, or they may become "moral entrepreneurs" for "the cause," whether or not they actually participate in specific protests (Altman & Barnartt, 1993). Or they may be neither.

Allies can differ on a number of dimensions. One dimension is temporal – they may be short-term allies, for the duration of one protest, or they may become the longer-term allies which Carey, Block, and Scotch (2019) discuss. Another dimension is ideological – they may support an entire ideological system which underpins the specific protest, or they may be aligned with a specific issue (such as income inequality) which appears across an ideological continuum. A third dimension is the degree of collectivity. Some allies in protests are there as individuals, while others are there as members of organized groups. They may differ in formality, or the degree to which they are formally coprotesters – or whether they are not actually supporters but are there to gain attention to their own (related) issue. Finally, allies may differ in the extent to which they are helpers who may or not actually be physically present in the protest but may contribute time, money, goods (such as food or sleeping bags), supportive statements, recruitment, or skills such as stuffing envelopes, personal care assistance, or sign language interpreting. (See Halley (2018) and his chapter in this volume.)[2]

Allies may be internal or external. "Internal allies" are supporting groups from within the movement. These groups organize the action, participate, or support from the side lines. Internal allies are long-term, ideological, partners, who share a collective consciousness (Barnartt, 1996) whether they participate in protests or not.

"External allies" are not "of the movement," but they can be involved in individual protests conducted by the movement. (This is one reason why focusing on protest allies may give scholars different information than focusing on social movements allies.) External allies are more likely than internal allies to be temporarily or occasionally active, or they may only be involved in one part of a movement's agenda. They may be allies who support only some of the movement's larger agenda: An example would be people who identified with the AIDS movement but who shared goals relating to SSDI support for people with disabilities and who participated in several protests. Alternatively, the agenda of external allies may coincide only with the goals of one protest. In this case, it is possible that some or all of the members of the social movement actually disagree with these external allies on most or all other issues. An example of the latter occurred when so-called "right to life" groups participated in a number of disability protests related to assisted suicide (Barnartt, 2007), since euthanasia and abortion are issues on which disability activists disagree among themselves (Asch, 2000, 2005).

Allies may also include individuals who are not part of organized groups. These people may participate in specific protests, but they are less likely to be counted as part of the social movement, since their presence may be sporadic or "spur of the moment." However, they do have to have identified themselves in some way to those writing about the protest, or they would not be identified in the current data.

Social movements have trajectories (Tarrow, 1998) in many aspects of their existence, and allies are no exception. At the beginning of a movement, preexisting organizations are crucial in order to have a base upon which to build (McAdam, 1982; Morris, 1984).[3] But if an incipient movement is to succeed and grow, it needs to expand from its original base and develop new allies. Tarrow (1998, p. 154) notes that the number of alliances a movement has is related to its success. A proliferation of organizations widens the possible appeal and therefore mobilization potential as well as spreading out the work of that social movement. In the women's movement, for example, protesters for abortion rights and for lesbian rights came to see themselves as being part of the feminist movement over time but not initially; Ferree and Hess (1994) point out that such increasing organizational diversity is likely to make a social movement stronger.

There are several ways in which allies emerge as a social movement grows. One is through diffusion. Tactics, members, or organizations may diffuse geographically within one movement or from one movement to another (Strang & Soule, 1998), and this may create allies for new movements. A second way is through early successes, which have the potential to create new allies. Successes may attract existing organizations to the new movement, or new organizations might emerge to take advantage of the success: New groups, nonaffiliated groups, and already affiliated groups become more likely to "jump on the bandwagon" (Barnartt, 1997). Thirdly, groups from an existing movement may become allies by helping the new movement utilize their own movement framing; such frame extension is often important for the growth and success of newer social movements (Snow & Benford, 1992; Snow, Rochford, Worder, & Benford, 1986) but also reinforces the status of the older movement. Finally, as a movement grows, new groups or organizations may see value in coming to identify as being part of a movement, or they may form specifically in response to new movement issues.

This chapter examines social movement allies as identified by their participation in protests which were part of the actions of the disability movement from 1970 to 2016.[4] It examines their characteristics and overall participation levels as well as changes over time in the trajectory of this part of the social movement.

METHODOLOGY

The methodology for this chapter is based upon event history analysis of media and other reports of protests, in which the unit of analysis is the protest event (Olzak, 1989). Reports of protests were initially located in newspapers using print indices (and then expanding to online indices). Additionally, reports of protests from newspapers and magazines published within or about the deaf and disability communities, as well as books, professional journal articles, and other publications, were included. More recently, electronic news lists which discussed protest events and websites of organizations involved in protests have been used to locate media accounts of protest events.

To be included as a disability protest, a protest event had to satisfy certain operational criteria. These specified that the event had to be collective, not individual; that it demanded social, not individual, change; that the issue was related to disability, whether the protesters themselves had identified as having disabilities or not; that it did not constitute politics as usual (Tarrow, 1998), and that the event was reported in the past, not as a "planned" event.[5] Actions related to fund-raising or self-help were not included, nor were noncontentious actions considered part of the normal political process such as voter registration drives or lobbying (Barnartt & Scotch, (2001). A large number of variables were coded for each protest incident, and the data were entered into an SPSS/Windows system file for analysis. The N for all disability-related protests in the United States between 1970 and the end of 2016 was 1712. The N used in this chapter is 1,268 because not all protests included allies, so those were eliminated for this purpose.

Several variables were coded related to the type of ally. "Internal allies" are groups who are centrally identified with disability issues and tend to have the word disability in their organizational title. Examples of this type of organization are discussed in some depth by Carey et. al. (2019).[6] The organizations were identified by the authors of the media reports through the speakers or other protest participants or by participants' signs or other types of identification, such as t-shirts or hats. Two variables, "organization 1" (the primary organization) and "organization 2" (one or more secondary organizations), were coded by name. While the variable "organization 1" was coded by a specific name, "organization 2" also included the categories of "other" and "many." "Other" organizations are extremely variable: Some are established organizations which participated very infrequently, while others are relatively newly formed organizations which did not originally show up in disability protests.[7] "Many" indicated more than one organizational ally participated in addition to the one which was coded under "organization 1." Because of this coding, the results reflected how many times a specific organization participated in any protest rather than the number of protests which included a specific organization.

The second type of organizational variable is "external allies." These are groups which do not necessarily share the disability-related aspect of the protest demand but who nevertheless supported one or more specific demands being made in the protest. The original codes were based upon the organization's name or mission, plus the categories "other" and "many." For purposes of the present analysis, larger categories were constructed by the author based upon the organizational name, type of members (for example, veterans), or the primary issue identified with the group. The issues spanned the gamut from those related to race or ethnicity, age, or gender to those related to specific medical conditions such as AIDS or cancer to those related to social issues such as poverty or "right to life." Some of these groups were likely to include people who may have had disabilities, such as veterans or older people, while others were not.

A third set of variables relates to the presence or absence of allies protesting as individuals. Eight variables, not all of which are reported here, were coded as to presence or absence. These included parents, teachers, medical or other treatment professionals such as audiologists or physical therapists, nondisabled children, and nondisabled adults – a category which could include politicians as well as public or private officials. Usually these people were identified by signs which were visible to media reporters; otherwise, they made speeches or participated in actions such as handling out fliers and so were identified that way. Sometimes people were described by reporters in other ways: For example, an article might report the presence of people pushing wheelchairs of children, who were described as being parents, family members, or caregivers (correctly or incorrectly) and coded as such. Other individuals were mentioned in passing or obliquely in the articles. For example, if a sentence mentioned "adults using wheelchairs" and others "walking," with no other function attributed to them, the latter were coded as "nondisabled adults" or, if children, were coded as "nondisabled children."

One type of allyship which will not be examined here is the presence of supporters or helpers who did not participate in the protest but who assisted in it. Although this type of allyship was an important factor in some disability protests, such as the 1977 HEW building takeover in San Francisco and the 1988 Deaf President Now protests (Christiansen & Barnartt, 1995), this information is not as likely to show up in media reports unless the group publicized it. It was coded if mentioned, but that occurred in only a few cases so it is not analyzed here.

RESULTS

Table 1 presents the basic numbers of instances in which the three types of allies showed up. There were 1067 instances in which internal organizational allies were present in protests. This does not equal either the number of protests or the number of organizations because the variable "organization 2" could name zero, one, or "many" organizations. There were 325 instances which included external organizational allies; again, some included more than one organization, but these were not specified. Finally, there were 798 instances of individual protesters. Because there were eight distinct variables indicating the presence of one type of protester, one protest could have between 0 and 8 different types.

Table 2 presents frequency and percentage distributions for the internal ally organizations involved in protests. There were 991 protests which included one internal ally organization and an additional 76 which included one or more

Table 1. Types of Allies Involved in Protests.

Type of Ally	N[a]
Internal organizational allies	1067
External organizational allies	325
Individual protesters	798

[a]Each protest could have one, two, or three of the types of allies. Because there were eight variables which indicated the presence or absence of individual protesters of a specific type, one protest could include more than one type of individual protester.

Table 2. Percentage Distributions of Internal Ally Organizations (N = 1067)

Organization	Primary		Secondary	
	N = 991	%	N = 76	%
ADAPT	285	28.8%	2	2.6%
Disabled in Action	12	1.2		
Jerry's Orphans	18	1.8		
National Association of the Deaf (NAD)	34	3.4		
National Foundation of the Blind (NFB)	120	12.0		
American Coalition of Citizens with Disabilities (ACCD)	14	1.4		
Not Dead Yet	24	2.4	3	3.9
Concrete Change	5	0.5		
Concerned Rail Corridor Users	2	0.2		
FDR in a Chair	25	2.5		
TASH	2	0.2		
The ARC	7	0.7		
American Council for the Blind (ACB)	7	0.7		
Any Independent Living Center or the National Council on Independent Living (NCIL)	5	0.6	8	10.5
National Spinal Cord Injury Association	1	0.1		
Disabled People's Liberation Front	3	0.3		
Atlantis	4	0.4		
MindFreedom International (formerly SCI)	15	1.5		
Deaf Grassroots Movement (DGM)	49	4.9		
Paralyzed Veterans of America (PVA)	8	0.8		
Disabled American Veterans (DVA)	144	14.5	2	2.6
Any State or Local Branch of a National Organization	70	7.0	15	19.7
Many			20	26.3
Other	129	13.0	26	34.2

secondary organizations. The most common primary organization was ADAPT, while Disabled American Veterans was the second most frequent primary organization.[8] Others which were the primary organization in at least 4% of the protests were the Deaf Grassroots Movement, state or local level branches of (unspecified) national organizations, Disabled American Veterans, and the National Federation of the Blind (NFB). "Other" organizations were the primary organization for 13% of the protests. Secondary organizations were most likely to be "other," "many," or "state or local level" branches.

Table 3 disaggregates those internal allies coded as specifically named organizations into three categories initially presented by Barnartt and Scotch (2001). The first type, "single impairment, multiple issue" organizations, is comprised of primarily older organizations which were not originally social movement (i.e., activist) organizations but were service or advocacy organizations. Some of these are quite

Table 3. Percentage Distributions of Organizations by Type of Organization

Type of Organization	**(N = 799)**
Single Impairment, Multiple Issue	**(N = 184)**
National Association of the Deaf [NAD]	18.5% (34)
National Foundation of the Blind [NFB]	65.2 (120)
The ARC	3.8 (7)
American Council for the Blind	3.8 (7)
National Spinal Cord Injury Association	0.5 (1)
Support Coalition International	8.2 (15)
Multiple Impairment, Multiple Issue	**(N = 202)**
Disabled in Action [DIA]	5.9% (12)
American Coalition of Citizens with Disabilities [ACCD]	6.9 (14)
TASH	1.0 (2)
Disabled People's Liberation Front	1.5 (3)
Atlantis	2.0 (4)
Disabled American Veterans [DAV]	72.3 (146)
NICL or any specific independent living center	6.5 (13)
Paralyzed Veterans of America	3.9 (8)
Multiple Impairment, Single Issue	**(N = 413)**
ADAPT	69.5% (287)
Jerry's Orphans	4.4 (18)
Not Dead Yet	6.5 (27)
Concrete Change	1.2 (5)
Concerned Rail Corridor Users	0.5 (2)
FDR in a Chair	6.1 (25)
Deaf Grassroots Movement	11.9 (49)

Note: Categories "State-level Organizations,""Other,"and "Many"Not Included.

long-standing and well-known. For example, the NAD was established in 1880. Others, established in the 1940s and 1950s, include The ARC (formerly The Association for Retarded Children) and NFB. Some of these groups did occasionally engage in activism even before disability protests became more common starting in 1970, but their activism was of the normative political variety and not the non-normative activism which characterizes social movements (Tarrow, 1996). The one exception was NFB, which organized some of the earliest protests.

These traditionally non-activist organizations show up the smallest number of times, a total of 184. The NFB – and later the NAD – were involved in most of the protests within this category: NFB was involved in about 65% of these protests, while NAD was involved in about 20%. Support Coalition International (SCI), an organization focused on psychiatric issues which changed its name to MindFreedom International in 2005 (https://mindfreedom.org/about-mfi/who-we-are-d2), was involved in about 8%. The other organizations were involved in 4% or fewer of protests in this category.

The second category consists of "multiple impairment, multiple issue," or "cross-disability," organizations. These organizations focused on multiple issues of potential interest to people with a wide variety of types of impairments. Cross-disability organizations have been seen by observers, such as Longmore (1997) and Young (1998), to be central to those successes which the disability movement has attained. Such organizations include the American Coalition for Citizens with Disabilities (ACCD) and Disabled in Action (DIA). It also includes some organizations whose constituencies and issues were somewhat more limited than ACCD and DIA but are still quite general, such as The Association for Severely Handicapped (TASH) and Paralyzed Veterans of American. Both of these groups are considered to be cross-disability organizations, although they are not completely so.

Organizations in this category showed up 202 times. The largest proportion (72%) involved DAV. The DIA, ACCD, and NCIL or other independent living centers showed up six to seven percent of the time. Other organizations showed up smaller numbers of times.

The two above categories of organizations were characterized by a wide focus on multiple issues which might be of importance to all people with any type of impairment, such as the passage of the Americans with Disabilities Act. In this, they were quite different from the third category of organizations. This category consists of "multiple impairment, single issue" organizations, so named because they coalesced around demands related to a single issue, although the issue was one which could be of interest to people with many types of impairments. These are relatively recently established organizations which were specifically formed to be activist social movement organizations, and they changed the organizational arena within the disability movement. ADAPT has received substantial media attention because its protests were often disruptive, using tactics such as chaining protesters to buses or blocking bus stations rather than the more usual marches or rallies. Other such organizations formed around this time (the 1980s) were Not Dead Yet, Jerry's Orphans, FDR in a Chair, and Concrete Change. Most recently (in 2015), there was the development of the Deaf Grassroots Movement, whose demands focus on getting sign language accessibility for deaf children to be mandated by state legislatures.

The table shows that ADAPT was involved in almost 70% of these protests, and the Deaf Grassroots Movement was involved in about 12%. Each of the other organizations was involved in about 6% or fewer – although even 6% of these protests is 25 events.

External allies are groups which are not part of or affiliated with the disability movement. Table 4 shows that 325 protests included one or more of such groups. Veterans groups were the most common (49%), followed by senior citizens groups (12.3%) and by unions (6.5%). There were many other types of groups involved, although in very small numbers. Some were racial or ethnic groups, some were church or religious groups, some groups focused on issues related to poverty, homelessness, or immigration, and some were "identity" groups, including transsexuals.

Table 4. Percentage Distribution of External Groups Involved in Protests (N = 325).

Focus of Group	%	N
Elderly	12.3%	40
Unions or workers	6.5	21
Veterans (not specifically related to disability)	48.9	159
Minority groups (blacks, Latinos)	1.8	6
Disease groups (includes cancer, AIDS, substance abuse)	2.8	9
Poverty, homelessness, or immigrants	4.9	16
Right to life	3.4	11
Parents' groups (not individuals)	2.5	8
Other groups or more than 1 group	16.9	55
Total	100.0%	325

Table 5 shows specific types of individuals who were involved in protests. They were not protesting as part of organized groups, although they might have been members. Usually they were identified in the reports as, for example, "parents or family members," or "parents and other supporters." Adults without disabilities appeared in 375 protests, while 295 included parents or others identified in the reports as family members. Only about 74 of the protests included professional, treatment personnel, or caregivers, and smaller numbers included teachers and children without disabilities (who were usually either siblings or fellow students).

Table 6 shows the participation of internal and external allies in protests across the decades. All decades except the 1990s had external allies in fewer than 12% of the protests in that decade. The decade of the 1990s saw the highest proportion (232 or about 30% of the protests) with external allies. The two decades with the highest participation of internal allies were the 1980s (63%) and the 1990s (almost 69%), but even in the partial 2010 decade and in the decade of the 1970s a majority (more than 51%) of the protests had internal allies involved.[9] Only the first decade of new century saw a substantially lower involvement of internal allies. Taken together, the decade of the 1990s had the

Table 5. Numbers of Individual Protesters, by Type[a].

Type of Individual Protesters	N
Adults without disabilities	375
Children without disabilities	21
Parents	295
Teachers	33
Professional or treatment personnel	74

[a]These are separate variables, so each protest could have more than one type of individual ally. Therefore, these numbers cannot be totaled to indicate numbers of protests.

Table 6. Percentages of Ally Organizations by Decade and Type[a].

Decade	External Allies	Internal Allies
1970–1979 (N = 72)	8.3% (6)	51.4% (37)
1980–1989 (N = 234)	8.1 (19)	63.2 (148)
1990–1999 (N = 765)	30.3 (232)	68.3 (523)
2000–2009 (N = 359)	9.4 (34)	25.1 (90)
2010–2016 (N = 276)	11.6 (32)	51.8 (141)

[a]Numbers differ from those on other tables because of missing dates for some protests.

largest participation of either internal or external allies, with almost 99% of the protests having one or more of both types of allies participating.

Table 7 shows changes in individual participant types by decade. Parents and family members participated in the largest proportion of protests (28%) during the 1990s and the smallest percentages (6% and 9%) in the 2000s and 2010s, respectively. (These differences by decade were statistically significant.) Participation rates for professionals and for teachers were very low in all decades and showed only small and nonsignificant differences by decade. Participation by teachers peaked at about 4% of protests in the 1970s, and participation by treatment personnel ranged between about 2% and 6%, with the largest number being seen in the 1980s.

DISCUSSION

The results presented here suggest two topics which need more attention. The first is that of how allies in disability protests compare to those in protests in other social movements, both in relative proportions and in the distinction between internal allies and external allies. The second question relates to changes over time in the presence and types of allies.

Table 7. Percentages of Protests with Individual Ally Protesters, by Type and Decade[b].

Decade	Parents	Teachers	Prof/Carers
1970–1979	16.7%	4.2%	5.6%
1980–1989	10.3	1.3	6.0
1990–1999	28.1	2.4	4.8
2000–2009	5.8	1.4	3.3
2010–2016	8.9	1.6	2.7
Total			
Chi square[a]	115.5 (sig < 0.000)	3.8 ns	4.8 ns

[a]For differences between decades
[b]Percentages are not additive.

Comparisons with Other Social Movements

There are two types of comparisons which researchers might want to make between the organizational allies of different social movement. One relates to how many protests include organizations, and the other relates to the variety of organizations involved as well as their overall frequency of participation.

In order to evaluate how disability protests compare to those of other social movements, we have to consider one of the frequent criticisms of event history analysis. A number of scholars (e.g., McCarthy, McPhail, & Smith, 1996; Mueller, 1997; Van Driel & Richardson, 1988) suggested that more disruptive protests would be more likely than less disruptive protests to be reported by news and other media and so would underestimate the numbers of less disruptive protests. However, whether a protest is reported in the media is a less relevant methodological issue here than exactly what was reported. Media reports of protests vary extensively. Whether allies are mentioned in the coverage depends upon if those individuals or organizations have publicized their presence or have taken pains to make that information known. Allied groups which did not have signs, did not introduce themselves to reporters, or did not otherwise make themselves visible might not have been identified in news reports and so were not, for purposes of this chapter, "there." Also, if the reporters were protesters themselves, as they might have been if the reports came from organizational websites, they might not have wanted to publicize other allies so as to enhance the reputation of their own organization.

Overall, over 70% of the 1716 protests in this database included the presence of one or more internal or external organizational allies, without considering the presence of individual allies. It is somewhat difficult to evaluate this number because so much social movements research is done within one or a few social movement organizations and so is not likely to indicate the presence or frequency of participation of other organizations. Perhaps this number is low, given the assumption by many social moment theorists of the centrality of organizational allies in social movement activities – but that assumption is also driven by the within-organizational research methodologies which characterize a large amount of social movements research.[10]

The current results show smaller numbers of disability protests having external allies than internal allies, about 33%–66%. How might this compare to other social movements? It is possible that the presence of external allies is smaller among disability protests than it might be in other social movements because disability protests are somewhat isolated from potential external ally groups from other social movements. This may be true even though the issues of some of these groups would seem to have a large amount of overlap with disability protest issues, and therefore the groups ought to share some of the goals of the disability movement. There are several reasons why this isolation might be the case.

For one thing, even though disability as a protest issue is not new in the United States, with protests having occurred as early as the late 1800s (Barnartt, 2008), scholarly recognition of disability protests remains low. The literature about social movements rarely acknowledges disability protests: They are almost never included in collections of articles about social movements or referred to in theoretical discussions about movement processes or issues. Nor have acknowledgments about overlaps with disability issues been common in social movements' own publications.[11] One exception was some discussions and a few publications about the overlap between disabled women's and lesbian women's issues in the late 1970s and early 1980s in the women's movement (Corbman, 2018), although these discussions did not lead to collective actions. Otherwise, analyses within and about the movement tended to ignore disability and disabled women until fairly recently (Arenas-Conejo, 2013).[12] Similarly, the large empirical overlap between aging and disability has not led to coalitions between disability organizations and seniors' groups or even to consensus on what the issues are.

The second reason why external allies may be less frequently seen in disability protests may relate to the stigmatized condition which disability remains, despite social and legal changes such as the passage of the Americans with Disabilities Act. Perhaps this was the cause of the outright refusal by civil rights activists Rosa Parks and Jesse Jackson to join in, or even support, a disability-related bus protest in Detroit in 1986 (Johnson, 1997; Shapiro, 1993, p. 128). While race is also stigmatized category, disability may be more so. Erkulwater (2018, p. 368) attributes her refusal to Rosa Parks "not wanting to embarrass the black political establishment of her hometown..." which suggests that a fear of the increased stigma might weaken the symbolic power of the bus protest if the civil rights movement shared it with other groups but particularly with disabled people.

Even though there seems to be less overlap between disability protests and those of other social movements, it is likely that the disability movement could not have succeeded even as well as it has without the extension of the frame of civil rights to disability which occurred as part of the passage of the Americans with Disabilities Act in 1990 (Altman & Barnartt, 1993). However, this frame extension occurred with less overlap of personnel than there was, for example, in the extension of the frame of civil rights to the feminist movement, since that movement included a number of women who had also been early participants in the civil rights movement. Activists with disabilities were less able to participate in protests or organizations in the civil rights or feminist movements because of physical or other barriers, and the earlier, more service-oriented disability organizations were completely separate from organizations in those movements anyway. This lack of overlapping personnel, with its resultant lessening of the possibility of overlapping networks as well as frame extensions, is another reason why disability protests seem to remain relatively isolated from external allies.

There were some "conscience constituents" (Goffman, 1963) among the external organizational allies and individual allies who participated in protests, although there did not seem to be many. This was different from, for example, the Black civil rights movement, which, especially during "Freedom Summer," had recruited white college students and other conscience constituent groups (McAdam, 2003, p. 56).

Later in the civil rights movement and the feminist movement, negative identities or motivations began to be attributed to whites and males, respectively, so they became less welcome in their respective social movement actions. In the disability movement, also, negative attributions to people who are "not deaf enough" (Christiansen, 2010) or "not disabled enough" may have produced internal pressure to keep some potential external allies out, in addition to external stigma against people with disabilities which kept potential conscience constituents away from disability protests.

Finally, although Tarrow (1998, p. 87) emphasizes the ways in which allies help a social movement by expanding the political opportunity structure, he also notes that allies or coalitions can have both positive and negative consequences for protesting groups. On the one hand, a larger protesting group can be more disruptive and so attract more attention. Allies can mobilize more constituencies as well as imply more political power than a protest which appears to represent only one group or point of view. McAdam (1982, pp. 154–155) also argued that, although allied organizations in the civil rights movement competed for resources and support, they also contributed "vitality and diversity" to the civil rights movement. On the other hand, a protesting group may not want to weaken or dilute its issue by adding other aspects or nuances to it, and there may be competition for resources and recognition among possible ally organizations (McAdam, 1982, p. 168; Meyer, 2003). Finally, as can be seen in protests occurring across the United States as this chapter is written, protest allies can hijack a protest "for their own agenda," with extremely negative consequences for the protest. [13] So the line between the more helpful and the less helpful presence of allies in a protest may be more blurry than perhaps it is in other situations such as money raising or the mobilization of supporters.

Changes over Time

McAdam's (1982, p. 147) presentation of data about organizational change over time shows the diminution of participation in the Civil Rights Movement by church-related allies and the concomitant increase in participation of what he calls "formal movement organizations" from the 1955–60 period to the 1961–1965 period. He also paints a picture of a social movement with an extremely concentrated core of four formal organizations which over time were more likely to act as allies in events even though they were at odds over issues and resources (1982, p. 156).

The clearest change in allies in disability protests over the years has been changes in the types of internal organizational allies. Organizations in the 1970s decade were basically single or multiple impairment, multiple issue organizations. The establishment of ADAPT and other multiple impairment, single issue organizations, whose expressed purpose was activism, fueled both the large increase in numbers of protests and the increasing participation of allies in protests which were seen in the 1980s and 1990s.

The early disability-related ally organizations were primarily service organizations which were likely to have been identified, for tax purposes, as 501C3 organizations. Such organizations "may not be an **action organization**, i.e., may not attempt to influence legislation as a substantial part of its activities..." (Internal Revenue Service, n.d.). In other words, they are not supposed to become involved in protests. TASH is one example of a 501C3 organization which calls itself an advocacy organization, not an activist organization. This tax status helps explain the relatively lower participation of internal organizational allies during the decade before the newer, activist organizations such as ADAPT emerged.

It is clear that the advent of the multiple impairment, single issue organizations spurred the growth of disability protests in general. It is not clear, however, how the growth of these organizations related to the increase in levels of external ally participation. McAdam (1982, pp. 121–122) suggests that increases in ally participation in the Civil Rights movement was a result, rather than a cause, of increased protest activity. The higher levels of external ally participation in the disability protests in the 1980s and, especially, the 1990s support that notion. Those levels may also have been a consequence of successes which have been attributed to some of the earlier disability protests (Altman & Barnartt, 1993). But, also, during the first two decades of disability protests, many protest demands were related to issues of civil rights and overlapped with demands made by other minority groups.[14] One might have predicted that the presence of external allies who shared those issues would have been higher in those decades before the ADA was passed in 1990 and dealt with some of those issues. During the 1990s, ADA enforcement demands in protests were quite common, but external allies who shared the focus on rights in general would have been less likely to be allies in protests over disability-specific issues such as whether Greyhound buses were violating the ADA. Thus, external ally presence in disability protests might have been expected either to stay at the same level or to decrease, instead of to increase to its highest level. More research on this question is clearly called for.

Changes in the participation of at least one category of individual allies – parents – across the time period are more difficult to explain. There were a number of successes won by parents' groups, including the passage of PL 94–142 (originally called the Education for all Handicapped Children Act, now called IDEA or the Individuals with Disabilities Education Act). Some sociological theories (e.g., Smelser, 1962; Westhaus, 1972) might suggest that the successes won by the organized parents' groups would lead to the cessation of parents' individual protest involvement. However, some parents had problems with that success and others (Carey, Block, & Scotch, 2020); their individual participation in subsequent protests may have reflected that dissatisfaction, despite the overall successes of the organized parents' movement.

CONCLUSION

More work on the conceptualization of allies as well as research on the trajectory of protests and allied groups across the history of disability protests would seem to be called for. In a recent obituary for Marca Bristo, who was a strong disability movement advocate and participant, Judy Heumann, also an early disability activist and protest leader, was quoted as saying, "She (Marca) recognized that in order to effect change that would have an impact … she needed to be working in coalitions" (Obituary Brisco, 2019). There is no question that she was correct, but what exactly constitutes an ally or a coalition within the framework of social movement activities? Is a group marching with another group an ally simply by its presence? To what degree should protesters actually share that social movement's demands and goals? Or does it matter, because it is all a "numbers game?" What if the co-participant ally groups actually see the ultimate goals as being different? This seems quite likely to have happened. The demand for equal rights in employment provides an example. If one group is demanding equal opportunity in jobs wants completely "blind" hiring for jobs, while another demands recognition that sometimes equal opportunity is not exactly the same for all groups, they may be allied in a protest for the sake of numbers (or some other reason), but are they truly allies?

Furthermore, what do allied groups actually do? These data can only tell us that the allied groups participated in a protest. Did they march, carry signs and placards, or hand out information? Were they involved in planning or recruiting? Did they provide speakers? Or did they, as in a recently described AIDS protest from 1990, form a human snake and run through the main protesting crowd setting off colored smoke bombs (Bernard, 2020)!

Such questions suggest that the concept of allyship within the context of social movements needs to become more developed and nuanced. Because the social movements literature, with only a few exceptions, has not really grappled with questions related to coalitions and allies, this chapter raises questions for future research regarding allies in both the disability movement and other social movements. Such research needs to be both qualitative and quantitative. Additionally, because of the amorphous natures both of social movements and of allyship, in order to get a good picture of how allies function at any point in time in a movement, let alone over the longer periods of time during which a social movement may exist, longitudinal data across multiple actions and actors are necessary.

NOTES

1. Social movements conduct contentious, non-normative actions, which is how they differ from traditional political processes, although they may also work "within the system." In the American context, non-normative political actions include tactics such as marches, sit-ins, takeovers, or strikes, while normative actions include lobbying, filing lawsuits, or conducting letter-writing campaigns. In other cultural contexts, however, different types of actions may be viewed as protests. These can include building houses in Vietnam or starting disability-run attendant-care programs in Japan (Barnartt, 2010). Also, even tactics such as voter registration drives, which fall into the category of politics as usual in the United States, may be disruptive in some American cultural or political contexts, such as in the deep South during the Civil Rights movement.

2. There are, however, those who see such people as being in a different category from protesters because they are not risking anything and so are not "accomplices" but are "missionary allies" perhaps motivates by guilt (Indigenous Action, 2014).

3. However, there is an argument among scholars about whether internal or external allies are more important in the genesis of a social movement (McAdam, 1982).

4. This chapter avoids the question of whether there is one disability movement or several. Pfeiffer (1988), for example, identified a disability rights movement and a movement for disability services. Others have identified a separate independent living movement, a Psychiatric Survivors Movement, among others. However, most of the protests related to these movements are subsumed under this database, and some were analyzed separately (Barnartt & Scotch, 2001).

5. Thus, a protest conducted by a person with disabilities, such as Stephen Hawking, on a topic not specifically related to disability, such as war in Iraq, would not be included. Protests related to health conditions such as obesity, AIDS, cancer, or other conditions were included if the issue was related to disability rights, services, portrayals, or other issues of interest to the disability community (Barnartt & Scotch, 2001).

6. The organizations are not always run by people with disabilities. Some organizations are "for" people with disabilities, while others are organizations "of" people with disabilities. If that became an issue in a protest, it was coded as a demand being made in the protest and is not discussed here.

7. These data collection began before groups representing people with some types of impairments, such as autism and learning disabilities, began developing advocacy stances or demands and identifying themselves in protests.

8. Its acronym originally stood for Americans Disabled for Public Transit but was later renamed Americans Disabled for Attendant Programs Today. Barnartt (2012) presented a more in-depth discussion of ADAPT's changing and complicated role in disability protests.

9. However, there were many fewer protests in the 1980s than in any other decade.

10. This does raise a question about how the disability protests which did include recognized allies differ from those which did not – a question which would be worth further research.

11. It is in fact that case that some issues in, for example, the civil rights movement, are actually different legally than those with the same name for the disability movement (Barnartt & Seelman, 1988).

12. It is ironic that the reverse is also true. Erkulwater (2018) notes "the paucity of scholarly attention to the black disability experience in disability studies" and that disability activism focuses on "the experiences and achievements of whites." In general, these problems reflect the lack of focus on intersectionality in social movements, even though the added mobilization potential of coordinating social movements would seem to favor coalitions more than any possible competition for resources or support would favor their separation.

13. Thus, an activist participating in the protests in Denver said he and others were asking some of those apparently participating as allies "not to escalate the protests (by using violence) on our behalf" (Tay Anderson on PBS Newshour, June 1, 2020).

14. However, while some might argue that civil rights are rights for all people, Burgdorf (1983) argued that this is not the case – and he argued that this was acceptable, a position which was controversial at the time and remains so.

REFERENCES

Altman, B., & Barnartt, S. (1993). Moral entrepreneurship and the passage of the ADA. *Journal of Disability Policy Studies*, *4*(1), 21–40.

Andrews, K. T. (2002). Creating social change: Lessons from the civil rights movement. In D. Meyer, N. Whittier, & B. Robnett (Eds.), *Social movements: Identity, culture and the state* (pp. 105–117). New York, NY: Oxford University Press.

Arenas-Conejo, M. (2013). At the intersection of feminist and disability rights movements: From equality in difference to human diversity claims. In S. Barnartt & B. Altman (Eds.), *Research in social science and disability* (Vol. 7, pp. 23–46). Bingley: Emerald Publishing Limited.

Asch, A. (2000). Why I haven't changed my mind about prenatal diagnosis: Reflections and refinements. In E. Parens & A. Asch (Eds.), *Prenatal testing and disability rights* (pp. 234–258). Washington, DC: Georgetown University Press.

Asch, A. (2005). Recognizing death while affirming life: Can end of life reform uphold a disabled person's interest in continued life? *Hastings Center Report*, *35*(Nov-Dec), S31–S36.

Barnartt, S. (1996). Disability culture or disability consciousness. *Journal of Disability Policy Studies*, *7*(2), 1–17.

Barnartt, S. (1997). The effect of success on social movement development: The case of the disability movement in the US. Presented at The International Sociological Association RC 48 First Regional Conference on Social Movements. Tel Aviv, Israel.

Barnartt, S. (2007). Assisted suicide protests in the disability and right-to life movements: A comparison of the trajectories of issue emergence and convergence. In T. Lillie & J. WerthJr (Eds.), *End of life issues and people with disabilities* (pp. 156–166). Austin, TX: PRO-ED, Inc.

Barnartt, S. (2008). *Protest. Encyclopedia of disability history*. New York, NY: Facts on File.

Barnartt, S. (2010). The globalization of disability protests, 1970–2005: Pushing the limits of cross-cultural research? *Comparative Sociology*, *9*, 222–240.

Barnartt, S. (2012). Americans disabled for public Transit. In L. Dumenil (Ed.), *Oxford encyclopedia of American social history* (Vol. 1, pp. 36-37). New York, NY: Oxford University Press.

Barnartt, S., & Scotch, R. (2001). *Disability protests: Contentious politics 1970- 1999*. Washington, DC: Gallaudet University Press.

Barnartt, S., & Seelman, K. (1988). A comparison of federal laws toward disabled & racial/ethnic groups in the USA. *Disability, Handicap & Society*, *3*(1), 37–48.

Bernard, D. (2020, May 24). Three decades before coronavirus, Anthony Fauci took heat from AIDS protesters. *Washington Post*, C5.

Burgdorf, R. (1983). *The legal rights of handicapped persons*. Towson, MD: Paul Brookes Publishing Co.

Carey, A., Block, P., & Scotch, R. (2019). Sometimes allies: Parent-led disability organizations and social movements. *Disability Studies Quarterly*, *39*(1).

Carey, A., Block, P., & Scotch, R. (2020). *Allies and obstacles: Disability activism and parents of children with disabilities*. Philadelphia, PA: Temple University Press.

Christiansen, J. (2010). *Reflections: My life in the deaf and hearing worlds*. Washington, DC: Gallaudet University Press.

Christiansen, J. B., & Barnartt, S. N. (1995). *Deaf president now: The 1988 revolution at Gallaudet University*. Washington, DC: Gallaudet University Press.

Corbman, R. (2018). Remediating disability activism in the lesbian feminist archive. *Continuum: Journal of Media & Cultural Studies*, *32*(1), 18–28.

Erkulwater, J. (2018). How the nation's largest minority became white: Race politics and the disability rights movement 1970-1980. *Journal of Policy History*, *30*(2), 367–399.

Ferree, M. M., & Hess, B. B. (1994). *Controversy and coalition: The new feminist movement across three decades of change*. (Revised edition). New York, NY: Twayne Publishers.

Finnegan, W. (2003). Affinity groups and the movement against corporate globalization. In J. Goodwin & J. M. Jasper (Eds.), *The social movements reader: Cases and concepts* (pp. 210–218). Malden, MA: Blackwell Publishers.

Goffman, E. (1963). *Stigma*. Englewood Cliffs, NJ: Prentice-Hall.

Halley, M. (2018). Interpreting dissent: Narratives about American Sign Language-English interpreting for the deaf president now protest. Gallaudet University. Unpublished Dissertation.

Indigenous Action. (2014, May 4). Accomplices not allies: Abolishing the ally industrial complex. Retrieved from http://www.indigenousaction.org/accomplices-not-allies-abolishing-the-ally-industrial-complex

Internal Revenue Service. (n.d.). Exemption requirements – 501 (3) (c) organizations. Retrieved from https://www.irs.gov/charities-non-profits/charitable-organizations/exemption-requirements-501c3-organizations

Johnson, M. (1997). Progressives and disability rights: They just don't get it. *Ragged Edge*, (Nov/Dec), pp. 16–18.

Longmore, P. (1997). Political movements of people with disabilities: The league of the physically handicapped, 1935 - 1938. *Disability Studies Quarterly*, *17*(2), 94–98.

McAdam, D. (1982). *Political process and the development of black insurgency, 1930 - 1970*. Chicago, IL: University of Chicago Press.

McAdam, D. (2003). Recruits to civil rights activism. In J. Goodwin & J. M. Jasper (Eds.), *The social movements reader: Cases and concepts* (pp. 55–63). Malden, MA: Blackwell Publishers.

McCarthy, J., McPhail, C., & Smith, J. (1996). Images of protest: Dimensions of selection bias in media coverage of Washington demonstrations, 1982 and 1991. *American Sociological Review*, *61*(3), 478–499.

Meyer, D. (2003). The "smothering" allies of the nuclear freeze movement. In J. Goodwin & J. M. Jasper (Eds.), *The social movements reader: Cases and concepts* (pp. 261–267). Malden, MA: Blackwell Publishers.

Morris, A. (1984). *The origins of the civil rights movement: Black communities organizing for change*. New York, NY: Free Press.

Mueller, C. (1997). International press coverage of East German protest events, 1989. *American Sociological Review*, *62*(October), 820–832.

Obituary for Brisco, M. (2019, September 15). *Washington Post*, C7.

Olzak, S. (1989). Analysis of events in the study of collective action. *Annual Review of Sociology*, *15*, 119–141.

Pfeiffer, D. (1988). Divisions in the disability community. *Disability Studies Quarterly*, *8*(2), 1–3.

Piven, F. F., & Cloward, R. (1979). *Poor people's movements: Why they succeed, How they fail*. New York, NY: Random House.

Shapiro, J. (1993). *No pity: People with disabilities forging a new civil rights movement*. New York, NY: Times Books.

Smelser, N. (1962). *Theory of collective behavior*. New York, NY: Free Press.

Snow, D. A., & Benford, R. D. (1992). Master frames and cycles of protest. In A. D. Morris & C. M. Mueller (Eds.), *Frontiers in social movement theory* (pp. 133–155). New Haven: Yale University Press.

Snow, D. A., Rochford, E. B., Jr, Worder, S. K., & Benford, R. D. (1986). Frame alignment processes, micromobilization and movement participation. *American Sociological Review*, *51*(August), 464–481.

Strang, D., & Soule, S. (1998). Diffusion in organizations and social movements: From hybrid corn to poison pills. *Annual Review of Sociology*, 265–290.

Tarrow, S. (1996). Social movements in contentious politics: A review article. *American Political Science Review*, *90*(4), 874–883.

Tarrow, S. (1998). *Power in movement: Social movements and contentious politics*. (2nd ed.). New York, NY: Cambridge University Press.

Van Driel, B., & Richardson, J. T. (1988). Print media coverage of new religious movements: A longitudinal study. *Journal of Communications*, *38*(3), 37–61.

Westhaus, K. (1972). *Society's shadow: Studies in the sociology of countercultures*. Toronto, ON: McGraw-Hill Ryerson Ltd.

Whittier, N. (1997). Political generations, micro-cohorts, and the transformation of social movements. *American Sociological Review*, *62*(October), 760–778.

Young, J. (1998, April). The President's Committee on the Handicapped and the origins of cross-disability organizing. Presented at the Society for Disability Studies Meeting, Oakland, CA.

PART II

RELATIONAL DYNAMICS OF ALLIANCE BUILDING

Chapter 6

NOTHING ABOUT "US" WITHOUT WHOM? (RE)COGNIZING ALLIANCE BETWEEN DISABLED PEOPLE AND CARE WORKERS IN DIRECT-FUNDED ATTENDANT SERVICES

Erika Katzman

ABSTRACT

Purpose: *This chapter problematizes the philosophical origins of direct funding models in a normative conception of independence that ignores and obscures the fundamentally relational nature of care work.*

Approach: *The study adopts a reflexive ethnographic methodological approach. In-depth, semistructured interviews were conducted with 19 participants variously involved with direct-funded attendant services (disabled "self-managers," "attendant" employees, other members of self-managers' support networks, and program staff). Additional data sources included the author's reflexive journaling and publicly available policy and program materials. The present analysis interrogated the impact of systemic constraints (i.e., limited funding) on the organization and management of attendant services.*

Findings: *The data illuminate how systemic constraints draw the interests of self-managers and attendants into tension, despite the affective relationality of the work they do together. The findings present four strategies self-managers adopt to maximize support hours, including: splitting shifts, strategic hiring, dynamic resource management, and supplementing remuneration. These findings suggest it is not vulnerability to each other that represents an ongoing*

Disability Alliances and Allies
Research in Social Science and Disability, Volume 12, 133–153

ISSN: 1479-3547/doi:10.1108/S1479-354720200000012010

concern for self-managers and attendants, so much as exploitation by a system that capitalizes on the oppression of both groups.

Implication/ Value: *Disabled people and care workers have been and continue to be constructed as opposing interest groups. However, there is great potential in disabled people and care workers joining a united front to lobby for their common, often interrelated interests. Direct funding models are an important evolution of support services, but where they fail to attend to the relational nature of care work, we must continue to pursue more inclusive solutions.*

Keywords: Disability; direct funding; direct payments; attendant care; interdependence; affective relationality

> People who are said to need caring for are assumed to be unable to exert choice and control. One cannot, therefore, have care and empowerment, for it is the ideology and the practice of caring which has led to the perception of disabled people as powerless (Morris, 1997, p. 54).

> [...] the growth in power of one group implicitly means that power is being redistributed and there are other groups who are – or should be – losing ground. [...] I shall argue that there are other groups of care deliverers, particularly those who actually deliver "hands-on" care, who are also relatively powerless, and that their position in a situation of redistributed power has also to be considered (Ungerson, 1997, p. 46).

> [A]s they spend most of their waking hours together, they start acknowledging each other's vulnerable circumstances or at times co-experiencing the vulnerable moments together, which causes many to start feeling sympathy for their care partners and building a sense of solidarity together: vulnerability infused with intimacy (Nishida, 2016, p. 154).

Direct-funded attendant services deliver cash grants that enable disabled people to hire support staff. The model is distinct from conventional models which entrust community agencies to organize and manage state-funded support services on behalf of disabled people. Direct funding came about in response to the activist efforts of Independent Living Movements, which argued that disabled people have a right "to live in their chosen communities, rather than warehoused in an asylum or institution" (Lord, 2010, p. 16). Resisting a conventional medical or rehabilitation conception of independence as physical ability to act without supports, the Independent Living Movements articulated a renewed definition of independence as "decisional autonomy" (Shakespeare, 2014, p. 180), emphasizing individual self-determination, service user direction, and control of resources at the community level (DeJong, 1983/2001; Lord, 2010). Direct funding models are widely recognized to empower disabled people by repositioning passive *receivers* of personal support services as active (self-)*managers* (Lord, 2010; Yoshida, Willi, Parker, & Locker, 2004).

Although a narrative of praise has dominated activist and scholarly conversations about direct-funded attendant services, the model has been met with some resistance and critique. Whereas public support for direct funding owes at least in part to claims to cost-effectiveness (Slasberg & Beresford, 2015), several studies observe a tendency for market logic to trump the model's social justice orientation (Mladenov, Owens, & Cribb, 2015; Pearson, 2000; Pearson et al., 2005;

Spandler, 2004). This literature highlights the potential for direct funding models to marketize, individualize, and privatize social support services, contributing to the erosion of social service infrastructure (Hande & Kelly, 2015; Mladenov et al., 2015; Scourfield, 2005, 2007). Others have questioned the ethical implications of conditioning access to the benefits of direct funding on contributions of labor, and of cost-savings accrued at the expense of labor contributed by disabled people and their support networks (Katzman & Kinsella, 2018; Katzman, Kinsella, & Polzer, 2019). A significant literature has traced issues with remuneration and protections for attendants (Church, Diamond, & Voronka, 2004; Cranford, 2005; Leece, 2010; Marfisi, 2002; Riddell et al., 2005; Scourfield, 2005; Spandler, 2004; Ungerson, 1997), a predominantly feminized and racialized workforce (Christensen, 2012; Kelly, 2016; Leece, 2004, 2010; Scourfield, 2005; Spandler, 2004). Complicating praise for direct funding models, these critiques suggest that direct funding may at once empower and oppress disabled people and their support networks.

Through qualitative data from a recent study, this chapter will illustrate practical tensions between the interests of disabled "self-managers" and their "attendant" employees that arise in the everyday organization and management of direct funding in one program in Ontario, Canada. The data showcase tensions arising primarily from systemic constraints upon the resources that are available to self-managers. This, I will argue, is a problem that affects and should concern self-managers and attendants *together*, and one that would be best addressed by disabled people and care workers *together*. Where disabled people and care workers have been and continue to be constructed as opposing interest groups, there is great potential in disabled people and care workers joining a united front to lobby for their common, often interrelated interests. This chapter concludes with a discussion of the political power and potential in building formal alliances between disabled people and care workers.

DIRECT FUNDING IN ONTARIO, CANADA: SELF-MANAGED ATTENDANT SERVICES

Independent Living Movements began to develop in the 1960s in the United States (DeJong, 1983/2001) and the United Kingdom (Morris, 1997) as

> ...disabled people who were incarcerated in residential homes started to agitate for more control over their lives and to articulate a social theory (the social model of disability) to support what became a campaign for civil rights (Morris, 1997, p. 57).

The movement reached Canada in the 1980s, and over the next decade, direct funding programs began to develop across the country (Lord, 2010).

In 1994, extensive efforts on the part of a local community of service users who demanded an alternative to conventional agency-managed attendant services instigated the launch of the Ontario "Self-Managed Attendant Services" program (Yoshida et al., 2004). Demand for the Ontario program has grown steadily since its inception. Initially funding 100 self-managers, the program had 720 participants in

2006 and over 300 people on a waiting list (Spalding, Watkins, & Williams, 2006). In 2014, the province announced it would expand the program, with the goal of delivering funding to 1,000 self-managers by 2016 (OMHLTC, 2014). In 2017, there were 900 self-managers using direct funding in Ontario (CILT, 2017). To contextualize these numbers in relation to other service delivery models in the province, "the number of people using Direct Funding in Ontario makes up less than 1 percent of long-term care service users and roughly 11.6 percent of attendant services users" (Kelly, 2016, p. 8).

The Ontario program is the largest direct funding program in Canada (Kelly, 2016) and is unique in that it was designed and continues to be managed "mainly by consumers working in partnership with the Ontario Government" (Parker, Self, & Willi, 2000, p. 3). The program is funded by the Ontario Ministry of Health, which transfers funding to the largely consumer-run Centre for Independent Living in Toronto (CILT). CILT administers the program, in collaboration with independent living centers around the province. CILT has historically been involved with lobbying for direct funding (Yoshida et al., 2004); however, as a nonprofit organization with charitable status, their government funding stipulates that they may not engage in political activity, such as collective advocacy (Kelly, 2016).

Eligibility for the program is outlined in provincial policy, which characterizes a self-manager as someone who "understands the nature of his or her disability and its impact on his or her *[sic]*[1] ability to carry out the essential activities of daily living" (MCSS, 1994, para. 2.2.f);

> ...is aware of the type of attendant services he or she requires, the times at which he or she requires the attendant services, the number of hours of attendant services he or she requires and the manner in which the attendant services should be provided (para. 2.2.g);

and "is capable of evaluating the attendant services he or she would receive and of communicating his or her evaluation to others" (para. 2.2.m). Applicants must be at least 16 years old and have stable attendant support needs related to a permanent physical disability. The application process includes a self-evaluation and a peer evaluation to determine eligibility for a number of funded support hours, up to 7 hours per day (212 hours per month).

As self-managers, disabled people accept full responsibility to recruit, hire, train, schedule, manage, fire (if necessary), and pay attendants. This structure is intended to address power differentials between disabled people and their attendants; as Kelly (2014) explains, "attendants have a form of physical power over self-managers and self-managers counter this with the power associated with making decisions and acting as an employer" (p. 134). Parker et al. (2000) acknowledge that this model grants "sole authority" (p. 15) to self-managers but emphasize evidence that indicates attendants are generally happy with the arrangement, citing benefits such as flexibility, informality, and better working relationships with the people they support.

That attendants working in direct funding arrangements enjoy their jobs and describe positive relationships with their employers should not, however, be taken to mean that direct funding creates fair working conditions for attendants. As the

Ontario direct funding program developed, organized labor contingents raised concern about

> ...the rights of the employee: employees working without a contract; not having wage parity, having no direct supervisor to lodge concerns; overall working environment safety and abuse of employees by the disabled employers (Yoshida et al., 2004, p. 196).

Proponents of direct funding have argued that, as "vulnerable employers," self-managers are unlikely to abuse the people they rely on for vital supports (Parker et al., 2000; Yoshida et al., 2004). Yet, as a predominantly feminized, racialized, and low-income workforce, attendants too often represent vulnerable groups (Cranford, 2005). As subsequent sections of this chapter will demonstrate, it is not vulnerability to each other that represents an ongoing concern for self-managers and attendants, so much as exploitation by a system that capitalizes on the oppression of both groups.

INDEPENDENT LIVING: A PENDULUM SWUNG TOO FAR?

The quintessential manifestation of Independent Living Movements, direct funding models enact a shift that is both structural and discursive, subverting a pervasive "ideology of caring" (Morris, 1997, p. 54) that has long constructed disabled people as dependent upon families and social welfare systems, entrusting "professionals" to manage state-funded supports. It is a core contention of Independent Living Movements that disabled people possess expert knowledge of their needs, that support needs are not inherently medical in nature, and that physical impairment need not constitute a barrier to one's ability to ensure one's own needs are met (Yoshida et al., 2004). Following these principles, direct funding models intentionally wrench control over the organization and management of services away from professionals, restoring choice and flexibility through "consumer control" (Yoshida et al., 2004). Direct funding models recognize not just the capability, but also the right of disabled people to determine when, how, and with whom support services will take place.

The structure of direct funding models is practical, in that it places self-manager-employers in direct control over attendant-employees, empowering disabled people to teach attendants how to provide support in a way that is customized to their own preferences and needs. There is also discursive significance in the inversion of conventional caregiving relationships that are undeniably power-laden (Kelly, 2010; Morris, 1997), and in reframing paternalistic care as "taking responsibility for" (Morris, 1997, p. 54) in strictly physical terms. At the same time, however, these reframings have often relied upon constructions of the attendant role as menial and unskilled, a construction with implications for the physical, emotional, and material well-being of attendants (Kelly, 2016; Leece & Peace, 2010; Marfisi, 2002) that is further compounded by failures to acknowledge attendants as "vulnerable employees." As Ungerson (1997) has argued,

> ...it is important to unpack the notion of "empowerment" in community care so that the position of those who provide "hands-on" care is scrutinised alongside the empowerment of "users" of care (p. 45).

Yet, where innovation of and advocacy for direct funding has been led by and for disabled people, the interests of "carers" have often been overlooked.

Tensions between feminist and "malestream" disability perspectives are long-standing and well documented (see, for example, Kelly, 2014; Kröger, 2009; Mauldin, 2017). Activists and scholars have critiqued the "white-dominated, single-issue, civil rights approach" (Piepzna-Samarasinha, 2018, p. 40) characteristic of disability rights and Independent Living Movements, pointing out limitations of disability activism that fails to address disability experiences shaped by gender, sexuality, race, class, status, and other intersectional identities. Independent Living Movements, in particular, placed significant emphasis on the pursuit of a normative, individualist independence (Fritsch, 2010; Hughes, McKie, Hopkins, & Watson, 2005) and a rejection of intimate and embodied care practices in favor of a supposedly disembodied and detached "help" or "assistance" (Shakespeare, 2006; Watson, McKie, Hughes, Hopkins, & Gregory, 2004).

With their emphasis on independence, Independent Living Movements reinforce "repressive systems that exclude disabled people" (Gibson, 2006, p. 190); they reify a normative, individualist notion of societal participation, obfuscating and devaluing alternative ways of being in the world. Specifically, discourses of independence belie the interdependent relationships that sustain not only direct funding models (Fritsch, 2010; Hughes et al., 2005; Yoshida et al., 2004), but all human life (Kittay, 1999; Reindal, 1999). With full regard for the successes, achievements, and value of the Independent Living Movements, it is important to recognize how these movements reproduce binary conceptions of dependence and independence, as well as carer and cared-for roles, and the ways in which these dichotomies uphold systems that oppress both disabled people and care workers. In subsequent sections, I will argue that the redistribution of power in direct funding models overcorrects the historical problem of prioritizing institutional interests ahead of individual needs and preferences. Where direct funding models center the needs and preferences of disabled people, we must begin to consider the shared interests and collective needs of disabled people and care workers *together*.

METHOD

The findings presented in this chapter are from a reflexive ethnographic study of direct-funded attendant services. The study focused on one direct funding program in Ontario, Canada. The primary focus of the study was to understand the work self-managers and their support networks do to organize and manage attendant services. The study drew on theories of work developed in disability studies (Abberley, 2002; Barnes & Roulstone, 2005; Church, Frazee, Panitch, Luciani, & Bowman, 2007; Kittay, 1999) and critical feminist scholarship (DeVault, 2014; Glazer, 1993; Hochschild, 1983; Lanoix, 2013; Smith, 2002) to theorize tasks and activities performed in the service of direct funding as "work."

A key finding of the overarching study was that positive outcomes of direct funding resulted from the efforts of self-managers and their support networks, work that was frequently relational (Katzman et al., 2019), most often invisible (Katzman & Kinsella, 2018), and that contributed to the achievement of positive outcomes by mitigating systemic constraints. The analysis presented here illuminates how systemic constraints draw the interests of self-managers and attendants into tension, despite the vital relationality of the work they do together.

A critically reflexive methodological approach was sought to prioritize ongoing interrogation of operations of power in the research process, itself a social relationship imbued with power (Kinsella & Whiteford, 2009). Reflexive ethnography (Denzin, 2003; Ellis & Bochner, 2003; Lather, 2001a, 2001b) was adopted as a means to name, describe, and better understand the work of self-managing attendant services; a key goal was to incite and promote discussion about a phenomenon – the work of self-managing attendant services – that has, to this point, remained largely unrecognized. This approach encouraged collection of diverse perspectives, including explicit engagement with my own positionality relative to the research as an attendant to three women (separately and at different times, though sometimes overlapping) over the past 15 years. I acknowledge that my own experiences provided the impetus for the research: it was through these experiences that I came to ask questions about the labor disabled people and their support networks contribute to the organization and management of direct-funded attendant services; throughout the research process, I inevitably filtered new ideas through the lens of my past experiences; iteratively, my analytic lens transformed as I integrated new learning throughout the research process.

In light of feminist epistemological insights emphasizing the situatedness of knowledge (Grosz, 1994; Harding, 1991), methods were chosen to interrogate the situated knowledges of a range of people who participate in self-managed attendant services. With approval from the research ethics board at Western University, participants were recruited via adverts posted in public locations (libraries, grocery stores) and with the support of administrative staff at independent living centers in two separate cities. Purposive sampling (Merriam, 2009) was used to recruit participants with varied experiences (i.e., length of involvement with and nature of relationship to self-managed attendant services). Semi-structured, in-depth interviews were conducted with 11 self-managers, three attendants, three program administrators, one self-manager's spouse, and one self-manager's parent. In accordance with principles of emancipatory research, and recognizing disparities in the potential consequences of the research for different stakeholder groups, my own experiences and the insights of nondisabled research participants were included but decentered in order to "[prioritize] disabled people's knowledge and experience" (Barnes, 2009, p. 463). To protect confidentiality, exclusion criteria prevented the participation of self-managers and attendants who work together (i.e., if a self-manager was participating, their attendants could not). In addition to my own reflexive journaling and interviews, publicly available policy and program materials were also collected and analyzed.

Interviews were audio-recorded and transcribed verbatim. The qualitative data management software *Quirkos* was used to code the data and organize emerging themes. Data analysis was guided by the primary research question, "What is the 'work' of self-managing attendant services?" and subquestions, including: "Who performs the various associated forms of work? When and where? Are they paid? By whom/with whose money?"; "How is the work of self-managing attendant services understood/represented by the people who perform it?"; "In what ways is work represented in 'official' accounts of Self-Managed Attendant Services?"; and "What assumptions about disabled people do the policies reveal?". Analysis was conducted following Srivastava and Hopwood's (2009) framework for analytic reflexivity – a process of "reflexive iteration" that continuously asks: "What are the data telling me?"; "What is it I want to know?"; and "What is the dialectical relationship between what the data are telling me and what I want to know?". For each code that was developed, a list of questions informed by the overarching research questions was created. This process led to an organic exploration of the dialectical relationship between what the data were telling me (codes) and what I wanted to know (questions). The analysis was approached with openness to multiple possible meanings, intentional integration of various "stakeholder views, perspectives, claims, concerns and voices" (Lincoln, Lynhman, & Guba, 2018, p. 242), and awareness of the researcher's positionality. Consultation with colleagues and research mentors throughout the analytic processes informed refinement of the analysis and findings.

FINDINGS

These findings highlight the power self-managers hold to make decisions that shape attendants' working conditions, and the structural factors that influence self-managers' decision-making. In the context of limited and insufficient funding, self-managers adopt resourceful strategies to maximize support hours. These strategies include *splitting shifts, strategic hiring, dynamic resource management, and supplementing remuneration.* While the findings are organized to illustrate tensions between self-managers and attendants that arise from the organization of direct funding models, the data clearly demonstrate the "mutually respectful, trusting and balanced relationship between the employer and the employee [that is] vital in order for attendant services to work" (Yoshida et al., 2004, p. 196). As the discussion that follows will address, the structure of direct funding models imperils the self-manager–attendant relationships that are vital to this model's success.

Strategy 1: Splitting Shifts

Self-managers in Ontario receive a budget of *up to* seven hours per day. As self-manager Kimberly noted, however, some self-managers might only have three or four hours of funded daily support.[2] In order to see needs met at different times of the day, self-managers need to organize support needs into shifts. Kimberly explained that this either requires attendants to come and go throughout the day, or self-managers to block activities they need support with into a single shift. Referring either to CILT or the policies that govern direct funding more generally, Kimberly said,

> I'll tell you what they want. They want someone to come in for an hour to get up and an hour to put you to bed and an hour to groom. They want the person to go and come. Well, it's very hard to get people that way. No one is going to get paid seven hours but take 14 hours to do the job. I know what they're trying to do 'cause it's good financially, economically, but in personal reality, it's not going to happen, no matter what angle you try to show. I know people that only have, like, four hours a day. So, what do they do? They can't find anyone to go and come back, so they choose the best four hours of their day and just hire somebody for that. No one is going to go and come back. That's ridiculous. And I don't even know why they put that in the program, because that is so unrealistic. It's not even, like, it's a joke. Like, I want to laugh at it. Get paid for seven hours and have to work over 14 hours. 'Cause I get up at seven am and it's seven o'clock [pm] now, so that's 12. And I always go to bed at 11 or 12 midnight. So, 17 hours and you only get paid seven. But oh, yeah, you have to be available 17. And then to do those hours you have to pay your car or your bus to get to the consumer's home or self-manager's home. It's ridiculous.

Kimberly's frustration is evident as she discusses the challenge downloaded to self-managers to manage budgeted hours of support, leaving her to navigate the fine balance of meeting her own needs while creating a schedule that is fair and attractive enough to retain workers.

Voicing remarkably similar concerns, Brenda offered an attendant perspective on this issue:

> The other thing is, is \$16.65 an hour, when you take away \$6.00 for public transit, is \$10.65 an hour, which is not a living wage in a city like Toronto. The average rent is about \$1,000 a month and most shifts run from between one to three hours. [...] nobody can work fulltime doing this kind of work because there is no eight-hour shift. There just isn't. There's no way that I can get – do somebody for an hour, hour and a half, and then go to another place, and get eight hours in. So, I have to have multiple jobs, that obviously pay more than what [direct funding] pays.

Brenda described attendant work as "incredible," "incredibly satisfying," and "incredibly gratifying" work that she "loves" but cannot afford to do full-time. Brenda later explained that she'd had to "cut back" the number of shifts she works for one of her employers, "'cause he's far away and I can't really afford it." These examples illustrate how participation in direct funding is shaped by self-managers' and attendants' efforts to balance their own and each other's needs.

Anita, who works as a bookkeeper for several self-managers, expressed similar concerns about funding constraints and the impact of split shifts on both attendants who must put in extra hours of travel to make their wages, and self-managers who struggle to attract and keep workers. Invoking formal workers' rights policy (which self-managers are expected to adhere to), Anita said,

> I wish they could change that there's a minimum of two hours, not one hour, 'cause one hour is not reasonable for a person to get up in the morning and just get up the client for one hour. [They should get] at least two hours, plus give them a half an hour travel for the worker to go to work. Two and a half, at least, you know what I mean? If they can improve that, maybe it will work for more people because right now most of my clients will say, "I'm really having hard time finding somebody to put me to bed at night just for one hour." I said, "you have to ask

> CILT to increase your hours so you can offer two hours for the employee." [...] I think it will be better if they get more hours for workers, so they, the client, can keep the worker. 'Cause nobody will survive for two hours in the morning, one hour at lunch and two hours in the evening or one hour in the evening.

Addressing the impact of shift length on attendants, Anita said,

> They should extend more hours because these people have their own family, they have to make a living, and working for two hours, one hour, half an hour is not enough. I think, even though, let's say there's nothing to do, at least, please, because people have to travel to go to a client, at least pay them at least three hours including the travel.

Anita's comments highlight the impact of split shifts on attendants, who work fewer hours per shift, losing valuable time to extra travel. The consequences extend to self-managers, whose management responsibilities are in turn challenged by the difficultly of filling impractical shifts.

Strategy 2: Strategic Hiring

In addition to the length and timing of shifts, Kimberly expressed frustration with the limited remuneration afforded for attendants, and the related challenges that poses for hiring; namely, high rates of turnover. "Can you imagine?", she asked.

> You're advertising to someone part-time, no benefits, and no really room for growth. Who's gonna take a job like that? They will in the short term, especially if it's the only job they can find. And/or they have no experience and they want to get into the field. But long term, you can say goodbye to them in one or two years.

Mary, who used to self-manage her attendant services but has since returned to a more conventional model, similarly suggested that unattractive compensation impacted her ability to hire good staff. In Mary's words,

> mostly for me, there were people that seemed to be, couldn't get other jobs. You know, it's really hard to get quality people and pay them the wages that they give you to pay them on the direct-funding program.

Adapting to systemic constraints around scheduling and remuneration, some self-managers adopted strategic hiring practices that targeted employees who had the most flexible schedules or who were most desperate for work. An attendant working for multiple self-managers and with experience working as an attendant in other contexts, Brenda described the demographic of attendants she saw being hired as "people who are brand new to the country, and their English is not very good; students who need to augment their income; or, people who are between jobs." For self-managers who were students themselves, hiring other students appeared to be a natural choice. Self-manager Karen explained it was important to her to hire people who were close in age and who "understand my lifestyle." As self-manager Lydia explained, hiring students could also be a strategy to stretch her budget: "I didn't know if how much I pay an hour was on par with other [personal support workers], so I thought students would expect less money, you know [laughing]? Which they did. There've never been any complaints about the wages." Karen, too, had success hiring university students because, in her words,

> ...a lot of people [...] want a 9-5 job, [...] want to be paid full time, and that's exactly why the university students work great. They only need to come in for one hour a day. They're doing it more for the experience, being able to put it on their resumé. They want to be doctors, nurses, things like that. So that's really helpful.

Given the intentional orientation of direct funding models to hiring support staff without medicalized training, it was interesting to note that several participants chose to recruit students in health professional programs. The practice of hiring attendants with complementary skills, assets, or needs, however, extended beyond students. Self-manager Denise, for example, explained that "the person I've hired [...] took early retirement from their job so they kinda like just [having] something to do. And, they're very flexible." For Mary,

> ...my neighbor right next door had been my support person at night for, I think nine or [...] ten years [...]. It was a perfect job for her. She had, um, like a mentally challenged *[sic]* daughter and she could leave her for a bit alone. And we were, like, it was townhouses, so the next wall was her unit.

Kimberly was one of a small number of participants who discussed opportunities to stretch allocated budgets by hiring live-in caregivers and flexibility afforded by on-call shifts. In the following quote, Kimberly describes her use of a government program to recruit live-in caregivers from overseas.

> The live-in caregiver is the best way to maximize the hours that you have. And they can also get paid a bit less because under [Canadian immigration law] they don't live here. So, I don't pay them less because I have to pay them according to the hourly wages of direct funding, but what I do, I give them less hours. But they actually do more, so, it kind of balances out. But that's the unique way of maximizing the hours that you have.

Kimberly explained that, although she had to pay for her worker's international flight, it was still more economical because:

> She lives here. [...] I don't need a lot of overnight care because I generally sleep, but if I do, she's available, right? See, I could never hire a person on the hours [provided through direct funding] 'cause if I get sick overnight, if I start vomiting, then I need some help. But if you hire someone that doesn't live in, you have to give them an on-call wage.

Kimberly was not the only self-manager to discuss scheduling on-call shifts; however, there was disagreement among participants as to whether attendants were required to be paid an on-call wage. After this research was completed, a new law in Ontario was introduced which specified a requirement to pay a minimum rate for on-call shifts. It is a practical challenge for direct funding models that individuals as employers are expected to act in accordance with provincial labor laws that are ever in flux.

Strategy 3: Dynamic Resource Management

Self-managers' budgets are allocated based on a maximum rate of pay allowed for a determined number of hours of support. Self-managers are then responsible to manage that budget as they see fit. Accountability measures require that self-managers maintain a positive balance in a dedicated bank account that holds their funding, and keep records showing that the funds are spent on allowable expenses (primarily support hours, with a few other allowances, such as hiring a bookkeeper to help with accounting). As Kimberly explained above, she is not legally required to pay her live-in caregiver at the minimum rate set by direct funding, so she adjusts her books by recording fewer hours paid at a higher wage. In another example, Karen explained that, while budgets are allocated based on a maximum rate of pay, self-managers determine the actual rate that their attendants are paid.

> I also don't pay people at the max because I found that I have the same attendant for so long that the minimum, or the maximum you can pay a person or – what is it, $16.20 an hour, it kept going up so often that I was like, I don't want to like keep paying everyone something increasing when they haven't really done – they haven't deserved it yet. So, I start my person off at $14.90 an hour. So, I actually have a lot of extra hours that I use for either emergency or shopping.

This example shows how attendants' rate of pay correlates to the number of hours of support a self-manager has. In this case, Karen indicated, a lower rate translates to hours she can save for emergency use or for an activity like shopping that might not have many, or any hours allocated. In another notable instance, Brenda claimed that both of her employers "have to budget me in there [for extra overnight hours] 'cause I'm worth it. It stresses them out, but it's worth it."

In Karen's own words, "I pay people pretty fair. If you work an hour, I pay you an hour. If you work, um, less than an hour, I'll still give you the hour." While straightforward hourly pay applies in most situations, Karen described instances in which she needed to "negotiate a lump sum." One example she outlined was occasional trips home to visit her family over the weekend.

> I get six hours a day, so on Fridays I'll give someone three hours, then I'll give someone six, 'cause I don't go home 'til the afternoon. So, I'll give them three hours, I'll give them six hours, and then on Sunday we're not going back 'til late so I'll give them five hours. So that's fourteen, but you're with me the whole weekend.

Karen described instances where she had encountered conflict with an attendant about this payment arrangement, relating two cases in which attendants questioned the amount of money they received for travel. In one case, Karen had traveled with an attendant for 12 days and felt the $2000 she paid the attendant was "plenty of money," noting that on top of wages, she "paid for everything." Notably, Karen was among a minority of participants who claimed to have sufficient funding to meet their support needs and adequately compensate attendants.

Discussing his overnight support needs and budget, self-manager Ed explained he pays attendants a flat rate for overnights, but due to budgetary constraints, adjusts the rate paid based on actual services he requires during a given night.

> I have two different flat rates depending on how much I need and how many turns and things like that. [...] I can pay $50.00 overnight, per overnight half the nights of the month, and the other nights $82.50. I would like to have the $82.50 every night because it was [allocated] based on my needs [and] overnights are not always the same, in terms of how many turns I need. But realistically though, if the worker has to stay here [...] the sacrifice of that or whatever, you know, like, I'd rather be able [to pay them the full amount].

Ed was one of several participants who expressed awareness and concern for the low wages attendants receive for their labor, work that is often valued very highly by self-managers.

Strategy 4: Supplementing Remuneration

Participants shared several examples of creative means self-managers adopt to supplement formal remuneration. In one example, attendant Mark described his employer as:

> ...good in that she will overcompensate. [...] For example, yesterday I was doing a shift from 12:30 to 5:30 and that was planned, and then one of her attendants was sick, actually, and so I was there and she's like, "can you cover that shift?" And I was like, "maybe. Can you ask someone else?" And then she couldn't find anyone else, so I was like, "sure, I'll do it." And so, instead of me going all the way back home I was like, "well, I'm just going to stick around here in between, like the two hours." And so, she gave me money for supper. She'll do stuff like that a lot. Or like, I covered New Years and she paid for a cab ride home. So, she'll do stuff like that all the time, which is really nice.

In addition to paying out of pocket for tangible material benefits, multiple self-managers described offering their attendants nonmonetary supports, such as emotional availability. In Lydia's words,

> I have attendants where they'll like, tell me problems with their relationships, problems with their family and [...] I want to help. Even if it's just nothing but just listening and letting them cry and letting them unburden themselves. I don't mind that [...]. I may not necessarily tell you everything about myself because when it comes to my problems I go to my best friends or my family. But, if you want to unburden yourself on me, in order just to let it out, have a good cry, that's fine. Um, and in some cases, obviously that's something I can easily deal with as long as in everything else you're a good attendant.

As these latter examples demonstrate, the resources self-managers draw from to recognize and compensate attendants' work may extend beyond program funding to include personal material and other (i.e., emotional or affective) resources.

In the context of systemic constraints upon wages and scheduling, it appeared to be an important strategy for self-managers and attendants to enter into mutually beneficial relationships whose benefits extend beyond remuneration. Consistent with Brenda's comments above, several participants described attendants as people who are seeking more than monetary compensation from their job. Karen explained that online hiring platforms could be challenging since "you have to weed out more people because they're from the general public and I just get people who are in it for the money." According to Judy, a program administrator,

> People don't do this because they make a lot of money. They do it because they find the work kind of rewarding, what they want to do. I've found, uh, over the years, [I've] seen attendants that [say], well, I like this. I mean, I know everybody's hung up on this idea right now of precarious employment. Like, I think that's [unintelligible] but it does suit some people too, like, if you're a student or if you have other family responsibilities, if this is just extra income for you, you know. So, and it's really not precar – like, once you're in, you're in. It's not precarious really.

These examples raise challenging questions about the value of immaterial benefits and nonmonetary forms of compensation; an issue that is complicated by the intersectional nature of economic marginalizations experienced by many care workers. For instance, do workers choose to engage in relational work because it is spiritually satisfying? Do they ascribe meaning to help endure low-waged work that can be physically and emotionally challenging? What does it mean to frame affect and relationship as forms of compensation for labor? And, to what extent do hiring practices reflect unjust social systems that justify inequitable forms of compensation owed to particular workers (especially women/femmes and people of color) for particular kinds of (especially care) work? Although these questions center on attendants' labor and working conditions, they arise in relation to the labor self-mangers contribute, often in pursuit of agreeable outcomes for themselves and their attendants within the bounds of systemic constraints.

DISCUSSION

The data showcased here illuminate tensions between the interests and needs of self-managers and attendants that arise from systemic constraints on the quantity of funding available to self-managers to hire attendant supports. Direct funding models put disabled people in charge of decision-making related to the organization and management of attendant services, decisions that impact not only disabled people but also the care workers who provide their support as well. Self-manager-employers are empowered to make decisions surrounding who to hire and when to schedule services but must also take into account the preferences and needs of their attendant-employees. Beyond adherence to provincial labor laws, self-managers are not formally required to take any consideration for the well-being of attendants. Yet, the findings suggest that self-managers do consider and take steps to protect the well-being of their attendants. As "vulnerable employers," the motive for self-managers to treat attendants well may be self-protective (Parker et al., 2000; Yoshida et al., 2004); self-managers were seen to mitigate suboptimal working conditions (i.e., unattractive working hours, low wages, no extended health-care benefits) by providing extra material supports paid out of pocket, or by contributing emotional labor to offer emotional support. Indeed, these kinds of efforts may improve self-managers' sense of safety with workers who are happier or more comfortable, which may in turn contribute to longer-term worker retention.

While the data demonstrate how the interests of self-managers and attendants may be drawn into tension, the evidence does not suggest that self-managers set out to exploit attendants, to compensate them unfairly, or to create precarious working conditions for their own gain. On the contrary, the data clearly show that self-managers are often conscious of their attendants' working conditions and their personhood, and, therefore, desire to compensate them more than they are able to within the constraints of their direct funding budgets. These findings suggest it is something more than self-protection that motivates self-managers to consider and act in favor of attendants' interests; something more akin to the "affective relationality." Nishida (2016) has observed to emerge from "recursive practices of care routines" that "allow [disabled people and care workers] to ontologically learn one another's bodies and movements and to adapt to their particular capacities, needs, desires, and rhythms" (p. 153).

Nishida (2016) describes affective relationalities as "interdependent, mutually caring, and co-capacitating in nature" (p. 154). They are relationships that emerge from shared experiences of injustice within oppressive systems that administer care and support. Specifically, Nishida describes the "neoliberal public health-care assemblage": a system that binds disabled people and care workers to an expansive care industry that constructs both groups as "consumable and disposable populations" (p. 132). Through shared care practices and shared experiences of exploitation by this system, disabled people and care workers are drawn into solidarity. Evidence of this solidarity can be seen in the findings of the current research as well, which offers numerous examples of self-managers expressing concern for the well-being of attendants and of attendants expressing concern for the well-being of self-managers. These findings further portray a complex economy of material and affective resources exchanged between, and in efforts to support, members of both groups.

Shaped by affective relationalities, Nishida suggests the care practices disabled people and care workers engage in are resistive in that they "destroy and change the flows of the public health-care assemblage from within" (p. 149). Amid a system that

> ...exploits the good intentions of those who enter care work or forces many to enter care labor; [that] also controls, manages, and debilitates those who require long-term care [...] some care recipients and providers are always and already engaging in collective caring, healing, resisting, and destroying of the neoliberal public health-care assemblage (p. 171).

Indeed, interdependence and mutual caring challenge "malestream" characteristics of direct funding as public policy "that is commensurate with its masculinist ethic and idealizes masculinist notions of autonomy" (Hughes et al., 2005, p. 263) while at the same time making important meaning and bringing great value to our lives.

As long as resistive practices operate under the radar, however, they subsidize a system of sexist and ableist norms that profits from the labor of care workers and disabled people. While the demographic profile of attendants employed through direct funding in Ontario appears to differ somewhat from that of care workers in other settings (Kelly, 2014), attendant work, like other care work, remains feminized, often racialized, and supports global labor flows that channel immigrant women into "minimum or lower than minimum wage work" (Nishida, 2016, p. 104; see also; Kelly, 2016). As the findings of this research have shown, it is not just care workers but disabled people as well who contribute unrecognized, undervalued, and unpaid labor to the organization and management of direct-funded attendant services. The portrait of self-managers' labor that is presented here illuminates the vital care work that many disabled people contribute within relationships of care and support that are often imagined to be unidirectional; care work that is skilled and whose performance taxes personal resources of energy and time.

THE FUTURE IS ALLIED: (RE)IMAGINING CARE AS MUTUAL INTERDEPENDENCE

Insofar as direct funding models rely on binary constructions of dependence and independence, and of carer and cared-for roles, these systems reproduce ideologies that oppress both disabled people and care workers. With philosophical origins in a normative conception of independence that ignores and obscures the fundamentally relational nature of care work, direct funding models that imagine attendants as "substitute arms and legs" fail to recognize affective aspects of the attendant role (Fritsch, 2010; Kelly, 2016). Such constructions bolster systemic constraints upon the resources available to disabled people through the Ontario direct funding program and contribute to the creation of precarious working conditions for attendants, to the detriment of both attendants and self-managers. Furthermore, the Ontario direct funding program as it is currently structured does not formally recognize the labor disabled people contribute in the self-manager role (Katzman & Kinsella, 2018). This study's findings illustrate how, in the context of systemic constraints, self-managers contribute extra labor and other personal resources to compensate for systemic lacks. Given the shared consequences for self-managers and attendants of underfunding and the devaluation of affective and relational labor, there is great potential in disabled people and care workers joining a united front to lobby for their common and interrelated interests.

While proponents of direct funding have argued that self-managers are vulnerable employers, advocates for care workers' rights have similarly characterized attendants as some of "the most vulnerable workers" (Ungerson, 1997, p. 51; see also; Cranford, 2005). Attendants employed by self-managers may at times be among the most vulnerable, since they work in isolation and without regulations or protections that are standard in more formal workplaces. Emphasizing our shared struggle, Ungerson (1997) situates carers and disabled people as two economically marginalized groups whose interests are drawn into competition as "they are both seeking recognition and satisfaction of their own needs and desires within an extremely constrained context of highly rationed and seriously depleted public resources" (p. 46). As Ungerson emphasized, it is not primarily vulnerability to their direct employers that is a concern for attendants; rather, it is exploitation by a system that saves money at the expense of fair working (and living) conditions. This system survived the Independent Living Movements by keeping the interests of self-managers and attendants in tension and retaining an individualist discourse of independence and competition. Going forward, we must target this system and these discourses, and work to build meaningful alliances between disabled employers and their attendants.

Recognizing the shared vulnerabilities of self-managers and attendants, Cranford (2005) urges workers and service users to join a united political front by engaging in "a broader community unionism, one that recognizes the important role played by the government as funder" (p. 135). While solidarity within and against the system represents one potential way forward, collective forms of care demonstrate an alternative possibility. Care collectives that "combine the political commitments to self-care as well as politicized notions of interdependency and disability solidarity" (Hande & Kelly, 2015, p. 969) represent an increasingly common survival strategy, particularly within queer, trans, and BIPOC communities. Sick and disabled individuals whose lives are shaped by intersecting marginalized identities are among those most impacted by the general precarity of state-funded care, systems that demonstrate pervasive forms of ableism, racism, queerphobia, and transphobia (Piepzna-Samarasinha, 2018). Grounded in principles of mutual aid and respect, collective approaches to care normalize need and embrace a diversity of forms and modes of contribution to collective well-being. While mutual aid between and among those most affected can increase safety, it can also lead to burnout and cannot always ensure that no one is left behind (Piepzna-Samarasinha, 2018). Consequently, Piepzna-Samarasinha concludes crossability allyship rooted in deep understanding and respect is vital. Without losing sight of the potential for such alternative systems to be "neatly co-opted into the systemic, neoliberal austerity agenda as this informal care work is removed from the paid labor sector" (Hande & Kelly, 2015, p. 970; see also; Katzman, 2016), collective care and mutual aid offer important principles to guide our way forward.

The history of care as a construct in relation to disability is inevitably fraught and has likely impeded the development of formal alliances between disabled people and care workers. However, this research contributes to a growing literature that attests to the profoundly affective and relational character of care work and to the political potential of these sites. As people who "live with" disability in a relational sense (Kafer, 2013) (i.e., who regularly interact with disabled people or who spend time in disability cultural spaces), care workers often come to know disability in intimate, experiential, and embodied ways (Katzman et al., 2019). Although certainly not true of *all* attendants, many do demonstrate allyship on a spectrum from "affirmation (focused on demonstrating interpersonal qualities such as respect, caring, and connection) [to] informed action (focused on acknowledging identity-based differences and taking action to address discrimination)" (Ostrove, Kornfeld, & Ibrahim, 2019, p. 925). As this research has shown, many self-managers are also attuned to the material circumstances of their employees; several participants' contributions demonstrated awareness of forces that marginalize attendants and a political commitment to supporting attendants' interests.

As we continue to dream new models for organizing care work into existence, we may consider revisiting the hallmark mantra, *nothing about us without us*. If direct funding models are any indication, care workers have often been excluded from the proverbial "us." In the spirit of solidarity that is observable in so many relationships between disabled people and care workers, there may be value in unpacking taken-for-granted notions of "us" that are reinforced when this mantra is invoked. Following Fritsch (2010), there is incredible potential in a radical reformulation of care as mutual interdependence; while an individualist approach to care asks what one can do for another, a relational approach asks, "what can we create together?". Care as mutual interdependence opens up "the possibility of undoing the grounds upon which capitalist labour relations depend as it radically shifts our sense of one another and changes our ethical responsibilities toward each other" (p. 11). Amid global discussion of "care crises," state-funded support services have little choice but to begin to (re)cognize the interdependent, affective, and relational nature of care work performed by disabled people and care workers.

ACKNOWLEDGMENTS

This work owes a debt of gratitude to the research participants for their invaluable contributions; to Anne Kinsella, Pamela Cushing, Shanon Phelan and Jessica Polzer for their support and contributions to this research; to Susan Mahipaul and Alessia DiVirgilio for their ongoing encouragement; and to the volume's editors and anonymous reviewers for their generous feedback and guidance.

NOTES

1. The author notes the need for policy language to be changed to align with gender inclusivity.
2. Pseudonyms are used throughout to protect the participants' anonymity.

REFERENCES

Abberley, P. (2002). Work, disability, disabled people and European social theory. In C. Barnes, M. Oliver, & L. Barton (Eds.), *Disability studies today* (pp. 120–138). Cambridge: Polity Press.

Barnes, C. (2009). An ethical agenda in disability research: Rhetoric or reality? In D. M. Mertens & P. E. Ginsberg (Eds.), *The handbook of social research ethics* (pp. 458–473). Thousand Oaks, CA: SAGE Publications.

Barnes, C., & Roulstone, A. (2005). 'Work' is a four-letter word: Disability, work and welfare. In A. Roulstone & C. Barnes (Eds.), *Working futures? Disabled people, policy and social inclusion* (pp. 315–328). Bristol: The Policy Press.

Centre for Independent Living in Toronto (CILT). (2017). News release: February 15, 2017. Retrieved from https://www.cilt.ca/about-us/

Christensen, K. (2012). Towards sustainable hybrid relationships in cash-for-care systems. *Disability & Society*, *27*(3), 399–412. doi:10.1080/09687599.2012.654990

Church, K., Diamond, T., & Voronka, J. (2004). In profile: Personal support workers in Canada. Ryerson University: RBC Institute for Disability Studies, Research and Education.

Church, K., Frazee, C., Panitch, M., Luciani, T., & Bowman, V. (2007). Doing disability at the bank: Discovering the work of learning/teaching done by disabled bank employees. Ryerson University: RBC Foundation Institute for Disability Studies, Research and Education.

Cranford, C. J. (2005). From precarious workers to unionized employees and back again?: The challenges of organizing personal-care workers in Ontario. In C. J. Cranford, J. Fudge, E. Tucker, & L. F. Vosko (Eds.), *Self-employed workers organize: Law, unions and policy* (pp. 96–135). Montreal, PQ: McGill-Queens University Press.

DeJong, G. (1983/2001). Defining and implementing the independent living concept. In N. M. Crewe, & I. K. Zola (Eds.), *Independent living for physically disabled people* (pp. 4–27). San Jose, CA: People With Disabilities Press.

Denzin, N. K. (2003). Performing [auto] ethnography politically. *The Review of Education, Pedagogy & Cultural Studies*, *25*(3), 257–278. doi:10.1080/10714410390225894

DeVault, M. L. (2014). Mapping invisible work: Conceptual tools for social justice projects. *Sociological Forum*, *29*(4), 775–790. doi:10.1111/socf.12119

Ellis, C., & Bochner, A. P. (2003). Autoethnography, personal narrative, reflexivity: Researcher as subject. In N. K. Denzin & Y. S. Lincoln (Eds.), *Collecting and interpreting qualitative materials.* (2nd ed., pp. 199–258). Thousand Oaks, CA: SAGE Publications.

Fritsch, K. (2010). Intimate assemblages: Disability, intercorporeality, and the labour of attendant care. *Critical Disability Discourse*, *2*, 1–14.

Gibson, B. E. (2006). Disability, connectivity and transgressing the autonomous body. *Journal of Medical Humanities*, *27*(3), 187–196.

Glazer, N. (1993). *Women's paid and unpaid labor: The work transfer in health care and retailing.* Philadelphia, PA: Temple University Press.

Grosz, E. (1994). *Volatile bodies*. Bloomington, IN: Indiana University Press.

Hande, M. J., & Kelly, C. (2015). Organizing survival and resistance in austere times: Shifting disability activism and care politics in Ontario, Canada. *Disability & Society*, *30*(7), 961–975.

Harding, S. (1991). Strong objectivity and socially situated knowledges. *Whose science? Whose knowledge? Thinking from women's lives* (pp. 138–163). Ithaca, NY: Cornell University Press.

Hochschild, A. R. (1983). *The managed heart*. Berkeley, CA: University of California Press.

Hughes, B., McKie, L., Hopkins, D., & Watson, N. (2005). Love's labours lost? Feminism, the disabled people's movement and an ethic of care. *Sociology*, *39*(2), 259–275. doi:10.1177/0038038505050538

Kafer, A. (2013). *Feminist, queer, crip*. Bloomington, IN: Indiana University Press.

Katzman, E. (2016). Self-management and the government of disability: Reinforcing normalcy through the construction of able-disabled subjectivities. In J. Polzer & E. Power (Eds.), *Neoliberal governance and health: Duties, risks and vulnerabilities* (pp. 307–329). Montreal: McGill-Queen's University Press.

Katzman, E., & Kinsella, E. A. (2018). 'It's like having another job': The invisible work of self-managing attendant services. *Disability & Society*, *33*(9), 1436–1459. doi:10.1080/09687599.2018.1497949.

Katzman, E., Kinsella, E. A., & Polzer, J. (2019). 'Everything is down to the minute': Clock time, crip time and the relational work of self-managing attendant services. doi:10.1080/09687599.2019.1649126

Kelly, C. (2010). The role of mandates/philosophies in shaping interactions between disabled people and their support providers. *Disability & Society*, *25*(1), 103–119.

Kelly, C. (2014). Re/moving care from the Ontario direct funding program: Altering conversations among disability and feminist scholars. *Social Politics*, *21*(1), 124–147.

Kelly, C. (2016). *Disability politics and care: The challenge of direct funding*. Vancouver, BC: UBC Press.

Kinsella, E. A., & Whiteford, G. (2009). Knowledge generation and utilization in occupational therapy: Toward epistemic reflexivity. *Australian Occupational Therapy Journal*, *56*(4), 249–258. doi:10.1111/j.1440-1630.2007.00726.x.

Kittay, E. F. (1999). *Love's labor: Essays on women, equality, and dependency*. New York, NY: Routledge.

Kröger, T. (2009). Care research and disability studies: Nothing in common? *Critical Social Policy*, *29*(3), 398–420. doi:10.1177/0261018309105177.

Lanoix, M. (2013). Labor as embodied practice: The lessons of care work. *Hypatia*, *28*(1), 85–100.

Lather, P. (2001a). Postbook: Working the ruins of feminist ethnography. *Signs*, *27*(1), 199–227.

Lather, P. (2001b). Postmodernism, post-structuralism, and post(critical) ethnography: Of ruins, aporias and angels. In P. Atkinson (Ed.), *Handbook of ethnography* (pp. 477–492). Thousand Oaks, CA: SAGE Publications.

Leece, J. (2004). Money talks, but what does it say? Direct payments and the commodification of care. *Practice*, *16*(3), 211–221.

Leece, J. (2010). Paying the piper and calling the tune: Power and the direct payment relationship. *British Journal of Social Work*, *40*, 188–206.

Leece, J., & Peace, S. (2010). Developing new understandings of independence and autonomy in the personalised relationship. *British Journal of Social Work*, *40*, 1847–1865.

Lincoln, Y. S., Lynham, S. A., & Guba, E. G. (2018). Paradigmatic controversies, contradictions, and emerging confluences, revisited. In N. K. Denzin & Y. S. Lincoln (Eds.), *Handbook of qualitative research*. (5th ed., pp. 108–150). Thousand Oaks, CA: SAGE Publications.

Lord, J. (2010). *Impact: Changing the way we view disability: The history, perspective, and vision of the Independent Living Movement in Canada*. Ottawa, ON: Creative Bound International.

Marfisi, C. (2002). Personally speaking: A critical reflection of factors which blur the original vision of personal assistance services. *Disability Studies Quarterly*, *22*(1), 1–7.

Mauldin, L. (2017). A feminist technoscientific approach to disability and caregiving in the family. In M. Rembis (Ed.), *Disabling domesticity*. New York, NY: Palgrave Macmillan.

Merriam, S. B. (2009). *Qualitative research: A guide to design and implementation*. San Francisco, CA: Jossey-Bass.

Ministry of Community and Social Services (MCSS). (1994). O. Reg. 367/94: Grants for persons with disabilities. Retrieved from https://www.ontario.ca/laws/regulation/940367

Mladenov, T., Owens, J., & Cribb, A. (2015). Personalisation in disability services and healthcare: A critical comparative analysis. *Critical Social Policy*, *35*(3), 307–326.

Morris, J. (1997). Care or empowerment? A disability rights perspective. *Social Policy and Administration*, *31*(1), 54–60.

Nishida, A. (2016). Affecting neoliberal public health care: Interdependent relationality between disabled care recipients and their care providers. Unpublished doctoral dissertation, The City University of New York, NY.

Ontario Ministry of Health and Long-Term Care (OMHLTC). (2014). Helping Ontarians with disabilities live independently: Ontario expanding program to help more people self-manage care. Retrieved from https://news.ontario.ca/mohltc/en/2014/01/helping-ontarians-with-disabilities-live-independently-1.html

Ostrove, J. M., Kornfeld, M., & Ibrahim, M. (2019). Actors against ableism? Qualities of nondisabled allies from the perspective of people with physical disabilities. *Journal of Social Issues*, *75*(3), 924–942. doi:10.1111/josi.12346

Parker, I., Self, H., & Willi, V. (2000). *Power shift*. Toronto, ON: CILT.

Pearson, C. (2000). Money talks? Competing discourses in the implementation of direct payments. *Critical Social Policy*, *20*(4), 459–477.

Pearson, C., Barnes, C., Jolly, D., Mercer, G., Priestley, M., & Riddell, S. (2005). Personal assistance policy in the UK: What's the problem with direct payments? *Disability Studies Quarterly*, *25*(1), 1–15.

Piepzna-Samarasinha, L. L. (2018). *Care work: Dreaming disability justice*. Vancouver, BC: Arsenal Pulp Press.

Reindal, S. M. (1999). Independence, dependence, interdependence: Some reflections on the subject and personal autonomy. *Disability & Society*, *14*(3), 353–367.

Riddell, S., Pearson, C., Jolly, D., Barnes, C., Priestly, M., & Mercer, G. (2005). The development of direct payments in the UK: Implications for social justice. *Social Policy and Society*, *4*(1), 75–85.

Scourfield, P. (2005). Implementing the community care (direct payments) act: Will the supply of personal assistants meet the demand and at what price? *Journal of Social Policy*, *34*(3), 469–488.

Scourfield, P. (2007). Social care and the modern citizen: Client, consumer, service user, manager and entrepreneur. *British Journal of Social Work*, *37*, 107–122.

Shakespeare, T. (2006). *Disability rights and wrongs*. London: Routledge.

Shakespeare, T. (2014). *Disability rights and wrongs revisited*. New York, NY: Routledge.

Slasberg, C., & Beresford, P. (2015). Building on the original strengths of direct payments to create a better future for social care. *Disability & Society*, *30*(3), 479–483.

Smith, D. (2002). Institutional ethnography. In T. May (Ed.), *Qualitative research in action* (pp. 17–52). London: SAGE Publications.

Spalding, K., Watkins, J. R., & Williams, A. P. (2006). *Self managed care programs in Canada: A report to health Canada*. Retrieved from https://www.canada.ca/en/health-canada/services/publications/health-system- services/self-managed-care-programs-canada-report-to-health-canada.html

Spandler, H. (2004). Friend or foe? Towards a critical assessment of direct payments. *Critical Social Policy*, *24*(2), 187–209.

Srivastava, P., & Hopwood, N. (2009). A practical iterative framework for qualitative data analysis. *International Journal of Qualitative Methods*, *8*(1), 76–84.

Ungerson, C. (1997). Give them the money: Is cash a route to empowerment? *Social Policy and Administration*, *31*(1), 45–53.

Watson, N., McKie, L., Hughes, B., Hopkins, D., & Gregory, S. (2004). (Inter) dependence, needs and care: The potential for disability and feminist theorists to develop an emancipatory model. *Sociology*, *38*(2), 331–350.

Yoshida, K., Willi, V., Parker, I., & Locker, D. (2004). The emergence of self-managed attendant services in Ontario: Direct funding pilot project – an independent living model for Canadians requiring attendant services. In J. J. Kronenfeld (Ed.), *Chronic care, health care systems and services integration. Research in the sociology of health care* (Vol. 22, pp. 177–204). Bingley: Emerald Publishing Limited. doi:10.1016/S0275-4959(04)22010-5

Chapter 7

AUTISTIC ADULT AND NON-AUTISTIC PARENT ADVOCATES: BRIDGING THE DIVIDE

Helen Rottier and Morton Ann Gernsbacher

ABSTRACT

Purpose: *Due to the developmental nature of autism, which is often diagnosed in preschool or elementary school-aged children, non-autistic parents of autistic children typically play a prominent role in autism advocacy. However, as autistic children become adults and adult diagnoses of autism continue to rise, autistic adults have played a more prominent role in advocacy. The purpose of this chapter is to explore the histories of adult and non-autistic parent advocacy in the United States and to examine the points of divergence and convergence.*

Approach: *Because of their different perspectives and experiences, advocacy by autistic adults and non-autistic parents can have distinctive goals and conflicting priorities. Therefore, the approach we take in the current chapter is a collaboration between an autistic adult and a non-autistic parent, both of whom are research scholars.*

Findings: *The authors explore the divergence of goals and discourse between autistic self-advocates and non-autistic parent advocates and offer three principles for building future alliances to bridge the divide between autistic adults and non-autistic parents.*

Disability Alliances and Allies
Research in Social Science and Disability, Volume 12, 155–166

ISSN: 1479-3547/doi:10.1108/S1479-354720200000012011

Implications: *The chapter ends with optimism that US national priorities can bridge previous gulfs, creating space for autistic adult and non-autistic parent advocates to work together in establishing policies and practices that improve life for autistic people and their families and communities.*

Keywords: Advocacy; disability; autism; priorities; autistic adults; non-autistic parents

INTRODUCTION

Autism is the shooting star of the disability advocacy world. Although the condition was considered rare and mysterious through most of the twentieth century, it experienced a dramatic rise in diagnoses and awareness in the 1990s (Gernsbacher, Dawson, & Goldsmith, 2005). Autism advocacy was initially spearheaded by non-autistic parents and professionals, which is common for a developmental disability. Parent-advocacy groups prioritized earlier screening for autism (catching autism as soon as possible) and earlier intervention (intervening against autism as soon as possible), along with research identifying the cause of autism and its cure (Ne'eman, 2010).

However, autistic[1] children grew up to be autistic adults, the increasing number of autism diagnoses included an increasing number of adults being diagnosed, and the rise of the Internet allowed autistic adults who were otherwise geographically dispersed to connect across space and time, with no need to read body language or make eye contact. Thus, was born the autistic self-advocacy movement, which prioritizes acceptance, support, and quality of life (Blume, 1997, 1998; Dekker, 1998; Harmon, 2004).

These discordant priorities – caricatured as find the cure versus increase the quality of life – underlie much of the conflict between autistic adults and non-autistic parents. Tensions have escalated into in-person and online protests (Brown, 2012; Luterman, 2015; Wallis, 2009), Twitter skirmishes (V. Hughes, 2015), boycotts of companies that donate to certain parent-led organizations (Owlia, 2019; WikiHow, 2019), and other publicly aired battles (Dejean, 2017). Entire websites and blog posts, such as "We Are Like Your Child" (http://wearelikeyourchild.blogspot.com), have been authored by autistic adults to counter a recurring parental claim that autistic adults "are nothing like my child" and are, therefore, unauthorized to contribute to the discussion (Endow, 2018). Complete dissertations have documented the conflicts between autistic adults and non-autistic parents (J. M. F. Hughes, 2015; Linehan, 2014). Here, we hope to do something more.

In this chapter, we begin by exploring the conflicting principles and priorities that have driven discord between autistic adults and non-autistic parents. We then offer examples of convergent advocacy, drawing from other disabilities and from outside the realm of disability. We end by offering three principles for building future alliances between autistic adults and non-autistic parents to bridge the divide.

NON-AUTISTIC PARENT ADVOCACY

The history of non-autistic parent organizations contributes to the current tension between autistic adult and non-autistic parents.[2] Although our focus is on US-based organizations, we see a similar pattern in the United Kingdom (Fletcher-Watson et al., 2019), Canada (Orsini, 2012), the Netherlands (van den Bosch et al., 2019; Waltz, van den Bosch, Ebben, van Hal, & Schippers, 2015), France (Chamak, 2008; Chamak & Bonniau, 2013), Sweden (Bertilsdotter Rosqvist, O'Dell, & Brownlow, 2015), and other countries.

In 1965, Bernard Rimland founded the Autism Society of America, which was the first autism-specific parent advocacy organization in the United States. Rimland, who had trained as an experimental psychologist, turned to the scholarly literature when his son began exhibiting characteristics that Rimland, through his readings, diagnosed as autism. Rimland's subsequent book, *Infantile Autism: The Syndrome and Its Implications for a Neural Theory of Behavior,* was instrumental in shifting the then-dominant explanation of autism's origin from Bruno Bettelheim's psychoanalytically based "refrigerator mother theory" to hypotheses based on genetics, biochemistry, and neurophysiology (Rimland, 1964).

In the 1970s and 1980s, the Autism Society of America played an instrumental role in advocating for several key disability laws (e.g., Section 504, the Developmental Disabilities Act, and the Education for All Handicapped Act, which later became the Individuals with Disabilities Education Act) (Autism Society, n.d.). In the early 1990s, the Autism Society argued before Congress against the use of aversives, such as the shock used at the Judge Rotenberg Center (Holden, 1990). However, the Autism Society of America was founded by non-autistic parents and, for the most part, has been run by non-autistic parents, along with non-autistic professionals.

The 1990s witnessed the onset of three new parent-founded and parent-run autism organizations: The National Alliance for Autism Research was founded by two non-autistic parents in 1994 with the mission of accelerating biomedical research and treatment for a "disorder ... every bit as devastating as the worst of the psychiatric diseases" (London, 1997); Cure Autism Now was founded by two non-autistic parents in 1995 with the mission to "cure autism now"; and Talk About Curing Autism was founded in 2000 by a non-autistic parent based on "the hope of recovery" (Ackerman, n.d.). In 2005, Autism Speaks was founded by to non-autistic grandparents (Gernsbacher, 2009). In 2006 and 2007, Autism Speaks quickly absorbed the National Alliance for Autism Research and Cure Autism Now, respectively, along with the Autism Coalition for Research and Education (Autism Speaks, n.d.).

Until 2016, Autism Speaks' mission statement described its organization as "dedicated to funding research into the causes, prevention, treatments, and a cure for autism." Their more recent mission statement disavows a cure, because, as stated in a section of their website titled "For the Record," they believe "there is no single 'autism'"; therefore, "there will be no single 'cure'" (Autism Speaks, n.d.).[3] Their website also promises that their organization's "goal is for all people on spectrum, no matter how they self-identify, to be appreciated for whom they are and the contributions they make to society."

Unfortunately, as many scholars have noted, very little of Autism Speaks' outreach has been in the service of "all people on the spectrum"; rather, the majority has been in the service of non-autistic parents of autistic children (Stevenson, Harp, & Gernsbacher, 2011). Moreover, quite a bit of Autism Speaks' rhetoric has been incongruent with a message of appreciation; indeed, much of their public rhetoric has been incongruent with the fundamental tenets of disability rights, including the basic human right, as established by Article 10 of the United Nations Convention on the Rights of Persons with Disabilities, to live life as a disabled person.

For example, in Autism Speaks' promotional video "Autism Every Day," one of the organization's non-autistic board members articulates her desire to murder her autistic daughter and confesses her reluctance to do so hinges only on the existence of her other, non-autistic, daughter (this scene is shot with her autistic daughter in full view; Yergeau, 2010). In another Autism Speaks' promotional video, "I Am Autism," autism is portrayed as a terrifying monster that destroys marriages, bankrupts families, steals children along with their non-autistic parents' dreams, and removes all parental hope (J. M. F. Hughes, 2015; Nicolaidis, 2012; Thibault, 2014; Wallis, 2009).

In full-page magazine and Internet ads (underwritten by the US Ad Council), Autism Speaks has warned parents that the odds of their child being diagnosed as autistic are horrifically worse than their child becoming critically injured in a car crash, contracting life-threatening hypothermia, and suffering other distressing outcomes (McGuire, 2011). Other parent-led autism advocacy groups have used rhetoric less extreme than that of Autism Speaks (Carey, Block, & Scotch, 2019), and not all non-autistic parents endorse Autism Speaks and their advocacy tactics (e.g., the cover of a recent issue of *Autism Parenting* magazine and its accompanying editorial decry Autism Speaks; Burby, 2014). However, Autism Speaks and its brand of parent advocacy have evoked some of the most notable conflict with autistic adults.

AUTISTIC ADULT ADVOCACY

The history of autistic adult advocacy also dates to the 1990s. After feeling excluded in conferences and listservs run by and for non-autistic parents, autistic adults first formed their own listservs and then organized their own in-person conferences (Sinclair, 2010). Although these early organizations (e.g., Autism Network International and Autreat) were motivated more by the desire to socialize and interact with other autistic adults than to advocate and campaign for societal change (Dekker, 1998), their early organization laid the groundwork for later autistic-run advocacy groups.

In 2006, the US-based Autistic Self Advocacy Network was founded with the mission to "advance the principles of the disability rights movement with regard to autism"; the goal of "a world in which autistic people enjoy equal access, rights, and opportunities"; the purpose of "empower[ing] autistic people across the world to take control of our own lives and the future of our common community"; the motivation of "organizing the autistic community to ensure our voices are heard in the national conversation about us"; and the mantra, "Nothing About Us, Without Us!" (Autistic Self Advocacy Network, n.d.).

In December 2007, the fledgling all-volunteer group of autistic adults gained initial visibility with a well-orchestrated protest of an egregiously ill-conceived publicity campaign promoted by non-autistic partents and produced by the NYU Child Study Center (Kaufman, 2007a). Posted on billboards, subway placards, and kiosks were signs designed to mimic kidnappers' ransom notes, for example, "We have your son. We will make sure he will not be able to care for himself or interact socially as long as he lives. This is only the beginning." The ransom notes were signed by the metaphorical kidnapper, "Autism" (Kras, 2010).

The campaign was intended to garner hundreds of millions of impressions over a few months (Ne'eman, 2007a). But the Autistic Self Advocacy Network sprang into action, empowering other autistic adults (and their allies), as well as people with other disabilities, to demand that the campaign organizers remove the signs. The controversy made the pages of *The New York Times* (Kaufman, 2007a) and the *Wall Street Journal* (Wang, 2007a). After a dozen days of protest, the campaign was halted, and all signs were removed, showcasing an autistic advocacy victory that again made the pages of *The New York Times* (Kaufman, 2007b) and *Wall Street Journal* (Wang, 2007b), as well as the *Washington Post* (Shulman, 2007) and other outlets.

The autistic adults' successful advocacy was driven by the power of the Internet coupled with their cross-disability – and even non-autistic parent – alliances. As Ari Ne'eman reported (2007b):

> Twenty-two disability rights organizations came together to ensure the withdrawal of this advertising campaign. Our response to this campaign stretched continents, with e-mails, letters and phone calls coming from as far away as Israel, Britain and Australia. The disability community acted with a unity and decisiveness that has rarely been heard before and we are seeing the results of our strength today.

The successful resolution to the ransom notes campaign and other successes placed autistic adults squarely in what Michael Wehmeyer, Hank Bersani Jr., and Ray Gagne (2000) proposed would be the third wave of advocacy: The first wave had been driven by professionals, the second had been driven by parents, and the last wave would be and must be driven by people with disabilities. As Ne'eman (2007b) warned:

> Our success sends an inescapable message: If you wish to depict people with disabilities, you must consult us and seek our approval. Anything less will guarantee that we will make our voices heard. We are willing to help anyone and any group that seeks to raise awareness of disability issues, but those efforts must be done with us, not against us.

No longer were autistic adults relegated to providing only what Sinclair (1994) deemed "self-narrating zoo exhibits." By this expression, Sinclair referenced the most common reason autistic adults had been welcomed at parent-led autism conferences and listservs: to describe their autistic lives to non-autistic parents who then led "discussion of ways to make us other than what we are, and … create a world in which we don't exist at all." Autistic adults had shown the world that they not only did exist, but they had allies, they could wield power, and they aspired to the mantle of advocacy.

BRIDGING THE DIVIDE

Despite the past and current tensions between autistic adults and non-autistic parents, we believe avenues for increased and mutually rewarding alliance are viable. We propose that non-autistic parents can best ally with autistic adults by honoring the three requirements Tom Shakespeare (1993) identified as vital to self-advocacy movements: resources, recognition, and autonomy.

Resources

It should come as little surprise that non-autistic parents have accrued more resources for advocacy than have autistic adults, if only by dint of longevity. These resources need to be freely shared with autistic adults. And by resources we mean both the tangible and the intangible.

With regard to intangible resources, a more plaintive appeal could not have been made than that issued, nearly three decades ago, by Jim Sinclair (1993, reprinted in Sinclair, 2012). When addressing an audience full of non-autistic parents at the International Conference on Autism in Toronto, Sinclair pleaded, "We need you. ... Your world is not very open to us and we won't make it without your strong support." The rest of Sinclair's address, which was titled, "Don't Mourn for Us," became the bedrock of autistic advocacy. However, the address is just as much a clarion call to non-autistic parents for alliance as anything. For example, Sinclair encouraged non-autistic parents to reframe their perspective and take action:

> Yes, there is tragedy that comes with autism: not because of what we are, but because of the things that happen to us. Be sad about that, if you want to be sad about something. Better than being sad about it, though, get mad about it – and then *do something about it.* (p. 3, emphasis added)

Undoubtedly, one of the most valuable intangible resources that non-autistic parents can share with autistic adults is their activism.

As for tangible resources, all the types of assets denoted by the dictionary definition of tangible resources, namely, money, equipment, land, or buildings, can and should be offered. For example, Nancy Bagatell (2010) described an autistic adult group, going strong since the early 1990s, that is only loosely associated with a non-autistic parent-led group. Nonetheless, the non-autistic parent group provides financial support and meeting space for the autistic adults – and has for years.

Non-autistic parents, Kathleen Seidel and Shannon Des Roches Rosa exemplify the process of garnering resources. In Seidel's case, she founded, financed, and curated the Neurodiversity.com website for many years, and then she and her spouse ran the Neurodiversity.Weblog (Seidel, 2019). Des Roches Rosa procured resources for the website, *The Thinking Person's Guide to Autism*, which is co-led by autistic adults and non-autistic parents (Greenburg & Des Roches Rosa, 2019).

The key for each of these parents was observing the quack treatments promoted for autistic children and the societal disdain proffered to autistic adults.

Recognition

Allyship requires recognition, which in the case of autistic adults and non-autistic parents means acknowledging autistic adults' existence, validity, and value. Decades ago, Martijn Dekker (1998) pinpointed the conditions that he considered autistic utopia. Those conditions were simple: non-autistic people who listen, respect, and accept autistic people. That is the recognition upon which fruitful alliance can be built.

A fruitful alliance can also be built on the willingness to address past harm (Rosenblatt, 2018; Taylor-Parker, 2016). Grappling with the past will require humility from non-autistic parents and their organizations, along with an understanding that prior conversations and ongoing tensions have been fueled by fear and anger. We believe bridges can be built, and trust can be restored with effective apologies (Kador, 2009). As social psychologists have noted, an earnest apology "not only renders a transgression less offensive but also…provides evidence that the offender acknowledges the [other's] worth" (Janoff-Bulman & Werther, 2008, p. 19).

Recognition will also require an overt and acknowledged shift in power and roles. Parents of offspring with other disabilities have already modeled this shift. For example, in some organizations, non-disabled parents have moved from working on behalf of people with learning disabilities to working beside them (Ryan & Griffiths, 2015; Walmsley, Tilley, Dumbleton, & Bardsley, 2017). One of the clearest demonstrations of a shift from "working for" to "working with" has been demonstrated by parents of gay and lesbian offspring; indeed, the entire organization of PFLAG (Parents and Family of Lesbians and Gays) was founded on the concept of straight parents walking beside, not in place of, their gay and lesbian offspring (Broad, 2011; Conley, 2011; Starr, 1986). We are now seeing a similar alliance with cisgender parents and their transgender offspring (Wahlig, 2015).

Recognition must be more than tokenism, as it has unfortunately been in the past (Petri, Beadle-Brown, & Bradshaw, 2017; Robison, 2013). And the conditions for recognition must not be set solely by non-autistic parents (Carter & Wilson, 2006). Autistic adults' right to exist as they are, and to be valued as they are, must be the basis of any bridges built.

Autonomy

Bridges of alliance can also be forged by respecting autistic adults' autonomy. Perhaps in no greater way has autistic adults' autonomy been challenged as when debating the issue of representation. Simultaneously, autistic adults have been told they are too autistic to represent other autistic people (and thus, non-autistic parents will represent them), and they are not autistic enough to represent other autistic people (recall the "not like my child" criticism we discussed before). This paradox, which Melanie Yergeau (2018) calls "demi-rhetoricity," must be abolished if we are to truly honor autistic adults' autonomy and the abolishment needs to remain enacted within the autistic adult community, as well.

Honoring autistic adults' autonomy also means respecting their choice of rhetoric, for example, when they choose identity-first over person-first language (Gernsbacher, 2017); when they decry the use of functioning labels (simply Google "functioning labels" to see why); and when they denounce the use of puzzle piece imagery (see Gernsbacher, Raimond, Stevenson, Boston, & Harp, 2018, p. 119, for links to nearly a dozen autistic adult's essays against puzzle piece imagery, as well as empirical evidence that puzzle piece imagery evokes negativity in the general public). Honoring autistic adults' autonomy means respecting autistic-only space, be it the #ActuallyAutistic Twitter hashtag or an in-person enclave.

CONCLUSION

We began by describing autistic adults' and non-autistic parents' separate histories and their divergent perspectives, here in the United States. Across the pond, we see more evidence of shared priorities. For example, in the UK, non-autistic parents and autistic adults correlate more than they segregate on national research priorities (Gotham et al., 2015; Pellicano, Dinsmore, & Charman, 2014). Both groups agree that identifying the best ways to improve the lives of autistic people and creating the best public services to meet the needs of autistic people are higher priorities than researching etiology or epidemiology (Pellicano, Dinsmore, & Charman, 2013; see also Gotham et al.'s, 2015 study demonstrating tight alignment in research priorities between large samples of autistic adults who do and do not have legal guardians).

We are optimistic that the United States can follow suit and that our national priorities can also bridge previous gulfs. We are beginning to glimpse hints of positive change. For example, a decade ago, the US Department of Health and Human Services' Interagency Autism Coordinating Committee (2009) organized their research funding priorities around six questions, which were clearly written from the perspective of non-autistic parents distressed about their autistic children. The questions included "When should I be concerned?" and "What caused this to happen and can it be prevented?" A decade later, the US Department of Health and Human Services' Interagency Autism Coordinating Committee (2019) organized their research funding priorities around questions relevant to autistic adults, for example, "What kinds of services and supports are needed to maximize quality of life for people on the autism spectrum?" and "How can we meet the needs of people with ASD as they progress into and through adulthood?" These are steps that will bridge the divide.

NOTES

1. We use identity-first language (e.g., autistic people, non-autistic people) rather than person-first language (e.g., people with autism, people without autism) because identity-first language is preferred by autistic people (Kenny et al., 2015), is recommended by APA (Dunn & Andrews, 2015), and is less likely to contribute to stigma (Gernsbacher, 2017).

2. We acknowledge that many autistic people are also parents of autistic and non-autistic offspring. See Ashkenazy (2009) for an excellent essay written by an autistic parent.

3. We note also that the parent-advocacy organization Talk About Curing Autism (TACA), founded in 2000, recently renamed their organization The Autism Community in Action (TACA), deleting the mention of cure from their name.

REFERENCES

Ackerman, L. (n.d.). A letter from Lisa Ackerman, Founder. *TACA: The Autism Community in Action*. Retrieved from https://tacanow.org/who-we-are

Ashkenazy, E. (2009, December 16). Parents in the autism world. *Autistic Self Advocacy Network*. Retrieved from https://autisticadvocacy.org/2009/12/parents-in-the-autism-world

Autism Society. (n.d.). Retrieved from https://www.autism-society.org/about-the-autism-society/his-tory

Autism Speaks. (n.d.). Retrieved from https://www.autismspeaks.org/about-us.

Autistic Self Advocacy Network. (n.d.). Retrieved from https://autisticadvocacy.org/about-asan/our-history.

Bagatell, N. (2010). Rethinking autism, rethinking anthropology. *Ethos*, *38*, 33–55. doi:10.1111/j.1548-1352.2009.01080.x

Bertilsdotter Rosqvist, H., O'Dell, L., & Brownlow, C. (2015). "An association for all" - Notions of the meaning of autistic self-advocacy politics within a parent-dominated autistic movement. *Journal of Community & Applied Social Psychology*, *25*, 219–231. doi:10.1002/casp.2210

Blume, H. (1997, June 30). Autistics are communicating in cyberspace. *The New York Times*. Retrieved from http://www.nytimes.com/library/cyber/techcol/063097techcol.html.

Blume, H. (1998, September). Neurodiversity. *The Atlantic*. Retrieved from http://www.theatlantic.-com/magazine/archive/1998/09/neurodiversity/305909.

van den Bosch, K. E., Krzeminska, A., Song, E. Y., van Hal, L. B. E., Waltz, M. M., Ebben, H., & Schippers, A. P. (2019). Nothing about us, without us: A case study of a consumer-run organization by and for people on the autism spectrum in the Netherlands. *Journal of Management and Organization*, *25*, 464–480. doi:10.1017/jmo.2018.54

Broad, K. L. (2011). Coming out for parents, families and friends of lesbians and gays: From support group grieving to love advocacy. *Sexualities*, *14*, 399–415. doi:10.1177/1363460711406792

Brown, L. X. Z. (2012, November 5). Protesting autism speaks. *Autistic Hoya*. Retrieved from https://www.autistichoya.com/2012/11/protesting-autism-speaks.html

Burby, L. A. (2014). Editor's letter. *Autism Parenting Magazine*. Retrieved form https://www.autismparentingmagazine.com/issue-14-asd-options-living-independently

Carey, A. C., Block, P., & Scotch, R. K. (2019). Sometimes allies: Parent-led disability organizations and social movements. *Disability Studies Quarterly*, *39*(1). Retrieved from http://dsq-sds.org/article/view/6281/5183

Carter, I., & Wilson, R. (2006). Reflections on face-to-face and online self-help group participation: Comparing the views of persons with autism with those of parents speaking for their autistic children. *International Journal of Self Help and Self Care*, *5*, 353–369. doi:10.2190/SH.5.4.g

Chamak, B. (2008). Autism and social movements: French parents' associations and international autistic individuals' organisations. *Sociology of Health & Illness*, *30*, 76–96. doi:10.1111/j.1467-9566.2007.01053.x

Chamak, B., & Bonniau, B. (2013). Autism and social movements in France: Exploring cross-cultural differences. In M. Orsini, & J. Davidson (Eds.), *Worlds of autism: Across the spectrum of neurological difference* (pp. 239–257). Minneapolis, MN: University of Minnesota Press.

Conley, C. L. (2011). Learning about a child's gay or lesbian sexual orientation: Parental concerns about societal rejection, loss of loved ones, and child well being. *Journal of Homosexuality*, *58*, 1022–1040. doi:10.1080/00918369.2011.598409

Dejean, A. (2017, April 17). The White House turned blue for "autism awareness." That's actually bad for autistic people. *Mother Jones*. Retrieved from https://www.motherjones.com/politics/2017/04/trumps-autism-awareness-effort-not-show-support-autistic-people

Dekker, M. (1998). On our own terms: Emerging autistic culture. Autism99 Internet Conference. Retrieved from http://www.autscape.org/2015/programme/handouts/Autistic-Culture-07-Oct-1999.pdf

Dunn, D. S., & Andrews, E. E. (2015). Person-first and identity-first language: Developing psychologists' cultural competence using disability language. *American Psychologist*, *70*, 255–264. doi: 10.1037/a0038636

Endow, J. (2018, March 07). Realities of being an autistic therapist. *Spectrum*. Retrieved from https://www.spectrumlife.org/blog/realities-of-being-an-autistic-therapist-121

Fletcher-Watson, S., Adams, J., Brook, K., Charman, T., Crane, L., Cusack, J., ... Pellicano, E. (2019). Making the future together: Shaping autism research through meaningful participation. *Autism*, *23*, 943–953. doi:10.1177/1362361318786721

Gernsbacher, M. A. (2009). A conspicuous absence of scientific leadership: The illusory epidemic of autism. In G. R. Goethals, & J. T. Wren (Eds.), *Leadership and discovery* (pp. 157–169). New York, NY: Palgrave MacMillan.

Gernsbacher, M. A. (2017). The use of person-first language may accentuate stigma. *Journal of Child Psychology and Psychiatry*, *58*, 859–861. doi:10.1111/jcpp.12706

Gernsbacher, M. A., Dawson, M., & Goldsmith, H. H. (2005). Three reasons not to believe in an autism epidemic. *Current Directions in Psychological Science*, *14*, 55–58. doi:10.1111/j.0963-7214.2005.00334.x

Gernsbacher, M. A., Raimond, A. R., Stevenson, J. L., Boston, J. S., & Harp, B. (2018). Do puzzle pieces and autism puzzle piece logos evoke negative associations? *Autism*, *22*, 118–125. doi: 10.1177/1362361317727125

Gotham, K., Marvin, A. R., Taylor, J. L., Warren, Z., Anderson, C. M., Law, P. A., ... Lipkin, P. H. (2015). Characterizing the daily life, needs, and priorities of adults with autism spectrum disorder from Interactive Autism Network data. *Autism*, *19*, 794–804. doi:10.1177/1362361315583818

Greenburg, C., & Des Roches Rosa, S. (2019). Two winding parent paths to neurodiversity advocacy. In S. K. Kapp (Ed.), *Autistic community and the neurodiversity movement: Stories from the frontline* (pp. 155–166). Singapore: Palgrave Macmillan. doi:10.1007/978-981-13-8437-0

Harmon, A. (2004, December 20). How about not 'curing' us, some autistics are pleading. *The New York Times*. Retrieved from https://www.nytimes.com/2004/12/20/health/how-about-not-curing-us-some-autistics-are-pleading.html

Holden, C. (1990, August 31). What's holding up "aversives" report? *Science*, *249*, 980–981. doi: 10.1126/science.2396100

Hughes, J. M. F. (2015). Changing conversations around autism: A critical, action implicative discourse analysis of U.S. Neurodiversity advocacy online. Communication Graduate Theses & Dissertations, *52*. Retrieved from https://scholar.colorado.edu/comm_gradetds/52

Hughes, V. (2015, February 23). Autistic people spark twitter fight against Autism Speaks. *BuzzFeed News*. Retrieved from https://www.buzzfeednews.com/article/virginiahughes/autistic-people-spark-twitter-fight-against-autism-speaks

Janoff-Bulman, R., & Werther, A. (2008). The social psychology of respect: Implications for delegitimization and reconciliation. In A. Nadler, T. Malloy, & J. D. Fisher (Eds.), *Social psychology of inter-group reconciliation: From violent conflict to peaceful co-existence* (pp. 145–171). Cambridge: Cambridge University Press.

Kador, J. (2009). *Effective apology: Mending fences, building bridges, and restoring trust*. San Francisco: CA: Berrett-Koehler Publishers.

Kaufman, J. (2007a, December 14). Campaign on childhood mental illness succeeds at being provocative. *The New York Times*. Retrieved from http://www.nytimes.com/2007/12/14/business/media/14adco.html

Kaufman, J. (2007b, December 20). Ransom-note ads about children's health are canceled. *The New York Times*. Retrieved from https://www.nytimes.com/2007/12/20/business/media/20child.html

Kenny, L., Hattersley, C., Molins, B., Buckley, C., Povey, C., & Pellicano, E. (2015). Which terms should be used to describe autism? Perspectives from the UK autism community. *Autism*, *20*, 442–462. doi:10.1177/1362361315588200

Kras, J. F. (2010). The 'Ransom Notes' affair: When the neurodiversity movement came of age. *Disability Studies Quarterly*, *30*(1). doi:10.18061/dsq.v30i1.1065

Linehan, T. B. (2014). Neurodiversity and disability: An analysis of social movement framing in dialog between parents and autistic self-advocates. Theses & Dissertations, *130*. Retrieved from https://digitalcommons.plymouth.edu/etd/130

London, E. (1997, November 1). A psychiatrist's journey from parent to founder of research advocacy organization. *Psychiatric Times*. Retrieved from https://www.psychiatrictimes.com/schizoph-renia/psychiatrists-journey-parent-founder-research-advocacy-organization

Luterman, S. (2015, October 9). What it's like to be David. *NOS Magazine*. Retrieved from http://nosmag.org/why-protest-autism-speaks

McGuire, A. (2011). Representing autism: A sociological examination of autism advocacy. *Atlantis: Critical Studies in Gender, Culture & Social Justice*, *35*, 62–71. Retrieved from http://journal-s.msvu.ca/index.php/atlantis/article/view/918/914

Ne'eman, A. (2007a, December 19). Victory! The end of the ransom notes campaign. *Autistic Self Advocacy Network*. Retrieved from https://autisticadvocacy.org/2007/12/victory-the-end-of-the-ransom-notes-campaign

Ne'eman, A. (2007b, December 8). An urgent call to action: Tell NYU Child Study Center to abandon stereotypes against people with disabilities. *Autistic Self Advocacy Network*. Retrieved from https://autisticadvocacy.org/2007/12/tell-nyu-child-study-center-to-abandon-stereotypes

Ne'eman, A. (2010). The future and the past of autism advocacy, or why the ASA's magazine *The Advocate* wouldn't publish this piece. *Disability Studies Quarterly*, *3*(1). Retrieved from http://dsq-sds.org/article/view/1059/1244

Nicolaidis, C. (2012). What can physicians learn from the neurodiversity movement? *Virtual Mentor*, *14*, 503–510. doi:10.1001/virtualmentor.2012.14.6.oped1-1206

Orsini, M. (2012). Autism, neurodiversity and the welfare state: The challenges of accommodating neurological difference. *Canadian Journal of Political*, *45*, 805–827. doi:10.1017/S0008423 91200100X

Owlia, A. (2019, April 26). Autism Speaks: They don't speak for the spectrum. *Triangle*. Retrieved from https://www.thetriangle.org/opinion/autism-speaks-they-dont-speak-for-the-spectrum

Pellicano, E., Dinsmore, A., & Charman, T. (2013). *A future made together: Shaping autism research in the UK*. London: Institute of Education. Retrieved from http://discovery.ucl.ac.uk/1495583/1/A_Future_Made_Together_1.2_LR.pdf

Pellicano, E., Dinsmore, A., & Charman, T. (2014). What should autism research focus upon? Community views and priorities from the United Kingdom. *Autism*, *18*, 756–770. doi:10.1177/1362361314529627

Petri, G., Beadle-Brown, J., & Bradshaw, J. (2017). "More honoured in the breach than in the observance"—self-advocacy and human rights. *Laws*, *6*(4), 26. doi:10.3390/laws6040026

Rimland, B. (1964). *Infantile autism: The syndrome and its implications for a neural theory of behavior*. New York, NY: Appleton-Century-Crofts.

Robison, J. E. (2013, November 13). I resign my roles at Autism Speaks. *Look Me in the Eye*. Retrieved from http://jerobison.blogspot.com/2013/11/i-resign-my-roles-at-autism-speaks.html

Rosenblatt, A. (2018). Autism, advocacy organizations, and past injustice. *Disability Studies Quarterly*, *38*(4). Retrieved from http://dsq-sds.org/article/view/6222/5137

Ryan, T. G., & Griffiths, S. (2015). Self-advocacy and its impacts for adults with developmental disabilities. *Australian Journal of Adult Learning*, *55*, 31–53.

Seidel, K. (2019). Neurodiversity.com: A decade of advocacy. In S. K. Kapp (Ed.), *Autistic community and the neurodiversity movement: Stories from the frontline* (pp. 89–108). Singapore: Palgrave Macmillan. doi:10.1007/978-981-13-8437-0

Shakespeare, T. (1993). Disabled people's self-organisation: A new social movement? *Disability, Handicap & Society*, *8*, 249–264. doi:10.1080/02674649366780261

Shulman, R. (2007, December 20). Child Study Center cancels autism ads. *Washington Post*. Retrieved from http://www.washingtonpost.com/wp-dyn/content/article/2007/12/19/AR2007121902230.html

Sinclair, J. (1994, January 22). Autobiographies. *Bit.Listserv.Autism*. Retrieved from https://groups.google.com/forum/#!msg/bit.listserv.autism/XCMbupxu2sk/7yvdOOnh7ZEJ

Sinclair, J. (2010). Cultural commentary: Being autistic together. *Disability Studies Quarterly*, *30*(1). doi:10.18061/dsq.v30i1.1075

Sinclair, J. (2012). Don't mourn for us. *Autonomy, the Critical Journal of Interdisciplinary Autism Studies*, *1*(1). Retrieved from http://www.larry-arnold.net/Autonomy/index.php/autonomy/article/view/AR1

Starr, A. (1986). Foreword. In C. W. Griffin, M. J. Wirth, & A. G. Wirth (Eds.), *Beyond acceptance: Parents of lesbians & gays talk about their experiences* (pp. xi–xii). New York, NY: St. Martin's Press.

Stevenson, J. L., Harp, B., & Gernsbacher, M. A. (2011). Infantilizing autism. *Disability Studies Quarterly*, *31*(3). doi:10.18061/dsq.v31i3.1675.

Taylor-Parker, L. (2016, October 21). The future of autism Speaks. *Autistic Future*. Retrieved from http://autisticfuture.com/2016/10/21/the-future-of-autism-speaks

Thibault, R. (2014). Can autistics redefine autism? The cultural politics of autistic activism. *Trans-Scripts*, *4*, 57–88.

U.S. Department of Health and Human Services. (2009). Autism spectrum disorder research 2008 portfolio analysis report. Interagency Autism Coordinating Committee. Retrieved from https://iacc.hhs.gov/publications/portfolio-analysis/2008/portfolio_analysis_2008.pdf

U.S. Department of Health and Human Services. (2019). 2016 autism spectrum disorder research portfolio analysis report. Interagency Autism Coordinating Committee. Retrieved from https://iacc.hhs.gov/publications/portfolio-analysis/2016/portfolio_analysis_2016.pdf

Wahlig, J. L. (2015). Losing the child they thought they had: Therapeutic suggestions for an ambiguous loss perspective with parents of a transgender child. *Journal of GLBT Family Studies*, *11*, 305–326. doi:10.1080/1550428X.2014.945676.

Wallis, C. (2009, November 6). 'I Am Autism': An advocacy video sparks protest. *Time*. Retrieved from http://content.time.com/time/health/article/0,8599,1935959,00.html

Walmsley, J., Tilley, L., Dumbleton, S., & Bardsley, J. (2017). The changing face of parent advocacy: A long view. *Disability & Society*, *32*, 1366–1386. doi:10.1080/09687599.2017.1322496

Waltz, M., van den Bosch, K., Ebben, H., van Hal, L., & Schippers, A. (2015). Autism self-advocacy in the Netherlands: Past, present and future. *Disability & Society*, *30*, 1174–1191. doi:10.1080/09687599.2015.1090954

Wang, S. (2007, December 14). Ads about kids' mental health problems draw fire. *Wall Street Journal*. Retrieved from http://blogs.wsj.com/health/2007/12/14/ads-about-kids-mental-health-problems-draw-fire

Wang, S. (2007, December 19). NYU bows to critics and pulls ransom-note ads. *Wall Street Journal*. Retrieved from http://blogs.wsj.com/health/2007/12/19/nyu-bows-to-critics-and-pulls-ransom-note-ads

Wehmeyer, M., Bersani, H., Jr, & Gagne, R. (2000). Riding the third wave: Self-determination and self-advocacy in the 21st century. *Focus on Autism and Other Developmental Disabilities*, *15*, 106–115. doi:10.1177/108835760001500206

WikiHow. (2019, September 30). How to boycott autism Speaks. *WikiHow*. Retrieved from https://www.wikihow.com/Boycott-Autism-Speaks

Yergeau, M. (2010). Circle wars: Reshaping the typical autism essay. *Disability Studies Quarterly*, *30*(1). Retrieved from http://dsq-sds.org/article/view/1063/1222

Yergeau, M. (2018). *Authoring autism: On rhetoric and neurological queerness*. Durham, NC: Duke University Press Books.

Chapter 8

BECOMING ALLIES: THE TRANSMOGRIFICATION OF THE ROLE OF AMERICAN SIGN LANGUAGE/ENGLISH INTERPRETERS DURING THE DEAF PRESIDENT NOW PROTEST

Mark Halley

ABSTRACT

Purpose: *In this chapter, I explore how American Sign Language/English interpreters came to enact an ally role with members of the American deaf community during the 1988 Deaf President Now (DPN) protest. The DPN protest, led by students at Gallaudet University in Washington, DC, was a historic moment in the deaf community's struggle for civil rights (Christiansen & Barnartt, 1995). During the events that unfolded over the week-long rebellion, students engaged in a variety of claims-making activities (Lindekilde, 2013), such as participating in media interviews and organizing rallies. To share their message with the world, the deaf protesters developed alliances with American Sign Language/English interpreters, who mediated a wide variety of protest-related activities.*

Method: *The data I analyze in this chapter come from (1) archival review and (2) semistructured interviews I conducted with DPN stakeholders, including interpreters and protesters.*

Disability Alliances and Allies
Research in Social Science and Disability, Volume 12, 167–188

ISSN: 1479-3547/doi:10.1108/S1479-354720200000012012

Findings: *Through these data, I explore how the protesters and interpreters came to develop shared understandings and expectations of allyship, including the roles that interpreters enacted in the protest.*

Implication/Value: *I frame this discussion within the context of a variety of metaphors that have been used to describe the role of signed language interpreters (Roy, 1993, 2002) and the concept of role-space (Llewellyn-Jones & Lee, 2014) to demonstrate the process of interpreters becoming allies in contentious political settings.*

Keywords: Protest; ally; interpreting; deaf president now; deaf; role

INTRODUCTION

Gallaudet University, located in Washington, DC, is the world's only liberal arts university for deaf and hard-of-hearing students. Frequently referred to as the "mecca" of the deaf world, it is a place deaf people come together in a shared community of linguistic and cultural unity (Armstrong, 2014).[1] In 1988, the university underwent a search for its seventh president. When the candidates were narrowed down to three, two were deaf (Dr. I. King Jordan and Dr. Harvey Corson). Since the founding of Gallaudet in 1864, six individuals had served as president, all of whom were hearing, white men. The deaf community eagerly anticipated that the Gallaudet University Board of Trustees, after months of interviewing the finalists, would finally have its first deaf president.[2] However, the board selected Dr. Elisabeth Ann Zinser – the only hearing finalist. As word spread of the decision, students, faculty, staff, and other members of the American deaf community responded by launching a week of protest, locking down the university campus and garnering national media attention. After eight days of protest actions of different kinds, the board of trustees complied with the students' four demands: (1) Zinser's resignation, to be replaced by a deaf individual, (2) the resignation of the Jane Bassett Spilman, chair of the board of trustees, (3) a 51% deaf majority on the board of trustees, and (4) no reprisals against demonstrators. After a week of insurrection, the board announced that Dr. I. King Jordan had been selected as the first deaf president of Gallaudet University in its 124-year history.

To share their message and make their claims known to the public, the protesters worked with American Sign Language/English interpreters. Gannon (1989) reported that, on one day of the protest, approximately 70 interpreters were working on Gallaudet's campus. Interpreters provided language mediation in a number of settings, including on-campus rallies and protester interviews with reporters. In this way, the interpreters facilitated the protesters' *claims-making activities*, or "the formulation of a political demand with a specific content (the claim) and the public staging of this demand (claims-*making*)" (Lindekilde, 2013, p. 201, emphasis in original). In the case of Deaf President Now (DPN) and the wider disability rights movement, activists made claims about social problems related to the social status of people with disabilities. In a nod to interpreters,

Christiansen and Barnartt (1995) cite interpreters' work as one of the many factors that facilitated DPN protesters' demands being met.

One area of scholarly interest in DPN is the roles that interpreters enacted in the protest, including how they came to enact their roles, what they understood about their roles, and the views about their roles from users of interpreting services (e.g., protesters and other stakeholders). Despite their ostensibly "neutral" positioning, evidence suggests that interpreters are active participants in communication encounters (see Hauser, Finch, & Hauser, 2008; Llewellyn-Jones & Lee, 2014; Metzger, 1999; Roy, 2000; Wadensjö, 2004). Historically, professional signed language interpreters have struggled to determine and explain the "role" they should assume when providing their services (see Cokely, 1984; Frishberg, 1986; Ingram, 1985; Witter-Merithew, 1986). But what is the role of interpreters and translators in forms of collective action like protests? In this chapter, I take up the DPN protest as a key moment in deaf and interpreting history, using it as an exemplar for the analysis of interpreter role in contentious political settings. This analysis of events that took place more than three decades ago provides a contemporary look on a historical moment, thereby allowing for a nuanced investigation of the interpreters' work. Further, it sets the stage for future research on interpreters working in protest environments, particularly in those involving deaf people and/or signed languages.

LITERATURE REVIEW

Scholars and practitioners have used several definitions, models, and metaphors to describe the role of an interpreter, as well as the challenges interpreters face when assuming their role.[3] These models include the helper model, the conduit model, the communication-facilitator model, the bilingual–bicultural (bi-bi) specialist model, and, most recently, the ally model.[4] Under the *helper model*, early interpreters saw themselves as individuals who sought to help deaf people. While altruism may be a noble endeavor, the model was considered by many deaf people and others to be paternalistic in that "helping" deaf people "reflected attitudes that deaf individuals were not able to take care of their own business, be it personal, social, or professional without the intervention of the helper" (Roy, 1993, p. 139). The *conduit model*, which developed partly in reaction to the helper model, saw interpreters as machines, a view that was demonstrated in codes of ethics that emphasized neutrality, divorcing interpreters from their humanity.[5] Informed by academia and communication theory, interpreters then adopted the *communication-facilitator model*, in which interpreters "made communication easier by adapting to the particular linguistic system desired by each individual deaf person" (Roy, 1993, p. 144). Despite this slight shift in definition, Roy (1993) argues that the communication-facilitator model is, in fact, "the conduit notion in disguise" because the metaphor still focuses on the mere transfer of information between two forms (p. 146). In a shift that took a step forward in recognizing the humanity and actual presence of interpreters in communicative situations, the *bi-bi specialist model* was developed. In the bi-bi model, the interpreter must "bridge, in a meaningful manner, the gap that separates both sender and receptor audience" (Arjona, 1978, p. 36). In this model, informed by an understanding that users of different languages bring with them different cultural backgrounds, values, and norms, interpreters were expected to perform cultural mediation between parties, a process that would ideally make communication effective.[6]

Finally, the most recent model of interpreting is the *ally model*, which

> ...implies that because of the common power imbalance between Deaf and hearing people, interpreters are in a unique position to provide information about the interaction to the Deaf participants so that they can make empowered decisions on how to proceed (Janzen & Korpiniski, 2005, p. 171).

How then can we make a distinction between the ally model and the earliest model of interpreting, the helper model? The critical factor that differentiates the two models is that interpreters who see themselves as helpers work through a sense of paternalism (Mindess, 1999). Rather than acting out of paternalistic attitudes toward deaf people, an interpreter who adopts the ally model "focuses on the recognition of oppression in our society and strives to create partnerships with deaf people that will reduce the power imbalances that exist" (Witter-Merithew, n.d.). Considering the broader contributions of translators and interpreters, Baker (2006) boldly states

> ...neutrality is an illusion, and thus uncritical fidelity to the source text or utterance also has consequences that an informed translator or interpreter may not wish to be party to (p. 128).

This perspective underlies the ally model: that the interpreter embodies a role in which they make choices with the aim of having decisive impacts in support of a particular community or cause.

These role metaphors have some value for describing the work of interpreters to students or others wishing to understand interpreting on the surface. However, they have the unfortunate consequence of distilling the very complex concept of role into overly simplified and bastardized conceptualizations. This is made abundantly clear when one begins to tease out the models and finds their inadequacies. Recall, for example, that differences between the conduit and communication-facilitator models are so granular that one is forced to conclude the latter is merely "the conduit notion in the disguise of communication facilitator" (Roy, 2002, p. 351).[7] Another key weakness of role descriptions and metaphors is that they "carry double messages... reminding everyone that the interpreter is uninvolved on any other level" while they also "encourage interpreters to be flexible, which usually means to be involved" (Roy, 2002, p. 347).

How can we address this apparent paradox? Let us first begin by delving into what precisely is meant by the term "role." Turner (1956) defined role as "a collection of patterns of behavior which are thought to constitute a meaningful unit and deemed appropriate to a person occupying a particular status" (p. 1). However, note that in this description of role, Turner (1956) is referring to "behavior rather than position, so that one may *enact* a role but cannot *occupy* a role" (p. 317, emphasis in original). Applying this notion to interpreting, we can say that interpreters do not assume or occupy roles; they enact roles according to their behaviors and actions.

Proposing a model that leans upon the sociological work of Mead (1934), Linton (1936), Newcomb (1950), Turner (1956, 1962), and Goffman (1961, 1972, 1990), Llewellyn-Jones and Lee (2014) offer a new paradigm to describe interpreter role that does not rely on problematic descriptions and metaphors. Instead, they argue that

> ...rather than a rule-based description of 'role,' a more complete and usable notion is that interpreters' behaviors are governed by the *role-space* they create and inhabit in any given situation (Llewellyn-Jones & Lee, 2014, p. 10, emphasis in original).

The particular role-space an interpreter creates can be visually represented within a three-dimensional plot defined by three axes: participant alignment (x), interaction management (y), and presentation of self (z).[8]

Let us briefly explore each of the three components of role-space. A low *presentation of self* refers to "not interacting, not presenting information," whereas a high presentation entails "speaking for one's self, providing information etc" (Llewellyn-Jones & Lee, 2014, p. 15). Along the *alignment* axis, we consider the extent to which an interpreter converges or diverges with participants on a sociolinguistic and psycholinguistic level. Finally, the axis of *interaction management* refers to how an interpreter manages discourse between interlocutors and participates in "regulating the flow of the interaction" (Llewellyn-Jones & Lee, 2014, p. 57). Interaction management includes the decisions an interpreter makes about a variety of communication events and challenges, such as managing overlapping speech and regulating turn-taking in an interpreted encounter.[9]

This paradigm offers a dynamic and nuanced approach to analyzing interpreter work and role beyond the static models described above. In this model, the role-space an interpreter creates may shift according to the context in which they are working; for example, an interpreter may have a relatively low presentation of self in one situation (e.g., when interpreting for a speaker at a conference), while demonstrating a relatively high presentation of self in a situation in which they more closely resemble a helper (e.g., when working with a child).

METHODOLOGY

This project was approved by the Gallaudet University Institutional Review Board (IRB). The data analyzed were collected from two sources: (1) historical archives and (2) semistructured interviews with DPN participants. Whereas the historical information uncovered in archives was helpful to describe the context in which DPN interpreting occurred, the data gathered in the interviews were useful for analyzing the roles interpreters enacted in the protest and how they came to see themselves as allies. In this chapter, I present data collected from both archival sources and interviewees.

In the following pages, I apply role-space theory to analyze the work of interpreters in DPN, while also demonstrating how the interpreter models (helper, conduit, communication facilitator, bi-bi specialist, and ally) do not adequately describe the roles of interpreters in the protest. Instead, I explore the particular roles interpreters enacted and the role-spaces they embodied during DPN, focusing on interpreters who acted as allies to the protesters. The data show how interpreter actions cannot be neatly categorized according to a role description (e.g., helper); however, by analyzing the role-space an interpreter embodies, we are better poised to understand what it means for an interpreter to act as an ally, particularly within protest settings. Considering the historical and limiting roles prescribed to professional interpreters through ethical codes (e.g., beliefs that interpreters should act as neutral conduits), I predicted that participants would share narratives detailing the challenges of balancing roles of both activist and professional interpreter. I further anticipated that this balancing act would be a considerable source of internal strife for participants and that they would report facing significant external pressures to conform to professional standards and roles.

Potential interviewees were identified by: (1) names in the archived material, (2) professional contacts, and (3) referrals from interviewees.[10] Interviewees represented two primary groups. One group consisted of American Sign Language/English interpreters who provided interpreting services during the protest, including the events leading up to the protest, protest events, and events organized by the board of trustees. This group included both interpreters who volunteered their services as well as those who were paid to interpret. They were contacted through an email request. I interviewed interpreters who worked with the protesters and interpreters who worked for the board of trustees. Three interpreters worked for the board and provided interpreting services for events such as board meetings that included both deaf and hearing participants. Of the 18 interpreters I interviewed who provided interpreting services to protesters, 14 identified primarily as volunteers. Those who worked with the protesters and were paid recalled being compensated from sources other than the protesters (e.g., an interpreter who worked with an interpreting agency that sent him to work on campus during the protest).

The second group of interviewees consisted of DPN protesters and organizers who worked with interpreters throughout the protest. These individuals were identified through archival materials, professional contacts, and interviewee referrals. They included protesters who were interviewed by reporters, organizers who met with members of Congress, student leaders who met with the board of trustees for negotiations, as well as individuals who assisted with scheduling and coordinating the provision of interpreting services. I recruited these participants through email contact.[11]

Data Collection

I used semistructured oral history interviews as a primary data collection tool. Semistructured interviews are commonly used in case studies because they have the potential to elicit rich descriptions from participants about their personal experiences (Blee & Taylor, 2002). In-depth interviewing of social movement participants is helpful for researchers addressing "central questions on the micro-dynamics of alternative forms of political participation" (della Porta, 2014, p. 258), making interviews particularly helpful for collecting data about interpreters in political movements. Questions in the interview guide (Weiss, 1994) included those related to their activities during the protest; questions were refined according to data collected in the archival review. Question topics centered around the participants' experiences in the protest, their views on interpreting in the protest, and their understanding of interpreter role. Some archival materials were also shown during the interviews to trigger memories and elicit narratives from the participants. For example, in one set of questions, I provided interviewees with archival materials (videos of their interpreted work) and posed questions to evoke detailed responses (e.g., "Can you tell me about how you coordinated the dialogue in this clip?").

Before beginning the interviews, I conducted a pilot interview with an American Sign Language/English interpreter with experience working in protest settings. In addition to the pilot interview with a mock interpreter, I met with a deaf native American Sign Language user to advise me on best practices for conducting an interview in American Sign Language.[12]

Participants completed informed consent forms and videotaping consent forms. Participants were then individually scheduled to meet with me, either via video-conferencing software (e.g., Skype, Google Hangouts, FaceTime) or in person. I recorded the interview data from each meeting. For interviews conducted remotely, I used screen recording software (QuickTime or SimpleScreenRecorder). Two interviews were conducted face-to-face and recorded using high-definition video cameras.

Whether interviews were held in person or remotely, participants were given the option of selecting the language in which the interview was conducted (American Sign Language or spoken English). Each of the nondeaf participants chose to conduct the interview primarily in spoken English. Due to technological limitations, three interviews were conducted by audio only. In total, 33 hours and 52 minutes of interview data were recorded and transcribed (average interview length: 75 minutes). All data (video, audio, and resulting transcripts) were stored electronically with password protection.

I used the interview questions as a guide. After reading from an opening script, I posed the questions to the participants and encouraged them to provide as much detail as possible. Additionally, because semistructured interviews are purposefully flexible in nature, I encouraged participants to elaborate by asking for clarification and posing follow-up and probing questions. At the conclusion of each interview, I collected demographic information from participants. Participants were offered $20 in compensation in their preferred manner (check, PayPal, Amazon gift card) for their participation.

For interviews conducted in English, bimodal bilingual participants sometimes exhibited code-switching or code-blending (Emmorey, Borinstein, Thompson, & Gollan, 2008), that is, using both English and American Sign Language. A bimodal bilingual is an individual who has some degree of fluency with two languages that are perceived and produced in different modalities (e.g., English and American Sign Language). This unique feature of discourse in bimodal bilinguals (e.g., the interpreters) also provided insight into which language interpreters used when discussing particular topics. For example, in an interview conducted primarily in spoken English, one participant began using American Sign Language when recounting a specific protest chant. For this reason, even interviews conducted in spoken English were audio and video recorded when possible.

Participant Demographics

Here, I report demographic information about the interviewees, beginning first with the 21 individuals who interpreted during the protest. Fifteen identified as female, and six identified as male. Nineteen identified as white, one identified as Asian, and one identified as being of mixed race. Age at the time of the protest ranged from 20 to 48 years of age. Age of their signed language acquisition ranged from 0 to 33 years. Sixteen participants reported not having deaf parents, and five had at least one deaf parent. Seven of the 21 were faculty or staff at Gallaudet, and five were contract interpreters working for Gallaudet during the time of the protest. Nineteen were certified American Sign Language/English interpreters at the time of the protest, 18 of whom held certifications granted by the Registry of Interpreters for the Deaf (RID).[13] One held a state-level qualification. Two held no interpreting credentials.

Of the five deaf protesters I interviewed, four identified as male, and one declined to state a gender identity. Four identified as white, and one declined to state a race or ethnic identity. The age of the protesters at the time of the protest ranged from 20 to 44 years. All the protesters acquired a signed language at birth and had at least one deaf parent.[14]

Demographic information of all participants is presented in Table 1.[15]

Data Analysis

After transcribing each interview, I offered participants the opportunity to review the transcripts for accuracy. No participants chose to review their transcript. Interviews with interpreters were conducted in English and interviews with deaf participants were conducted in American Sign Language (my second language) and translated into English transcripts. I then retained a native language user to verify the accuracy of my translations.

The data were examined using thematic analysis. Thematic analysis has been described as a tool that uses data collection, transcription, coding, listing of patterns of experience, identifying data related to the patterns, combining the patterns into subthemes, and developing an argument grounded in both the data and previous scholarship (Aronson, 1995).[16] In this way, thematic analysis may be understood as a "hypothetico-deductive approach" in which a researcher makes discoveries and argues the merit of such discoveries based on thematic patterns within a dataset (Hayes, 1997, p. 179). I note here that scholars have suggested that thematic analysis is not a research approach, but an analytic tool (Boyatzis, 1998) or an analytic process (Ryan & Bernard, 2000).

Table 1. Demographic Information of Participants.

#	Role	Gender	Age during DPN	Age of Signed Language Acquisition	Interpreting Credentials	Deaf parent(s)
1	Interpreter (Board)	Female	39	25	RID	No
2	Interpreter (Board)	Female	29	Birth	RID	Yes
3	Interpreter (Board)	Female	36	21	RID	No
4	Interpreter (and coordinator)	Female	31	Birth	RID	Yes
5	Interpreter (and coordinator)	Female	42	33	No	No
6	Interpreter	Female	28	20	RID	No
7	Interpreter	Female	43	Birth	RID	Yes
8	Interpreter	Male	23	19	No	No
9	Interpreter	Male	25	19	RID	No
10	Interpreter	Female	39	Birth	RID	Yes
11	Interpreter	Male	42	22	RID	No
12	Interpreter	Female	28/29	16	RID	No
13	Interpreter	Female	32	7	State	No
14	Interpreter	Female	29/30	22	RID	No
15	Interpreter	Female	28	18	RID	No
16	Interpreter	Male	26	19	RID	No
17	Interpreter	Female	27	18	RID	No
18	Interpreter	Female	32	20	RID	No
19	Interpreter	Male	Late 30s	Early 20s	RID	No
20	Interpreter	Female	30	Early 20s	RID	No
21	Interpreter	Male	38	Birth	RID	Yes
22	Protester	Male	24/25	Birth	No	Yes
23	Protester	N/A	20	Birth	No	Yes
24	Protester	Male	44	Birth	No	Yes
25	Protester	Male	29	Birth	No	Yes
26	Protester	Male	34	Birth	No	Yes

FINDINGS

In this section, I present the findings of my analysis. Specifically, I focus on two key themes that I elucidated from the data: (1) interpreter understanding of role as "conduit allies" and (2) interpreter enactment of role according to the role-space model.

Interpreter Understanding of Role as "Conduit Allies"

The interpreters who worked during DPN consistently described their roles in the protest in ways that suggested allyship with the deaf community, as well as conduits or impartial communication facilitators. In the following illustrative examples from the data, I demonstrate how interpreters' understanding of their roles often overlap various role metaphors described above, suggesting contradictions in the models and in how interpreters see their work.[17]

First, let us explore how interpreters who volunteered their time for various protest events during DPN described their development of the roles they enacted. The interpreters suggested that their roles grew from expectations in the deaf community. As one interpreter stated:

> I didn't feel any ethical conflicts over my role. We just went with it. We were in the community. And we were really taking our cues about what interpreters were from the community. And it may have conflicted with what I learned in class. But they were happy with the work we were doing, and that's all that mattered. (Participant #19)

Other volunteer interpreters echoed these sentiments, describing no internal turmoil or ethical conflicts between their role as interpreters and as quasi-protest participants. This suggests that the interpreters viewed themselves as enacting a role that most closely aligns with the ally model, a clear departure from earlier views such as the conduit model. By being allies "in the community" as the above interpreter suggested, the interpreters emphasized how deaf community expectations about the role of interpreters – not ethical principles taught in a classroom – were the fundamental factors influencing how they assumed their role as allies.

Such perspectives underscore a shift away from the helper and conduit models and toward the ally model. By describing how they came to create their roles according to the needs and desires of deaf people, the interpreters detailed how their alignment with the deaf community moved them to strive not to be conduits for communication, but allies for change.

Despite seeing themselves as allies, the interpreters painted an apparent contradiction of terms when describing their day-to-day activities in the protest. On the one hand, they considered themselves allies to the community. On the other, they described their work as mere facilitators of communication between protesters and onlookers. One interpreter shared the following perspective about the evolution of how she viewed the role of signed language interpreters:

> I didn't really think about it much during the week, but what was very obvious to me that I ultimately looking back felt like it was a really, really good lesson that I could take with me for the rest of my time on this planet, was that we hearing people are facilitators and nothing more. So at that moment, we definitely were in the back seat, as interpreters, as hearing people, and I felt that had a cleanness to it and a separation of role that was just right. In terms of empowerment of the deaf community and so on, whenever I walk into a new situation now, 30 years later, this whole rest of my life, I've been involved in so many different kinds of situations where deaf people are trying to do something, and you know there's a little bit of a negotiation going on about who's in charge. But my impulse is always, "Now step back." Even if you disagree or you think that you could do something in a different way, let the deaf person handle it. When it's over you might advise or provide a comment, but when the moment comes for decisions to be made, you step back. (Participant #13)

Although the interviewee did not share a particular experience that brought about this realization, these comments suggest that seeing deaf people rise up in insurrection during DPN may have had a profound impact on how she viewed her responsibilities as an interpreter toward deaf people. By seeing deaf people take care of themselves, she learned to "step back" in future interpreting work. In essence, the interpreter has described moving from the role of a helper, but it is unclear whether she is moving toward allyship or apparent conduit. Another volunteer interpreter and Gallaudet faculty member shared similar sentiments saying,

> They did this. That shifted my perspective about how much hearing people should do for deaf people, and it made me change my view of myself in terms of being in the helper mode or anticipating their needs. (Participant #10)

Above all, these responses point toward a shift in interpreter understanding, leading them to consider more carefully how to be allies to the deaf community while not at the same time disempowering deaf people from leading their own lives.

Deaf protesters generally suggested seeing DPN interpreters, particularly those who volunteered, as their allies. As one protester explained,

> I didn't look at them as interpreters but as allies… we all had our role to play in the protest. I saw interpreters as being on our team and on the same side. (Participant #25)

Other deaf protesters suggested seeing interpreters as fellow activists and protesters working toward a common goal. As one explained:

> There were a lot of illegal actions during DPN. But sometimes civil rights actions take precedence. Like when we marched without a permit. Or when someone pulled the fire alarm, and Spilman wasn't sure how to react, which led to her being filmed walking across the stage angrily and saying things like, "You can't hear me now!" We all looked at her and were like, "We're deaf. If you were deaf we could communicate." So that moment stuck out to me. But anyway, then we also had students who illegally deflated the bus tires. They took over the campus and closed the entrances. That wasn't safe! Now, in some situations the press would talk with a student, and the student may not have been the best communicator. I have a gut feeling that interpreters might have played a role in bluffing a little bit. They were kind of embellishing the language, playing it up. Now keep in mind that during the 1988 protest interpreters were volunteers. So not necessarily everyone who was there was a professional interpreter. But my suspicion is the protest was very flexible, and some interpreters were like, "Fuck it!" (Participant #22)

By framing interpreters as fellow rulebreakers, he suggests that they are not only allies, but perhaps accomplices in the protest. He suggests that the actions they took, while falling outside ethical and professional norms, were performed out of a sense of allyship with the community. For example, he argues that interpreters did not follow the general ethical guideline that interpreters must interpret impartially, suggesting that they instead chose to embellish the language protesters used when interpreting for media interviews.[18] With this description and his comparison of interpreters' and protesters' actions, he frames interpreters as activists, fellow protesters, and allies to the deaf community.

However, this view was not ubiquitous. Some DPN protesters painted a different picture of interpreter involvement and role, suggesting some attributes of allies, while also alluding to the conduit model of interpreting. One protester recounted that interpreters were "friends in the community" but also argued:

> In the simplest view, an interpreter acts as a facilitator, a translator, a transmitter, a conduit, to facilitate the message to a signed message, and to a spoken message. My view of interpreters was always the same growing up. I see how some deaf people look at interpreters as "assistants" or "helpers," but I don't like that role. I'm in charge, not the interpreter. Now, it really depends on the interpreter's personality, like some interpreters are very dominant and like to take over or speak on behalf of deaf people. No, do not speak on behalf of the deaf person. Interpreters are to facilitate the floor for deaf individuals, not for themselves, so it depends on the interpreter's personality. But my view is that an interpreter's role is to interpret and facilitate. Now, back in 1988, on their "off duty time" interpreters were typically friends in the community… DPN interpreters did a great job. Most of the reporters would do interviews, and the interpreters wouldn't speak for themselves – they would defer to deaf people. Not like how when hearing people address all their questions to interpreters, who then answer everything. Instead, they brought in a deaf person to answer, so that was good…
>
> Interpreters served as ears to the outside world for us. I mean, interpreters knew where reporters were and who they were, so they would tell us things like when they arrived, like when ABC [News] or someone got there, they would pass on the word and inform us. Also the police would tell us about things like road closures, and interpreters kept us informed, so they were our ears to what was happening out there, which helped so we didn't have to do a lot of checking into things, they would let us know as our ears. (Participant #23)

With these comments, the interviewee suggests viewing interpreters both as both professionals and as allies. Although they underscore aspects of interpreting inherent in the conduit and communication facilitator models of interpreting, they also describe close personal relationships between protesters and interpreters. By suggesting that interpreters acted as the protesters' "ears to the outside world" and recounting actions they took beyond interpreting, the protester frames interpreters as "friends in the deaf community." Specifically, they recount interpreters enacting a different role on their "off duty time," demonstrating a critical attention to the roles interpreters enact, especially highlighting interpreters' work as allies. The protester's perspective indicates an overlap of interpreter role according to the various role descriptions.

Data from interviewees – both protesters and interpreters – suggest two conclusions: (1) that DPN participants saw interpreters as creating and enacting a nuanced role that cannot neatly fit into any one of the role metaphors of interpreting and (2) that the role metaphors do not neatly encapsulate interpreter role. As Roy (1993, 2002), Wilcox and Shaffer (2005), and others have argued, the role metaphors frequently lead back to mechanistic views of communication and the interpreting process. In the case of DPN, they lead to a confusing picture of "interpreter as conduit ally."

Analyzing DPN Interpreting through the Role-space Model

Here, I provide a nuanced analysis of interpreter role in the protest according to the role-space model (Llewellyn-Jones & Lee, 2014). Specifically, I analyze data that speak to the three components of role-space: participant alignment, interaction management, and presentation of self.

The interpreters demonstrated a high level of participant alignment with the protesters. As I have argued elsewhere, this alignment is borne out of a shared identity and sense of group belonging – referred to by Polletta and Jasper (2001) as *collective identity* – between interpreters and members of the deaf community (Halley, 2019). This alignment was consistently emphasized by the interpreters and was made clear by their very rationale behind participating in the protest: the interpreters suggested they were there *because* of their deaf friends or family who were protesting. Were it not for their personal connections and alignment with the protesters, they would not have been present to interpret in the first place. Llewellyn-Jones and Lee (2014) refer to this as the work of a "prealigned interpreter," in which the interpreter "will, inevitably, already know or perhaps be related to some of the people they might have to interpret for" (p. 50).

Interpreters in DPN were generally more closely aligned with deaf people (and therefore the protesters) than with hearing people due to existing personal and community-based relationships. Consider, for example, the numerous interpreters who had prior or current connections with Gallaudet University, including those who had taught, studied, or worked at the university. Contrast this with their nonexisting relationships with hearing people (e.g., reporters, members of the administration), and we see that interpreters in the protest enacted an alignment toward the protesters.[19] As one interpreter recounted:

> I taught at Gallaudet for six years on and off. Most of that was in the English Department… I was totally immersed in the deaf world in DC. I lived with deaf people, worked with deaf people, and my friends were deaf people. (Participant #13)

Such sentiments were common among the interpreters who volunteered to work in the protest. More than half of the interpreters I interviewed (12 out of 21) were formally affiliated with the university at the time of the protest (e.g., as contract interpreters, administrative staff, etc.), and several others had former ties to the university (e.g., former students or faculty).

Through archival review, it was also possible to identify some aspects of how interpreters approached interaction management in their work during the protest. The demands of instantaneous communication broadcast across the airwaves, coupled with the imperfections of simultaneous interpretation, exacerbated the challenges the DPN interpreters faced when interpreting in news media environments. A key example of this occurred during a live, televised interview on ABC's *Nightline* with Elisabeth Zinser, Greg Hlibok, and deaf actress Marlee Matlin, which included the work of at least two interpreters (one who interpreted Hlibok's comments into English, and one who interpreted Matlin's). At numerous points during the interview, individuals spoke over one another, a common challenge faced by interpreters who work with dialogic and interactive participants. Such challenges may be exacerbated when interpreters and participants do not all have direct access to one another, such as during the *Nightline* interview, when Hlibok and Zinser were not in the same location. A clear example of the interpreter's need to manage the interaction occurred when Dr. Zinser said, "I believe very strongly that a deaf individual, one day, will not only be the president of Gallaudet–" and was immediately cut off by interpreted responses from Matlin and Hlibok: "Why not now? Why not now? Look at me! Look at me" and "No, that's old news! I'm tired of that statement, 'One day,' again and again, 'Some day a deaf person...'"

It is also worth noting that interaction management issues were not unique to interpreters who were volunteering their services in the protest. In one event organized by the board, a deaf member of the faculty, Dr. Harvey Goodstein, took to the stage to interrupt comments from board chair, Jane Bassett Spilman. As Goodstein addressed the crowd in American Sign Language and the event devolved into chaos, a deaf member of the audience began to address Spilman, who indicated to the interpreter – a paid contractor for the board – that she was not interested in hearing what he had to say. As the interpreter explained:

> So, I was standing on the stage next to Spilman, and there was somebody signing down at the stage. And she said, "Nope, nope, nope! I'm not, until they quiet down, I'm not going to have any conversation." That moment was, "Huh? What do I do now?" You know, I can see him talking, and so I actually think I made a pretty good decision in the moment. I didn't come back over and stand next to her to say, "This is what he's saying." I just stood there and did it. Just talked so that she could hear. Well as much as anybody could hear in that moment. But I felt like I was not going to deny him a voice, and I wasn't going to shove it down her throat, but at the moment I think it was the right decision. Even looking back I think it was the right decision. I didn't dismiss him... (Participant #1)

One can imagine that an interpreter behaving as an ally might make decisions that support the ability of a particular participant to make themselves heard (e.g., talking over a hearing person if they attempted to interrupt when a deaf person was signing). At this point, it is also worth noting how issues of alignment may play into interaction management. Both interpreters who worked with Matlin and Hlibok during the *Nightline* special were in the same physical location as the deaf person for whom they were interpreting; conversely, the interpreter employed by the board of trustees was physically and financially aligned with Spilman (i.e., she was paid by the board and stood on the stage with the board chair). Despite this, all the interpreters made decisions regarding interaction management that supported the ability of deaf people to participate more fully and meaningfully.

Finally, we come to the third component of role-space: presentation of self. Recall that a low presentation of self refers to "not interacting, not presenting information," whereas a high presentation entails "speaking for one's self, providing information etc" (Llewellyn-Jones & Lee, 2014, p. 15). Throughout the interviews, no interpreters ever suggested participating in the protest in such a way that they allowed their presentation of self to overshadow the work of deaf students and community members leading the protest. Interviewees consistently described the importance of deferring to the protesters and the deaf community, rather than speaking on behalf of them, potentially indicating a relatively low presentation of self. However, as one interpreter explained:

> Once the media got hold of this, it was amazing how many interpreters suddenly climbed out of the woodwork and wanted to come and interpret. Because there was a camera there, and so there was a little bit of showcasing that occurred. You did see a little bit of people who liked the limelight, but it was minimal in terms of the overall movement. (Participant #18)

Despite this contention, note that there was generally a low presentation of self from interpreters while actively interpreting. The interpreters did not report regularly partaking in "speaking for one's self" (Llewellyn-Jones & Lee, 2014, p. 15) while working in the protest. As another interpreter suggested, "Who really cares who is in the limelight? We felt like we had a job, a purpose, a mission to accomplish." Further, few of the interpreters reported any ancillary participation in the protest (e.g., holding signs), although some recalled minimal participation in claims-making activities (Lindekilde, 2013) like being with protesters during a march. For example, one interpreter opined about the optics of simply being present:

> If we take an aerial view of the crowd, you're in there somewhere... but to be a protester to me means you really had to have your own voice... I couldn't and didn't do that. (Participant #11)

The interpreters suggested that they enacted a relatively low presentation of self because doing so supported the goals of the protesters. In a protest that was ostensibly led by and intended for deaf people, the interpreters argued that taking a role in which they made decisions or weighed in too heavily with their perspectives would undermine the movement as a whole. As one interpreter stated,

> I can remember feeling that this was the time to stand ready and be supportive but not do anything else. So, I felt like my job was just to stand at the ready and respond when asked. (Participant #15)

Taken together, the data presented herein suggest that DPN interpreters embodied a role-space in which they demonstrated a relatively high participant alignment with protesters, a relatively high level of interaction management, and a relatively low presentation of self. Future analyses might examine interpreters acting as allies in other settings to better understand how and why they enact and create particular role-spaces. More specifically, these data have demonstrated interpreter role-space of ally-like behavior in a singular contentious political situation (the DPN protest). The role-space of interpreters enacting ally-like role-spaces in other situations will shed light on the work of interpreters in a variety of settings.

DISCUSSION

The lived experiences of hearing people are not the same as members of the deaf community (Lane, Hoffmeister, & Bahan, 1996). Despite this, deaf studies scholar Paddy Ladd (2003) writes that some hearing people who have forged relationships with deaf people (e.g., interpreters) are sometimes granted "partial membership" in the deaf community (p. 42). Recognizing the role of DPN interpreters as allies, interviewees in this study seem to support this idea of interpreters being quasi-members of the deaf community. A partial membership and allyship with the deaf community appear to go hand in hand.

Another area worthy of note is the concept of self-identification as an ally in contrast to being *granted* the title ally. Who decides whether one is an ally to a given community and how that allyship is defined? Although the interpreters interviewed in this study described seeing themselves as allies and the deaf protesters generally agreed with this description, this may not always be the case. Marginalized groups who seek allies have the right to engage in gatekeeping activities that determine who should be considered an ally and what actions contribute toward a sense of allyship. For example, in activism surrounding children with disabilities, Carey, Block, and Scotch (2019) have described the "tense" alliances between organizations of parent activists and organizations led by people with disabilities. Although the data in this study reveal no tension over allyship between interpreters and protesters, it is not difficult to imagine tensions rising as practitioners and community members further refine the meaning of allyship and potentially find areas of conflict. These considerations also raise issues for the meaning of interpreter actions toward allyship more generally; what does ally behavior entail *outside* of role-space, and how can interpreter educators distill these lessons into pedagogical outcomes for future generations of interpreters who strive to be allies to deaf people?

Despite the positive image of the ally behavior I have painted in this chapter, interpreter actions toward allyship during DPN may not have been without negative consequences. This is particularly so when interpreters' actions are viewed by those not in the community as inappropriate or overextending boundaries. In these cases, interpreters who behave as allies are seen as destructive. In the case of DPN, archival review uncovered numerous occasions in which members of Gallaudet's administration viewed interpreters with, at best, suspicion and, at worst, outright distrust. In the following striking example of distrust from administrators, President Zinser describes an interpreter who enacted a role-space in which they demonstrated – via body language – a strong alignment with protesters and a high presentation of self. In an interview transcript unearthed in the Gallaudet University Archives, President Zinser recounted a meeting in which she engaged in negotiations with student protesters:

> [Two] of [the students] were sitting on the bed and [two] of them were sitting on another bed. I sort of leaned against the dresser, now this is a hotel room, and their interpreter was there, very hostile, in fact, I must tell you, the interpreters through this whole thing were very hostile... It was their affect, just glaring at me, what are you doing here, kind of look on their faces. They were very much involved in it all, I could really tell. I had my own [interpreter] and I was just as happy that I had my own. (Zinser, n.d., p. 22)

Unfortunately, no member of the board of trustees agreed to be interviewed for this study, making it difficult to analyze their perspectives. However, such views may help us to problematize interpreters who act as allies, analyze their behavior in new ways, and continue to refine role-space theory applied to both allyship and roles in contentious settings. This preliminary analysis suggests potential unintended consequences that may arise due to an interpreter behaving as an ally to any given party in an interpreted encounter. Specifically, when an interpreter demonstrates aligning with one party coupled with a high presentation of self in a contentious situation, suspicions may arise, contributing to a general breakdown of trust and uncertain or unintended consequences. This example also suggests that the role-space of an interpreter acting as an ally may not be static: in this case, the interpreter presented a high presentation of self, unlike interpreters at other points in the protest. Allyship, it seems, may be manifest according to a variety of role-spaces that interpreters create.

Finally, it is also worth considering not only the role of individual interpreters in the protest but also the role of interpreters as a collective body. During DPN, a variety of institutions offered their support for the protest (e.g., publicity and financial support from the American Postal Workers Union). Documents produced by the RID also provide evidence of formal institutional support from interpreters. Although no interviewees in this study indicated learning about the protest through the organization, the national RID office compiled an "Advocacy Action Notice" packet during the protest, which was distributed to affiliate RID chapters. In the packet, RID Executive Director Don Roose shared RID's position statement on the protest:

> The membership and organization of the Registry of Interpreters for the Deaf (RID) support the struggle of deaf people to achieve and win the necessary power over their own destiny. Therefore, the deaf and hearing members of the RID are in total support with the goals of the Gallaudet University faculty, staff and student body in their fight to obtain decision-making control of their Gallaudet community.

In addition to the official position statement, RID and the local affiliate chapter (the Potomac Chapter of the Registry of Interpreters for the Deaf, PCRID) used the packet to encourage members to engage in a number of activities to support the protest. For example, RID members were asked to share RID's position statement, contact the university and members of Congress, and make donations in support of DPN through RID. Additionally, RID sent a representative – Don Renzulli – to speak at several DPN rallies and meetings, reiterating the organization's support. At one protest rally, Renzulli addressed the crowd:[20]

> All over America and Canada our members have been calling us, and they've been calling our national office, which is here in Washington, and they want you to know that they support your efforts one hundred percent, and we will continue to support your efforts one hundred percent. Thank you!

By issuing such statements, RID verbally affirmed its support for the protesters and suggested it was mobilizing interpreting resources. The comments and actions by RID indicate allyship toward the deaf community not only on an individual level but also nationally. Through its engagement with members and physical presence at the protest, RID's advocacy contributed to the network that pushed the protest forward.

Since its founding in 1964, RID has been the national organization for the profession of American Sign Language/English interpreters. In its national role, RID has provided its support for social and political changes that are central to the deaf community. In the case of DPN, Renzulli, Roose, and other members of RID's leadership spoke on behalf of interpreters in favor of the protest. RID's supportive role as an organization with ties to the deaf community was not unique to DPN. For example, when an unqualified individual posed as an interpreter at the funeral of Nelson Mandela in 2013, RID responded by advocating for the linguistic rights of deaf people across the globe. In a statement, RID leadership wrote, "The United Nations recognizes access to language as a basic human right. The very rights for which Mandela fought were violated for Deaf people during his memorial ceremony..."[21]

CONCLUSION

Through their participation in the DPN protest, the American Sign Language/English interpreters who did so behaved as allies to the protesters and the wider American deaf community. Reflecting on DPN, interpreter and former president of the Registry of Interpreters for the Deaf, Lou Fant (1990) suggested that interpreters must "learn to walk the narrow path between advocacy as individuals, and objectivity as professional interpreters" (p. 87). However, as Ladd (2003) argues, due to social status and power imbalances between deaf and hearing people, "an interpreter attempting a fully neutral stance will end up reinforcing the energies emanating from the more powerful group" (p. 447). By shifting away from the role of interpreter as disinterested party and moving toward instead becoming allies, the DPN interpreters rejected a notion of strict neutrality and instead embraced participating in social change.

Finally, it is interesting to note that although the interpreters described their work in ways that suggest allyship, their role in DPN predates the development and widespread use of the ally model among interpreters. However, this may not be surprising, and it may even be promising for the future of interpreting. Rather than uncritically following ethical codes and prescribed role standards of the time, the DPN interpreters forged their own path in collaboration with the deaf community.[22] This bodes well for the continued evolution of how interpreters enact various roles and how we come to understand them. As interpreters face the new challenges of the twenty-first century – and contemporary politics – they may continue to modify the ways in which they enact their roles according to the demands they face.

ACKNOWLEDGMENTS

This chapter is a result of my PhD dissertation research conducted at Gallaudet University. I thank the members of my dissertation committee for their support: Dr. Brenda Nicodemus (chair), Dr. Mona Baker, Dr. Keith Cagle, Dr. Emily Shaw, and Dr. Sharon Barnartt. I especially thank Dr. Barnartt for her review of this manuscript, Daniel LeMay for his insightful comments on role-space, and Arien Peppers for her editorial review. Finally, I thank the Gallaudet University Office of Research Support and International Affairs (RSIA) for their generous financial support of this project.

NOTES

1. People with hearing loss identify in numerous ways including deaf, hard-of-hearing, and deafblind, among others. In using the term "deaf," I do not seek to make broad

generalizations about this diverse group of people. Rather, I use the term as a simple and inclusive means of encompassing the wide variety of individuals with hearing loss.

2. To be "hearing" is to be not deaf or hard-of-hearing.

3. Historically, signed language interpreters have taken up a greater interest in interpreter role than their spoken language counterparts. Because spoken language interpreters frequently work in conference settings (i.e., in a booth without direct access to speakers), social aspects of spoken language interpreting have garnered less attention in the literature (Roy, 1993, 2002). However, because signed language interpreters have traditionally worked in dialogic community settings (e.g., medical appointments), theorists have been more apt to describe the ways in which these interpreters enact their role(s) using metaphors and models.

4. These models have been described by a variety of authors, including Roy (1993, 2002), Witter-Merithew (1986), Baker-Shenk (1991), McIntire and Sanderson (1993), and Frishberg (1986).

5. Angelelli (2004) also notes that conduit model stems from beliefs about the role of conference interpreters.

6. This model shares much with the work of Venuti (1995), who discussed *domestication* and *foreignization* in translation, a construct to examine how a translation conforms with the cultural norms and values of the culture of the target reader (domestication) or the original author (foreignization).

7. By employing the framework of cognitive linguistics, Wilcox and Shaffer (2005) further suggest that most descriptions of interpreter role and function of interpreters still employ "conduit thinking" about human communication, reinforcing views of both communicative and social neutrality. They instead argue in favor of a cognitive model of interpreting, which "permits interpreters to break through the impossibility of achieving neutrality" and "recognize their role in making meaning" (p. 48).

8. Although I do not create them in this chapter, for visual representations of role-spaces enacted by interpreters in various settings on a three-dimensional plot, see Llewellyn-Jones and Lee (2014).

9. Roy (2000) identified four possible approaches an interpreter may employ to address overlapping speech: 1) the interpreter stops one speaker and allows the other to continue, 2) the interpreter momentarily ignores the overlapping speech and interprets it later, 3) the interpreter ignores the overlapping speech altogether, and 4) the interpreter momentarily ignores the overlapping speech and then offers a turn to the one creating overlapping speech.

10. The interpreters I interviewed were primarily identified through a handwritten list of nearly 100 interpreters' names located in the Gallaudet University Archives. However, some were also identified through professional contacts and referrals from other DPN participants.

11. In addition to the protesters and interpreters, I also interviewed one deaf member of Gallaudet's administration. Requests to speak with members of the board of trustees yielded no interviews.

12. I thank Drs. Keith Cagle and Paul Harrelson for offering their time.

13. RID, founded in 1964, is the national professional association of American Sign Language/English interpreters in the United States. The organization advocates in the interpreting profession and administers a nationally recognized interpreter credentialing system.

14. I also interviewed one individual who was a member of Gallaudet's administration during DPN. He identified as a white, deaf male and was 44 years of age at the time of the protest. He began learning American Sign Language at the age of 22 and did not have deaf parents.

15. Note that two of the interpreters also took up leadership roles in coordinating interpreting services, and three of the interpreters worked primarily with the Gallaudet University Board of Trustees, did not interpret in student-led protest events, and are not analyzed here as activist interpreters. These interpreters are noted as Participants 1–5 in Table 1. Further, note that while participants were asked to share their race and ethnicity,

this demographic information is not reported in the table. Because this small pool of participants was predominantly white, I choose to protect their identities by not reporting this individualized and potentially identifiable data.

16. All data were compiled in a Google Sheets document. Although spreadsheet software packages are often associated with quantitative forms of analysis, they are also used in qualitative research to code, organize, and analyze large sets of data, such as interview transcripts (Meyer & Avery, 2009). I used McCracken's (1988) approach to coding, in which the data are filtered through three *readings*: I first observed the data for content, then I interpreted the observations on their own and according to the rest of the data and existing literature (e.g., role-space theory and earlier models of interpreter role), and I finally connected the observations identified in the coding process.

17. Some of the illustrative examples in this chapter also appear in Halley (2019), in which I analyzed the data through the lens of social movement studies. However, the data reported here are analyzed through the descriptions of role and the role-space model and offer new insight into interpreter enactment of role.

18. Although this is an interesting point to consider, a linguistic analysis of the interpreting *product* is outside the scope of this chapter. However, see Christiansen and Barnartt (1995), who also suggest that interpreters may have been "embellishing" their spoken English interpretations of the protesters' American Sign Language message (p. 184).

19. However, this is not necessarily the case for the interpreters who worked for the board of trustees. In addition to their payment coming from the board, the interpreters described forming close bonds with both deaf and hearing members of the board.

20. Renzulli addressed the crowd using American Sign Language. The words in this chapter reflect the English interpretation of his comments provided by an interpreter working during the rally.

21. RID's full statement, available in English and American Sign Language, is available at https://rid.org/the-registry-of-interpreters-for-the-deaf-inc-rid-issues-statement-about-interpreting-services-at-the-nelson-mandela-memorial-services/.

22. Numerous interpreters described DPN as a transformational moment for them, frequently sharing stories of seeing deaf people take control of their own destinies for the first time. Further analysis is necessary and forthcoming, but it seems that interpreter allyship and alliances may come about as a consequence of political unrest and upheaval.

REFERENCES

Angelelli, C. (2004). *Revisiting the interpreter's role: A study of conference court, and medical interpreters in Canada, Mexico, and the United States*. Amsterdam: John Benjamins.

Arjona, E. (1978). Intercultural communication and the training of interpreters at the Monterey Institute of Foreign studies. In D. Gerver & H. W. Sinaiko (Eds.), *Language interpretation and communication*. NATO Conference Series (Vol. 6, pp. 35–44). Boston, MA: Springer. Retrieved from https://link.springer.com/chapter/10.1007/978-1-4615-9077-4_5

Armstrong, D. (2014). *The history of Gallaudet University*. Washington, DC: Gallaudet University Press.

Aronson, J. (1995). A pragmatic view of thematic analysis. *Qualitative Report*, *2*(1), 1–3.

Baker, M. (2006). *Translation and conflict: A narrative account*. New York, NY: Routledge.

Baker-Shenk, C. (1991). The interpreter: Machine, advocate, or ally? *Expanding horizons: Proceedings of the 1991 RID convention*, (pp. 120–140). Silver Spring, MD: RID Publications.

Blee, K., & Taylor, V. (2002). Semi-structured interviewing in social movement research. In B. Klandermans & S. Staggenborg (Eds.), *Methods of social movement research* (pp. 92–117). Minneapolis, MN: University of Minnesota Press.

Boyatzis, R. (1998). *Transforming qualitative information: Thematic analysis and code development*. Thousand Oaks, CA: SAGE Publications.

Carey, A., Block, P., & Scotch, R. (2019). Sometimes allies: Parent-led disability organizations and social movements. *Disability Studies Quarterly*, *39*(1). Retrieved from https://dsq-sds.org/article/view/6281/5183

Christiansen, J., & Barnartt, S. (1995). *Deaf president now: The 1988 revolution at Gallaudet university*. Washington, DC: Gallaudet University Press.

Cokely, D. (1984). Response to Etilvia Arjona on evaluation. In M. McIntire (Ed.), *Proceedings of the fourth national conference of interpreter trainers: New dialogues in interpreter education* (pp. 139–150). Silver Spring, MD: Registry of Interpreters for the Deaf.

Emmorey, K., Borinstein, H., Thompson, R., & Gollan, T. (2008). Bimodal bilingualism. *Bilingualism: Language and Cognition, 11*(1), 43–61.

Fant, L. (1990). *Silver threads: A personal look at the first twenty-five years of the Registry of interpreters for the deaf*. Alexandria, VA: RID Publications.

Frishberg, N. (1986). *Interpreting: An introduction*. Silver Spring, MD: Registry of Interpreters for the Deaf.

Gannon, J. (1989). *The week the world heard Gallaudet*. Washington, DC: Gallaudet University Press.

Goffman, E. (1961). *Encounters: Two studies in the sociology of interaction*. Indianapolis, IN: Bobbs-Merrill.

Goffman, E. (1972). *Interaction ritual: Essays on face-to-face behavior*. London: Allen Lane.

Goffman, E. (1990). *The presentation of self in everyday life*. London: Penguin.

Halley, M. (2019). Interpreting as ideologically-structured action: Collective identity between activist interpreters and protesters. *New Voices in Translation Studies, 20*, 54–85.

Hauser, P., Finch, K., & Hauser, A. (2008). (Eds.), *Deaf professionals and designated interpreters: A new paradigm*. Washington, DC: Gallaudet University Press.

Hayes, N. (1997). Theory-led thematic analysis: Social identification in small companies. In N. Hayes (Ed.), *Doing qualitative analysis in psychology* (pp. 93–114). Hove: Psychology Press.

Ingram, R. (1985). Simultaneous interpretation of sign languages: Semiotic and psycholinguistic perspectives. *Multilingua, 4*(2), 91–102.

Janzen, T., & Korpiniski, D. (2005). Ethics and professionalism in interpreting. In T. Janzen (Ed.), *Topics in signed language interpreting: Theory and practice* (pp. 165–169). Amsterdam: John Benjamins.

Ladd, P. (2003). *Understanding deaf culture: In search of deafhood*. Tonawanda, NY: Multilingual Matters Ltd.

Lane, H., Hoffmeister, R., & Bahan, B. (1996). *A journey into the deaf-world*. San Diego, CA: DawnSignPress.

Lindekilde, L. (2013). Claims-making. In D. Snow, D. della Porta, B. Klandermans, & D. McAdam (Eds.), *The Wiley-Blackwell encyclopedia of social and political movements* (Vol. 1, pp. 201–203). Malden, MA: Blackwell Publishing Ltd.

Linton, R. (1936). *The study of man*. New York, NY: Appleton-Century-Crofts.

Llewellyn-Jones, P., & Lee, R. G. (2014). *Redefining the role of the community interpreter: The concept of role-space*. Lincoln: SLI Press.

McCracken, G. (1988). *The long interview*. London: SAGE Publications.

McIntire, M., & Sanderson, G. (1993). Bye-bye! Bi-bi!: Questions of empowerment and role. In J. Plant-Moeller (Ed.), *A confluence of diverse relationships, proceedings of the thirteenth national convention of the Registry of Interpreters for the Deaf* (pp. 94–118). Silver Spring, MD: RID Publications.

Mead, G. H. (1934). *Mind, self, and society from the standpoint of a social behaviorist*. Chicago, IL: University of Chicago Press.

Metzger, M. (1999). *Sign language interpreting: Deconstructing the myth of neutrality*. Washington, DC: Gallaudet University Press.

Meyer, D., & Avery, L. (2009). Excel as a qualitative data analysis tool. *Field Methods, 21*(1), 91–112.

Mindess, A. (1999). *Reading between the signs: Intercultural communication for sign language interpreters*. Yarmouth, ME: Intercultural Press.

Newcomb, T. M. (1950). *Social psychology*. New York, NY: Dryden Press.

Polletta, F., & Jasper, J. (2001). Collective identity and social movements. *Annual Review of Sociology, 27*, 185–203.

della Porta, D. (2014). In-depth interviews. In D. della Porta (Ed.), *Methodological practices in social movement research* (pp. 228–261). Oxford: Oxford University Press.

Roy, C. (1993). The problem with definitions, descriptions, and the role metaphors of interpreters. *Journal of Interpretation, 6*(1), 127–154.

Roy, C. (2000). *Interpreting as a discourse process*. New York, NY: Oxford University Press.

Roy, C. (2002). The problem with definitions, descriptions, and the role metaphors of interpreters. In F. Pöchhacker & M. Shlesinger (Eds.), *The interpreting studies reader* (pp. 345–353). London: Routledge.

Ryan, G., & Bernard, H. (2000). Data management and analysis methods. In N. K. Denzin & Y. S. Lincoln (Eds.), *Handbook of qualitative research* (2nd ed., pp. 769–802). Thousand Oaks, CA: SAGE Publications.

Turner, R. H. (1956). Role-taking, role standpoint, and reference-group behavior. *American Journal of Sociology*, *61*. 316–328.

Turner, R. H. (1962). Role taking: Process versus conformity. In A. M. Rose (Ed.), *Human behavior and social processes: An interactionist approach* (pp. 20–40). Boston, MA: Houghton Mifflin.

Venuti, L. (1995). *The translator's invisibility: A history of translation*. London: Routledge.

Wadensjö, C. (2004). Dialogue interpreting: A monologising practice in a dialogicallyorganized world. *Target*, *16*(1), 105–124.

Weiss, R. (1994). *Learning from strangers*. New York, NY: Free Press.

Wilcox, S., & Shaffer, B. (2005). Towards a cognitive model of interpreting. In T. Janzen (Ed.), *Topics in signed language interpreting: Theory and practice* (pp. 27–50). Amsterdam: John Benjamins.

Witter-Merithew, A. (1986). Claiming our destiny. RID VIEWS.

Witter-Merithew, A. (n.d.). From benevolent care-taker to ally: The evolving role of sign language interpreters in the United States of America. Retrieved from http://www.interpretereducation.org/wp-content/uploads/2014/04/From-Benevolent-Caretaker.pdf

Chapter 9

CAN WE BROADEN THE NEURODIVERSITY MOVEMENT WITHOUT WEAKENING IT? PARTICIPATORY APPROACHES AS A FRAMEWORK FOR CROSS-DISABILITY ALLIANCE BUILDING

Kristen Gillespie-Lynch, Patrick Dwyer, Christopher Constantino, Steven K. Kapp, Emily Hotez, Ariana Riccio, Danielle DeNigris, Bella Kofner and Eric Endlich

ABSTRACT

Purpose: *We critically examine the idea of neurodiversity, or the uniqueness of all brains, as the foundation for the neurodiversity movement, which began as an autism rights movement. We explore the neurodiversity movement's potential to support cross-disability alliances that can transform cultures.*

Methods/Approach: *A neurodiverse team reviewed literature about the history of the neurodiversity movement and associated participatory research methodologies and drew from our experiences guiding programs led, to varying degrees, by neurodivergent people. We highlight two programs for autistic university students, one started by and for autistics and one developed in collaboration with autistic and nonautistic students. These programs are*

Disability Alliances and Allies
Research in Social Science and Disability, Volume 12, 189–223

ISSN: 1479-3547/doi:10.1108/S1479-354720200000012013

contrasted with a national self-help group started by and for stutterers that is inclusive of "neurotypicals."

Findings: *Neurodiversity-aligned practices have emerged in diverse communities. Similar benefits and challenges of alliance building within versus across neurotypes were apparent in communities that had not been in close contact. Neurodiversity provides a framework that people with diverse conditions can use to identify and work together to challenge shared forms of oppression. However, people interpret the neurodiversity movement in diverse ways. By honing in on core aspects of the neurodiversity paradigm, we can foster alliances across diverse perspectives.*

Implications/ Values: *Becoming aware of power imbalances and working to rectify them is essential for building effective alliances across neurotypes. Sufficient space and time are needed to create healthy alliances. Participatory approaches, and approaches solely led by neurodivergent people, can begin to address concerns about power and representation within the neurodiversity movement while shifting public understanding.*

Keywords: Neurodiversity; autism; stuttering; cross-disability alliances; participatory research; university

INTRODUCTION

> Autism is a way of being. It is *pervasive*; it colors every experience, every sensation, perception, thought, emotion, and encounter, every aspect of existence. It is not possible to separate the autism from the person – and if it were possible, the person you'd have left would not be the same person you started with. (Sinclair, 1993/2012, p. 1)

The misconception that autism fundamentally disrupts the ability to connect meaningfully with others was once so widespread that the first autistic people to publicly share their experiences being autistic introduced themselves as "recovered" from autism (e.g., Grandin, 1990; Kanner, 1943; Pripas-Kapit, 2020). After weathering misconceptions about autism for decades, Jim Sinclair, Donna Williams, and Xenia Grant met for the first time in an "autistic space," free of nonautistic people and their expectations about how people should interact. Together Jim, Donna, and Xenia cofounded the first autistic-led advocacy organization, Autism Network International (ANI) in 1992 (Sinclair, 2010). Within a few years, the ideas sparked by this initially "autistic only" alliance would inspire a dialogue between autistic people and people with and without other conditions that would lay the foundation for a new type of civil rights movement, the *neurodiversity movement*. The neurodiversity movement challenges deficit-oriented conceptualizations of autism, reframing autism as a valuable minority identity that needs no cure (Kapp, 2020; Kapp, Gillespie-Lynch, Sherman, & Hutman, 2013).

In the late 1990s, Judy Singer (2017) and Harvey Blume (1998) coined the term *neurodiversity*, or the uniqueness of *all* brains, based on discussions in an autistic-run online group, InLv, that included autistic people and nonautistic allies (Dekker, 2020). The term called forth a new "Politics of Neurodiversity" (the neurodiversity movement) by situating neurological differences at the intersections of other minority identities and providing a framework to critique discrimination (Singer, 2019): "Just as biodiversity is essential to ecosystem stability, so neurodiversity may be essential for cultural stability" (Singer, 2017, loc. 1079).

In 2006, Ari Ne'eman and Scott Michael Robertson founded the Autistic Self Advocacy Network (ASAN) to address a lack of autistic representation in dialogues about autism. In 2007, Ne'eman led a campaign against a stigmatizing "public service campaign" framing autism as a kidnapper (Kras, 2010). This effective campaign, which elicited support from autistic advocates and the broader disability rights community, increased ASAN's influence and situated the neurodiversity movement as part of a cross-disability coalition for human rights and social justice.[1] The central premise of this chapter is that the neurodiversity movement's rapid expansion out from its roots in the autism rights movement fosters both within- and across-disability alliances that can transform cultures, making them increasingly supportive of the diversity that nourishes them.

Indeed, the term neurodiversity has taken on a life of its own, helping autistic self-advocates and their allies identify like-minded people to band together with to challenge and reshape public and scientific narratives about autism, research priorities, and services (e.g., Fletcher-Watson et al., 2019; Kapp, 2020). The neurodiversity movement inspired the emergence of participatory approaches to autism research, wherein autistic people are meaningfully involved in developing, enacting, and disseminating research initiatives (Nicolaidis, 2012). The idea of neurodiversity is also appealing to other disability communities. Observing the promising impacts of neurodiversity-aligned advocacy on autism research and policy, scholars and writers have begun to explore how neurodiversity-aligned perspectives can be applied to other conditions, e.g., stuttering, dyslexia, mood disorders, anxiety, ADHD, intellectual and learning disabilities, and schizophrenia (Antonetta, 2007; Armstrong, 2010; Constantino, 2018; Fenton & Krahn, 2007; Griffin & Pollak, 2009; Jamison, 1995). For example, Christopher Constantino (2018), a stuttering researcher, clinician, stutterer, and an author of this report, recently published a paper describing how the idea of neurodiversity can be used to improve stuttering research and practice. He shared how neurodiversity-aligned approaches to stuttering (e.g., exploring different ways of stuttering and benefits of stuttering) promote well-being.

This chapter was inspired by informal dialogues at the National Stuttering Association's (NSA, 2019) Research Symposium, designed by Christopher Constantino and Vivian Sisskin to bring stuttering experts in contact with neurodiversity-aligned practices and perspectives from other communities (i.e., the autistic and Deaf communities). Although the autistic and stuttering communities[2] have developed largely independently of one another, autism and stuttering share key commonalities. They are both neurodevelopmental disorders (or believed to be characterized by brain atypicalities early in development that may change over time) that impact self-expression (American Psychiatric Association, 2013; Casartelli, Molteni, & Ronconi, 2016; Chang, Zhu, Choo, & Angstadt, 2015). Both conditions often have a strong genetic component (Frigerio-Domingues & Drayna, 2017; Geschwind & State, 2015). However, genetic contributions are highly complex and variable. Both stutterers and autistic people face high levels of discrimination (e.g., bullying and difficulty obtaining jobs) that can contribute to heightened anxiety over time (Alm, 2014; Botha & Frost, 2020; Pierre, 2012). Both autistic people and stutterers feel empowered by opportunities to engage with people like them, particularly when they are able to help others (Boyle, 2013; Dwyer, 2019a; Morrison et al., 2019; Sinclair, 2010; Yeoman, 2019).

However, misconceptions about autism and stuttering can make it very difficult for autistic people and stutterers to take on leadership positions helping others (Hughes, 2016; Robertson, 2010; Yeoman, 2019). For example, a speech-language pathologist who develops and leads innovative support groups for young stutterers almost gave up on the career she now excels at when her professor told her that she could not become a successful speech-language pathologist because she herself stutters. Stigmatizing misconceptions often have their roots in the research and advocacy communities that develop their agendas without substantive guidance from the people they are purportedly trying to serve (Hughes, 2016; Raymaker & Nicolaidis, 2010). For example, major autism and stuttering organizations have explicitly sought to cure autism and stuttering, leading to outrage from some neurodivergent[3] people (Singh, Illes, Lazzeroni,& Hallmayer, 2009; Yeoman, 2019).

Participatory autism research emerged in 2006 with the explicit goal of correcting misconceptions fostered by a research tradition that had developed for over half a century with minimal autistic input (Feinstein, 2011; Raymaker & Nicolaidis, 2010). Growing from other social justice–oriented approaches, including action research, Freire's critical pedagogy, and feminism, participatory approaches use democratic decision-making processes to maximize the participation of people affected by research in the research process (Call-Cummings, Hauber-Özer, & Ross, 2019; Groot et al., 2019; Raymaker & Nicolaidis, 2013; Wilson, Kenny, & Dickson-Swift, 2018). Participatory approaches, which position community members as experts about their own lived experiences, vary along a continuum of involvement from consultation to authentic collaboration to fully equal partnerships.

Until very recently, participatory approaches to autism research were very rare; researchers tended to believe that their work was far more inclusive than community members felt that it was (Pellicano, Dinsmore, & Charman, 2014b). Although autism is often associated with research skills, such as attention to detail and pattern matching skills (Samson, Mottron, Soulières, & Zeffiro, 2012), participatory collaborations with autistic adults emerged years after participatory collaborations with adults with intellectual disabilities (ID) gained support from researchers and policy makers (e.g., March, Steingold, Justice, & Mitchell, 1997; Minkes, Townsley, Weston, Williams, & Tyrell, 1995;

Raymaker & Nicolaidis, 2010; Walmsley, 2001; Williams, Simons, & Swindon People First Research Team, 2005). However, people with ID have most commonly been involved in research in advisory capacities, meaning that they are called upon by researchers to give advice but are not involved as full collaborators (Bigby, Frawley, & Ramcharan, 2014). This approach can result in tokenistic involvement.[4]

Although the aim of participatory research is the democratization of knowledge, it often takes place in hierarchical settings where people with a diagnosis seek help from an "expert." Therefore, as interest in participatory approaches grows rapidly, so do concerns about potential consequences of uneven power dynamics such as tokenistic involvement, academics co-opting marginalized people's identities, and privacy concerns (e.g., Bigby et al., 2014; Schwartz, Kramer, Cohn, & McDonald, 2019). Recent review papers revealed that most of the early "participatory" research about neurodevelopmental conditions provided insufficient detail to determine if the studies were actually participatory. For example, Jivraj, Sacrey, Newton, Nicholas, and Zwaigenbaum (2014) concluded that only two participatory studies involved collaborators in all stages of the process and provided detail about how consensus was achieved and dissent handled.[5] Both of these studies were headed by the mother of an autistic individual, Christina Nicolaidis, and her autistic co-PI, Dora Raymaker. One of their projects, Academic Autism Spectrum Partnership in Research and Education (AASPIRE), which Steven K. Kapp (a coauthor of this report) is a member of, brings together academics, autistic adults, family members, and providers around the world. Nicolaidis' and colleagues' groundbreaking work set a precedent that has recently inspired rapid growth in participatory autism research (see Crane, Adams, Harper, Welch, & Pellicano, 2019 for a strong example).

Although Nicolaidis' et al. (2019) work has resulted in influential academic papers and applied tools, they initially had to overcome pronounced resistance to the very possibility of participatory autism research. Reviewers expressed biases about autism, including that autistic people lack understanding of themselves and others and are very inflexible, to support their doubts that autistic people could act as coresearchers. When evidence of the success of their work began to accrue, reviewers questioned if the people they were collaborating with were *really* autistic. Over time, feedback became much more positive. However, some academics continue to attribute problems that may arise during collaborations with autistic people to characteristics of autism. A recent paper describing participatory approaches as essential for improving autism research also highlighted biases about autism as barriers to full inclusion (Fletcher-Watson et al., 2019).

In contrast to the exclusionary history of autism research, speech-language pathology has a long tradition of disabled people helping others as scientists and clinicians (e.g., Quesal, 2012). Some of the earliest pioneers in speech-language pathology stuttered, such as Samuel Potter, Wendell Johnson, and Charles Van Riper (Duchan, 2011). For close to a century, stutterers have conducted research about stuttering (e.g., Boyle, 2013, 2018; Constantino, 2016, 2018; Johnson,

1930; Pierre, 2012). Some of this research has included stutterers who are not trained as researchers as authors (e.g., Krauss-Lehrman & Reeves, 1989; Yaruss et al., 2002). Perhaps because stutterers are often clinicians and researchers, no published research about stuttering uses an explicitly "participatory" methodology, wherein the power to steer the research is consciously shared between researchers and community members. Explicitly participatory methodologies may provide practical guidance to foster alliances across neurotypes that are more equitable.

AIMS AND METHODOLOGY

In this chapter, a neurodiverse team, comprised of autistic scholars, a scholar who stutters, and researchers without an unidentified disability, critically examines the theoretical roots and practical applications of the idea of neurodiversity in order to illuminate its potential as a framework for both disability-specific and cross-disability alliances.[6] We draw examples from our combined experience leading programs that were developed, to varying degrees, by neurodivergent people. We describe two peer support program models for autistic university students: one led by and including only autistic students and one developed by a nonautistic academic in collaboration with autistic and nonautistic mentees and mentors. We also describe a self-help group for people who stutter that was started by stutterers but is inclusive of "neurotypical" people. By exploring a few of the diverse ways in which neurodiversity-aligned support groups can develop through the lens of two communities that have not traditionally been in close contact (autistics and stutterers), we identify strategies for effective alliance building within and across neurotypes.[7] Our reflections on our connections to these programs, communities, and the neurodiversity movement more generally can be viewed in Table 1.

Given that concerns about power, representation, and shared purpose disrupt effective alliance building, we use and explore the history of participatory research methods focused on neurodevelopmental disorders in this chapter. The authors collaboratively generated ideas for this chapter in a Google planning document and through Skype. First we conducted a literature review focused on the history of the neurodiversity movement, participatory research methods with people with neurodevelopmental disorders, and other methods for eliciting insights from a broader range of neurodivergent people than are typically included in research. Then, the first, second, and third authors wrote reflections on the programs used as practical examples of alliance building. The first author transformed the planning dialogue and literature review into a paper draft which the other authors added to and revised. Excerpts from our planning document are directly quoted in this chapter when we considered the pattern of dialogue illuminating. After receiving constructive feedback from anonymous reviewers and the editors of this volume, we collaboratively revised the chapter.

Table 1. Reflexivity Statements.

Dr Kristen Gillespie-Lynch began working with autistic people as a caregiver for nonspeaking youth 19 years ago. She was immediately struck by the depth and uniqueness of the autistic young people she worked with and initially educated herself by reading scientific articles and autobiographies. She became interested in the neurodiversity movement during her doctoral research at UCLA and developed a survey to study neurodiversity which she was not able to successfully recruit for until she started collaborating with Steven K. Kapp. Kristen's doctoral research was fairly medical model, focused on visual search and joint attention in relation to current and later skills in autism. However, she has many friends and family members who are autistic, so was drawn to the neurodiversity movement upon first encountering it. Soon after joining the Psychology Department at the College of Staten Island and the Graduate Center, Kristen started a mentorship program for autistic college students. She aimed for the program to be participatory but the process of becoming participatory took time, as described in this chapter.

Although Patrick Dwyer is an empirical researcher who has worked in research institutions that are influenced by a medical model, Patrick is also a neurodivergent autistic person and identifies as part of the neurodiversity movement and autistic community. The college peer-support communities in which Patrick has participated have been led by neurodivergent people, including Patrick, who are members of the communities, with only limited involvement from typically developing individuals. The communities have not been part of formal research studies, and statements regarding the programs are based on Patrick's subjective impressions.

Dr Christopher Constantino is a stutterer, speech-language pathologist, assistant professor in communication sciences and disorders, and active member of the stuttering self-help movement. Christopher believes that embracing stuttering as a neurodivergent trait, rather than a medical pathology, will reduce social stigma and discrimination, expose the positive aspects of stuttering, and improve the quality of life of his fellow stutterers.

The neurodiversity paradigm appealed to Dr Steven K. Kapp because its advocacy for practical support for autistic people's needs and rights to live fully in the community offered a compelling alternative to the harmful cure movement that dominated autism research and advocacy (especially in the surrounding Los Angeles area). Its complex view of autism resonated with his identity linked to autistic traits associated with both his strengths and weaknesses, and its origins from the autistic "grassroots" lent it legitimacy. The neurodiversity movement inspired him to become a researcher and activist, having influenced the revision of autism's diagnosis in the DSM-5, co-led trailblazing studies, edited a book featuring neurodiversity advocates' first-hand accounts, and now begun to develop a pioneering, broad neurodiversity studies university class.

Dr Emily Hotez is a research scientist at the UCLA Center for Healthier Children, Families, & Communities where she conducts life course intervention research for children and families. Prior to her current position, she collaborated on the development, implementation, and evaluation of a participatory research study of a summer transition program for incoming neurodiverse college students. Through this work, she gained a critical appreciation of the importance of ensuring that interventions are reflective of the needs, experiences, and priorities of the populations they seek to serve. In her current research, she prioritizes collaborations and partnerships that facilitate a codesign process for all interventions and educational programs.

Ariana Riccio is a doctoral candidate at the City University of New York in the final stages of her dissertation work focused on autistic identity development in autistic adolescents and young adults. Over the past four years, she has focused on using participatory methods in her research endeavors and has coordinated a mentorship program with and for autistic college students. These experiences have been the most relevant and informative aspects of her doctoral training, and she believes that partnerships with neurodivergent communities are essential to any and all research in this space. As a neurotypical person, she acknowledges the need to carefully consider one's positionality and aims to allow the experiences of neurodivergent communities to drive research and practice.

Dr Danielle DeNigris is a neurotypical assistant professor in the School of Psychology and Counseling at Fairleigh Dickinson University. Her interest in autism research began while pursuing her doctoral degree at the City University of New York which led to her collaboration with a neurodivergent group of researchers. Prior to her current faculty position, Danielle served as the coordinator for a peer-mentorship program for neurodiverse college students. These experiences

Table 1. (*Continued*)

informed her understanding of neurodiversity and the meaning of true participatory work. As a neurotypical female, Danielle has learned through collaborations with this participatory research group, that authentic collaboration requires the need to explore (and to personally consider) power imbalances and biases in order to yield an inclusive space where research can thrive.
Bella Kofner is a researcher who identifies as a part of the autistic community. Bella has been a part of Project REACH at CSI where she did the transition from mentee to mentor. She also does many presentations, including neurodiversity in the workplace and gender inequality in autism. Neurodiversity is about celebrating human differences, so Bella believes that every person deserves to have equal opportunity in the workplace by bringing their skills to the job regardless of who they are. Bella believes that women who are in STEM and who have autism can bring their skills to any career of their choice, especially for jobs that are in a male-dominant field.
As a psychologist, autistic adult, and parent of an autistic adult, Dr Eric Endlich knows well the impact on neurodivergent individuals of being marginalized. His personal experiences have led to a passionate pursuit of inclusion by speaking and writing about neurodiversity and helping neurodivergent teens successfully transition to higher education.

THEORETICAL BACKGROUND AND FRAMEWORK

What Is Neurodiversity?

An autistic scholar, Nick Walker (2014), distinguished between three related but distinct terms: *neurodiversity*, the *neurodiversity paradigm*, and the *neurodiversity movement*. *Neurodiversity* refers to the simple fact that *all* brains are different. The *neurodiversity paradigm* refers to the intertwined beliefs that the diversity of brains is valuable, the idea of a "normal" brain is socially constructed, and social dynamics toward neurodiversity mirror dynamics toward other minority identities by promoting power inequalities or, if diversity is embraced, creativity. The *neurodiversity movement* refers to a decentralized movement that includes people with diverse perspectives who advocate for civil rights, respect, and full inclusion, e.g., equal opportunities in education and work, for neurodivergent people.

The neurodiversity paradigm asserts that the fact that *all* people are neurodiverse (i.e., have unique brains) is essentially positive for society. This positive evaluation is not entirely consistent with Singer's and Blume's original conceptualization of neurodiversity as encompassing *all* neurological variations, including those that are harmful to oneself and/or others (Singer, 2019). Indeed, Dekker, the founder of InLv, where neurodiversity was coined, critiques the neurodiversity paradigm because he believes it excludes people who view autism more negatively.

> It is important to note that InLv's notion of neurodiversity was different from the "neurodiversity paradigm" that many contemporary activists subscribe to. These days it is often held that there is no such thing as a brain that is "less" or "broken" because "all neurologies are valid" [12]. By contrast, neurodiversity as an aspect of biodiversity includes and accepts people with suboptimal neurological configurations. While autistic people who would have preferred to be "cured" if possible were a minority in the InLv community, we never excluded or denounced them. (Dekker, 2020, p. 47)

What Are the Roots of the Neurodiversity Movement?

Early cross-disability alliances effectively challenged the medical model, wherein disabilities were defined as deficits within disabled bodies that treatments sought to erase, by embracing the social model, which attributes disability-related impairments to oppressive, conformist societal attitudes and structures that subjugate people who are different from "norms" (Baker, 2011). Although the social model's focus on the societal roots of oppression was essential for early advocacy, both the social and the medical models are reductionist, overlooking the degree to which living beings and their environments are interdependent and mutually shaped by dynamic systems of relationships (e.g., Lickliter & Witherington, 2017). The neurodiversity paradigm positions disability as a form of human variation like any other personal trait, e.g., friendliness. This allows for descriptions of disability that need not appeal to simplistic binaries like good/bad, sick/well, or oppressed/liberated. Instead, experiences of disability can be described with as much nuance as ethnic, racial, and/or gendered experiences. Unlike the social model, the neurodiversity movement frames neurological diversity as invaluable to the development of society, yet also challenging at times (e.g., Kapp et al., 2013).

The neurodiversity paradigm defines disabilities as natural aspects of human diversity that can offer both advantages and challenges, as well as traits that only become challenges as a result of societal structures that disadvantage neurodivergent people (e.g., Armstrong, 2010; Dwyer, 2019b). In contrast to the social model, which attributes challenges associated with disability solely to environmental factors, autistic activists often recognize that some challenges associated with autism may *not* be alleviated by improving society. Many of the leaders of the neurodiversity movement face pronounced challenges addressing co-occurring conditions and support individualized treatments to ameliorate such challenges (e.g., Ballou, 2018). Autistic self-advocates have noted that environmental accommodations alone will not eliminate all difficulties experienced by autistic people, indicating that both societal changes and individualized education/therapy may be needed (Ballou, 2018; Robison, 2013). Neurodiversity-aligned therapies build from people's strengths and toward self-determined goals rather than goals imposed by others. The neurodiversity paradigm asserts that neurodivergent people should be accepted for whom they are, and that attempts to eradicate evidence of their neurodivergence ("normalization") are stigmatizing and should not be a goal of treatment (AStrangerInGodZone, 2011; Dwyer, 2019b; Gillespie-Lynch, Kapp, Brooks, Pickens, & Schwartzman, 2017b).

Like autism itself, the neurodiversity paradigm and movement are dynamic social constructs; their nature changes based on public understanding of their meaning. "Normal" is also a socially defined construct that is highly contested (e.g., Fenton & Krahn, 2007). Sir Francis Galton, who transformed the idea of "normal" from a state of dynamic functional health to a fixed statistical relationship, also coined the term eugenics (Stephens & Cryle, 2017). Early proponents of eugenics used vague and poorly defined conceptions of "normal" to advocate for strict immigration laws and forcible sterilization of people with disabilities, poor, and "immoral" people (Stephens & Cryle, 2017). Many current neurodiversity advocates question the focus of vast amounts of funding on finding genetic markers for autism, concerned about the potential adaptation of genetic markers for eugenic purposes, as occurred with Down Syndrome (Nadesan, 2013; Thomas & Rothman, 2016; Yeoman, 2019). However, the neurodiversity movement has a complicated relationship with biogenetic conceptualizations of disability.

Is Essentialism Essential to Neurodiversity?

Consistent with autism's classification as a neurodevelopmental disorder (American Psychiatric Association, 2013) and with the definition of "neurodivergence," autistic self-advocates often endorse essentialist accounts of autism, viewing their brains as fundamentally different from the brains of "neurotypicals" and indicating that genes associated with autism are increasing due to natural selection (Brownlow & O'Dell, 2013; Kapp et al., 2013; O'Dell, Bertilsdotter Rosqvist, Ortega, Brownlow, & Orsini, 2016; Ortega, 2013; Reser, 2011). Although attributing autism to brain differences can lead to nonpathologized forms of identity and community, it can also conceal intersectional complexities of personhood (Ortega, 2013).

Biogenetic explanations were initially endorsed as a method for ameliorating stigma toward diverse conditions. However, subsequent research revealed that biogenetic explanations often increase stigma toward mental illnesses by essentializing differences and marking diagnostic characteristics as outside of a person's control (Angermeyer, Holzinger, Carta, & Schomerus, 2011). Indeed, the logic of eugenics requires differences to be essential to one's biology. Eugenics aims to move human populations closer to an idealized "normal" over time by decreasing the propagation of these differences through the gene pool (Wilson & Pierre, 2016). The neurodiversity framework turns this idealization of "normalcy" upside down, arguing that neurodivergence resulting from natural selection enriches society. This framing may more effectively challenge stigma than deficit-based biogenetic explanations as attitudes toward autism may be improving (White, Hillier, Frye, & Makrez, 2019).

Yet, a key challenge for the neurodiversity movement is that clear neurological differences between autistic and nonautistic people are far from clearly documented (e.g., Baker, 2011; Loth et al., 2017). Neuroimaging findings tend to be contradictory and often fail to replicate due to small sample sizes and heterogeneity associated with autism. Recent cross-site collaborations have revealed some evidence of reproducible functional connectivity differences between autistic and nonautistic samples (Holiga et al., 2019). However, autistic people with "low IQs" were excluded from the study to reduce variability, as they often are from neuroimaging research. Indeed, a large-scale neuroimaging study found that differences in functional connectivity between autistic and nonautistic participants tended to *not* be reproducible across data collection sites; autism symptoms and IQ also exhibited *opposite* patterns of associations with functional connectivity (King et al., 2019). Furthermore, similar neuroimaging patterns can sometimes be found in autism and other divergent neurotypes (e.g., Baribeau et al., 2019; Mogadam et al., 2019). These findings highlight the vast heterogeneity in neurotypes within the multidimensional autism constellation.[8] Similar inconsistencies in neuroimaging findings have been observed in stuttering research (Etchell, Civier, Ballard, & Sowman, 2018). Concerns about our ability to reliably distinguish between neurodivergence and "typical development" as well as the very high rate of co-occurring conditions (Simonoff et al., 2008) highlight a pragmatic reason for promoting cross-disability alliances; diagnostic categories are imprecise (Hyman, 2010) and vary as a function of social, cultural, and historical contexts (Engel, 1977; Grinker, 2008; Hacking, 2009).

In his book about the history of the neurodiversity movement, Steven K. Kapp (2020) describes the term *neurodiversity* as adopting a dimensional approach in which people's neurocognitive differences are recognized as largely lacking natural boundaries. The connection between a dimensional approach and group-based identity politics may at first seem contradictory. However, the neurodiversity framework draws from reactions to *existing* stigma. In other words, all brains vary along intersecting spectrums of difference, but society's reactions to certain differences form them into medical categories (Foucault, 1973/1994). These categories are reclaimed by negotiating their meaning into an affirmative construct. People who are not discriminated against do not have their neurological differences prescribed in this way; therefore, there is nothing for them to reclaim. These individuals likely benefit from neurotypical privilege (Harp, 2009) and arguably do not need corresponding legal protections and access to services.

Is the Neurodiversity Movement Opposed to Treatment?

A common misconception about the neurodiversity movement is that it consists of "high-functioning" autistics who wish to deny "low-functioning" autistics needed treatment due to perspective-taking difficulties, coupled with a dogmatic belief that autism is a difference rather than a deficit (Jaarsma & Welin, 2012; Costandi, 2019).[9] However, nonspeaking autistics and autistics with intellectual disabilities are also advocates within the neurodiversity movement (Kapp, 2020).

Although the neurodiversity movement opposes a cure for autism, it still supports certain treatments for autism (Kapp, 2020). Neurodiversity-aligned stutterers also tend to view seeking a cure for stuttering as deeply stigmatizing (Pierre, 2012; Yeoman, 2019). However, some stutterers who identify with the neurodiversity movement may be more open to the idea of a cure than autistic neurodiversity advocates are (Constantino, 2018). While autism is a lifelong condition, the vast majority of children who stutter no longer stutter by adulthood. Even people who continue to stutter as adults often experience periods of fluency. Therefore, stuttering may be a less pervasive aspect of some stutterers' identities than autism tends to be. This contrast highlights the degree to which the temporal and embodied aspects of one's experiences with neurodivergence may influence one's perspectives on the neurodiversity movement.

The distinction between cure and treatment has often caused misunderstandings. "Cure" refers to total *elimination* of autism or other forms of neurodivergence, whereas "treatment" supports *amelioration* of those features that impair adaptive functioning (Kapp et al., 2013). The neurodiversity movement seeks adaptive functioning and subjective well-being (happiness), which together constitute quality of life (Constantino, 2018; Ne'eman, 2010; Robertson, 2010). The movement recognizes that some features of neurodivergence may function neutrally (or as strengths) for the individual and for others. Challenges are recognized as contextual, arising primarily from social environments that do not afford opportunities for different types of people to thrive (Kapp, 2013). Therefore, the emphasis of treatment (which might be demedicalized as a form of "support") should be on helping the individual leverage their strengths and mitigate their difficulties to achieve a high quality of life.

Patrick Dwyer, an autistic self-advocate, doctoral student, and author of this report, provides a particularly cogent critique, in his blog, of the misconception that the neurodiversity movement is opposed to treatment (Dwyer; 2019b). Patrick states:

> We don't really need to call someone "deficient" or "disordered" to change them. We simply need to recognize that it would help them thrive, be happy, and enjoy better mental well-being if they possessed some skills... Furthermore, if we're going to strive to help the individual thrive and be happy, whether we do so by trying to change the individual or their environment, we probably don't want to insult them and say that their mind and brain are fundamentally "deficient" and "disordered."...Right now, when autistic people access services and supports, they often do so as petitioners, asking an expert neurotypical to generously offer their expertise to help the autistic person with their deficits and challenges. Furthermore, the services and supports that are offered are usually imperfectly matched to the individual's needs. Thus, this process is not only disempowering, but also inefficient.

Neurodiversity advocates call for research to shift its primary focus from basic mechanisms toward developing evidence-based strategies to improve the quality of life, self-determination, and inclusion of existing neurodivergent people across the lifespan (Kapp, 2013; Pellicano, Dinsmore, & Charman, 2014a; Yeoman, 2019). Members of the neurodiversity movement typically support interventions that promote adaptive functioning by building from strengths while mitigating characteristics that threaten quality of life, but reject attempts to normalize for normalization's sake (Constantino, 2018; Kapp et al., 2013). Although most people would likely support improving the quality of life of neurodivergent people, discussions about *who* the neurodiversity movement should represent tend to generate limited consensus.

Who Should the Neurodiversity Movement Include?

Christopher Constantino wrote in the planning document for this study:

> "In the same way that being black is not a failure at being white or being gay is not a failure at being straight, stuttering is not a failure at fluency but a way of speaking that exists independent of fluency." He described neurodiversity as "for anyone who wants to exist independent of a comparison to an ideal. It is for the autistic whose style of interacting is not simply a failure at normalcy, for the person with ADHD whose thought processes are not simply a failure to concentrate, the stutterer whose stutters are more than a failure of fluency."

Patrick Dwyer replied in the planning document for this study:

> All variation of minds and brains may be neurodiversity, factually speaking, but does all of it fall under the political neurodiversity paradigm?... I suspect we could agree that something like a brain tumor is clearly medical, right?... And then there is that gray area in between. Like, for example, is depression something we should count as a valuable, non-pathological form of neurodiversity? On the one hand, a neurodiversity approach to depression may reduce stigma; on the other hand, people may not identify with their depression and may strongly want to get rid of it... So perhaps all mental variation is, factually speaking, neurodiversity, but does all of this neurodiversity fall within the scope of the *political* neurodiversity paradigm? And if not, where is the boundary?

Does the neurodiversity paradigm apply to people who experience their disability as an impairment without associated strengths? Within autistic communities, pronounced disagreement exists about whether the neurodiversity framework should include people who experience autism solely as a difficulty. Martijn Dekker (2020), the founder of InLv, and Judy Singer (2019) have both indicated that the term neurodiversity was not meant to endorse an exclusively positive evaluation of neurodivergence (neurodiversity was meant to encompass all people) but has been used to exclude autistic people who view autism solely as a deficit.

Misidentification of the neurodiversity movement as a positive attitude toward all aspects of autism is also apparent among some autism researchers. Simon Baron-Cohen[10] attempted to reduce disagreements between neurodiversity-aligned and medical model–oriented viewpoints at INSAR's 2019 annual meeting, suggesting that tensions could be resolved by recognizing the diversity of autism. While INSAR has historically adhered to a medical model of autism, the neurodiversity approach has been gaining prominence in the organization. According to Baron-Cohen (2019), neurodiversity-aligned perspectives frame autism as a difference rather than a deficit and are applicable to autistic people who face less severe challenges. In contrast, autistic people who are intellectually disabled, who have limited speech, and/or who experience pronounced comorbidities may require a medical model orientation where their condition is recognized as a "disease" rather than a "difference." In response, Aiyana Bailin (2019), an autistic self-advocate, reminded Baron-Cohen that the neurodiversity movement recognizes intrinsic challenges associated with autism, as many neurodiversity advocates experience such challenges.

This discussion is a very recent example of a longstanding and often acrimonious debate within autism communities about what *neurodiversity* means and who the neurodiversity movement represents. People often question the degree to which autistic people who speak and/or are not intellectually disabled can represent the viewpoints of autistic people who cannot communicate fluently or who are cognitively delayed (e.g., Fletcher-Watson, 2017; McCready, 2019). However, there is some evidence that autistic people often process things in similar ways despite pronounced differences in communication and cognitive skills (Dawson, Mottron, & Gernsbacher, 2008). In addition, this question about representation can easily be turned back on the academic community, as people who do not speak or who have intellectual disabilities are woefully underrepresented in extant research (Jack & Pelphrey, 2017).

There is evidence that the heterogeneity of the autism constellation complicates collaborative advocacy efforts within autism communities (Robison, 2019; Sinclair, 2010). These complications highlight potential pitfalls for building further alliances across different types of conditions. Inter-disability alliances necessarily increase heterogeneity and may thus spark disagreements and dilute advocacy aims. Indeed, interviews with 12 autism researchers in the UK suggest that some researchers continue to blame their difficulties collaborating with the autism community on the heterogeneity of autism and perceived social-communicative difficulties associated with autism (Hollin & Pearce, 2019). The researchers described feeling bewildered by conflicting feedback from the autism community, e.g., autism is a difference to be respected versus a deficit to cure, and overwhelmed by blunt communication styles. They felt that debates were dominated by a few particularly vocal autistic people who could not understand the perspectives of autistic people who were more severely affected. Although several researchers participating in an online survey strongly endorsed the value of collaborating with autistic people, other researchers expressed similar concerns to those noted above about the lack of a consistent voice within the autism community and challenges communicating with autistic people (Pellicano et al., 2014b). Even neurodiversity-aligned researchers have elected to conduct focus groups with different stakeholder groups separately to avoid having potential disagreements cloud interpretations (Pellicano et al., 2014a).

Nevertheless, the neurodiversity movement as applied to autism aims to function inclusively, in that activists include nonautistic people as allies, and it accepts and fights for the full developmental spectrum of autistic people (including those with intellectual disabilities and no or minimal language). Marginalization of autistic people by nonautistic relative–led autism organizations catalyzed the movement (Pripas-Kapit, 2020; Sinclair, 2012). Thus, it seeks to help families advocate for acceptance, understanding, and support to positively impact people across the autism spectrum and their parents (Kapp, 2018). Celebratory acts by parents of autistic children such as learning to speak their child's language and accepting autism as part of their child's identity – and ameliorative acts like teaching their child adaptive coping skills – elicit support in varied autism communities, including "pro-cure" parent groups and "pro-acceptance" autistic groups (Kapp et al., 2013). Yet many of the more powerful parental organizations have behaved in dehumanizing and polarizing ways toward autistic people, such as using fear and pity as fundraising strategies and seeking an end to autism (daVanport, 2020). They have appropriated self-advocacy by using language such as "families with autism" (whereas if anyone "has" autism, autistic people do). They have also claimed autistic people cannot advocate for policy affecting people with comorbid conditions, even though some autistic activists themselves have the same comorbidities, e.g., intellectual disabilities (Ballou, 2018).

Similar debates about neurodiversity have emerged in other communities. In response to the publication of *Stammering Pride and Prejudice* (Campbell, Constantino, & Simpson, 2019), a book using the social model of disability and neurodiversity paradigm to explore new, positive, narratives around stuttering, some people who stutter took to social media to decry it. They insist that stuttering is not a condition to be celebrated but a serious malfunction that is inherently negative (Weidig, 2019). Given the substantial diversity of perspectives on neurodiversity within disability-specific communities, how can we effectively promote cross-disability alliances under the banner of the neurodiversity movement?

How Can Tensions within the Neurodiversity Movement Inform Alliance Building?

Thus far, we have come to see that the neurodiversity movement, like neurodivergence itself, may be misunderstood partially because it is so multidimensional. People who identify as members of the neurodiversity movement may differ in their viewpoints about who the movement should include, what the goals of the movement should be, and how we can work toward these goals. For example, some (but certainly not all) neurodiversity advocates agree that the movement should not exclude people who view their neurodivergence solely as a source of suffering. However, there is less consensus about how the movement should respond to people who are harmful to others (like some psychopaths).

Given that the neurodiversity movement has been (and will continue to be) interpreted in so many different ways, it is helpful to hone in on the essential aspects of the underlying neurodiversity paradigm. In his blog, Patrick Dywer (2019b) identifies three key ideas at the heart of the neurodiversity paradigm (paraphrased here): (1) there is no such thing as a "normal" brain and the reality of diversity (neurodiversity) is good for society, (2) neurodivergent people should be accepted as they are rather than pursuing "normalization" for its own sake, and (3) many (but not all) of the challenges neurodivergent people face arise from societal inequalities.

The neurodiversity movement aims to equalize power inequalities between different neurotypes. A dialogue between coauthors of this chapter about the implications of tensions within the neurodiversity movement for alliance building (see Table 2) illustrates how essential "critical consciousness" (Freire, 1970; Sakamoto & Pitner, 2005), or becoming aware of power imbalances that contribute to oppressive practices and working to rectify them, is for building effective alliances across diverse neurotypes.

Table 2. How Can Tensions within the Neurodiversity Movement Inform Alliance Building?

"When power dynamics give power to neurotypicals, emphasis is placed on changing autistic people rather than on changing how neurotypicals interact with autistic people."

–**Patrick Dwyer**, planning document

"The whole dynamic needs to change, as long as intervention is focused on making the 'person with the issue' more like 'people without the issue,' we're still operating with a medically driven paradigm. We're just using different words to describe it. The whole point of neurodiversity is to level the playing field and think about building spaces that allow as many people as possible to access resources and relationships within those spaces. The upshot is that everyone who contributes to those spaces may need to change, not just the people who carry medical diagnoses. At its most basic level, an ally is someone who is willing to change to create a space that accommodates a greater range of human diversity."

–Response from **Christopher Constantino**

"Perhaps being an ally means that you don't look at accommodations as something you provide for the autistic (or other) person, but something that the ally actually does themselves, making this idea of accommodations an active verb rather than a noun."

–Response from **Danielle DeNigris**, a "neurotypical" researcher and coauthor

"In so doing, the ally is often giving up a privileged position. To achieve equality, it is often not enough to try to raise someone up, sometimes you must lower yourself to their level and deal with their problems with them. The implication is allyship is not an attitude or an orientation but requires work. Someone can care about autistics without being an ally. What makes them an ally is their willingness to do, at their own expense, something about the situation."

–Response from **Christopher Constantino**

"I agree that the power differential is a critical element not just in terms of how neurodivergent people are treated, but how they are defined. Those who define neurodivergent individuals as deficient and in need of correction are able to do so in part because of their superior numbers, but also because of their perceived expertise and status. Perhaps some of us who are neurodivergent and also have some of the markers of expertise such as graduate degrees will be able to help facilitate communication between neurodivergent and neurotypical communities…It makes sense that an umbrella neurodiverse community (vs just an autistic or stuttering community) would be able to command more attention and respect – assuming we can organize."

–Response from **Eric Endlich**, an autistic psychologist and coauthor

"One background point might be the conventional power relationship in the delivery of supports and services, wherein the person providing the support has expertise, knowledge, etc. The support system is also an institution that defines the options available to support seekers; they must navigate within these options and not others."

–**Patrick Dwyer**

To move toward critical consciousness, allies must interrogate their multiple identities and perspectives to continuously learn how to become better allies. Active alliance building requires "neurotypical" allies to recognize that common ways of communicating and associated assumptions about people who diverge from norms promote inequalities. For example, early autism research described autistic people as lacking Theory of Mind (ToM), or the ability to understand others' perspectives (Baron-Cohen, Leslie, & Frith, 1985). Consequently, many interventions focus on teaching autistic people to think and act more like neuro-typical people despite limited evidence that interventions to promote ToM or "social skills" lead to generalizable improvements (Bottema-Beutel, Park, & Kim, 2018; Fletcher-Watson, McConnell, Manola, & McConachie, 2014). Damian Milton (2012) reframed these "ToM difficulties" as a "double empathy problem" wherein both autistic and nonautistic people may not intuitively grasp one another's perspectives. He noted that autistic people often try harder to understand nonautistic people than the reverse. Similarly, stutterers have pointed out that communication challenges associated with stuttering are bidirectional: "'broken speech' is constructed by *both* a speaker and a hearer (Pierre, 2012, p. 3)." Misunderstandings between people with different neurotypes may arise because people tend to make snap negative judgments about neurodivergent people (Alkhaldi, Sheppard, & Mitchell, 2019; Boyle, 2018; DeBrabander et al., 2019; Sasson et al., 2017).

In order to begin to address the societal inequalities identified by the neurodiversity paradigm, safe spaces are needed where neurodivergent people can feel free to be themselves (e.g., the "autistic space" where ANI was born). Supports are also needed to help "neurotypical" and "neurodivergent" people understand one another (e.g., ASAN and the NSA). Participatory approaches, which promote effective communication, collaboration, and careful documentation of deliberative processes, can be used to foster effective communication across neurotypes.

In order to begin to envision how the neurodiversity paradigm can be applied to better support diverse people, we share practical insights derived from our own experiences guiding neurodiversity-aligned programs. Two of the programs we will highlight (both of which are support programs for autistic university students) grew, in different ways, from the neurodiversity movement. The third program we will describe grew from advocacy by stutterers and only recently began to draw inspiration from the neurodiversity movement.

PRACTICAL EXAMPLES OF ALLIANCE BUILDING WITHIN AND ACROSS NEUROTYPES

Peer-led Support Groups

Programs to help autistic students adapt to university typically rely, at least to some extent, on peer mentor/support programs (Barnhill, 2016). Although a growing body of literature suggests that peer mentor programs are helpful for autistic college students (Kuder & Accardo, 2018), extant programming may inadvertently reify power imbalances favoring neurotypical over autistic perspectives by framing alliance building solely in terms of *nonautistic* mentors *helping autistic* mentees. Oftentimes support comes from a top-down, nondisabled perspective that assumes certain needs; while this is likely well intentioned, it may overlook the perspectives of the people being served and yield supports that lack social validity. Programs for autistic university students that are described in the existing literature have generally failed to provide opportunities for autistic students to *guide program development* (see Capozzi, Barmache, Cladis, Peña, & Kocur, 2019; Gillespie-Lynch et al., 2020; Hotez et al., 2018; Searle et al., 2019 for exceptions). Some autistic students have taken matters into their own hands and developed programs to support their autistic peers themselves.

Patrick Dwyer (2019a) has been a member and facilitator of two autistic-led peer-support communities for autistic students at two different postsecondary institutions and has also been involved in cross-disability student advocacy. In his experience, one of the various tensions that can affect small groups of neurodivergent individuals in local communities is the tension between providing a safe and supportive environment for neurodivergent members, who may encounter barriers and considerable stress in their daily lives, and the goal of advocating for cultural and systems change. While members of these peer-support communities have been involved in events and panel discussions aimed at engaging with the general campus community, members have sometimes offered feedback that such advocacy can be threatening, given that the community may reject messages advanced by self-advocates. Moreover, a tension has sometimes emerged between openness to allyship and a desire to preserve an atmosphere of supportive community for neurodivergent people. While some members of peer-support communities have suggested engaging more deeply with neurotypical allies, others have feared that opening regular group meetings to "neurotypical" allies would change the supportive atmosphere of the community. Although formal participatory strategies can be used to support collaboration among "neurotypical" and "neurodivergent" people, the personalities of individuals may play a larger role in shaping the culture of informal community groups. To preserve the safe space provided by a "neurodivergent only" zone while also working with nonautistic people to promote neurodiversity appreciation, Patrick is involved with two separate groups. One group is a "neurodivergent only" group (started by autistics) and one is a "neurotypical-neurodivergent" group started by "neurotypicals" interested in autism. This clear demarcation of group compositions according to their desired function allows Patrick and his peers to participate flexibly in both disability-specific and cross-disability alliances.

It is noteworthy that the peer-support community Patrick currently facilitates theoretically describes itself as being open to neurodivergent people more generally in addition to autistic people, but almost all members self-identify as autistic. This highlights the difficulties of achieving cross-disability collaborations in practice; it is difficult to attract members from other neurotypes when different disability communities often operate in segregation from one another. These dynamics may reinforce themselves: because the group consists of autistic people, it therefore becomes understood by its members and others in the community as an "autism group," in spite of its theoretically more open purpose.

Mentorship Program Created for and with Autistic University Students

In 2013, Kristen Gillespie-Lynch developed a mentorship program for autistic students in collaboration with students, the Center for Student Accessibility (CSA), and other academics. Some autistic students were wary of an autism-specific program, describing feeling isolated in high school and wanting to interact with diverse people but being forced to practice "social skills" with other autistics. Some nonautistic students didn't want to be excluded. Therefore, we broadened the program to include students with diverse disabilities, though it is majority autistic.

Danielle DeNigris, Emily Hotez, and Ariana Riccio (coauthors of this report) helped shape the program when they were doctoral students; Bella Kofner (also a coauthor) took on a notable leadership role while still an undergraduate.

Although we intended for the program to be participatory since its inception, neurodivergent students only slowly assumed leadership roles. Since the program began, students have been informed that it is shaped by student input.[11] We have described the initial processes by which the program became more participatory in other papers (Gillespie-Lynch et al., 2017a; Hotez et al. 2018). Although students have expressed pride that their ideas have helped shape the program since it began, early opportunities to shape the program were not sustained or structured enough to enable students to exert a powerful influence on program structure. In retrospect, our early claims that the program was participatory were more of an aspiration than a reality.

In Fall 2016, we formed a participatory research group to guide program evaluation and development. Core members of this group (three autistic students, one autistic scholar, one autistic psychologist, and three nonautistic scholars, with additional members joining less frequently) typically meet every three weeks during the school year. This group has focused primarily on improving the program and on researching autistic identity development, as most group members are interested in understanding the process and consequences of developing a neurodiversity-aligned perspective (e.g., DeNigris et al., 2018; Riccio et al., 2020).

Three other autistic students were disinterested in the participatory research group, but enjoyed meeting more spontaneously with the lead author to adapt an autism training designed to reduce stigma and increase knowledge (Gillespie-Lynch et al., 2015) by sharing their lived experiences being autistic. The participatory autism training was more effective than a nonparticipatory training in improving autism knowledge and stigma. Seven autistic students in the program also give talks to increase autism understanding in the community.

Thus far, 17 students/alumni with disabilities (12 autistic) have become mentors. Students with other disabilities besides autism, e.g., sensory, were the earliest mentees to transition into mentor roles. Transitioned mentors often inspired their mentees to become mentors, highlighting the value of cross-disability alliances for promoting leadership.

In 2018, we hired a neurodiversity specialist (an autistic college student) to help make the groups more autism friendly and to colead groups. In 2019, an autistic student, Bella Kofner, and an actor with ADHD, colead group meetings. They qualitatively coded critiques of the program, after obtaining reliability, in order to more systematically improve programming (see next paragraph). Bella joined the program as a mentee in the fall of 2016; her mentor had transitioned from mentee to mentor herself. She feels that the program allowed her many opportunities to take on leadership roles including presenting, coauthoring papers, and becoming a researcher and a mentor. For Bella:

> Project REACH means that no person with disabilities will ever feel excluded (as it will) provide support so that people with disabilities can learn how to take what they learned in Project REACH and apply it to their lives. So, Project REACH helps people with

disabilities grow individually and develop skills that will help them deal with college and life outside of college. Project REACH teaches people with disabilities vital skills such as self-advocacy, time-management, and socializing with others.

Student input has helped make our program increasingly engaging. Between 2016 and 2018, we observed improvements in GPA associated with joining the program that were not apparent during early semesters of the program (p = 0.003; data available for 19 students). Qualitative coding of responses by 24 autistic mentees, nine mentors without disabilities, and six mentors with disabilities to end-of-the-term questions about what they liked about the program and how it could be improved revealed that autistic mentees enjoyed learning things (75%) and giving and/or gaining social support (40%). Mentors without disabilities particularly liked learning things (67%), especially appreciation of diversity (44%). Mentors with disabilities particularly enjoyed giving and/or gaining social support (67%) relative to mentors without disabilities (33%). Mentors with disabilities (80%), mentors without disabilities (22%), and autistic mentees (27%) often said the program did not need improvement. All three groups' (~40%) most common recommendation for improving the program was to broaden its reach. Mentors without disabilities (44%) noted a need for better social supports, particularly more effective mentor–mentee matching (22%), that mentors with disabilities (0%) and autistic mentees (12%) did not note as frequently. Students' accounts revealed that they generally enjoyed a program wherein students with diverse neurotypes could learn from one another and wanted the program to grow. However, a need for more explicit support connecting mentees and mentors was noted.

Student input has improved assessments, helped us more effectively guide mentees into becoming mentors, and has led to more opportunities for students to connect on their own terms. Opening the program to diverse types of students created opportunities for them to learn from one another. However, the diversity of our program is not without challenges. Some students visit the popular group meetings once or twice, are overwhelmed by the diversity of voices they encounter there, and decide to focus solely on one-on-one mentorship.

In mentorship group meetings, we promote civil discourse by developing shared promises at the beginning of each term and referring back to them at the beginning of each meeting. Patrick Dwyer (2019a) also developed this practice in his autistic-led support group. Although we have tried to use guidelines for participatory research that were recently published by AASPIRE (Nicolaidis et al., 2019) to obtain consensus on key decisions during our research meetings, we use rules inconsistently, partially because meeting participation fluctuates, reducing clarity about decision-making, which may disadvantage less assertive members. Review of AASPIRE's guidelines highlights the need to collaboratively develop clearer communication protocols for our research group. We do most of our planning in Google Docs, with periodic Skype meetings. Google Docs has an advantage of leaving a permanent record of edits and of being easier to manage, as we often run into technical difficulties when using Skype that leads some researchers to type their ideas into a textbox. Collaborators mark their ideas with their initials in Google Docs, but the use of multiple communication modalities leads to some ambiguity about the origin of ideas. As Ted Chiang (2019) noted:

> Before a culture adopts the use of writing, when its knowledge is transmitted exclusively through oral means, it can very easily revise its history…(technologically-mediated records) acknowledge our fallibility and make us less judgmental about the fallibility of others. (p. 222)

One weakness that our participatory research group shares with the field is that it does not sufficiently represent the autism constellation (Bigby et al., 2014; Fletcher-Watson et al., 2019; MacLeod, 2019). Although we developed a multimodal emotion rating scale to try to communicate with nonspeaking people (Riccio et al., 2020), our efforts to invite nonspeaking people to collaborate have thus far been unsuccessful. The lead author, who used to be a caregiver for nonspeaking autistic people, attended a workshop and a conference about ways to communicate with nonspeaking people. Yet, attempts to forge collaborations with nonspeaking people have not yet borne fruit. As Kristina Chew, the mother of a mostly nonspeaking autistic child wrote:

> Bearing witness to our own insufficiency, to the inscrutability of the otherness we are trying to speak for and represent, across unfathomable distance— this recognition of the necessity and futility of our attempts to know can leave us speechless. (2013, p. 313)

The National Stuttering Association as a Source of Self-help

Christopher Constantino is a member of the NSA, the world's largest self-help organization for people who stutter. The NSA was founded by two people who stutter, Michael Sugarman and Bob Goldman, in 1977 to help bring about "a world without prejudice, full of self-help groups, advocacy, and public awareness" (Sugarman, 1999). The NSA has traditionally welcomed neurotypical people as members and even leaders of the organization. Although the autistic advocacy and the stuttering advocacy communities developed largely independently of one another, similar neurodiversity-aligned ideas emerged in both communities. Very recently, members of the NSA (e.g., Chris Constantino) have suggested that supports for stutterers could be strengthened by explicitly aligning them with the principles of the neurodiversity movement.

Chris's first experience with the NSA was at a local support group run by other people who stutter. He then started participating in national conferences. This led to him starting and leading his own local support groups, helping to organize conferences, and presenting workshops at conferences. Chris believes that the NSA's primary strength is its ability to empower people who stutter. It's local and national structures create a network of people who stutter who can serve as witnesses and support for each other's growth and struggles. Importantly, they also serve as friends. The NSA creates a unique environment where stuttering is no longer the stigmatized, minority way of speaking but, rather, the norm. Within this context, it often becomes glaringly clear to people who stutter that many of their struggles stem not from how they speak but from the prejudice of others. In this section, Christopher synthesizes research[12] about the NSA to highlight neurodiversity-aligned themes and associated tensions that have arisen within the stuttering community.

Empirical investigations of the effect of involvement in the NSA on the lives of people who stutter have largely been positive (Trichon & Tetnowski, 2011). Involvement with the NSA is often the first time stutterers meet other people who stutter. The experience is often one of empowerment and improved self-image (Tetnowski & McClure, 2010). Perhaps most importantly, people who stutter simply enjoy being at the NSA, it provides a place to share feelings, experiences, and challenges (Krauss-Lehrman & Reeves, 1989). It provides a sense of community (Trichon, Tetnowski, & Rentschler, 2006).

While the NSA has many functions, its original and primary function has been to facilitate local self-help groups throughout the United States. Self-help can reduce anxiety and improve motivation and self-concept, making speaking easier (Gathman, 1986; Ramig, 1993; Yaruss et al., 2002). Most of these local groups are led by a chapter leader who stutters, although some are led by fluent speakers with an interest in stuttering. The founders saw self-help as an important force in changing the way people who stutter view themselves and are viewed by others. The groups also acted as local cells for advocacy and activism. Local groups have protested companies that discriminate against people who stutter as well as media that portrays people who stutter negatively (Sugarman, 1999).

In 2001, the NSA started hosting joint symposiums for scientists, clinicians, and people who stutter (National Stuttering Association, 2019). These research symposiums have become yearly meetings of professionals and stutterers to talk about the latest research and therapies for stuttering. They have proved fertile ground for thought-provoking conversation and have provided a way for stutterers to have a say in researchers' and therapists' agendas. The research symposium for 2019 was cochaired by Constantino. Its title was *Stuttering: Perspectives on Disability, Diversity and Culture,* and it brought together experts on neurodiversity – such as Judy Singer and Kristen Gillespie-Lynch – as well as researchers in the fields of disability studies and speech-language pathology.

Despite this apparent progress, there are still tensions between stutterers and professionals within the NSA. There are disagreements over who holds power and whether these people should be stutterers. Additionally, not all members of the NSA embrace neurodiversity. The issue of *cure* has been problematic. Many stutterers desire a cure for stuttering and donors often specifically want their money to fund research seeking a cure. In 2016, the NSA explicitly made it part of its vision statement to fund research searching for stuttering's "cause and cure" (Maguire & Reitzes, 2016). There was an immediate backlash from some in the stuttering community who felt this was antithetical to the cause of embracing stuttering and furthered stigma. The NSA has since removed any mention of cure from its vision statement; nonetheless, this continues to be a wedge issue for people who stutter.

Another recent conflict has been over local chapters' ability to control attendance at their local meetings. Many chapters do community outreach and allow professionals to attend their meetings. However, the primary function of these groups is for stutterers to mutually support each other, not to educate the fluent public. Some NSA chapters have started holding stutterer-only events. Fluent SLPs were very critical of these meetings. They worried they would stoke hostility toward therapy and were a step backward into old antagonisms. In response, the NSA insisted on a policy of "inclusivity" and stopped sanctioning these events. This has resulted in local groups dissociating themselves from the NSA in order to hold stutterer-only conferences (NYC Stutters, 2018). The NSA is a powerful example of how neurodivergent groups can take control of their own narratives and professional assistance. At the same time, it shows how trying to include all stakeholders can become problematic. It shows how easily power shifts from the hands of the neurodivergent to the neurotypical when both are involved in the same organization.

DISCUSSION

How Can We Use Neurodiversity to Support Cross-disability Alliances?

The neurodiversity paradigm provides a framework that can help people recognize that superficially dissimilar experiences may have shared underlying causes, e.g., stigma as a cause of unemployment and unequal access to health care. The preceding examples of alliance building within and across neurotypes highlight benefits of cross-neurotype alliances (e.g., creating models for self-advocacy and spreading neurodiversity appreciation). However, challenges were also apparent (e.g., power imbalances favoring neurotypical people and a potentially overwhelming diversity of viewpoints). Attempts at cross-disability advocacy may at times promote battles over limited resources. This may be especially true if cross-disability alliances are imposed from above as a forced requirement that ignores real differences between people with different conditions (Friedner, Ghosh, & Palaniappan, 2018). When using neurodiversity as a framework to help people recognize and achieve shared aims, it is important to avoid assuming commonalities that the communities in question have not identified themselves.

People who share a specific disability may need space to decide whether or not to enter into cross-disability coalitions. Cross-disability alliances are likely to be most effective when spaces that allow many people to access resources and relationships are available, yet some spaces are reserved for people who share a specific condition and/or advocacy aim. This approach aligns with evidence that people tend to mobilize for causes that affect them (Putnam, 2005). Protests focused on disability-specific issues are usually led by people with the specific condition that the issue affects (e.g., the fight for a Deaf president of Gallaudet; Christiansen & Barnartt, 2003; and the protest of stuttering's portrayal in *A Fish Called Wanda*; Horn, 1989), while protests addressing systemic issues that affect many types of people draw from cross-disability alliances (e.g., the Independent Living Movement; Penney & Bassman, 2007).

Aspiring allies need to recognize that people who have been disadvantaged by society may need space away from more privileged people, even if the latter view themselves as allies with the best intentions. Indeed, it is important to remember that participatory research is not the *only* way for neurodivergent people to take on leadership roles. Neurodivergent people can also lead initiatives *without* collaborating with "neurotypicals." Fletcher-Watson et al. (2019) highlighted the value of having some autistic-only decision-making spaces. Spaces for smaller groups may also spark innovation (Pellicano et al., 2014a). Indeed, meeting spaces that are open only to people with a specific neurotype may be as important for the strength of society as spaces where people with different neurotypes can work together.[13] Although it can be challenging to recognize that alliances can be strengthened by one's own absence, boundaries can serve as a "means of communication, as opposed to division" that are "essential to the circulation of knowledge and information across social worlds" (Seale, Nind, Tilley, & Chapman, 2015, p. 485).

Fletcher-Watson et al. (2019) expressed hope that the growing neurodiversity movement will help people understand differences rather than always seeking consensus. If we wish to truly engage with diverse others, including people whose viewpoints we may not agree with, our aim cannot always be to obtain consensus by resolving or avoiding all controversies (Pellicano & Stears, 2011). Purposefully balancing the number of people representing each identity in a larger group (or over-representing people with an identity that has traditionally been disempowered) may foster civil discourse (Schwartz et al., 2019). Strategies from political organizing may also be helpful for making sure that each group's unique perspectives are heard, including securing "translators" to convey information between disability-specific groups and cross-disability groups and collaboratively developing guidelines about the communication preferences of different groups. Intergroup dialogue, wherein peer facilitators representing different identities lead dialogues about group identity and work through any conflicts that arise, may combat stigma and promote cross-disability alliances (Sakamoto & Pitner, 2005). Credibility checking is a promising strategy for documenting diversity in opinions (MacLeod, 2019). Efforts to promote fair representation must be developed collaboratively, so that the processes by which power is conferred are visible and guided by the degree to which groups are directly affected by an issue (Bertilsdotter et al., 2019; MacLeod, 2019; Pellicano & Stears, 2011).

Participatory research groups have developed clear strategies that we can use to collaborate with diverse others in increasingly equitable ways. These strategies, which are designed to counter power imbalances and create transparent decision-making processes, have the potential to strengthen both cross-disability and disability-specific alliances (as even people who share a specific disability often differ in other aspects of their identities and aims). Participatory research focused on ID has increasingly highlighted strategies such as establishing trust, shared purpose, and clear roles; developing democratic and reflexive strategies for managing power imbalances; making information accessible (e.g., using simple language and pictures); compensating fairly; and allowing practices to evolve as people learn (Di Lorito, Bosco, Birt, & Hassiotis, 2018; March et al., 1997; Nind & Vinha, 2014; Schwartz et al., 2019; Vaughan et al., 2019). Experienced participatory researchers emphasize that participatory research is a process, with some studies becoming more participatory over time as collaborators grow more empowered (Call-Cummings et al., 2019; Schwartz et al., 2019).

Nicolaidis et al. (2019) recently published recommendations derived from their experiences leading participatory initiatives focused on autism and other neuro-developmental conditions since 2006 (e.g., AASPIRE). Their recommendations, which often align with recommendations from the ID literature, include working together to build trust, e.g., visioning exercises to identify shared goals, and jointly creating clear roles and effective communication processes. They rely primarily on communication via chat during meetings to reduce power imbalances by requiring nonautistic researchers to communicate through a less preferred modality. They recommend discussing processes regularly, e.g., reserving the last few minutes of each meeting to reflect and using change logs to document how materials are altered based on feedback.

The AASPIRE guidelines, and our own experiences, highlight the value of protocols that document the process of seeking consensus (when consensus is sought) for decreasing power imbalances and helping everyone involved understand their roles and responsibilities. At the same time, opportunities to interact that are *not* structured a priori are also needed, as such spaces may foster unexpected connections and discoveries. Fletcher-Watson et al. (2019) describe benefits of unstructured engagements wherein questions can emerge slowly through dialogue, rather than being limited by an agenda.

By unstructured spaces we do not mean the absence of needed accommodations. The most heated debates about whom the neurodiversity movement can represent tend to focus on people who do not speak (e.g., McCoy, Liu, Lutz, & Sisti, 2020). Although participatory research is designed to empower disempowered people to share their own expertise about their lives, underrepresentation of people with the greatest communicative challenges has been a consistent refrain across papers describing participatory approaches with varied populations (e.g., Bertilsdotter et al., 2019). Creative strategies to involve people who struggle to speak are increasingly used (Beresford, Tozer, Rabiee, & Sloper, 2004; Milner & Frawley, 2018; Nicholas, Orjasaeter, & Zwaigenbaum, 2019; Tesfaye et al., 2019). However, participatory research continues to rely primarily on speaking or typing words, both of which can be challenging for people with dyspraxia.[14] To effectively engage the community, we must become more creative in how we seek out collaborators and communicate (MacLeod, 2019; Pellicano et al., 2014b). As Dawn Eddings Prince (2013), an autistic anthropologist, writes:

> Academic writing serves to empty the fullness of the thing it seeks to unequivocally contain. It kills the patient in its very prescription. A cutting thing, a surgery of words, it makes the many into one rather than loaning itself to the cause of connection (p. 330).

CONCLUSION

In this chapter, we examined how the term neurodiversity has been conceptualized and applied in order to better use it as a framework to support cross-disability alliances. We learned that the "neuro" in neurodiversity refers to a constellation of differences that often lack clear demarcations from "normal." Societal expectations shape these dimensional differences into categories. These categories can hurt people by marking them as less than some imagined ideal. These categories can also help people by securing them access to supports they may need in order to live self-determined lives. These categories can be changed and reimagined when people work in concert to change them. Neurodiversity provides a conceptual framework that people with diverse conditions can use to identify shared forms of oppression and work together to change them. Participatory approaches, and approaches that are solely led by neurodivergent people, have shifted public understanding of autism, stuttering, and other conditions and have great potential to continue improving research and practice. The iterative process of participatory work can strengthen alliances, much as stuttering slows and thus deepens communication, "Stuttering interrupts this hegemonic order of time (Pierre quoted by Yeoman, 2019)."

Although small percentages of the population may have any given diagnosis, together people with diagnoses make up a very sizable chunk of the population. These numbers are useful politically, such as when fighting for accommodations and services. But they are also useful personally. They increase the odds that those with diagnoses will come into contact with messages that support their neurodivergent identity rather than diminish it. They are also a source of social solidarity and friendship.

As the neurodiversity movement grows, it will be strengthened by more consistently demonstrating the appreciation of diversity that it advocates for. In order to foster cross-disability alliances that have the power to transform cultures, we must find ways to navigate difference by listening and communicating more effectively. Greta Thunberg, an autistic teenager who sparked a global climate crisis advocacy movement, provides an excellent example of the power of identifying a key shared objective (e.g., reducing carbon emissions) and communicating it simply and clearly for forging effective alliances. As Tisoncik, an autistic activist whose work was inspired by the civil rights movement, wrote:

> We are tied in a single garment of destiny. Autistic activism is but one branch of an eternal great struggle, to set right what is wrong, to lift up those who have been pushed down, and to make space for joy in this world. (2020, p. 75)

ACKNOWLEDGMENTS

We would like to thank all of the people who have contributed to each of the programs described in this report. We would like to thank Chris Frka for his help with qualitative coding of mentor/mentee feedback about Project REACH and for coleading the Project REACH group in the fall of 2019. We would also like to thank Ibrahim Khan for his insights about effective strategies to build political alliances (derived from his volunteer work for the Bernie Sanders campaign). We would also like to thank the reviewers of this manuscript and the editors, particularly Tara Fannon, for their exceptionally constructive feedback.

NOTES

1. ASAN (2020) seeks "to advance the principles of the disability rights movement with regard to autism" by advocating for "policy positions on issues of importance to autistic people and others with disabilities."

2. While advocates for the social model often call for "person-first language" to emphasize that people are much more than their disabilities (Dunn & Andrews, 2015), this form of distancing tends to be undesirable for people who view their diagnosis as central to their sense of self, who prefer "identity-first language," e.g., "autistic person" (Kapp et al., 2013; Kenny et al., 2016). While some neurodiversity-aligned researchers in the stuttering community prefer the term "stutterer," others prefer "person who stutters," or use both terms interchangeably (Constantino, 2018; Pierre, 2012). To align our writing with the preferences of the communities we are writing about, we use identity-first terms to refer to autistic people and both person-first and identity-first terms to describe stutterers.

3. *Neurodivergent* is defined as having a brain that functions differently from dominant societal norms, e.g., a brain that produces behaviors, cognitions, or experiences that society would recognize as disability. Conversely, *neurotypical* means having a brain that falls within societally accepted definitions of "normal."

4. Indeed, a recent review paper revealed that "participatory" research with people with ID has often lacked transparency about the origin of ideas, resulting at times in accusations of neurotypical researchers using coresearchers with ID as puppets (Bigby et al., 2014). Instances of people with ID feeling disempowered by being asked for their help but then not having sufficient support to actually contribute were also documented. However, the authors noted improved documentation of roles and supports in more recent papers.

5. Jivraj and colleagues' use of strict inclusion criteria requiring that studies either clearly document the participatory process or outcomes revealed only *seven* participatory studies focused on collaborations with adults with neurodevelopmental disorders, five of which focused on ID and only two of which focused on autism. *Fifty four* papers were excluded for not meeting their criteria. However, another recent review article by Di Lorito et al. (2018) documented early participatory research wherein people with ID were meaningfully involved as coauthors (e.g., Williams et al., 2005). Therefore, the selection criteria used by Jivraj and colleagues led some participatory ID research to be overlooked. Nevertheless, both sets of authors highlighted the need for greater clarity about what constitutes a participatory study, recommending that collaborators be involved in framing questions, interpreting results, and disseminating findings.

6. The initial aim of this paper was to share the process through which some of its authors developed a participatory mentorship program in which neurodivergent college students play leadership roles in developing curriculum, forging alliances as mentors, and/or evaluating programming as researchers. When delivering talks at the National Stuttering Association, the authors learned how valuable cross-disability alliances can be. We broadened the focus of this paper as we realized that our collective experiences developing different programs for neurodivergent people illuminate strengths and challenges of neurodiversity-aligned cross-disability alliances.

7. Neurotypes means different types of brains, often inferred from behavioral differences.

8. Regarding the term "constellation," see Fletcher-Watson & Happé (2019, pp. 34–35).

9. Functioning levels are placed in quotation marks because neurodiversity advocates (and recent academic research) reject them as imprecise; they fail to distinguish between different types of functioning and ignore how functioning varies across contexts (Alvares et al., 2019; Courchesne, Meilleur, Poulin-Lord, Dawson, & Soulières, 2015; Sequenzia, 2013).

10. Simon Baron-Cohen was the president of the International Society for Autism Research, INSAR in 2019.

11. At an initial pizza party to let students know about the new program, we asked students to identify topics they were most interested in learning about. We continue to conduct needs assessments at the beginning of each term to guide program development. Patrick Dwyer (2019a) conducts similar needs assessments in his autistic led group.

12. This section draws more from published research than the prior practical examples because the NSA has been around for much longer than the other example programs, so there is much more published research about it.

13. Given that internalized stigma may prevent some people from engaging with groups of people who share their diagnosis, strategies to reduce stigma and spaces where people do not need to disclose a diagnosis to join are also essential.

14. Dyspraxia refers to difficulties with motor coordination and motor initiation. Motor difficulties are believed to underly the challenges many nonspeaking autistic people face when trying to speak (Donnellan, Hill, & Leary, 2013).

REFERENCES

Alkhaldi, R. S., Sheppard, E., & Mitchell, P. (2019). Is there a link between autistic people being perceived unfavorably and having a mind that is difficult to read? *Journal of Autism and Developmental Disorders*, doi:10.1007/s10803-019-04101-1

Alm, P. A. (2014). Stuttering in relation to anxiety, temperament, and personality: Review and analysis with focus on causality. *Journal of Fluency Disorders*, *40*, 5–21.

Alvares, G. A., Bebbington, K., Cleary, D., Evans, K., Glasson, E. J., Maybery, M. T., & Whitehouse, A. J. (2019). The misnomer of 'high functioning autism': Intelligence is an imprecise predictor of functional abilities at diagnosis. *Autism*. doi:10.1177/1362361319852831

American Psychiatric Association. (2013). *Diagnostic and statistical manual of mental disorders (DSM-5®)*. Arlington, VA: American Psychiatric Pub.

Angermeyer, M. C., Holzinger, A., Carta, M. G., & Schomerus, G. (2011). Biogenetic explanations and public acceptance of mental illness: Systematic review of population studies. *The British Journal of Psychiatry*, *199*(5), 367–372.

Antonetta, S. (2007). *A mind apart: Travels in a neurodiverse world*. New York, NY: Penguin.

Armstrong, T. (2010). *Neurodiversity: Discovering the extraordinary gifts of autism, ADHD, dyslexia, and other brain differences*. Cambridge, MA: Da Capo Lifelong Books.

ASAN. (2020). ASAN: About ASAN. Retrieved from https://autisticadvocacy.org/about-asan/. Accessed on April 26.

AStrangerInGodZone. (2011, November 14). Behavioural therapy - 'normalization' vs 'teaching of skills'. [Blog post]. Retrieved from http://strangeringodzone.blogspot.com/2011/11/behavioural-therapy-normalization-vs.html

Bailin, A. (2019). Clearing up some misconceptions about neurodiversity. *Scientific American*. [Blog post]. Retrieved from https://blogs.scientificamerican.com/observations/clearing-up-some-misconceptions-about-neurodiversity/

Baker, D. L. (2011). *The politics of neurodiversity: Why public policy matters*. Boulder, CO: Lynne Rienner Publishers.

Ballou, E. P. (2018). What the neurodiversity movement does- and doesn't- offer. *Thinking Person's Guide to Autism*. [Blog post]. Retrieved from http://www.thinkingautismguide.com/2018/02/what-neurodiversity-movement-doesand.html.

Baribeau, D. A., Dupuis, A., Paton, T. A., Hammill, C., Scherer, S. W., Schachar, R. J., & Anagnostou, E. (2019). Structural neuroimaging correlates of social deficits are similar in autism spectrum disorder and attention-deficit/hyperactivity disorder: Analysis from the POND Network. *Translational Psychiatry*, *9*(72). doi:10.1038/s41398-019-0382-0

Barnhill, G. P. (2016). Supporting students with Asperger syndrome on college campuses: Current practices. *Focus on Autism and Other Developmental Disabilities*, *31*(1), 3–15.

Baron-Cohen, S. (2019). The concept of neurodiversity is dividing the autism community. *Scientific American*. [Blog post]. Retrieved from https://blogs.scientificamerican.com/observations/the-concept-of-neurodiversity-is-dividing-the-autism-community/

Baron-Cohen, S., Leslie, A. M., & Frith, U. (1985). Does the autistic child have a "theory of mind? *Cognition*, *21*(1), 37–46.

Beresford, B., Tozer, R., Rabiee, P., & Sloper, P. (2004). Developing an approach to involving children with autistic spectrum disorders in a social care research project. *British Journal of Learning Disabilites*, *32*(4), 180–185.

Bertilsdotter Rosqvist, H., Kourti, M., Jackson-Perry, D., Brownlow, C., Fletcher, K., Bendelman, D., & O'Dell, L. (2019). Doing it differently: Emancipatory autism studies within a neurodiverse academic space. *Disability & Society*, *34*(7–8), 1082–1101. doi:10.1080/09687599.2019.1603102

Bigby, C., Frawley, P., & Ramcharan, P. (2014). Conceptualizing inclusive research with people with intellectual disability. *Journal of Applied Research in Intellectual Disabilities*, *27*(1), 3–12.

Blume, H. (1998). Neurodiversity. *The Atlantic*, *30*, pp. 09–90.

Botha, M., & Frost, D. M. (2020). Extending the minority stress model to understand mental health problems experienced by the autistic population. *Society and Mental Health*, *10*(1), 20–34.

Bottema-Beutel, K., Park, H., & Kim, S. Y. (2018). Commentary on social skills training curricula for individuals with ASD: Social interaction, authenticity, and stigma. *Journal of Autism and Developmental Disorders*, *48*(3), 953–964.

Boyle, M. P. (2013). Psychological characteristics and perceptions of stuttering of adults who stutter with and without support group experience. *Journal of Fluency Disorders*, *38*(4), 368–381.

Boyle, M. P. (2018). Enacted stigma and felt stigma experienced by adults who stutter. *Journal of Communication Disorders*, *73*, 50–61.

Brownlow, C., & O'Dell, L. (2013). Autism as a form of biological citizenship. In J. Davidson, & M. Orsini (Eds.), *Worlds of autism: Across the spectrum of neurological difference* (pp. 97–114). University of Minnesota Press.

Call-Cummings, M., Hauber-Özer, M., & Ross, K. (2019). Struggling with/against the unintentional reproduction of power structures in participatory research: Using reconstructive horizon analysis. *Action Research*. doi:10.1177/1476750319837324

Campbell, P., Constantino, C. D., & Simpson, S. (Eds.). (2019). *Stammering pride and prejudice: Difference not deficit*. Albury: J&R Press.

Capozzi, S., Barmache, D., Cladis, E., Peña, E. V., & Kocur, J. (2019). The significance of involving nonspeaking autistic peer mentors in educational programs. *Autism in Adulthood*, *1*(3), 170–172.

Casartelli, L., Molteni, M., & Ronconi, L. (2016). So close yet so far: Motor anomalies impacting on social functioning in autism spectrum disorder. *Neuroscience & Biobehavioral Reviews*, *63*, 98–105.

Chang, S. E., Zhu, D. C., Choo, A. L., & Angstadt, M. (2015). White matter neuroanatomical differences in young children who stutter. *Brain*, *138*(3), 694–711.

Chew, K. (2013). Autism and the task of the translator. In J.Davidson & M.Orsini (Eds.), *Worlds of autism: Across the spectrum of neurological difference* (pp. 305–515). Minneapolis, MN: University of Minnesota Press.

Chiang, T. (2019). *Exhalation: Stories*. New York, NY: Knopf.

Christiansen, J. B., & Barnartt, S. N. (2003). *Deaf president now!: The 1988 revolution at Gallaudet University*. Washington, DC: Gallaudet University Press.

Constantino, C. D. (2016). Stuttering gain. International Stuttering Association. International Stuttering Awareness Day Online Conference 2016. Retrieved from http://isad.isastutter.org/isad-2016/papers-presented-by-2016/stories-and-experiences-with-stuttering-by-pws/stuttering-gain-christopher-constantino/.

Constantino, C. D. (2018). What can stutterers learn from the neurodiversity movement? *Seminars in Speech and Language*, *39*(04), 382–396.

Costandi, M. (2019). Against neurodiversity. *Psyche*. Retrieved from https://aeon.co/essays/why-the-neurodiversity-movement-has-become-harmful

Courchesne, V., Meilleur, A. A. S., Poulin-Lord, M. P., Dawson, M., & Soulières, I. (2015). Autistic children at risk of being underestimated: School-based pilot study of a strength-informed assessment. *Molecular Autism*, *6*(1)12.

Crane, L., Adams, F., Harper, G., Welch, J., & Pellicano, E. (2019). 'Something needs to change': Mental health experiences of young autistic adults in England. *Autism*, *23*(2), 477–493.

daVanport, S. (2020). Out of searching comes new vibrance. In S. K. Kapp (Ed.), *Autistic community and the neurodiveristy movement: Stories from the frontline*. Singapore: Palgrave Macmillan.

Dawson, M., Mottron, L., & Gernsbacher, M. A. (2008). Learning in autism. In J. Byrne & H. L. I. Roediger (Eds.), *Learning and memory: A comprehensive reference* (Vol. 2, pp. 759–772). Oxford: Elsevier.

DeBrabander, K. M., Morrison, K. E., Jones, D. R., Faso, D. J., Chmielewski, M., & Sasson, N. J. (2019). Do first impressions of autistic adults differ between autistic and nonautistic observers? *Autism in Adulthood*, *1*(4), 250–257.

Dekker, M. (2020). From exclusion to acceptance: Independent living on the autistic spectrum. In S. K. Kapp (Ed.), *Autistic community and the neurodiversity movement: Stories from the frontline*. Singapore: Palgrave Macmillan.

DeNigris, D., Brooks, P. J., Obeid, R., Alarcon, M., Shane-Simpson, C., & Gillespie-Lynch, K. (2018). Bullying and identity development: Insights from autistic and non-autistic college students. *Journal of Autism and Developmental Disorders*, *48*(3), 666–678.

Di Lorito, C., Bosco, A., Birt, L., & Hassiotis, A. (2018). Co-research with adults with intellectual disability: A systematic review. *Journal of Applied Research in Intellectual Disabilities*, *31*(5), 669–686.

Donnellan, A. M., Hill, D. A., & Leary, M. R. (2013). Rethinking autism: Implications of sensory and movement differences for understanding and support. *Frontiers in Integrative Neuroscience*, *6*, 124.

Duchan, J. F. (2011). A history of speech-language pathology. Retrieved from http://www.acsu.buffalo.edu/~duchan/1900-1945.html

Dunn, D. S., & Andrews, E. E. (2015). Person-first and identity-first language: Developing psychologists' cultural competence using disability language. *American Psychologist*, *70*(3), 255.

Dwyer, P. (2019a). Establishing an autism peer support community. *Stairway to STEM*. Retrieved from https://www.stairwaytostem.org/establishing-a-peer-support-community-for-autistic-students/

Dwyer, P. (2019b). On neurodiversity, Part III: What is the neurodiversity paradigm [blog post]. Retrieved from http://www.autisticscholar.com/what-is-neurodiversity/

Engel, G. L. (1977). The need for a new medical model: A challenge for biomedicine. *Science*, *196*(4286), 129–136.

Etchell, A. C., Civier, O., Ballard, K. J., & Sowman, P. F. (2018). A systematic literature review of neuroimaging research on developmental stuttering between 1995 and 2016. *Journal of Fluency Disorders*, *55*, 6–45.

Feinstein, A. (2011). *A history of autism: Conversations with the pioneers*. Hoboken, NJ: John Wiley & Sons.

Fenton, A., & Krahn, T. (2007). Autism, neurodiversity, and equality beyond the "normal". *Journal of Ethics in Mental Health*, *2*(2), 1–6.

Fletcher-Watson, S. (2017, March 24). Autistic voices, and the problem of the 'vocal minority.' Retrieved from https://dart.ed.ac.uk/vocal-minority/.

Fletcher-Watson, S., Adams, J., Brook, K., Charman, T., Crane, L., Cusack, J., & Pellicano, E. (2019). Making the future together: Shaping autism research through meaningful participation. *Autism*, *23*(4), 943–953.

Fletcher-Watson, S., & Happé, F. (2019). *Autism: A new introduction to psychological theory and current debate*. Abingdon: Routledge.

Fletcher-Watson, S., McConnell, F., Manola, E., & McConachie, H. (2014). Interventions based on the Theory of Mind cognitive model for autism spectrum disorder (ASD). *Cochrane Database of Systematic Reviews*, *2014*(3), doi:10.1002/14651858.CD008785.pub2.

Foucault, M. (1973/1994). *The birth of the clinic*. A. Sheridan (Trans.). New York, NY: Vintage Books.

Freire, P. (1970). *Pedagogy of the oppressed*. New York, NY: Continuum.

Friedner, M., Ghosh, N., & Palaniappan, D. (2018). "Cross-Disability" in India?: On the limits of disability as a category and the work of negotiating impairments. *South Asia Multidisciplinary Academic Journal*.

Frigerio-Domingues, C., & Drayna, D. (2017). Genetic contributions to stuttering: The current evidence. *Molecular Genetics & Genomic Medicine*, *5*(2), 95–102.

Gathman, B. (1986). Clarifying the focus and function of self-help. *The Speak Easy Newsletter*, *6*, pp. 5–6.

Geschwind, D. H., & State, M. W. (2015). Gene hunting in autism spectrum disorder: On the path to precision medicine. *The Lancet Neurology*, *14*(11), 1109–1120.

Gillespie-Lynch, K., Brooks, P. J., Someki, F., Obeid, R., Shane-Simpson, C., Kapp, S. K., … Smith, D. S. (2015). Changing college students' conceptions of autism: An online training to increase knowledge and decrease stigma. *Journal of Autism and Developmental Disorders*, *45*(8), 2553–2566.

Gillespie-Lynch, K., Bublitz, D., Donachie, A., Wong, V., Brooks, P. J., & D'Onofrio, J. (2017a). "For a long time our voices have been hushed": Using student perspectives to develop supports for neurodiverse college students. *Frontiers in Psychology*, *8*, 544.

Gillespie-Lynch, K., Hotez, E., Zajic, M., Riccio, A., DeNigris, D., Kofner, B., … Luca, K. (2020). Comparing the writing skills of autistic and non-autistic university students: A collaboration with autistic university students. *Autism*. doi:10.1177/1362361320929453

Gillespie-Lynch, K., Kapp, S. K., Brooks, P. J., Pickens, J., & Schwartzman, B. (2017b). Whose expertise is it? Evidence for autistic adults as critical autism experts. *Frontiers in Psychology*, *8*, 438.

Grandin, T. (1990). Needs of high functioning teenagers and adults with autism (Tips from a recovered autistic). *Focus on Autistic Behavior*, *5*(1), 1–16.

Griffin, E., & Pollak, D. (2009). Student experiences of neurodiversity in higher education: Insights from the BRAINHE project. *Dyslexia*, *15*(1), 23–41.

Grinker, R. R. (2008). What in the world is autism? A cross-cultural perspective. *Zero to Three*, *28*(4), 5–10.

Groot, B. C., Vink, M., Haveman, A., Huberts, M., Schout, G., & Abma, T. A. (2019). Ethics of care in participatory health research: Mutual responsibility in collaboration with co-researchers. *Educational Action Research*, *27*(2), 286–302.

Hacking, I. (2009). How we have been learning to talk about autism: A role for stories. *Metaphilosophy*, *40*(3–4), 499–516.

Harp, B. [bev] (2009, August 7). Check list of neurotypical privilege: New draft [Blog post]. Retrieved from http://aspergersquare8.blogspot.com/2009/08/checklist-of-neurotypical-privilege-new.html.

Holiga, Š., Hipp, J. F., Chatham, C. H., Garces, P., Spooren, W., D'Ardhuy, X. L., … Dukart, J. (2019). Patients with autism spectrum disorders display reproducible functional connectivity alterations. *Science Translational Medicine*, *11*(481), eaat9223. doi:10.1126/scitranslmed.aat9223

Hollin, G., & Pearce, W. (2019). Autism scientists' reflections on the opportunities and challenges of public engagement: A qualitative analysis. *Journal of Autism and Developmental Disorders*, *49*(3), 809–818.

Horn, J. (1989). Oscar demonstrators line up on eve of awards show. Associated Press. Retrieved from https://apnews.com/191442d2cadf0722d4efdcf902c053d7

Hotez, E., Shane-Simpson, C., Obeid, R., DeNigris, D., Siller, M., Costikas, C., & Gillespie-Lynch, K. (2018). Designing a summer transition program for incoming and current college students on the autism spectrum: A participatory approach. *Frontiers in Psychology*, *9*, 46.

Hughes, J. M. F. (2016). Nothing about us without us: Increasing neurodiversity in disability and social justice advocacy groups. Retrieved from https://autisticadvocacy.org/wp-content/uploads/2016/06/whitepaper-Increasing-Neurodiversity-in-Disability-and-Social-Justice-Advocacy-Groups.pdf

Hyman, S. E. (2010). The diagnosis of mental disorders: The problem of reification. *Annual Review of Clinical Psychology*, *6*, 155–179.

Jaarsma, P., & Welin, S. (2012). Autism as a natural human variation: Reflections on the claims of the neurodiversity movement. *Health Care Analysis*, *20*(1), 20–30.

Jack, A., & Pelphrey, A. (2017). Annual Research Review: Understudied populations within the autism spectrum–current trends and future directions in neuroimaging research. *Journal of Child Psychology and Psychiatry*, *58*(4), 411–435.

Jamison, K. R. (1995). Manic-depressive illness and creativity. *Scientific American*, *272*(2), pp. 62–67.

Jivraj, J., Sacrey, L. A., Newton, A., Nicholas, D., & Zwaigenbaum, L. (2014). Assessing the influence of researcher–partner involvement on the process and outcomes of participatory research in autism spectrum disorder and neurodevelopmental disorders: A scoping review. *Autism*, *18*(7), 782–793.

Johnson, W. (1930). *Because I stutter*. New York, NY: D. Appleton.

Kanner, L. (1943). Autistic disturbances of affective contact. *Nervous child*, *2*(3), 217–250.

Kapp, S. (2013). Interactions between theoretical models and practical stakeholders: The basis for an integrative, collaborative approach to disabilities. In E. Ashkenazy, & M. Latimer (Eds.), *Empowering leadership: A systems change guide for autistic college students and those with other disabilities* (pp. 104–113). Washington, DC: Autistic Self Advocacy Network (ASAN).

Kapp, S. K. (2018). Social support, well-being, and quality of life among individuals on the autism spectrum. *Pediatrics*, *141*(Supplement 4), S362–S368.

Kapp S. K. (Ed.). (2020). *Autistic community and the neurodiversity movement: Stories from the frontline*. Singapore: Palgrave Macmillan.

Kapp, S. K., Gillespie-Lynch, K., Sherman, L. E., & Hutman, T. (2013). Deficit, difference, or both? Autism and neurodiversity. *Developmental Psychology*, *49*(1), 59.

Kenny, L., Hattersley, C., Molins, B., Buckley, C., Povey, C., & Pellicano, E. (2016). Which terms should be used to describe autism? Perspectives from the UK autism community. *Autism*, *20*(4), 442–462.

King, J. B., Prigge, M. B., King, C. K., Morgan, J., Weathersby, F., Fox, J. C., & Bigler, E. D. (2019). Generalizability and reproducibility of functional connectivity in autism. *Molecular Autism*, *10*(1), 27.

Kras, J. F. (2010). The "ransom notes" affair: When the neurodiversity movement came of age. *Disability Studies Quarterly*, *30*(1). Retrieved from https://dsq-sds.org/article/%C2%A0view/1065/1254

Krauss-Lehrman, T., & Reeves, L. (1989). Attitudes toward speech-language pathology and support groups: Results of a survey of members of the National Stuttering Project. *Texas Journal of Audiology and Speech Pathology*, *15*(1), 22–25.

Kuder, S. J., & Accardo, A. (2018). What works for college students with autism spectrum disorder. *Journal of Autism and Developmental Disorders*, *48*(3), 722–731.

Lickliter, R., & Witherington, D. C. (2017). Towards a truly developmental epigenetics. *Human Development*, *60*(2–3), 124–138.

Loth, E., Charman, T., Mason, L., Tillmann, J., Jones, E. J., Wooldridge, C., & Banaschewski, T. (2017). The EU-AIMS Longitudinal European Autism Project (LEAP): Design and methodologies to identify and validate stratification biomarkers for autism spectrum disorders. *Molecular Autism*, *8*(1), 24.

MacLeod, A. (2019). Interpretative phenomenological analysis (IPA) as a tool for participatory research within critical autism studies: A systematic review. *Research in Autism Spectrum Disorders*, *64*, 49–62.

Maguire, G., & Reitzes, P. (2016). The future of the national stuttering association. *StutterTalk*, *578*, May 2.

March, J., Steingold, B., Justice, S., & Mitchell, P. (1997). Follow the yellow brick road! People with learning difficulties as co-researchers. *British Journal of Learning Disabilites*, *25*(2), 77–80.

McCoy, M. S., Liu, E. Y., Lutz, A. S., & Sisti, D. (2020). Ethical advocacy across the autism spectrum: Beyond partial representation. *The American Journal of Bioethics*, *20*(4), 13–24.

McCready, J. (2019, July 15). The silencing of severe autism across the pond. National Council on Severe Autism. Retrieved from https://www.ncsautism.org/blog//the-silencing-of-severe-autism-across-the-pond.

Milner, P., & Frawley, P. (2018). From 'on'to 'with'to 'by:'people with a learning disability creating a space for the third wave of Inclusive Research. *Qualitative Research*. doi:10.1177/1468794118781385

Milton, D. E. M. (2012). On the ontological status of autism: The "double empathy" problem. *Disability & Society*, *27*(6), 883–887 doi:10.1080/09687599.2012.710008.

Minkes, J., Townsley, R., Weston, C., Williams, C., & Tyrell, J. (1995). Having a voice: Involving people with learning difficulties in research. *British Journal of Learning Disabilites*, *23*(3), 94–97.

Mogadam, A., Keller, A. E., Arnold, P. D., Schachar, R., Lerch, J. P., Anagnostou, E., & Pang, E. W. (2019). Magnetoencephalographic (MEG) brain activity during a mental flexibility task suggests some shared neurobiology in children with neurodevelopmental disorders. *Journal of Neurodevelopmental Disorders*, *11*, 19. doi:10.1186/s11689-019-9280-2.

Morrison, K. E., DeBrabander, K. M., Jones, D. R., Faso, D. J., Ackerman, R. A., & Sasson, N. J. (2019). Outcomes of real-world social interaction for autistic adults paired with autistic compared to typically developing partners. *Autism*. doi:10.1177/1362361319892701

Nadesan, M. (2013). Autism and genetics: Profit, risk, and bare life. In J. Davidson & M. Orsini (Eds.), *Worlds of autism: Across the spectrum of neurological difference* (pp. 117–142). Minneapolis, MN: University of Minnesota Press.

National Stuttering Association. (2019). About the NSA. Retrieved from https://westutter.org/about-the-nsa

Ne'eman, A. (2010). The future (and the past) of Autism advocacy, or why the ASA's magazine, the Advocate, wouldn't publish this piece. *Disability Studies Quarterly*, *30*(1). Retrieved from https://dsq-sds.org/article/view/1059/1244

Nicholas, D. B., Orjasaeter, J. D., & Zwaigenbaum, L. (2019). Considering methodological accommodation to the diversity of ASD: A realist synthesis review of data collection methods for examining first-person experiences. *Review Journal of Autism and Developmental Disorders*, *6*(2), 216–232.

Nicolaidis, C. (2012). What can physicians learn from the neurodiversity movement? *AMA Journal of Ethics*, *14*(6), 503–510.

Nicolaidis, C., Raymaker, D., Kapp, S. K., Baggs, A., Ashkenazy, E., McDonald, K., … Joyce, A. (2019). The AASPIRE practice-based guidelines for the inclusion of autistic adults in research as co-researchers and study participants. *Autism*. doi:10.1177/1362361319830523

Nind, M., & Vinha, H. (2014). Doing research inclusively: Bridges to multiple possibilities in inclusive research. *British Journal of Learning Disabilites*, *42*(2), 102–109.

NYC Stutters. (2018). One day conference for adults who stutter. Retrieved from http://www.nycstutters.org/

O'Dell, L., Bertilsdotter Rosqvist, H., Ortega, F., Brownlow, C., & Orsini, M. (2016). Critical autism studies: Exploring epistemic dialogues and intersections, challenging dominant understandings of autism. *Disability & Society*, *31*(2), 166–179.

Ortega, F. (2013). Cerebralizing autism within the neurodiversity movement. In J. Davidson & M. Orsini (Eds.), *Critical Autism Studies: Enabling Inclusion, Defending Difference* (pp. 73–95). Minneapolis, MN: University of Minnesota Press.

Pellicano, E., Dinsmore, A., & Charman, T. (2014a). What should autism research focus upon? Community views and priorities from the United Kingdom. *Autism*, *18*(7), 756–770.

Pellicano, E., Dinsmore, A., & Charman, T. (2014b). Views on researcher-community engagement in autism research in the United Kingdom: A mixed-methods study. *PloS One*, *9*(10), e109946.

Pellicano, E., & Stears, M. (2011). Bridging autism, science and society: Moving toward an ethically informed approach to autism research. *Autism Research*, *4*(4), 271–282.

Penney, D., & Bassman, R. (2007). The independent living movement and people with psychiatric disabilities: Searching for common ground. Retrieved from http://www.community-consortium.org/pdfs/ILC.pdf

Pierre, J. S. (2012). The construction of the disabled speaker: Locating stuttering in disability studies. *Canadian Journal of Disability Studies*, *1*(3), 1–21.

Prince, D. E. (2013). "All the things I have ever been" autoethnographic reflections on academic writing and autism. In J. Davidson & M. Orsini (Eds.), *Worlds of autism: Across the spectrum of neurological difference* (pp. 319–330). Minneapolis, MN: University of Minnesota Press.

Pripas-Kapit, S. (2020). Historicizing Jim Sinclair's "Don't mourn for us": A cultural and intellectual history of neurodiversity's first manifesto. In S. K. Kapp (Ed.), *Autistic Community and the neurodiversity movement: Stories from the frontline*. Singapore: Palgrave Macmillan.

Putnam, M. (2005). Conceptualizing disability: Developing a framework for political disability identity. *Journal of Disability Policy Studies*, *16*(3), 188–198.

Quesal, R. W. (2012). The person who stutters as a speech-language pathologist. In P. Reitzes, & D. Reitzes (Eds.), *Stuttering: Inspiring stories and professional wisdom* (pp. 219–228). Chapel Hill, NC: StutterTalk, INC.

Ramig, P. R. (1993). The impact of self-help groups on persons who stutter: A call for research. *Journal of Fluency Disorders*, *18*(2–3), 351–361.

Raymaker, D. M., & Nicolaidis, C. (2010). The dynamics of autistic-academic community partnerships. *Dynamics*, *9*. Retrieved from https://pdxscholar.library.pdx.edu/socwork_fac/17/

Raymaker, D., & Nicolaidis, C. (2013). Participatory research with autistic communities: Shifting the system. In J. Davidson & M. Orsini (Eds.), *Worlds of autism: Across the spectrum of neurological difference* (pp. 305–515). Minneapolis, MN: University of Minnesota Press.

Reser, J. E. (2011). Conceptualizing the autism spectrum in terms of natural selection and behavioral ecology: The solitary forager hypothesis. *Evolutionary Psychology*, *9*(2). doi:10.1177/147470491100900209

Riccio, A., Delos Santos, J., Kapp, S. K., Jordan, A., DeNigris, D., & Gillespie-Lynch, K. (2020). Developing the multidimensional visual scale assessing affect, anxiety, pride, and energy through a research partnership with autistic scholars. *Autism in Adulthood*, *2*(1), 87–100.

Robertson, S. M. (2010). Neurodiversity, quality of life, and autistic adults: Shifting research and professional focuses onto real-life challenges. *Disability Studies Quarterly*, *30*(1). Retrieved from https://dsq-sds.org/article/view/1069/1234

Robison, J. (2013, October 7). What is neurodiversity? Neurodiversity means many things to many people. Here's my first-person definition. *Psychology Today*. Retrieved from https://www.psychologytoday.com/us/blog/my-life-aspergers/201310/what-is-neurodiversity

Robison, J. E. (2019). Talking about autism—thoughts for researchers. *Autism Research*, *12*(7), 1004–1006.

Sakamoto, I., & Pitner, R. O. (2005). Use of critical consciousness in anti-oppressive social work practice: Disentangling power dynamics at personal and structural levels. *British Journal of Social Work*, *35*(4), 435–452.

Samson, F., Mottron, L., Soulières, I., & Zeffiro, T. A. (2012). Enhanced visual functioning in autism: An ALE meta-analysis. *Human Brain Mapping*, *33*(7), 1553–1581.

Sasson, N. J., Faso, D. J., Nugent, J., Lovell, S., Kennedy, D. P., & Grossman, R. B. (2017). Neurotypical peers are less willing to interact with those with autism based on thin slice judgments. *Scientific Reports*, *7*(40700). doi:10.1038/srep40700.

Schwartz, A. E., Kramer, J. M., Cohn, E. S., & McDonald, K. E. (2019). "That felt like real engagement": Fostering and maintaining inclusive research collaborations with individuals with intellectual disability. *Qualitative Health Research*. doi:10.1177/1049732319869620

Seale, J., Nind, M., Tilley, L., & Chapman, R. (2015). Negotiating a third space for participatory research with people with learning disabilities: An examination of boundaries and spatial practices. *Innovation: The European Journal of Social Science Research*, *28*(4), 483–497.

Searle, K. A., Ellis, L., Kourti, M., MacLeod, A., Lear, C., Duckworth, C., ... Simpson, J. (2019). Participatory autism research with students at a UK university: Evidence from a small-scale empirical project. *Advances in Autism*, *5*(2), 84–93.

Sequenzia, A. (2013). More problems with functioning labels. Retrieved from https://ollibean.com/problems-functioning-labels/

Simonoff, E., Pickles, A., Charman, T., Chandler, S., Loucas, T., & Baird, G. (2008). Psychiatric disorders in children with autism spectrum disorders: Prevalence, comorbidity, and associated factors in a population-derived sample. *Journal of the American Academy of Child & Adolescent Psychiatry*, *47*(8), 921–929.

Sinclair, J. (1993). Don't mourn for us. Our voice. *Autism Network International*, *1*(3). Retrieved from https://www.autreat.com/dont_mourn.html

Sinclair, J. (2010). Being autistic together. *Disability Studies Quarterly*, *30*(1). doi: 10.18061/dsq.v30i1.1075.

Sinclair, J. (2012). Autism network international: The development of a community and its culture. In J. Bascom (Ed.), *Loud hands: Autistic people, speaking* (pp. 17–48). Washington, DC: The Autistic Press. Retrieved from http://www.autreat.com/History_of_ANI.html

Singer, J. (2017). *Neurodiversity: The birth of an idea*. Sydney: Amazon Digital Services.

Singer, J. (2019). Neurodiversity 2.0: Reclaiming the Centre. Retrieved from https://neurodiversity2.blogspot.com/p/what.html

Singh, J., Illes, J., Lazzeroni, L., & Hallmayer, J. (2009). Trends in US autism research funding. *Journal of Autism and Developmental Disorders*, *39*(5), 788–795.

Stephens, E., & Cryle, P. (2017). Eugenics and the normal body: The role of visual images and intelligence testing in framing the treatment of people with disabilities in the early twentieth century. *Continuum*, *31*(3), 365–376.

Sugarman, M. (1999). Overview and brief history of the National Stuttering Association. *The Stuttering Homepage*. Retrieved from https://www.mnsu.edu/comdis/isad2/papers/sugarman2.html.

Tesfaye, R., Courchesne, V., Yusuf, A., Savion-Lemieux, T., Singh, I., Shikako-Thomas, K., & Szatmari, P. (2019). Assuming ability of youth with autism: Synthesis of methods capturing the first-person perspectives of children and youth with disabilities. *Autism*. doi:10.1177/1362361319831487

Tetnowski, J., & McClure, J. (2010). Experiences of people who stutter: National Stuttering Association 2009 survey. Paper presented at the Poster presentation at the Annual Conference of the American Speech-Language-Hearing Association, Philadelphia, PA.

Thomas, G. M., & Rothman, B. K. (2016). Keeping the backdoor to eugenics ajar?: Disability and the future of prenatal screening. *AMA journal of ethics*, *18*(4), 406–415.

Tisoncik, L. A. (2020). Autistics.Org and finding our voices as an activist movement. In S. Kapp (Ed.), *Autistic community and the neurodiversity movement: Stories from the frontline* (pp. 65–76). Singapore: Palgrave Macmillan.

Trichon, M., & Tetnowski, J. (2011). Self-help conferences for people who stutter: A qualitative investigation. *Journal of Fluency Disorders*, *36*(4), 290–295.

Trichon, M., Tetnowski, J., & Rentschler, G. (2006). Perspective of participants of self-help groups for people who stutter. Paper presented at the Research, treatment, and self-help in fluency disorders: New horizons. Proceedings of the fifth world congress on fluency disorders.

Vaughan, C., Khaw, S., Katsikis, G., Wheeler, J., Ozge, J., Kasidis, V., & Moosad, L. (2019). 'It is like being put through a blender': Inclusive research in practice in an Australian university. *Disability & Society*, *34*(7–8), 1224–1240.

Walker, N. (2014). Neurodiversity: Some basic terms and definitions. *Neurocosmopolitanism*. September, 27. Retrieved from https://neurocosmopolitanism.com/neurodiversity-some-basic-terms-definitions/

Walmsley, J. (2001). Normalisation, emancipatory research and inclusive research in learning disability. *Disability & Society*, *16*(2), 187–205.

Weidig, T. (2019). British stammering association stammering pride and prejudice publication facebook announcement. Retrieved from https://www.facebook.com/stammeringbsa/posts/10156233774551813?comment_id=1015623635430681

White, D., Hillier, A., Frye, A., & Makrez, E. (2019). College students' knowledge and attitudes towards students on the autism spectrum. *Journal of Autism and Developmental Disorders*, *49*(7), 2699–2705.

Williams, V., Simons, K., & Swindon People First Research Team (2005). More researching together: The role of nondisabled researchers in working with people first members. *British Journal of Learning Disabilites*, *33*(1), 6–14.

Wilson, E., Kenny, A., & Dickson-Swift, V. (2018). Ethical challenges in community-based participatory research: A scoping review. *Qualitative Health Research*, *28*(2), 189–199.

Wilson, R. A., & Pierre, J. S. (2016). Eugenics and disability. In P. Devlieger, B. Miranda-Galarza, S. E. Brown, & M. Strickfaden (Eds.), *Rethinking disability: World perspectives in culture and society* (pp. 93–112). Antwerp, BE: Garant.

Yaruss, J. S., Quesal, R. W., Reeves, L., Molt, L. F., Kluetz, B., Caruso, A. J., & Lewis, F. (2002). Speech treatment and support group experiences of people who participate in the National Stuttering Association. *Journal of Fluency Disorders*, *27*(2), 115–133.

Yeoman, B. (2019). Stammer time. *The Baffler*, *48*. Retrieved from https://thebaffler.com/salvos/stammer-time-yeoman

Chapter 10

A DIFFERENT STORY: NARRATIVE ALLYSHIP ACROSS ABILITY

Nicki Pombier

ABSTRACT

Purpose: *This chapter proposes narrative allyship across ability as a practice in which nondisabled researchers work with disabled nonresearchers to co-construct a process that centers and acts on the knowledge contained in and expressed by the lived experience of the disabled nonresearchers. This chapter situates narrative allyship across ability in the landscape of other participatory research practices, with a particular focus on oral history as a social justice praxis.*

Approach: *In order to explore the potential of this practice, the author outlines and reflects on both the methodology of her oral history graduate thesis work, a narrative project with self-advocates with Down syndrome, and includes and analyzes reflections about narrative allyship from a self-advocate with Down syndrome.*

Findings: *The author proposes three guiding principles for research as narrative allyship across ability, namely that such research further the interests of narrators as the narrators define them, optimize the autonomy of narrators, and tell stories with, instead of about, narrators.*

Implications: *This chapter suggests the promise of research praxis as a form of allyship: redressing inequality by addressing power, acknowledging expertise in subjugated knowledges, and connecting research practices to desires for social change or political outcomes. The author models methods by which others might include in their research narrative work across ability and demonstrates the particular value of knowledge produced when researchers*

Disability Alliances and Allies
Research in Social Science and Disability, Volume 12, 225–257

ISSN: 1479-3547/doi:10.1108/S1479-354720200000012014

attend to the lived expertise of those with disabilities. The practice of narrative allyship across ability has the potential to bring a wide range of experiences and modes of expression into the domains of research, history, policy, and culture that would otherwise exclude them.

Keywords: Oral history methodology; oral history ethics; Down syndrome; self-advocacy; participatory research; narrative; intellectual disability

INTRODUCTION: A DIFFERENT STORY

I was midway through my graduate studies in 2012 at Columbia University's Oral History Master of Arts program (OHMA) when I had my son, Jonah. He was diagnosed at birth with Down syndrome, soon after with sensorineural hearing loss, and several years later with autism spectrum disorder. Writing now, I want to delete the diagnoses and instead write – what? How do I narrate my disabled son into social science?

Jonah has eyes with long calico lashes and irises blueberry blue brushed with galactic streaks of hazel. He loves the ocean, the Beatles, and car rides. Lately, as a joke, he calls me Grandpa. "Who you calling Grandpa?" I reply, cracking him up. He needs repetition and routine the way I need breathing. He stims, using anything long and thin to tap his lap, ad infinitum. He loves going for walks in the neighborhood along a route he devises. He is often searching for something – a ceiling fan, a car in a driveway, a porch light always on. Humans he can take or leave. When he is alive to others, he is a source of light. He walks up to strangers and presses against their thighs, crooning, "Hi," which charms and worries me. He loves water, light, roller coasters, and rocking to some inner motion. He was born quietly, with neither name nor diagnosis until the next day, when the hospital pediatrician told me (postpartum and alone) that he has Down syndrome.

Where does my son belong? Where do I belong, as writer, oral historian, parent, scholar, ally? This chapter is not about my son, but my work here began with him. The days after his diagnosis were an abrupt beginning to the ongoing work of unlearning my ableism and learning from disability activists, scholars, artists, and self-advocates new ways of theorizing and acting in and on society. My beginning was as (inter)personal as it gets; I never had a meaningful encounter with a person with intellectual disability until I gave birth to one. As I began to process this fact in those early days, I saw that this was by design: the world, written by and for an idea of "normal," has kept us apart.

My political awakening to disability and my ongoing education in new language, frameworks, and ways of knowing began with that first encounter across difference and has proceeded over eight years along many lines: parent, oral historian, scholar, writer, friend, ally. It sometimes makes for a messy braid, but with this chapter, I am trying to twine all to one.

This chapter articulates a methodological approach to working as a narrative ally across ability by reflecting on my graduate thesis project, which included oral history interviews with self-advocates with Down syndrome, collaboratively edited into an online collection. In order to apply the methods of narrative allyship to the writing of this chapter itself, I include and analyze reflections on narrative allyship from a self-advocate with Down syndrome. This person, who wishes to remain anonymous and has expressed a desire to be referred to in this chapter as Advocate, shares my desire to tell more complex stories about experiences of intellectual disability. This is key in order to employ narrative as a "strategy of resistance" to narrowly construed notions of what's possible for people with intellectual disability (Green & Loseke, 2020, p. 5). For Advocate, that means working on autobiographical projects, including a book. For me, it has meant working on a range of projects using oral history to elicit and share first person stories from people with intellectual disability, in order to deepen and expand audiences' understanding of their history and humanity. Our stakes in this work are different; for Advocate, as our work below will show, telling a more complex story about their life requires living that story, which in turn is complicated by a range of barriers. For me, the stakes are personal and iterative. I want to enact in my parenting what I believe in my work and want my work to make possible the world in which I want to parent my child. I work and parent in the belief that where my tools are limited, it is incumbent on me to work differently; that my job is to serve my son and others' self-actualization; and that making space for new and different stories of intellectual disability can contribute to a world with fewer structural, social, and cultural barriers to self-determination for my son and all people with intellectual disability.

I also acknowledge that for me, the stakes in this work, including the authorship of this chapter, are professional. I work as an independent oral historian, and an educator and scholar at several higher educational institutions, and my career stands to gain through publication of an academic article. That is not to negate the value or meaning of this to Advocate, but rather to acknowledge "where the idealized world of inclusive research collides with the unequal world beyond" (Walmsley & Johnson, 2003, p. 181). The "unequal world" put real pressure on the writing of this paper as an act of narrative allyship.

I hope to offer methodological insights to encourage social science to take up the promise of narrative work, as Volume 11 in this series highlights, to "uncover and bring to the table voices missing in traditional scholarship" (Green & Loseke, 2020, p. 7). No voices may be more excluded from traditional scholarship, including oral history, than those of people with intellectual disabilities (Atkinson, 1998; Hirsch, 1995; Walmsley, 2009). I hope to not only model the methods by which others might include in their research narrative work across ability, but demonstrate the particular value of knowledge produced when researchers take seriously the foundational cry of the disability rights movement: nothing about us without us.

ORAL HISTORY PRAXIS AS ALLYSHIP

I entered the field of oral history as a graduate student in 2010, at a time of renewed commitment to activism within the discipline. I was drawn to its foundational dedication to radical inclusion, deep self-reflexivity, attention to power in the interview and beyond, and commitment to justice. I began interviewing when my son was a newborn; I was, in a literal and immediate way, learning from my narrators. In my interviews with John Anton, I learned about key structural injustices like the subminimum wages in sheltered workshops. From Mitchell Levitz, I learned the language of self-determination, and David Egan taught me the disability rights slogan "Nothing About Us Without Us." These are just a few examples. There was no false humility in my invitation to self-advocates with Down syndrome: I saw them as expert authors of experiences I needed to learn from, as a new parent, a would-be ally, and an oral historian. In the methods section below, I share more about how this dynamic played out in the project. While giving birth to a child with disability midway through a graduate degree program is not replicable (nor recommended!), research as allyship across ability, centering the lived expertise of narrators as co-researchers, is.

This has long been the work of oral history, which has evolved in dialogue with other practices committed to equitable, just, or emancipatory collaboration and alliance with communities of nonresearchers. What makes oral history unique is that it both generates narrative and is centered on the narrative process of long form life history interviewing. Our narrative work makes particular contributions not simply by creating personal historical narratives, but because of the processes that generate them, which are informed by a long history of research as allyship, including the popular education praxis of Paolo Freire and the community and participatory action research of Helen Lewis and others (Kerr, 2016). These social justice research praxes both informed and dovetailed with developments in oral history method and theory, as practitioners sought to leverage oral history research to mobilize knowledge from the bottom, attend to power within and beyond research dynamics, and seek egalitarian and nonexploitative relationships between researchers and participants. In the 1970s and 1980s, feminist oral history practitioners began to articulate oral history as a "feminist encounter" (Gluck, 1977, p. 5) that records women's experiences as historical and worthy of research; interrogates the ethic between interviewer and interviewee; sees the engagement between researcher and subject as the site where power structures can be challenged; and acknowledges the necessity of researcher's self-reflexivity and "self-critical examination" (Anderson & Jack, 1991; Gluck & Patai, 1991; Sheftel & Zembrzycki, 2016). Contemporary conceptions of queer oral history build on the "liberationist urge" in early feminist oral history, notably the commitment to taking up the "more challenging space" of critical social analysis, insisting on a rigorous attention to the intricacies of the research experience (Boyd & Ramírez, 2012, p. 6).

This self-reflexivity is central to other key concepts in oral history method and theory that articulate the particular value of the oral historical encounter, where power is negotiated across difference. In Alessandro Portelli's influential 1991 contribution to oral history methodology, *The Death of Luigi Trastulli and Other Stories,* he posits oral history research as an "experiment in equality" (Portelli, 1991). In this "experiment," equality and difference are interrelated. Without equality, difference iterates as hierarchy and subordination. Without difference, there is only sameness, which is not equality (Portelli, 1991). Portelli's scholarship situated oral history as a political encounter across difference, predicated on mutual recognition by researcher and subject, interviewer and interviewee, of the subjectivity of the other. Oral history is a political intervention when the interview and subsequent interpretive processes "stimulate others, as well as ourselves, to a higher degree of self-scrutiny and self-awareness," and "help [interviewees] grow more aware of the relevance and meaning of their culture and knowledge," and, finally, "raise the question of the senselessness and injustice of the inequality between them and us" (Portelli, 1991, p. 44). As Daniel Kerr points out, this echoes the concept of "accompaniment" developed decades prior in the popular education praxis of Staughton and Alice Lynd,

> ...where two people seeking to bridge a divide come together as they are, not pretending they are something they are not; recognize the expertise of the other; and walk "side by side with one another on a common journey." (Kerr, 2016, p. 376)

We can also hear this in Paolo Freire's call to the popular educator, who is neither the "proprietor of history," nor the "liberator of the oppressed," but is rather committed, "within history, to fight at their side" (quoted in Kerr, 2016, p. 378). The oral history researcher as ally does not erase or ignore the complexity of difference between interviewer and interviewee, but rather sees the mutual recognition and interrogation of that difference as a necessary precursor to the political work of grappling with inequality.

A key phrase in the field's lexicon, signaling oral history's intersubjectivity, is Michael Frisch's "shared authority," the titular term of his 1990 essay collection. Authority signifies both authorship and power, and Frisch's term gave the field a concise way to acknowledge that oral history researchers and subjects are bound to one another's respective authorities within the interview and in the processes by which those interviews are authored into a broader domain. Oral historian and subject each bring to the interview a particular positionality, set of tools and resources, and expertise. Frisch notes that experience and expertise have the same root, citing the etymology of "expert": "a person wise through experience" (Frisch, 2011, p. 128). What we author together through an oral historical process is marked by and a product of the negotiation of the respective and varied authorities of the researcher and subject. Authority is not the researcher's to share, but rather, *is shared.* Shared authority is a condition of the process that is not fixed, but can shift across a range of differences throughout the process. Oral historians working across difference while recognizing shared authority and investing in the political work of addressing power act on the knowledge that the dialogic process is not limited to the interview, but integral to the interpretive work beyond, so that shared authority is also shared authorship (Frisch, 2011; Grele, 2007; Shopes, 2014).

I have focused on a historiography of oral history method and theory because that is the field in which my work originated and developed. Below, I will briefly note some of the other theoretical and methodological frameworks that informed and guided my methods. Oral history method and theory is resonant with a range of other contemporary social justice praxes. For example, Phillips, Kristiansen, Vehviläinen, and Gunnarson (2015) describe a twenty-first century "dialogic turn" in contemporary social science collaborative research practices, in which the experiential knowledge of nonresearchers is brought, through dialogue and communication, onto equal footing with the researchers' "expertise." In the dialogic turn, as in the practice of oral history, difference constitutes strength, in that it generates knowledge that can be used to achieve individual or community empowerment (Phillips et al., 2015).

Second, in the legacy of Freire's critical pedagogy, the late Joe Kincheloe synthesized research bricolage and postformal psychology to argue that rigor in research comes from juxtaposition of difference and that postformalism, as a critical theory of cognition, "expands the boundaries of what can be labeled intelligence or sophisticated thinking" (Kincheloe, 2007, p. 3). Bricoleurs engage "the transformative politics of difference," and with attention to the power structures and social and historical forces that delineate difference, initiate "postformal conversations" as complex processes of developing "genuine and egalitarian interactions" across difference, alive to the socially constructed identities of researcher and nonresearcher and aimed at addressing systemic inequality (Kincheloe, 2007, p. 10). The valuing of subjugated knowledges and ways of knowing and the imperative for researchers to work with "radical humility" (Kincheloe, 2007, p. 10) are similar to the principles informing cultural humility, which Tervalon and Murray-Garcia (1998) propose as a training framework by which medical professionals learn how to listen differently and to see patients from "marginalized communities" as experts of their own experiences (Tervalon & Murray-Garcia, 1998, p. 123).

Kincheloe's postformalist bricolage is particularly relevant because he politicizes cognition by expanding what can be considered intelligence to include those whose ways of knowing are otherwise kept apart based on prejudicial or limited ideas about what constitutes cognitive ability (Kincheloe, 2007, p. 4). This is especially applicable to research with people with intellectual disabilities.

Sociologist Allison C. Carey also provides relevant analysis for my work. Carey's scholarship on the denial of and fight for civil, social, and human rights for people with intellectual disabilities in the United States shows both the stakes of our beliefs about the capacities of those with intellectual disabilities and how those beliefs have changed over time (Carey, 2009). People with intellectual disabilities have historically had their lives severely circumscribed by assumptions about their cognitive limitations. In the United States, this process has included forced sterilizations, mass institutionalization, segregation, denial of education and employment, pervasive exclusion and repression with little cultural representation, and stigmatization such that it is still common to hear the now-derogatory term "retarded" used as a synonym for a particularly derided form of stupidity.

This is both what we are up against and what we stand to gain when we, researchers as allies across ability, listen to and center the lived experiences of people with intellectual disabilities with whom we work. Narrative is both a subject and an actor. It contains history and makes it; contains culture and makes it; contains research and makes it. For individuals with intellectual disability, narrative work requires allyship to bring their wide range of experiences and modes of expression into the domains of research, history, policy, and culture that would otherwise continue to exclude them. They have long had their history and the policies that determine the scope of their lives written by others in language that labels, diagnoses, and emphasizes deficiency and lack (Atkinson, 1998; Atkinson, Richardson, & Ramcharan, 2005; Atkinson & Williams, 1990). But autobiographical accounts, authored through processes that take seriously the shared authority at the juncture of the researcher's tools and the subject's lived expertise, offer compelling rejoinders to the limited ideas about people with intellectual disabilities (Couser, 2009). These narratives show the many and complex ways of knowing for people with intellectual disabilities. They challenge myths of dependency, point out faulty assumptions about agency, and demonstrate life as a complex ecosystem of interdependence, contributing to the work that many in disability studies have done to challenge neoliberal idealization of individualism and self-sufficiency (see, for instance, Tabatabai, 2020). They are not easy narratives to draw out, interpret, or share; they challenge researchers to imagine new tools, praxes, stories, and ideas. This is the promise of narrative work in disability: new narratives, generated through new processes, might challenge existing stories about disability and the sociocultural processes, including research practices, those stories both reflect and enact (Green & Loseke, 2020).

What is the existing state of narrative work by and with people with intellectual disabilities? In the United States, it is still somewhat limited. Here, autobiographical works by people with intellectual disability include several written texts generated through a range of relationships and processes across ability that are not elaborated in the publications.[1] In the field of oral history, which has often overlooked the history of intellectual disability in the United States (Hirsch, 1995; Walmsley, 2009), recent work offers promising new developments. In 2007 and 2008, Joe Caldwell from the Department of Disability and Human Development at the University of Illinois at Chicago collected oral history interviews with leaders in the self-advocacy movement, which are archived at the Regional Oral History Office (ROHO) at the University of California, Berkeley (Caldwell, n.d.). In 2012, the Institute on Disabilities at Temple University began the Visionary Voices project, which documents the history of the intellectual disability rights movement in Pennsylvania through oral history interviews with movement leaders, including self-advocates (Visionary Voices, n.d.).[2]

In the United Kingdom, there is a much larger body of autobiographical work made by and with people with intellectual disabilities. Much of this work has been driven by the Social History of Learning Disability Research Group (SHLD) at the Open University.[3] Founded in 1994 by Dorothy Atkinson and Jan Walmsley to develop and disseminate scholarship that generates a history of intellectual disability through inclusive processes, research at SHLD is driven by the recognition that people with intellectual disabilities have lived expertise, knowledge, and valuable skills that are essential to the construction and interpretation of intellectual disability history (Social History of Learning Disability Research Group, n.d.). SHLD has published extensive reflections and analyses on the range of methodological approaches to working inclusively with people with intellectual disability, including texts centered on life history processes (Atkinson, 1998; Atkinson, Jackson, & Walmsley, 1997; Atkinson & Williams, 1990; Goodley, 2000; Walmsley, 2009); texts documenting and interpreting experiences of self-advocacy (Goodley, 2000; Mitchell et al., 2006; Walmsley, Johnson, & Wolfe, 2010); and texts exploring methodological challenges and approaches to working inclusively with people with intellectual disabilities (Atkinson, 1997; Atkinson & Williams, 1990; Booth & Booth, 1996; Goodley, 2000; Nind, 2008; Walmsley & Johnson, 2003).

I discovered SHLD's body of work while working on my graduate thesis and found in it a portrait of the possible and a standard against which I could measure my own methods. These methods and concepts, which I discuss further below, included self-reflexivity and transparency about process; a willingness to listen differently and adapt my tools to narrators' different modes of speech or remembering; collaboration with third parties (with the challenges this entails); a "do no harm" ethic alongside a foundational belief in the ability and right of narrators to make their own decisions about their participation; and the commitment to situating this work as part of a larger movement, in which individual narratives can accrue meaning and power by way of their connection to one another.

I, too, wanted to situate my own work as part of a broader movement, represented by SHLD's radically inclusive, social justice–oriented, and methodologically rich publications. One thing that makes my work distinct is that its primary and public form was a cultural product centering edited excerpts from interviews with self-advocates with Down syndrome. My creation of a digital collection of online stories, told primarily in audio, was influenced by my work at StoryCorps, a national nonprofit oral history project that has archived in the Library of Congress tens of thousands of 40-minute audio conversations between people who know each other (StoryCorps, n.d.).[4] While I did not produce stories, I was immersed in a culture that centered the power of the human voice. The aural quality to oral history, and the authenticity and primacy of the oral record over transcription, is well documented in the field (see, for instance, Frisch, 2011; Grele, 1991, 2007; Portelli, 1991). It is also, in a word, audist.[5] By privileging the oral – and by relying on cognitive processes of remembering and narrating the past – we leave many out.[6]

Nevertheless, I chose to focus on audio with narrative advocacy in mind. It was in *listening* to my narrators that I challenged my own ablest preconceptions about communication with people with Down syndrome; by listening to voices that sound different from those we typically hear in audio stories, I also wanted to serve as a proxy for others.

As an online collection of stories, my thesis entered a cultural landscape overflowing with "storytelling." Alexander Freund offers a critical assessment of the profusion of storytelling that masquerades as oral history, critiquing the work of StoryCorps in particular. He situates the twenty-first century's "storytelling craze" within therapy and self-help cultures, arguing that focusing on individual autobiographical accounts can erase historical grounding and elide social critique. He implores oral historians to critically engage with the "storytelling industrial complex" and embrace what makes oral history different: its capacity as a research practice to critically explore the social and historical factors that shape and are shaped by the life stories we cocreate (Freund, 2015). Though my project's digital platform Cowbird falls within the storytelling landscape Freund critiques, I hoped, in my framing of the project and my authorial decisions, to do more than offer individual stories in an historical vacuum. I hoped that the collection of stories from self-advocates would work in the service of their desires, which go beyond the individual to address the political, historical, and social. That is to say, I hoped to work as a narrative ally.

ENACTING NARRATIVE METHODOLOGY IN "NOTHING ABOUT US WITHOUT US"

I propose that narrative allyship across ability is a practice in which nondisabled researchers work with disabled nonresearchers to coconstruct a process that centers, and acts on, the knowledge contained in and expressed by the lived experience of the disabled nonresearchers. These processes can produce narrative work in a range of forms, from academic texts to cultural work. This practice should not differentiate the narrative products of research from the processes that generate them, such that narratives produced as acts of allyship should center the knowledge contained in the lived experience of disabled nonresearchers. Toward this end, I propose three guiding principles for the process and products of allyship. Narrative allyship across ability should:

(1) Further the interests of narrators, as the narrators define them.
(2) Optimize the autonomy of narrators.
(3) Tell stories with, instead of about, narrators.

In order to explore the potential of this practice, I will reflect on my oral history graduate thesis, a narrative project with self-advocates with Down syndrome. The discussion section that follows demonstrates my effort to enact narrative allyship in writing this chapter, with the inclusion and analysis of reflections from Advocate.

Oral History Thesis: Research Goals

Between September 2012 and September 2013, I conducted 12 life history interviews with eight self-advocates who have Down syndrome, collaborating to create an online collection of edited excerpts from these interviews.[7] My collaboration with narrators included communication and decision-making processes involving, to varying degrees, family members, staff, guardians, or other third-party carers.[8] The digital collection, along with a methodological paper, constituted my thesis submission for my MA in Oral History, which I obtained in October 2013.

The first phase of my research, from Jonah's birth in March through August 2012, centered on a partnership with the National Down Syndrome Society

(NDSS), which calls itself "The leading human rights organization for all individuals with Down syndrome" (National Down Syndrome Society, n.d.). I wanted to know how self-advocates were involved in defining the landscape of their own rights. NDSS connected me with self-advocates in their network, and I conducted four initial interviews in the fall of 2012. My official partnership with NDSS concluded in December 2012, and I did additional interviews in spring and summer 2013 with self-advocates I connected with through my own advocacy activities and outreach.

In my project design, I strove for a feminist critical theory approach and devised interviews that were a hybrid of broad-scope life history interviews and subject-oriented interviews about self-advocacy (Larson, 2007). My initial research goals were:

- To contribute to an understanding of how adults with Down syndrome think about their role in advocating for themselves and others;
- To celebrate in a new way the contributions self-advocates have made toward promoting the value, acceptance and inclusion of people with Down syndrome; and
- To consider how a project working with adults with an intellectual disability challenges the discipline of oral history.

To the third point, the field of oral history has done limited work with people with intellectual disability, as described in the background section above (Atkinson, 1998; Hirsch, 1995; Walmsley, 2009). I wanted to explore how this omission might reflect the limits of oral history's tools, rather than the abilities of would-be narrators with intellectual disability (Booth & Booth, 1996).

Interviews and Informed Consent

The oral history interview process begins well before the interviewer hits record and extends far beyond. The process centers narrator's rights and control over their story. Informed consent is key. When inviting a narrator to participate, the oral historian needs to be transparent about their goals, the process, the narrator's rights within the process, and how the interviews may be used. The oral historian must be clear that during the interview, the narrator can stop the recording at any time and does not have to answer any questions. After the interview, the oral historian shares the interview with the narrator for their review. The narrator can then decide whether and for what they give permission. They may make redactions, place restrictions, or decide not to release the interview at all. If and when the narrator decides to release the interview, the oral historian is responsible for stewarding the interview materials according to the agreement made (OHA, n.d.).

Oral history interviews are most often one-on-one encounters between the interviewee and narrator, in which the interviewer asks open-ended questions that elicit personal memory and invite meaning-making in historical context. The interview guide I developed before I started interviewing (Appendix) reflects this approach to asking oral historical questions. Interviewers often invite narrators to start at the beginning, meaning birth and early life, and proceed chronologically. Oral history interviewers with a set of research questions in mind typically bring to the interview knowledge of key historical events, turning points, moments or movements, and seek to elicit the narrator's experiences and perspective in relation to those. Interview sessions typically last at least an hour and are often conducted more than once with a single narrator.

Working with narrators who have Down syndrome, I anticipated needing to modify my methodology, but I did not know how. I did not know what literacy skills my narrators would bring to the process; whether they had legal rights to release their own interviews; or how I would know if they understood my explanations of the goals and potential outcomes of the interview. I did not want to presume deficiency or be paternalistic or patronizing. Because I did not know what challenges I would encounter, what I would or would not know, or how I would even know, I needed help from others. A key methodological adaptation, then, was to involve carers throughout the oral history process. These were people without disability who I understood to know the narrator well and believed might provide guidance or help if needed. This strategy walked a fine line between an ableist impulse to protect narrators and oral history's commitment to informed consent and obligation to the privacy, security, and rights of our narrators (Nind, 2008). In terms of my methodology, this meant including a third party, to varying degrees, in the process of inviting narrators to participate, interviewing them, sharing interview materials for their review, and choosing how interview materials could be used. I reflect on the impact of carers' involvement in the "optimizing autonomy" section below.

Modifications to the oral history interview itself took a range of forms. First, the involvement of a third party in the interview itself was a distinct methodological departure from the traditional one-on-one oral history interview format. Alternate interview configurations were sometimes planned in advance and sometimes happened in the field and include what I call co-interviews, supported interviews, and observed interviews. In co-interviews, the carer joined the self-advocate in narrating, and my questions were posed to the two, together, or to one or the other to invite response to what their co-interviewee said. Carers took a more active role in supported interviews, working more as a co-interviewer than co-narrator. In these interviews, I relied on both the carer's knowledge of the interviewee and understanding of my intentions with the interview. In observed interviews, a carer was present but neither posed questions nor responded to mine. Carers in these cases offered support in such forms as rephrasing my questions to the self-advocate, bringing forward photos and ephemera that might help the self-advocate remember, narrate, or explain, and bringing their experiential knowledge of the substance of the interview into post-interview processes of review and release.

Second, my approach to asking questions and listening to responses was as varied as my narrators' ways of remembering and expressing themselves. Some narrators were responsive to questions about their youth, while others had difficulty remembering the deep past. David Egan challenged the premise of questions about childhood, telling me that if I wanted to know what he was like as a kid, I should ask his parents. For some narrators, looking at photos or other meaningful objects proved useful in prompting reflections on the past, and some responded by dancing, gesturing, or making faces – all meaningful expressions lost on my audio recorder. Some narrators, by their timbre, inflection, syntax, word choice, or pronunciation, challenged me to listen harder or listen differently. It became clear that there was no single interview protocol for narrators with Down syndrome, which is not a homogenous group. Instead, these improvisational interviews confirmed oral history's mandate to be a self-reflexive, attentive, flexible, and rigorously curious listener, alive to what is said, suggested, or might be silenced (Booth & Booth, 1996; Goodley, 2000; Terkel & Grele, 1991; Thompson, 1988).

Finally, my preparation for the interviews did not include, as a typical oral history project would, robust advance research aimed at situating the lives of the narrators in an historical context of disability rights and self-advocacy. As a mother to a newborn with disability and a student with graduate school deadlines, I was learning that history concurrent with my interviewing; consequently, those I interviewed were a primary source in my own disability education.

Production

In December 2012, I concluded my partnership with NDSS, after working with five self-advocates and their carers, from invitation, to interview, review, and release. I shared interview materials with narrators and, with their permission, NDSS. As I considered how to move forward with my thesis project, I had to acknowledge the limitations of my interviews as research into the question of how self-advocates were included in defining the landscape of their own human rights. The interviews were initiated and arranged through partnership with NDSS, an organization they either worked for, volunteered at, or had contributed to as public speakers or members of the self-advocacy board. I had not afforded opportunities within the interview for narrators to speak back to NDSS or to other sites where their self-advocacy encountered barriers.

Off the record, however, I had some pivotal conversations late that fall with two of my narrators, David Egan and Sara Wolff. Following my interview with him in November, David asked many questions about the interview review and release process and expressed his desire to exert control over how his interview would be used. He spoke critically about existing media portrayals of people with disabilities and passionately about the capacity of stories to "open hearts and change minds." In my first interview with Sara on November 10, 2012, her mother had joined spontaneously as a co-interviewee, and she and Sara together told stories from Sara's upbringing.[9] After the interview, Sara pulled me aside to ask if we could do a second interview without her mother present. Her mother's presence had, naturally, impacted what Sara did and did not say. In December 2012, Sara and I met for coffee to discuss our second interview, and she shared with me some frustrations: "Everyone knows Sara the public speaker, NDSS takes me for granted, but no one knows what I'm really feeling." We talked about how further interviews might be a tool for potentially addressing those frustrations, and Sara told me in a follow-up email that she "totally agreed" and that "most definitely" I would be a great "resource." This marked a definitive shift, not only from the interference of the carer in the interview, but toward putting me in my place as an ally with particular tools that could serve Sara's needs and desires. I committed to follow-up interviews in the spring with Sara and David and began lasting relationships with these two self-advocates that would play a defining role in my work moving forward.

In January 2013, I initiated the production phase. My conversations with David and Sara suggested that my strengths as an author were relevant to their stated needs as self-advocates: for David, control over how his story was told and access to a larger audience; for Sara, a way to tell the story behind and beyond her role as a public speaker. This aligned with my own desires as a parent and would-be ally and advocate; one of my motivations for doing this work in the first place was a paucity of stories available from people with Down syndrome and my frustration with the limited kinds of stories that were told. Where were the stories showing the complexity of people with Down syndrome?

In February 2013, David Egan emailed me in advance of our follow-up interview to ask if he could partner with me in my oral history and advocacy work. At that time, I wanted to create a collaboratively authored, public-facing outlet for stories from self-advocates with Down syndrome, and David expressed an interest in helping me get these stories "out there." We agreed that a website would be ideal.

I had reservations about building a website from scratch; it was important to situate these stories where they could reach new audiences, not just those already in the Down syndrome or intellectual disability communities, and I doubted my capacity to direct mainstream attention to a stand-alone website created for these stories. Instead, I looked to the storytelling platform Cowbird, self-described as "the most beautiful place in the world to tell stories," whose community rules included "be decent, be humble, be legal, and be yourself" (Cowbird, 2013).

A platform designed to enable users to tell and discover new stories that could be posted as audio, image, and text and tagged and searchable by location, characters, and themes, Cowbird would enable me to create a mosaic portrait of self-advocates with Down syndrome. Further, it would allow me to situate these stories, individually and as a collection, alongside and in dialogue with stories from nondisabled storytellers around the world. In this way, the platform could situate the individual experience reflected in each self-advocate's story in a social context redrawn not according to the terms that have historically kept them apart, but according to terms set by the narrator within the story. Further, Cowbird offered a built-in audience beyond disability, with an ethos of connection that honored the individual and advanced social, participatory engagement. It was the best digital platform I could envision to meet the needs identified by Sara and David: to have a place to share their truth, as self-advocates, and to join a "bigger conversation." David agreed that Cowbird was a great fit for the project.

That February, I initiated a collaborative editorial process for this public collection of online stories edited from my interviews with self-advocates. First, I reconnected with the self-advocates I had interviewed in the fall, communicating my new intentions and giving them the opportunity to release, restrict, or retract their permission for my use of their interview for this purpose. I committed to sharing edited clips for their review, feedback, approval, or rejection and invited narrators to share with me passages or moments from their interview that they would like me to edit for the online platform. In all, I edited interviews with six self-advocates with Down syndrome into 36 stories published on Cowbird in a combination of audio, text, and images. I elaborate on the complexity of these dynamics in the discussion section below.

The Cowbird collection, entitled "Nothing About Us Without Us" at David's suggestion, was published in September 2013 and submitted along with a methodological paper as my thesis. David's interest in partnership led us to explore, in the spring and summer of 2013, Cowbird's potential as a platform where others could contribute their own stories. David and I initially connected over our shared birthplace: Madison, Wisconsin. In the summer of 2013, as David and his family were planning a trip to Madison, I planned my own visit home at the same time, and David and I gave a storytelling and self-advocacy workshop in Madison that July. We also copresented at the Down Syndrome Advocacy Foundation conference in Long Island on November 23, 2013, where we shared the project and our hope that others might add their own stories. We went back to Madison in October 2014, where we copresented at the Oral History Association (OHA) annual meeting along with Claire Bible, another self-advocate narrator from the project. This was the first time David had presented at a conference not specific to disability, and it was the first time I had seen someone with intellectual disability present at a nondisability conference. This was also the last collaboration between David and me around this project. Without a clear process for moving forward or a clear goal, we no longer work together, though I have maintained a friendship with David and his mother, Kathleen. I visited the family in Virginia for David's birthday in 2015, we communicate via Facebook and email, and in 2019, at Kathleen's request, I wrote a short contribution to David's memoir, *More Alike Than Different: My Life With Down Syndrome,* which will be published in September of 2020 (Egan & Egan, 2020). There is much to say about the evolution away from a narrative collaboration, but in order to speak to that, I would need to engage David in a shared process of reflection, which is beyond the scope of this chapter.

Beyond the Thesis: Writing Research as Narrative Allyship

Reflecting on my graduate thesis ought itself to be an act of allyship; otherwise, I risk performing academic expertise to the exclusion of people with intellectual disability. In order to enact narrative allyship in the authorship of this chapter, I invited another self-advocate to be in conversation with me as I write. I reached out to this particular self-advocate because I knew they were working on their own autobiographical projects and thought they would have valuable insight into how nondisabled allies might work across ability to tell stories of people with Down syndrome. We began our work on this paper with a defining conversation about narrative and allyship, and have proceeded in the months since through a process by which I write, share drafts with Advocate, and we have discussions by phone, FaceTime or Zoom about the sections where their words and ideas are represented and interpreted. I discuss the impact of this review process in sections below.

REFLECTING ON NARRATIVE ALLYSHIP

In this section, I discuss the three guiding principles I propose for narrative allyship across ability, namely that such work should:

(1) Further the interests of narrators, as the narrators themselves define them.
(2) Optimize the autonomy of narrators.
(3) Tell stories with, instead of about, narrators.

I begin with a conversation between Advocate and me, in order to center their expertise, and highlight and reinforce narrative allyship's guiding principles. Redactions are made where Advocate requested. I acknowledge that these redactions might disrupt the flow of the conversation for the reader; however, I prioritize Advocate's wishes to keep private, even beyond the privacy of anonymity, some of their specific desires.

NP: Okay. So, this article. It's going to be in a journal, an academic journal about, um, disability and allyship.

Advocate: Mm-hmm.

NP: So, I want to start by asking you what you think about, like, what makes a good ally?

Advocate: What do you mean by ally?

NP: Yeah. Is that a term that you use or have heard before—

Advocate: I never really use it.

NP: Yeah. It's kind of like, um, someone who is there to work alongside people with disabilities—

Advocate: Okay.

NP: —in support of realizing what's, like, the goals are that are important to people with disabilities—

Advocate: Mm-hmm.

NP: —themselves. So, it's a little different from advocacy, cause it's —

Advocate: Yeah.

NP: —it's like working with.

Advocate: Mm-hmm.

NP: So, like, bringing what strengths they have in partnership with people with disabilities, to sort of work alongside them.

Advocate: Okay.

NP: Um, so, I want to think about, or I — I want to write about what I'm calling narrative allyship. So, like, do you know what I mean by narrative? Is that a word that you use?

Advocate: Is it like, narrating a movie, or—

NP: Yeah.

Advocate: Or like a documentary—

NP: Totally, it's the same word, just a different use, so it's like basically telling stories.

Advocate: Yeah.

NP: A narrative is like a story.

Advocate: Okay.

NP: So, how can — what does it mean to be working as an ally with people with disabilities in telling stories—

Advocate: Awesome.

NP: Rather, not telling stories about, but with.

Advocate: Awesome.

NP: Awesome?

Advocate: Yeah.

NP: I'm curious like, when you think about stories, let's just say about people with Down syndrome, what are the stories that you think need to be told?

Advocate: I say powerful. Powerful stories, people to hear, to um—

NP: Yeah

Advocate: — [get their] message across.

NP: Yeah. What do you think makes a story powerful?

Advocate: Their story, their personal life, be real for themselves, cause I think that's more important—just be yourself.

NP: What are things that get in the way of people with Down syndrome telling those kinds of stories?

Advocate: It's their story to tell, I think. Like for me, for example. People like me with Down syndrome have so many barriers. [Redacted].

[Redacted]

NP: So that's like a barrier to you [Redacted].

Advocate: Yeah.

NP: What about a barrier to, like, telling your powerful stories?

Advocate: Cause you need to be yourself, right? That's not possible. For many people that is out of your comfort zone.

NP: Are there like, so I'm thinking about like allies. Right, and like what it means to tell stories with people, and not about them. Have there been times when you feel like stories are told about you, or about Down syndrome, by people who don't have Down syndrome—

Advocate: Yeah.

NP: Yeah? What is, what, tell me a little more. Tell me what you're thinking.

Advocate: Uh, yikes. Um. So many things I'm remembering.

NP: I want them all!

Advocate: Ugh, I don't think so. Um. Like, what do you want to know?

NP: You're kind of making a face like you're, like it bothers you.

Advocate: I don't know. So many things bother me.

NP: Is there a time—so I want to know about what bothers you about those stories. Or about when people without Down syndrome tell those stories.

Advocate: I don't know why I can't [Redacted]. Someday I wish I could. I wish I could go to the grocery store by myself because I like it.

NP: Yeah.

Advocate: It's comforting. Just—I don't drive, so the transportation part is going to be hard—

NP: Right. So, am I understanding you right, that there are stories, like—

Advocate: There's like other stories besides [Redacted].

[Redacted]

NP: Mm-hmm. Do you think that if your family had, um, a different story about what was possible—

Advocate: Yeah.

NP: —that they might act differently?

Advocate: Yeah. I don't know if they might act differently. I don't know what they want for me. I know what I want for myself.

NP: Yeah.

Advocate: Like I know I'm not just capable but, I know I'm capable of [Redacted].

[Redacted]

Advocate: I know I could do it. [Redacted].

NP: Right.

Advocate: So it's going to come natural for me.

NP: So if, when I think about, air quotes, narrative allyship, like telling stories that work to support what a person with Down syndrome needs, or like, what you say is important to you, that makes me think that like a, a role for me, if I am thinking of myself as a narrative ally, would be in helping you tell the story you want to tell with your life.

[Silence.]

Advocate: Yeah.

NP: Yeah? What are the ways that you would want, like that you think I could be helpful in doing that?

Advocate: Talking to my family.

NP: Talking to your family! [Laughs] No way!

Advocate: Yeah.

NP: Myself?

Advocate: Yeah.

NP: But that's not telling your story, that's—

Advocate: Like, my story, I don't know, I think it's more, it's helpful to come from someone else, besides me.

NP: That's interesting.

Advocate: They know what I want.

NP: Do they?

Advocate: Yeah. They just don't want me to do it. But if they hear it from somebody else [pause] it's a different story.

For Advocate, story is inseparable from living. Telling the story they want to tell with their life requires living the story they want to live. My insistence in this conversation on talking about "stories about people with Down syndrome" belies the privilege of my perspective. "Narrative" for me is an act of creation, be it an oral history thesis or an academic article, while for Advocate, story is an act of necessity: creating a life. Their lived expertise here pushes against my preconceptions about what constitutes story, until I at last absorb their meaning: in order to be *for* Advocate, narrative allyship would make it possible to live the story they want to tell with their life.

The tension between the story someone wants to tell with his or her life and the story others feel comfortable hearing shows a central problem for many people with intellectual disabilities. Nondisabled gatekeepers still have, believe, or tell limited stories about what is possible for people with Down syndrome, and these in turn limit what is possible in their lives. Advocate implies that a narrative ally would not steward the story as it is, but would intervene to address the limits imposed by nondisabled gatekeepers so that people with Down syndrome can tell the stories that they want to tell with their lives. Advocate knows the power that I have as a nondisabled ally and asks me to use it. Narrative allyship means telling a different story.

Who Is It for? Narrative Allyship and Narrators' Interests

Researchers who work as narrative allies across ability create processes that center and act on the lived expertise of their subjects. Many researchers who work as allies begin with their own research questions, intended outcomes, or ideas about how their tools and expertise may work in the interests of people with intellectual disability. Narrative allyship asks these researchers to exercise critical self-reflectiveness about the needs that are driving the research, the researcher's own as well as that of the subjects. Taking seriously the authority subjects bring to the research encounter, narrative allies "listen" for ways that people with intellectual disabilities may contest the premises of the research or offer a different story about their interests or what it means to further them. This may lead to rich dialogue across ability about what or who the research is for. Researchers should be open to adapting or subverting their own needs or interests to further the self-defined interests of those with intellectual disabilities.

My exchange with Advocate above illustrates this, as does my graduate thesis. As I've described, I began with a set of research questions that reflected my understanding of the interests of self-advocates with Down syndrome, namely how they are engaged in defining their rights in the Down syndrome advocacy landscape. I allowed my thesis to reflect what I learned from my narrators about what they really needed (with crucial flexibility and support from my graduate program). As I created an online collection of edited excerpts from my interviews with self-advocates, I invited their editorial participation, which I discuss in the following section on optimizing autonomy.

While editing interview excerpts for the online collection, I first selected passages that reflected my own understanding of what was important to each narrator. I looked for segments where the narrator was active, not only in what they described but how they described it to me. I wanted clips that showed narrators' authorship in action, as agents in their own lives and the stories of others, giving and receiving care and friendship, and engaging systems that would limit their opportunities for work, education, or to be understood. By collecting their stories into a mosaic portrait for the general public, I hoped to broaden limited views of people with Down syndrome, as my own views had radically expanded through listening to self-advocates.

Existing advocacy narratives tend to argue that people with Down syndrome belong because they are "just like us" or should be admired for their heroic accomplishments. In the years since concluding my graduate thesis, I have deepened my understanding of the need for "a different story" about what constitutes a meaningful life for people with Down syndrome. I say this in part to acknowledge the limitations of my graduate thesis, which had its origins in a partnership with the National Down Syndrome Society (NDSS). In my invitation to self-advocates, I framed my project goals in terms that echoed the NDSS mission, which in 2013 was to "be the national advocate for the value, acceptance, and inclusion of individuals with Down syndrome" (NDSS, 2013). This framing may have signaled that I expected stories that aligned with the NDSS mission and complicated any desire my narrators may have had to "talk back" to dominant advocacy narratives. These narratives predicate value, acceptance, and inclusion on positive imagery and a message of "greatness," evidenced in the 2013 NDSS public awareness initiative, the "My Great Story" campaign. A parallel campaign, the "More Alike Awareness Campaign," by the National Down Syndrome Congress (NDSC, 2013), argued for the value and inclusion of people with Down syndrome by way of their "likeness" to the rest of "us." This story-based messaging by major national advocacy organizations for people with Down syndrome can be understood in part as the legacy of the movement in the 1970s and 1980s to close institutions and make places for people with intellectual disability to live in community. Arguments that people with intellectual disability belong in "our" communities hinge on positive imagery and demonstrations of their capacity to behave in culturally normative ways (Walmsley & Johnson, 2003). The dominant advocacy narratives portray people with Down syndrome performing "normal" social activities: going to school, working in the community, having relationships, and achieving "normal" social milestones like attending prom, graduating from high school, going to college, and getting married. These stories are often framed as both inspirational and ordinary, suggesting simultaneously that people with Down syndrome face barriers to participation in society, but that they are heroically capable of living lives just like us.

That is the message that many of the self-advocates I interviewed for my graduate thesis convey in their public speaking. In fact, one of my thesis narrators, Sara Wolff, was prominently featured in the NDSS "My Great Story" campaign, including a poster in which she is posed on a rooftop, holding a megaphone aloft over a lush cityscape, beneath a sky inscribed with "My Great Story" in the clouds. She's on top of the world, heroic, in an actual cape, smiling back at the camera and poised at the brink, the image suggests, of her own great story. One of the stories that Sara and I edited together from our January 5, 2013. interview for the online collection on Cowbird was entitled "More than Public Speaking," and included her reflection that sometimes there is a disconnect between the story she tells *about* her life in her public speeches and the story *of* her life beyond (Pombier Berger, 2013).

Revisiting my graduate thesis as a narrative ally today, I would want to create space for people with Down syndrome to complicate narratives about inclusion and belonging, inviting narratives that show the complexity of self-advocacy when, as Advocate elucidates, telling the story one wants to tell of one's life means living that story in the first place. Additionally, rather than reinforcing the portrait of "normal" that existing advocacy narratives lean on, I would work as a narrative ally guided by the desire to make space for voices and perspectives that challenge the premise of normal and the subtext of existing advocacy narratives: that people with Down syndrome are worthy of inclusion inasmuch as they are capable of conforming to nondisabled norms. These narratives, including my graduate thesis, risk reifying rather than challenging what constitutes a life worth living, minimizing the value of difference. They risk obscuring the need for all people with intellectual disabilities to define and work toward a meaningful life on their own terms (Walmsley et al., 2010).

Optimizing Autonomy

One of the main implications of Advocate's reflections on narrative allyship is that stories are important tools for convincing others that people with Down syndrome are capable of living the stories they want to tell with their lives. Nondisabled third parties are often gatekeepers to agency for people with intellectual disability, creating power dynamics that researchers who work as allies across ability will need to understand and navigate. In this context, centering the lived expertise of narrators can be challenging for researchers. It is all too easy to privilege the perspective of a third-party carer, to seek their guidance before or instead of the narrator's, to shape the research in ways that reflect the carer's interests or interventions. At the same time, understanding the ways in which narrators with intellectual disability express and exert their own agency can take time, and carers who themselves are allies can be invaluable to researchers with that goal. Researchers working as narrative allies, taking seriously their subjects' authority, must go beyond simply recognizing that authority toward what G. Thomas Couser calls "optimizing autonomy" (Couser, 2004). This means developing a process, including third-party carers, that presumes the narrator's agency and seeks to understand its forms of expression. Researchers should be rigorously self-reflexive and transparent, allowing their understanding of narrators' autonomy to change over time, recalibrating their approach if needed in order to center and support narrator control in each stage of the research. They should establish ways to check third-party influences, so as to avoid overprotection and minimize external control that jeopardizes narrator's desires, authority, or expertise.

This complex process will look different for each narrator. Here, I offer a brief description of some of my experience navigating these dynamics in my graduate thesis, offering examples where narrators demonstrated their authorial control, where carer interventions were privileged over narrators, and where my own power as author intervened at the expense of my narrators' agency.[10]

Interviewee A: Narrator Authorship
Interviewee A exerted the most control over the presentation of their stories on the public website. They sent me a list of passages they wanted excerpted from our interviews together, and in an accompanying letter, they wrote:

> It's amazing. I listened to the whole interview this morning. I loved it. No restrictions. It really captures me. To listen to myself telling my own story really brought it home. I am so excited about being and becoming one of the voices of the movement.

The excerpts they proposed for the online collection were the same ones I had in mind, which affirmed my understanding of what was important to the narrator. I wanted to share two additional stories, which I played for the narrator over the phone, inviting their approval, feedback, or restriction. They requested edits to one clip, wanting to remove a segment where they sang, worried that a general public audience might make fun of their voice. They rejected the second clip entirely, out of concern for a friend included in the excerpt, saying that it was not their story to share. Interviewee A made their editorial decisions independent of a third-party carer, and consequently I am most confident of their sense of ownership and authorship of their stories in the collection.

Interviewees B and C: Carer-Initiated Interventions
The carer for interviewee B intervened in the release process, and interviewee C's in the editorial process. In both cases, the interventions reflected carers' explicit desires to protect the interviewee. In the case of Interviewee B, the carer called me following the interview to discuss two points of concern. The first was a small detail the interviewee shared about their professional work as an advocate that, if misconstrued, could damage their political work. The second was a more general concern about Interviewee B's characterization of their family. The carer worried that if Interviewee B's family members heard those passages, they may call into question plans already in motion for Interviewee B's professional advancement. Not wanting to put Interviewee B's professional life at risk, I took the carer's recommendation to remove the small detail of concern. Regarding the second concern, we devised an approach to restriction to preclude interference in the interviewee's plans. I asked that the carer discuss this with Interviewee B and sent a revised release form, prefilled with the recommended restriction.

Following my interview with Interviewee C, I emailed them and their carer an excerpt that I was particularly excited about sharing in the online collection. I thought the passage, which included Interviewee C's opinion about a hot button political topic, presented an image of someone with Down syndrome not often portrayed, passionate and civically engaged. I received a response from the carer's email account, written in the first-person plural, collapsing carer and Interviewee C into one pronoun: "We do not think this is an appropriate excerpt to share." They (plural) told me that such a passage could compromise the political neutrality essential to Interviewee C's work and requested that the passage be restricted from the interview entirely. When I asked Interviewee C about this episode later, they (singular) told me quite simply that they had not thought the excerpt was a problem. "It's just – parents. You know how they are." By acting to protect without providing Interviewee C a space to speak to the issue independently of their carer's influence, I eroded rather than optimized their autonomy.

Interviewees Y and Z: Researcher-Initiated Intervention

In both cases above, I took carers' desires to protect the interviewee at face value. It may be that my position as a parent influenced my response, causing me to act on an instinct to protect. This raises the question of my own power in the research and authorship process and when and how I might have intervened at the expense of narrators' autonomy. My work with two final narrators is illustrative.

Communication with Interviewees Y and Z was the most challenging among my narrators. In contrast to the other interviewees, these two individuals may not have identified as self-advocates. While both live with relative independence and actively participate in their communities, neither is directly involved in self-advocacy work, and their participation in this project was, to some degree, circumstantial. With Interviewees Y and Z, I needed and sought assistance from carers in order to be sure I was balancing consideration for their autonomy with the ethical imperative to do no harm.

What harm did I worry about causing? In both cases, I was concerned about posting excerpts from their interviews online. I shared the Cowbird website with both in person, demonstrating how it worked and explaining why I wanted to include their stories. With Interviewee Y, I shared edited excerpts from their interview and photos I wanted to include. We listened to the excerpts together in the presence of a carer, and the carer pointed out that the stories on the website could be heard by strangers. When prompted, Interviewee Y said they liked listening to the stories, and they laughed and nodded along while listening. They gave what I interpreted as an assenting sound as I showed the website and described my wish to include their stories. While this may well have constituted a "positive indicator of consent" (Nind, 2008, p. 8), it did not, to my mind, prove a demonstrable understanding of what it would mean to post their story online. I consulted with the carer, who agreed, and we decided that further discussion with other carers in Interviewee Y's life should follow.

Interviewee Z was excited to have their story posted online and insisted on signing and giving me a copy of the release form immediately following the interview, so I could get right to work editing. While a carer had been present during the interview and preinterview discussion of the review process, Interviewee Z and I were alone as I reiterated the process. I repeatedly, and, I hoped, respectfully, described the importance of their opportunity to listen to the interview before making any decisions regarding release. Eventually, Interviewee Z relented, taking back the copy of the signed release form and saying that they would wait until they had reviewed it with their carer.

In these cases, I do not think I could have acted ethically to optimize autonomy without enlisting the support of carers. However, the nature of my concerns suggest that my intervention, ultimately deciding not to include excerpts from Interviewee Y and Z in the collection, served to ignore the experiential authority in these narrators' stories and erase from the collective narrative of self-advocacy voices that might challenge existing stories and offer a more complex portrait of life with Down syndrome. I worried that online representations of these Interviewees might be inadvertently harmful by reinforcing some of the stigmas and stereotypes about individuals with Down syndrome, because the quality of their voices – their sound, cadence, and syntax – require effort to listen to and understand. I worried that the casual listener may, at best, not put forth that effort, and at worst, notwithstanding the "Cowbird culture" of kindness, would engage in the kind of hurtful language the Internet makes easy, language that is not infrequently directed toward individuals with Down syndrome. I worried that sharing their voices would make them vulnerable to potential harm reflective of the very stigma and prejudice I hoped to counteract. But my desire to protect them instead reinforced that stigma by erasing difference from my collection, excluding them despite their expressed desire to be included, and reproducing the many ways in which nondisabled people write a world that leaves out people with intellectual disabilities. Reifying the norm by excluding voices that challenged it, my collection perpetuated the dominant advocacy narratives about what kind of voice is worth listening to, instead of inviting audiences to listen differently and broaden our ideas about who belongs.

Advocate: Anonymity as Optimizing Autonomy

Writing this chapter with Advocate's involvement meant navigating their own dynamic with carers. Advocate was concerned that, if this was published using their real name, some carers who had not been involved in the process would be upset. But inviting carers into the interview and writing process would have, Advocate said, fundamentally changed what they could say. We worked for a while on making some revisions to the transcript that might assuage their worries about hurting the feelings of carers, but I began to worry that the central point Advocate made in our interview was being eroded, and told them as much. After many drafts, and many conversations, we decided that the mask of anonymity was the best way forward, with Advocate redacting certain parts of the interview. For me, this was crucial to the scholarship. Between the story Advocate told me in August 2019, and the story I worried their revisions were creating, was the beating heart of this paper. As a parent myself, I appreciated Advocate's sensitivity to the feelings and privacy of their carers, and could imagine and sympathize with the perspective of carers. As a researcher and narrative ally, I wanted to enact the lessons I learned by reflecting on my work on my graduate thesis and ensure a process that enabled Advocate to speak freely. I wanted to keep that central in our ongoing dialogue. Beyond the particulars of my work with Advocate, this begs the broader question: how can researchers further the interests of narrators with intellectual disability who, for whatever reason, feel they cannot speak freely? In some cases, this might be precisely where the "unequal world" meets an idealized process like the one I was trying to lead as a narrative ally (Walmsley & Johnson, 2003, p. 181). How can we optimize autonomy? Anonymity and redaction gave Advocate and me a way forward, a compromise that enabled Advocate to speak while still protecting the privacy and feelings of their carers, while allowing me to center Advocate's expertise.

Telling Stories with, Not about

It should be clear by now that narrative ally research requires critical self-reflexivity at every stage. In this final point, I urge researchers working as narrative allies to consider how research, in process and as authored to audiences, is itself a story that is told "with" our subjects in each stage. From start to finish, researchers as narrative allies should hold in mind and take seriously the disability rights movement's demand, nothing about us without us.

In the case of my graduate thesis, oral history interviewing is a narrative process in which the primary tool of the research – the interview – is by definition an act of telling stories "with." Oral history interviews, conducted by researchers as narrative allies, are sites of shared authority, in Michael Frisch's term, or in Alessandro Portelli's phrase, "experiments in equality" (Frisch, 2011; Portelli, 1991). The oral history interview is an encounter where the respective expertise of interviewer and interviewee co-exist, generating new historical records that are valuable precisely because they reflect the complexity of the dynamic between researcher and subject. Oral history interviews generate narratives "with," and the oral history researcher as narrative ally carries that "withness" into the authorship of their work in the public domain. With my graduate thesis, I wanted to author the research in a way consistent with my narrators' desires to be heard by new audiences. My voice is "with" theirs in that collection in several ways: in the choices I made as editor of the stories, in my recordings of brief introductions for each story, and in my written introduction to the collection, describing its provenance, purpose, and methodology. My voice is also present in the stories themselves, which I edited to include my own questions wherever possible, in the interest of transparency about my role and to dramatize the narrators' expertise, as they taught me. I included images that showed me with my narrators, suggesting visually the co-construction of these stories, and myself alongside the self-advocates as an ally. But I do not embed that collection in my research or contextualize it according to the questions, concerns, and methods I have outlined at length here. Instead, the collection of voices from self-advocates *is* the story. In that case, "telling with" meant stepping back, aiming for transparency without privileging my voice as a researcher. "Telling with" also meant including David Egan and Claire Bible in a presentation of the work to my colleagues at the Oral History Association Annual Meeting in 2014, where I told the story of the research with them, not about them.

Researchers working as narrative allies should carry their allyship through the final stages of research, when the work is constructed for an audience, authoring their work into the public domain with their narrators. In this way, the narrative work of the research reflects the centrality of the lived expertise of people with intellectual disability, who move from being objects of study to subjects in the story of the research. Telling *with* will look different across research projects, audiences, and forms, but researchers should explicitly endeavor to extend their narrative allyship through the process of communicating the research to others.

Many publications of the Social History of Learning Disability Research Group at the Open University offer instructive models for including the voices of narrators with intellectual disabilities alongside and in dialogue with the voices of researchers.

I have tried to do as much in this article. Including Advocate's reflections in the writing process does more than simply bring their voice into the research, which is itself an important opportunity presented by narrative across ability (Green & Loseke, 2020). Developing a process that keeps me in dialogue with a self-advocate with Down syndrome, as I am writing about them, has changed the knowledge this article might otherwise produce. One example came in our conversations about revision in April 2020, when Advocate expressed their concern with what I had written in my analysis of our summer 2019 conversation. I worried about losing one of my key points if Advocate wanted to cut it. I tried not to tip the scale in our dialogue, first seeking to understand their concerns before telling them what I thought. As a result, the passage that we addressed together is stronger. I assumed that they were concerned about compromising their ongoing conversations with their family about a key desire they have for their future. I was wrong. Advocate corrected me in two crucial ways: first, they felt protective of their family's feelings, not wanting them to feel hurt or be misunderstood. Second, Advocate reminded me that this is bigger than just them; rather than focus on what is their personal dialogue with their parents, I should broaden my language so it is clear that the point is relevant for all people with Down syndrome. Here was shared authority in action: Advocate's expertise as an author of their own relationships and an advocate for others, in dialogue with my own expertise as writer, coproduced language that makes a stronger argument for narrative allyship than the one I drafted, capable of reaching audiences Advocate alone would not.

The review process was rich with examples of shared authority in action, and how dialogue across difference can produce a better kind of knowledge. We had many honest and probing conversations that illuminated much about our respective motivations in publishing this work, and our roles. While we began by describing our collaboration as coauthorship, as the paper took shape, Advocate said they no longer wanted to be considered a coauthor. Instead, they wanted to highlight their own expertise as an advocate, someone who, in their words, "supported Nicki." "You wrote it," they said. It was a moment in which I had to contend with my own motivations in including Advocate as coauthor. While I wanted to demonstrate that "authorship" can be broadened beyond simply "writing," here Advocate was telling me that coauthor was a misnomer. Had I treated them with a kind of tokenism, I wondered, more interested in the idea of coauthorship than what it would have meant to *cowrite*? But a cowriting process would not have allowed me to write with the self-reflexivity necessary to narrative allyship, or the language required by this form.

Once we were no longer calling ourselves coauthors, I myself had a different sense of ownership over the writing. One example came as we engaged in a dialogue about how to make Advocate anonymous. They did not want to use a pseudonym and instead wanted to use a term they felt captured their identity. I thought the phrases and words they suggested would be distracting, and too far a departure from the expectations of a social science paper, which perhaps we are already pushing. At some point, a writing decision needed to be made. I suggested "Anonymous," and they suggested "Advocate," and the latter is where we landed.

Coauthoring this paper as an act of narrative allyship meant continual dialogue across difference, and across ability, right up to the deadline. In this way, the writing of research extends the political work of oral history as Portelli's "experiment in equality" (Portelli, 1991). In our conversations about what Advocate can freely say, for themselves, we each were stimulated to "a higher degree of self-scrutiny," and, finally, I am left with a profound sense of the "injustice of the inequality between [people with intellectual disability] and us" (Portelli, 1991, p. 44). Where I take pride in freely publishing this work under my name, the knowledge generated in this process only illuminates the complex pressures that complicate Advocate's freedom to do the same. What for me is the story of this research is for Advocate the story of their life. The story of this paper may end with publishing, which fixes something in print, but the demands of narrative allyship continue well beyond a book, beyond the static page on which it lives.

WE CAN TALK MORE ABOUT THIS, RIGHT?

Nicki Pombier [NP] with Advocate [Advocate], Summer 2019

NP: I'm thinking about the book you're working on—

Advocate: Yes.

NP: —and that is a very clear way for you to tell your story.

Advocate: Yes.

NP: On your terms.

Advocate: Yes.

NP: In your words.

Advocate: Yes.

NP: And you're including other people, too, like interviewing your family, and giving me assignments to write a chapter. So, how would I be a good ally to you in this?

Advocate: If you could like, not help me, but like guide me the right way. You know what I mean?

NP: What's the difference, do you think, between helping and guiding?

Advocate: Helping is more like telling you what to say, telling you how to do it. Guiding is different because you guide a person to like, you know. You know what guiding is [laughs].

NP: I know, but I want to know from you.

Advocate: Guide me in like direction.

NP: Yeah yeah yeah. Guide you in a direction.

Advocate: Yeah. So that I can move forward.

NP: Right, right. Well. [Waitress serves us lunch.] Food's here!

Advocate: Yeah.

NP: Recorder off!

Laughter.

NP: But we can talk more about this later, right?
Advocate: Yeah.
NP: Over and out.

My understanding of my role as an oral historian who wants to work as an ally with people with intellectual disability has been fundamentally changed by the dialogue I have had with self-advocates with Down syndrome through my graduate thesis work and beyond. My commitment to allyship challenges me personally and professionally and requires reciprocity well beyond the scope of what I might have imagined when I did my first oral history interview with a self-advocate, eight years ago. As writing this paper has prompted me to revisit that work, I have rededicated myself to stewarding the stories from self-advocates I interviewed when I was a graduate student. I am building a new website to house the stories, as Cowbird is unstable, and taking the occasion to reopen conversations with interviewees whose stories I left out. I am building out a password-protected page where, with permission from the narrators, I will make the full interviews and transcripts available to those who ask me and have relevant research, advocacy, or other interests.[11] I've chosen this approach, instead of submitting the interviews to an archive like the Oral History Research Office at UC – Berkeley or elsewhere, in order to retain my ability to contextualize the interviews. I believe that doing justice to the narratives of these self-advocates as historical authors requires understanding the provenance of the interviews, including my own limits as a novice oral historian new to disability, interviewing in partnership with NDSS. While I am attempting to do that work in this paper, I have not resolved the questions raised by archiving the interviews. In the meantime, the creation of a password-protected online "archive" that I can moderate myself is a compromise. But, as I said to Advocate in our conversation above, we can talk more about this later, and we will. Advocate has invited my own participation in their ongoing work telling stories, giving me prompts, deadlines, and letters of agreement, asking, in these ways, for reciprocity. Being subject to similar processes I ask of my narrators, or of Advocate in this writing process, is humbling. Narrative allyship is ongoing and reciprocal, and asks for continual self-reflexivity and dialogue.

As a parent, that commitment is necessarily lifelong. Jonah is now eight, and his complexity deepens the more I think I know him. The project of knowing Jonah may be without resolution, may ask me simply to persist from one question to the next and understand that he has ways of knowing that I have yet to learn. I have revised this paper in the midst of the COVID-19 pandemic. Under stay-at-home orders in Brooklyn, I have had the kind of sustained time with Jonah that our regular lives do not afford. I follow him around the apartment, trying to refract what I think I understand through his prism. What is he doing, as we walk in circles around my kitchen island: at the window, lift one wrist, tip the head, click the tongue, onward, repeat. What does his choreography mean? What does he want or get from this movement, or what does he say? What will he remember, and what will I, and how might I be an ally in revealing who he is or was in this moment and what he, and others with intellectual disability, have to teach?

In my own work, including my parenting, I embrace the challenging richness of narrative allyship. I try to parent in a way that optimizes his autonomy, centers his lived expertise, furthers his interests, enables him to set the terms of what those are, and I try to see our relationship as a story we're telling with one another. These are the principles that can guide research as narrative allyship across ability, which I have learned through working with and listening to people with intellectual disabilities and reading work from their narrative allies.

ACKNOWLEDGMENTS

I want to express my gratitude to the narrators who participated in my graduate oral history project, John Anton, Claire Bible, Chris Burke, David Egan, Mitchell Levitz, and Sara Wolff, and to the "carers," the friends, family members, and organizations, who helped me connect with these self-advocates in the first place. I am also grateful to those who supported me throughout my thesis process. I owe much to my peers and professors at Columbia, including my advisor Rachel Adams and our colleagues in the Future of Disability Studies Group at the Center for the Study of Social Difference, whom I had the privilege of learning from and thinking alongside as a graduate fellow in 2012–2013. Mary Marshall Clark's support has always been critical to my work. Amy Starecheski's early enthusiasm for this project spurred me on in crucial ways, and she has continued to afford me space to ask the broader questions raised by this work, including several opportunities to present as part of OHMA's Paul F. Lazarsfeld lecture series. My peers at OHMA listened to me patiently and endured early drafts of my thesis work. Marsha Hurst's Illness and Disability Narratives course in the Narrative Medicine program at Columbia greatly influenced my work on my thesis project and beyond. I have benefitted from rich and enriching conversations with Noelle McCormack, whose narrative work with people with profound and multiple learning disabilities points the way forward. I have been in dialogue since 2013 with Lisa Sonneborn, Direct of Media Arts and Culture at Temple University's Institute on Disabilities, and her support, guidance, imaginative rigor, and bravery are sources of inspiration and critical supports to my own thinking and work. I have profound gratitude to all whose labor and love give me time to work, reflect, and write, including my son's teachers, therapists, and caregiver, and my network of family and friends. Finally, thank you to my sons, Jackson, who made me a mother, and Jonah, who transformed me into this one.

NOTES

1. *Count Us In: Growing Up With Down Syndrome* (1994) by Jason Kingsley and Mitchell Levitz, cowritten with their parents; *New Voices: Self-Advocacy by People With Disabilities* (Dybwad & Bersani Jr., 1996), a collection of first-person reflections and critical essays by allies and people with intellectual disabilities, which historicize and reflect on the self-advocacy movement to date; and *Lost in a Desert World: The Autobiography of Roland Johnson (as told to Karl Williams)* (1999), published by the self-advocacy organization Speaking for Ourselves.

2. Coupled with a commitment to activate this history for the disability community and new audiences, these interviews ignited years of arts-based programming led by the Institute,

for which I have worked as an independent oral history artist since 2014. A review of that work, which emphasizes narrative co-construction and co-interpretation to address the needs and desires of people with intellectual disabilities, is beyond the scope of this chapter, but points toward future research. Such research is also warranted by recent cultural productions centering the lived experiences of people with intellectual disabilities, such as the documentary about a married couple with Down syndrome, *Monica and David,* directed by Alexandra Codina (2009), and *Born This Way,* a reality television show by executive producers Jonathan Murray and Laura Korkoian, featuring young adults with Down syndrome, which ran for five seasons from 2015 to 2019 and won two Emmys and a Critics Choice Award (Murray & Korkoian, 2015–2019). The nonprofit organization Sprout, which offers cultural, arts, and travel programming for adults with developmental disabilities, has a "Make-a-Movie" program, in which nondisabled filmmakers work with individuals with developmental disabilities to produce narrative and documentary films featuring people with disabilities in starring roles, on production teams, and as subjects (Sprout, n.d.). A group of self-advocates in Rhode Island, Advocates in Action, engaged with directors Bob Macaux and Jim Wolpaw to cocreate a documentary about the history of the Joseph H. Ladd Center through the perspectives of its former residents, including first-person reminiscences about the institution (Macaux & Wolpaw, n.d.). A review of the production processes and cultural impact of this contemporary film centering people with intellectual disabilities points toward future research into narrative allyship across ability.

3. In the United Kingdom, the terms "learning disability" or "learning difficulties" are used, as opposed to the common contemporary phrase in the United States of "intellectual disability," which I use throughout this chapter, except in cases when proper nouns include other terms.

4. I worked part- to full-time at StoryCorps from June 2010 through May 2014, where I led and/or worked on community engagement programs, primarily The National Teachers Initiative and StoryCorpsU.

5. Dr. Brian Greenwald, Director of the Drs. John S. & Betty J. Schuchman Deaf Documentary Center at Galludet University, said as much in his keynote address to the 2019 annual meeting of the Oral History in the Mid-Atlantic Region (OHMAR) professional association at Monmouth University in West Long Branch, New Jersey.

6. What would it look like to relinquish the oral in oral history and work toward a more radically inclusive practice? How can we acknowledge ways of knowing that challenge our limited ideas about memory and cognition and embrace nonverbal or nontraditional modes of self-expression? Are we willing to shift our conceptual frameworks entirely? These questions have fueled my oral history work since 2013. Potential models include the methodology developed by the Deaf Documentary Center at Gallaudet University for recording life history interviews with deaf narrators; Stacy Anne Clifford's proposition that we rethink self-advocacy in terms of spontaneity instead of empowerment to allow for different cognitive processes (Clifford, 2013); Howard Sklar's methodology for using comic narrative approaches to facilitate life story work with people with intellectual disability (Sklar, 2012); and Noelle McCormack's dissertation research proposing ethical methodologies for including nonverbal adults in the construction of their own life histories (McCormack, 2017). Perhaps it is time for a visual turn in the field of oral history, so that we might better align our methods with our theories of radical inclusion.

7. The online collection was originally published on the web platform Cowbird at the URL http://www.cowbird.com/nickipombierberger/collections. Cowbird is no longer a stable platform, and as of this writing in May 2020, I am in the process of creating a new website to house this content, which will be available at www.selfadvocatestories.com.

8. I use the term "carer" in this chapter to refer to an individual who played some part in the interview process. I use this more general term, as opposed to specifying parent, support person, sibling, and so forth, in order to maintain anonymity of interviewees as needed.

9. I had a technical issue with my recorder and this interview was lost.

10. I focus here on the postinterview processes of review, release, and authorship in the online collection, but the interviews themselves are another important site to interrogate

for the impact of power dynamics at play between the self-advocate, carer, and myself. This points toward future research.

11. For instance, those who may wish to analyze the in-interview power dynamics at play between self-advocates, carers and myself, as described above.

REFERENCES

Anderson, K., & Jack, D. C. (1991). Learning to listen: Interview techniques and analyses. In S. B. Gluck, & D. Patai (Eds.), *Women's words: The feminist practice of oral history* (pp. 11–26). London: Routledge.

Atkinson, D. (1997). *Auto/biographical approach to learning disability research*. London: Ashgate.

Atkinson, D. (1998). Autobiography and learning disability. *Oral History*, *26*(1), 73–80.

Atkinson, D., Jackson, M., & Walmsley, J. (1997). *Forgotten lives: Exploring the history of learning disability*. Birmingham: British Institute of Learning Disabilities.

Atkinson, D., Richardson, M., & Ramcharan, P. (2005). Narratives and people with learning disabilities. In G. Grant, P. Ramcharan, M. Flynn, & M. Richardson (Eds.), *Learning disability: A life cycle approach* (pp. 7–27). London: Open University Press.

Atkinson, D., & Williams, F. (Eds.). (1990). *'Know me as I am': An anthology of prose, poetry and art by people with learning difficulties*. London: Hodder & Stoughton in association with the Open University.

Booth, T., & Booth, W. (1996). Sounds of silence: Narrative research with inarticulate subjects. *Disability & Society*, *11*(1), 55–70.

Boyd, N., & Ramírez, H. N. R. (Eds.). (2012). *Bodies of Evidence: The practice of queer oral history*. New York, NY: Oxford University Press.

Caldwell, J. (n.d.). Leaders with developmental disabilities in the self-advocacy movement. Oral History Center, The Bancroft Library, University of California Berkeley. Retrieved from https://bancroft.berkeley.edu/ROHO/collections/subjectarea/ics_movements/self_advocacy.html

Carey, A. (2009). *On the margins of citizenship: Intellectual disability and civil rights in twentieth-century America*. Philadelphia, PA: Temple University Press.

Clifford, S. A. (2013). A narrative inquiry of self-advocacy: Rethinking empowerment from liberal sovereignty to Arendtian spontaneity. *Disability Studies Quarterly*, *33*(3). doi:10.18061/dsq.v33i3.3244

Codina, A. (Director) (2009). Monica and David [Film]. CineMia.

Couser, G. T. (2004). *Vulnerable subjects: Ethics and life writing*. Ithaca, NY: Cornell University Press.

Couser, G. T. (2009). *Signifying bodies: Disability in contemporary life writing*. Ann Arbor, MI: University of Michigan Press.

Cowbird. (2013). Retrieved from http://www.cowbird.com/. Accessed on February 9, 2013.

Dybwad, G., & Bersani, H. (Eds.). (1996). *New voices: Self-advocacy by people with disabilities*. Cambridge, MA: Brookline Books.

Egan, D., & Egan, K. (2020). *More alike than different: My life with down syndrome*. Buffalo, NY: Prometheus Books.

Freund, A. (2015). Under storytelling's spell? Oral history in a neoliberal age. *The Oral History Review*, *42*(1), 96–132. doi:10.1093/ohr/ohv002

Frisch, M. (2011). From a shared authority to the digital kitchen, and back. In B. Adair, B. Filene, & L. Koloski (Eds.), *Letting go? Sharing historical authority in a user-generated world* (pp. 126–137). London: Routledge. doi:10.4324/9780429333743-14

Gluck, S. (1977). What's so special about women? Women's oral history. *Frontiers: A Journal of Women Studies*, *2*(2), 3–17. doi:10.2307/3346006

Gluck, S. B., & Patai, D. (1991). *Women's words: The feminist practice of oral history*. London: Routledge.

Goodley, D. (2000). *Self-advocacy in the lives of people with learning difficulties: The politics of resilience*. London: Open University Press.

Green, S. E., & Loseke, D. R. (Eds.). (2020). *New narratives of disability: Constructions, clashes, and controversies*. Research in social science and disability (Vol. 11). Bingley: Emerald Publishing Limitied.

Grele, R. (1991). Movement without aim. In R. Grele, S. Terkel, J. Vansina, D. Tedlock, S. Benison, & A. Kellser Harris (Eds.), *Envelopes of sound: The art of oral history* (pp. 126–155). Santa Barbara, CA: Praeger.

Grele, R. (2007). Oral history as evidence. In T. L. Charlton, L. E. Myers, & R. Sharpless (Eds.), *History of oral history: Foundations and methodology* (pp. 33–91). Lanham, MD: Rowman & Littlefield.

Hirsch, K. (1995). Culture and disability: The role of oral history. *The Oral History Review*, *22*(1), 1–28. doi:10.1093/ohr/22.1.1.

Kerr, D. R. (2016). Allan Nevins is not my grandfather: The roots of radical oral history practice in the United States. *The Oral History Review*, *43*(2), 367–391. doi:10.1093/ohr/ohw074

Kincheloe, J. (2007). The power of difference in knowledge production: Multilogicality in the bricolage and postformalism. Retrieved from http://freireproject.org/wp-content/critical_pedagogy_reading_room/CP_research/BeyondReductionism.doc

Kingsley, J., & Levitz, M. (1994). *Count us in: Growing up with down syndrome*. Boston, MA: Mariner Books.

Larson, M. A. (2007). Research design and strategies. In T. L. Charlton, L. E. Myers, & R. Sharpless (Eds.), *History of oral history: Foundations and methodology* (pp. 95–124). Lanham, MD: Rowman & Littlefield.

Macaux, B., & Wolpaw, J. (Directors) (n.d.). *Best judgment: Ladd school lessons* [Film]. Advocates in Action Rhode Island, in association with Harken Media and the Down Syndrome Society of Rhode Island. Retrieved from http://www.laddfilm.com/

McCormack, N. (2017). Making memory sites: Extending opportunities for people with profound and multiple learning disabilities to participate in life story work. Unpublished doctoral dissertation. University of East London.

Mitchell, D., Traustadóttir, R., Chapman, R., Townson, L., Ingham, N., & Ledger, S. (2006). *Exploring experiences of advocacy by people with learning disabilities: Testimonies of resistance*. London: Jessica Kingsley Publishers.

Murray, J., & Korkoian, L. (Executive Producers) (2015–2019). *Born this way* [TV series]. A&E.

National Down Syndrome Congress. (2013). Retrieved from http://www.ndsccenter.org/. Accessed on March 5, 2013.

National Down Syndrome Society. (2013). Retrieved from https://www.ndss.org/. Accessed on March 5, 2013.

Nind, M. (2008). Conducting qualitative research with people with learning, communication and other disabilities: Methodological challenges. Review Paper. National Centre for Research Methods, Southampton.

Oral History Association. (n.d.). Best practices. Retrieved from http://www.oralhistory.org/.

Phillips, L., Kristiansen, M., Vehviläinen, M., & Gunnarson, E. (Eds.). (2015). *Knowledge and power in collaborative research: A reflexive approach*. London: Routledge.

Pombier Berger, N. (2013). Nothing about us without us: A thesis collection. *Cowbird*. Retrieved from http://cowbird.com/nickipombierberger/collection/nothing-about-us-without-us-a-/. Accessed on April 12, 2020.

Portelli, A. (1991). *The death of Luigi Trastulli, and other stories: Form and meaning in oral history*. Albany, NY: State University of New York Press.

Sheftel, A., & Zembrzycki, S. (2016). Who's afraid of oral history? Fifty years of debates and anxiety about ethics. *The Oral History Review*, *43*(2), 338–366. doi:10.1093/ohr/ohw071

Shopes, L. (2014). "Insights and oversights": Reflections on the documentary tradition and the theoretical turn in oral history. *The Oral History Review*, *41*(2), 257–268. doi:10.1093/ohr/ohu035

Sklar, H. (2012). Narrative empowerment through comics storytelling: Facilitating the life stories of the intellectually disabled. *Storyworlds: A Journal of Narrative Studies*, *4*, 123–149. doi:10.5250/storyworlds.4.2012.0123

Social History of Learning Disability Research Group. (n.d.). Retrieved from http://www.open.ac.uk/health-and-social-care/research/shld/

Sprout. (n.d.). Retrieved from https://gosprout.org/

StoryCorps. (n.d.). Retrieved from https://storycorps.org/

Tabatabai, A. (2020). Neoliberalism and the fight for the child: Narratives of queer mothering. In S. E. Green, & D. R. Loseke (Eds.), *New narratives of disability: Constructions, clashes, and controversies*. Research in social science and disability (Vol. 11, pp. 231–244). Emerald Publishing Limitied. doi:10.1108/S1479-354720190000011027.

Terkel, S., & Grele, R. (1991). Riffs and improvisations: An interview with studs Terkel. In R. Grele, S. Terkel, J. Vansina, D. Tedlock, S. Benison, & A. Kessler Harris (Eds.), *Envelopes of sound: The art of oral history* (pp. 10–49). Santa Barbara, CA: Praeger.

Tervalon, M., & Murray-Garcia, J. (1998). Cultural humility versus cultural competence: A critical distinction in defining physician training outcomes in multicultural education. *Journal of Health Care for the Poor and Underserved*, *9*(2), 117–125. doi:10.1353/hpu.2010.0233

Thompson, P. (1988). *The voice of the past*. Oxford: Oxford University Press.

Visionary Voices. (n.d.). Retrieved from https://disabilities.temple.edu/voices/.

Walmsley, J. (2009). Interviews with people with disabilities. In R. Perks, & A. Thomson (Eds.), *The oral history reader* (pp. 184–197). London: Routledge.

Walmsley, J., & Johnson, K. (2003). *Inclusive research with people with learning disabilities: Past, present and futures*. London: Jessica Kingsley.

Walmsley, J., Johnson, K., & Wolfe, M. (2010). *People with intellectual disabilities: Towards a good life?* Bristol: Policy Press.

Williams, K., & Johnson, R. (1999). *Lost in a desert world: The autobiography of Roland Johnson (as told to Karl Williams)*. Philadelphia, PA: Speaking for Ourselves.

APPENDIX: INTERVIEW GUIDE

Interview Guide: Self-Advocates with Down Syndrome Thesis, 9/20/12

Subject-specific questions

Research Question	Interview Questions
What motivates self-advocates?	Tell me about a time when you knew you had to speak up for people with Down syndrome.
	Tell me about a time when you felt nervous or reluctant about speaking up for people with Down syndrome What helped you overcome that (fear, nerves, shyness, etc.)?
	Tell me a story that shows why you do what you do, what keeps you going.
How do they define advocacy?	Tell me about a time when you helped someone else with DS.
	Tell me about a time when your advocacy helped someone who doesn't have DS.
	Tell me about a time when you felt like you were really successful as a self-advocate.
	Tell me about the first time you knew you wanted to be a self-advocate.
	Tell me about the time when you felt you had really become a self-advocate.
What about the world as they have seen and experienced it needs to change?	Tell me about a time when you were treated a certain way because you have DS.
	Tell me a story that shows how you think our society treats people with DS.
	Tell me about a time when you surprised someone who thought of you a certain way because you have DS.
	Tell me about a moment when you first realized you knew you had something called DS.

(Continued)

Research Question	Interview Questions
What vision of the future are they working toward?	My son who has DS is six months old. Paint a picture for me of what you would want the world to look like for him when he is your age.
How do they work with other advocates in the field?	Tell me about someone you see as a great advocate for people with DS.
	Tell me about a time when you felt understood by other advocates.
	Tell me about a time when you felt misunderstood.
	Who has been important to you as a self-advocate?
	Who have you been important to?
	Tell me about a time when you felt frustrated as a self-advocate.
	Tell me about a time when you felt proud as a self-advocate.
How do they see their work in an historical context?	Tell me about someone from an older generation who has had an influence on your work as a self-advocate.
	How do you think your life would have been different if you had been born 10 years earlier? Born to a different family? Born in a different place?
	Who have you looked up to in your work?
	Who has looked up to you?
	How do you think your life has been influenced by IDEA [other legislation]?
	Tell me a story that shows how the world is different now from when it was when you first started your work as a self-advocate.
	Tell me a story that shows how the world is different now from when it was when you were young.
What contributions do they think they have made?	Tell me about something you have accomplished as a self-advocate.
What changes to they take pride in?	Tell me about a moment when you felt proud to be a self-advocate.
	Tell me about a time when you felt proud to have DS.

Printed and bound by CPI Group (UK) Ltd, Croydon, CR0 4YY

13/09/2026

14961031-0002